Reading Ricoeur
through Law

Studies in the Thought of Paul Ricoeur

Series Editors: Greg S. Johnson, Pacific Lutheran University/Oxford University (ELAC) and Dan R. Stiver, Hardin-Simmons University

Studies in the Thought of Paul Ricoeur, a series in conjunction with the Society for Ricoeur Studies, aims to generate research on Ricoeur, about whom interest is rapidly growing both nationally (United States and Canada) and internationally. Broadly construed, the series has three interrelated themes. First, we develop the historical connections to and in Ricoeur's thought. Second, we extend Ricoeur's dialogue with contemporary thinkers representing a variety of disciplines. Third, we utilize Ricoeur to address future prospects in philosophy and other fields that respond to emerging issues of importance. The series approaches these themes from the belief that Ricoeur's thought is not just suited to theoretical exchanges, but can and does matter for how we actually engage in the many dimensions that constitute lived existence.

Recent Titles in the Series
Reading Ricoeur through Law, edited by Marc de Leeuw, George H. Taylor, and Eileen Brennan
Paul Ricoeur's Renewal of Philosophical Anthropology: Vulnerability, Capability, Justice, by Marc de Leeuw
A Hermeneutics of Contemplative Silence: Paul Ricoeur, Edith Stein, and the Heart of Meaning, by Michele Kueter Petersen
The Phenomenology of Revelation in Heidegger, Marion, and Ricoeur, by Adam J. Graves
Reading Religious Ritual with Ricoeur: Between Fragility and Hope, by Christina M. Gschwandtner
Reading Scripture with Paul Ricoeur, edited by Joseph A. Edelheit and James F. Moore

Reading Ricoeur
through Law

Edited by Marc de Leeuw,
George H. Taylor, and Eileen Brennan

LEXINGTON BOOKS
Lanham • Boulder • New York • London

Published by Lexington Books
An imprint of The Rowman & Littlefield Publishing Group, Inc.
4501 Forbes Boulevard, Suite 200, Lanham, Maryland 20706
www.rowman.com

86-90 Paul Street, London EC2A 4NE

Copyright © 2021 by The Rowman & Littlefield Publishing Group, Inc.

All rights reserved. No part of this book may be reproduced in any form or by any electronic or mechanical means, including information storage and retrieval systems, without written permission from the publisher, except by a reviewer who may quote passages in a review.

British Library Cataloguing in Publication Information Available

Library of Congress Cataloging-in-Publication Data

Names: De Leeuw, Marc, 1965- editor. | Taylor, George H. (George Howard), 1951- editor. | Brennan, Eileen (Writer of Reading Ricœur through law), editor.
Title: Reading Ricœur through law / edited by Marc de Leeuw, George H. Taylor, and Eileen Brennan.
Description: Lanham, Maryland : Lexington Books, an imprint of The Rowman & Littlefield Publishing Group, Inc., [2022] | Series: Studies in the thought of Paul Ricoeur | Includes index. | Summary: "This is the first collection of essays examining Paul Ricoeur's writings on law, bringing together eminent Ricoeur scholars from around the world to demonstrate the importance of Ricoeur's philosophy for the juridical field while offering new paths to extend and build on his work"—Provided by publisher.
Identifiers: LCCN 2021047160 (print) | LCCN 2021047161 (ebook) | ISBN 9781793600912 (cloth) | ISBN 9781793600936 (paperback) | ISBN 9781793600929 (epub)
Subjects: LCSH: Ricœur, Paul—Political and social views. | Law—Philosophy.
Classification: LCC K235 .R359 2022 (print) | LCC K235 (ebook) | DDC 340/.1—dc23/eng/20211029
LC record available at https://lccn.loc.gov/2021047160
LC ebook record available at https://lccn.loc.gov/2021047161

∞™ The paper used in this publication meets the minimum requirements of American National Standard for Information Sciences—Permanence of Paper for Printed Library Materials, ANSI/NISO Z39.48-1992.

Contents

Acknowledgments   vii

Introduction: Reading Ricoeur through Law   1
Marc de Leeuw, George H. Taylor, and Eileen Brennan

PART I: RICOEUR ON LAW, JUSTICE, AND PLURALITY

Introduction to Paul Ricoeur's "The Just Between the Legal and the Good"   19
Eileen Brennan

1   The Just Between the Legal and the Good   21
    Paul Ricoeur

2   The Plurality of Instances of Justice   37
    Paul Ricoeur

Reply to Paul Ricoeur   53
Ronald Dworkin

PART II: READING RICOEUR THROUGH LAW

3   Juridical Precedents and Reflective Judgment   59
    Roger W. H. Savage

4   The Subject of Rights and Responsibility in Ricoeur's Legal Philosophy: Toward a Prospective Idea of Responsibility   75
    Guido Gorgoni

5   Symbolism and the Generativity of Justice   91
    Antoine Garapon

6	Ricoeur, Narrative, and Legal Contingency *George H. Taylor*	107
7	Paul Ricoeur's Juridical Anthropology: Law, Autonomy, and a Life Lived-in-Common *Marc de Leeuw*	125
8	The Unbearable Between-ness of Law *Francis J. Mootz III*	139
9	Law and Metadiscourse: Ricoeur on Metaphysics and the Ascription of Rights *Geoffrey Dierckxsens*	157
10	Between Truth and Justice: Ricoeur on the Roles and Limits of Narrative in Legal Processes *Marie-Hélène Desmeules*	173
11	Law and (Dis)empowerment: On Ricoeur's Phenomenology of Judging *Hans Lindahl*	192
12	The "Crisis of Witnessing" and Trauma on the Stand: Attending to Survivors as an Obligation of Justice *Stephanie Arel*	209
13	The Interaction Between Love and Justice in the Legal System *Walter Salles*	229
14	Forgiveness at the Border of Law *Oliver Abel*	245
15	Law and Evil in Paul Ricoeur's Thought *Bertrand Mazabraud*	263
Index		279
About the Contributors		291

Acknowledgments

The idea for a book on Ricoeur's work on law emerged from our observation that Paul Ricoeur's work is mostly absent in the traditional legal philosophy field, an omission that needed correction. In most law schools, legal positivism and analytical philosophy dominate jurisprudential thinking, while critical reflections on law from an ethical, political, or social perspective now usually happens in philosophy, sociology, or political science departments. Ricoeur's exemplary ability to cross-pollinate and reconnect these fields while offering an affirmative anthropological perspective on the human condition made the need to showcase his original legal thinking in an accessible volume an urgent task yet to be fulfilled.

We would like to thank Anne Bernard Kearney (and the assistance of Joseph S. O'Leary), Laura Kassar and Karl Racette, and Norah Woodcock for their excellent translations, respectively, of the chapters by Oliver Abel, Marie-Hélène Desmeules, and Bertrand Mazabraud. Eileen Brennan translated Antoine Garapon's chapter and Paul Ricoeur's "Le juste entre le légal et le bon" ("The Just between the Legal and the Good"). The translations allowed us to add significantly to the quite interdisciplinary and international array of authors that the book offers. Our authors and editors are from Australia, Belgium, Brazil, Canada, France, Ireland, Italy, Netherlands, and the United States.

We also want to thank the editors of the "Studies in the Thought of Paul Ricoeur" at Lexington Books, Dan R. Stiver and Greg S. Johnson, for including our volume in their Series, which has grown into an impressive repository for new, original Ricoeur scholarship. We thank Jana Hodges-Kluck at Lexington for her endless patience, and for her ongoing advice in preparing this volume, and Sydney Wedbush for all her help in the last phase of this project.

In preparing the manuscript we would like to thank the members of the Document Technology Center at the University of Pittsburgh School of Law for extensive help with formatting, editing, and referencing control. We are also very grateful for the funding provided by the University of Pittsburgh and the University of New South Wales enabling professional translation and editing assistance. We also want to thank the Institute for Advanced Study in Princeton for offering the time and space to complete this project in pandemic times.

A special thanks also goes to Jean-Paul Ricoeur and Nathalie Ricoeur-Nicolaï who, as heirs of Paul Ricoeur, granted us permission to translate and republish free of charge "Le juste entre le légal et le bon," which previously appeared in Ricoeur's collected essays *Lectures I. Autour du Politique*, published by Seuil in 1991.

Finally, we of course want to acknowledge and thank all of our contributors whose hard work and original insights produced this unique collection of essays highlighting the ongoing importance of Ricoeur's legal thinking.

We wish to thank several publishers for permission to republish or cite works by Paul Ricoeur for which they hold the copyrights:

Paul Ricoeur, "The Just Between the Legal and the Good." Copyright © 1991 by Seuil. All rights reserved. Originally published as "Le juste entre le légal et le bon," *Lectures I. Autour du Politique*, Copyright © Éditions du Seuil, 1991. Used by permission of Jean-Paul Ricoeur and Nathalie Ricoeur-Nicolaï.

Paul Ricoeur, "The Plurality of Instances of Justice," *The Just.* Copyright © 2000 by The University of Chicago Press. All rights reserved. Originally published as *Le Juste*, Copyright © Éditions Esprit, 1995. Used by permission.

Republished with permission of John Wiley & Sons, from "Reply to Ricoeur," Ronald Dworkin, *Ratio Juris*, vol. 7, no. 3, 287–90, 1994, Copyright © John Wiley & Sons, permission conveyed through Copyright Clearance Center, Inc. All rights reserved. Used by permission.

Introduction

Reading Ricoeur through Law

Marc de Leeuw, George H. Taylor,
and Eileen Brennan

In *The Concept of Law* (1961), the most famous legal philosophy book of the twentieth century, H. L. A. Hart laments that compared to questions such as "What is chemistry?" or "What is medicine?," the question "What is law?" has only received vague and speculative answers. It is usually approached in ways comparable to stating that medicine is just "what doctors will do," and hence that law is simply what lawyers and judges do.[1] The question, for example, of how law voluntarily *obliges* persons to do something—how law differs from the request of someone pointing a gun—has, according to Hart, never sufficiently been answered. The "science" of law—Jurisprudence—is a rather recent "field," triggered by John Austin's *The Providence of Jurisprudence Determined* (1832). Austin states that law is nothing else than a command determined by an absolute authority, which itself does not take commands. For Austin to answer the question "What is law?," we mainly need to know how law is *declared* or posited. In addition, we need to know how law gains general acceptance. In fundamentally detaching law from religion and morality, Austin became the founding father of Legal Positivism, whose battle cry summarizes the key perspective through which most law students in Western liberal democracies still learn what constitutes the normativity of law: a moral violation does not need to be a legal violation, and a morally desirable rule does not need to be a legally desirable rule. Legal positivism's main goal is to overcome the subjective nature of law by neutralizing the influence of religious and political authority upon the judiciary and detaching law from morality. Unfortunately, this split also caused its greatest crisis in the aftermath of the Second World War: did the Nazi perpetrators of atrocities not correctly claim that they had done nothing wrong if the laws enforcing their regime were properly posited under a rule of law system? Could, according to legal positivism, a Nazi law completely void of morality still be a legitimate and valid law? This moral conundrum triggered fierce debates among the most important post-war legal philosophers (H. L. A. Hart, Lon Fuller, Ronald Dworkin, Joseph Raz) but also sparked the revival of natural law thinking (John Finnis), the formulation of universal human rights, Marxist critiques of law as ideology, socio-legal perspectives reviving Weber and Durkheim, as well as the law and economy approach of the Chicago School (Friedrich Hayek, Richard Posner), and the increasing influence of legal realism (Oliver Holmes). From the 1970s onward, critical legal studies, poststructuralism, feminist legal thinking, and postcolonial legal theory succeeded in significantly expanding the field of Jurisprudence by asking vital questions regarding law's power, politics, methods, ethics, and overall legitimacy. These considerations elicit the need to renew and rethink the philosophical foundations that undergird the legitimacy of law and legal institutions.

RICOEUR AND LEGAL THINKING

In his introduction to *The Just*, Paul Ricoeur observes that contemporary philosophers, although often engaging with questions of politics and ethics, mostly overlook *juridical* questions. This was not always the case. From Plato and Aristotle to Machiavelli and Hobbes, philosophy included an "explication of the origin and end of law."[2] Leibniz, Kant, and Hegel all wrote substantive and still influential treatises on law. Ricoeur notes that his own generation's thinking "on the sequence ethics-law-politics"[3] derived from their reading of Hegel's *Philosophy of Right* where, unfortunately, only the connection "between *ethics and politics* was the main object of concern."[4] This redefinition of Hegel's most important work on law as a *political* philosophy, Ricoeur laments, leaves the actual "impasse over the specific status of the juridical"[5] unresolved. Although Ricoeur accepts that the horrors of the twentieth century pushed philosophy towards the seemingly more important questions of *political* violence, the ignorance of the *legal within the political* must be traced back further to the terror of the French Revolution. This terror, Ricoeur argues, resulted from the *lack* of a "constitutional order" which should have defined the new French State as "based on the rule of law."[6] It is the need to reappraise the *juridical* aspects in Hegel's *Philosophy of Right* that informs Ricoeur's self-proclaimed starting point for his reflections on law and justice.

A second central moment of return for Ricoeur's reflections on law takes up his earlier work on the "political paradox"[7] signified by the tension between the free cooperation and reasoned self-governance of "the people" for the common good, and the simultaneous desire of politicians and the state to exercise power over rivals by unchallenged decisionism. It is the lack of philosophical attention to constitutionalism and the rule of law—the *juridical* in the political (Hegel)—together with the ongoing power struggle between "We the People" and political authority which we need to resolve, Ricoeur argues, before we can "do justice to the question of right and law."[8]

During the 1990s Ricoeur received several invitations for talks at the *Institut des hautes études pour la justice* and the *École nationale de la magistrature* in Paris. These talks allowed him to reflect on the "question of the *juridical* in the figure of the *judiciary*" while engaging with written laws, tribunals, judges, ceremonial processes, and sentences in their "proper setting."[9] Ricoeur concluded that *"war* is the insistent theme of political philosophy and *peace* that of the philosophy of law." Law symbolizes a "place within society" where "words do win out over violence."[10] Human conflict can end by the proclamation of a sentence in the courtroom, allowing law to facilitate "the consolidation of society as a cooperative enterprise."[11] Moving beyond the fundamental binary of conflict and peace, Ricoeur adds an anthropological and phenomenological layer—"a kind of ontogenetic order"[12]—to the question of the juridical by invoking our early childhood experiences of unfair treatment: the "cry of *indignation*"[13] over unequal shares, unkept promises, or disproportionate punishments triggers a deep, innate sense of injustice in most humans. Ricoeur deciphers in these primal emotions the "lineaments of the juridical order: penal law, the law of contracts and exchanges, distributive justice."[14] It is the transfer of our innate sense of injustice into abstract legal concepts that, Ricoeur states, generates a *"just distance"* between the antagonistic parties turning violent conflict into a clash of legal arguments. The "just distance" metaphor becomes the main trope through which Ricoeur perceives the legal process producing the fundamental equation between *justice* and *impartiality*: "Just distance, the mediation of a third party, and impartiality present themselves as the great synonyms of a sense of justice along the path down which indignation has led us from our earliest youth."[15]

Moving from law as institution to persons as subjects of law, Ricoeur admits the need for a double "corrective" to his "little ethics" as worked out in chapters 7–9 of *Oneself as Another*. It is the specific capacity of "imputability" which forms the "lynchpin"[16] between the acting and suffering human, enabling us to "recognize ourselves as accountable."[17] The second corrective refers to the "recognition of a rule that obligates us,"[18] evoked by the "circularity" of an "ethic passing through moral obligation."[19] The desire for a good life needs to pass through "the filter of moral judgment," for example, in the quest for a good—a *just*—medical, judicial, or environmental praxis. It is by way of the circularity between the ethical good and moral obligation that "the just" is established. Ricoeur reminds us, quoting Aristotle's *Nicomachean Ethics*, that a similar circularity applies to law: the just is "'what is lawful and what is fair, the unjust the lawless and the unfair.'"[20] It is the positing of *the legal in between the good and the ethical* that marks Ricoeur's main perspective on the *"impasse* over the specific status of the juridical."[21]

While Ricoeur's legal thinking returns to classical beginnings in figures such as Aristotle, Hobbes, Kant, and Hegel, he equally engages with contemporary colleagues in jurisprudence such as H. L. A. Hart, Hans Kelsen, Ronald Dworkin, Robert Alexy, and Manual Atienza, while also reflecting on socio-political aspects of law through the work of Max Weber, Hannah Arendt, John Rawls, Jürgen Habermas, Michael Walzer, Ottfried Höffe, Luc Boltanski, Laurent Thévenot, and Antoine Garapon. In dialogue with these authors Ricoeur arrives at law's most fundamental questions: how may we create a more just and equitable society; how can a legal verdict justify closure if interpretation is always open; how can legal reasoning reconnect with the ethical and political instead of being detached from them; how should we determine accountability and responsibility if human agency and selfhood are fragmented or fundamentally contested; in what manner can punishment act as just, reconcile, or establish social peace if it always echoes a form of vengeance; what does it mean to testify, judge, proclaim a sentence, or be sentenced; when should we forgive or pardon?

READING RICOEUR THROUGH LAW

The present collection is the very first solely focused on Ricoeur's thinking about law, bringing together both established and emerging scholars to offer a systematic and critical examination of Ricoeur's legal thinking. The "readings" offered by our contributors not only explain the specific contribution Ricoeur makes to the field of jurisprudence but also examine how Ricoeur's work on law fits, complements, or changes his overall anthropology, phenomenology, and hermeneutics and provide a complex insight into how law, ethics, and politics intertwine both from within law as normative rule setting, as well as through the wider socio-political and historical context in which law and legal institutions affect our interpersonal and collective human life as lived "with and for others in just institutions."[22]

The collection also contributes two texts by Ricoeur himself, and they open our volume. We offer for the first time in English "The Just between the Legal and the Good" ("Le juste entre le légal et le bon"). In this text Ricoeur examines how our ideas of the just, the good, and the legal attach or detach in constitutive juridical operations haunted by unresolved tensions evoked by the essential difference between *moral* or *legal* justice. In addition to applications of Kant's deontology to law, Ricoeur explicitly engages with John

Rawls's seminal *Theory of Justice*, where the deontological and teleological notion of justice becomes a quest for *fair* distribution, for a just *sharing* of goods. At stake here is the question who defines what economic, political, social, or legal equality (*équité*) actually stands for. Is equality an economic or rather social values problem? Can there be equality separate from egalitarianism? Ricoeur argues that while Rawls's notion of "justice as *fairness*" offers an imperfect formalism, by contrast Kant's "justice as *duty*" follows a perfect and hence absolute formalism. "We go then," Ricoeur concludes, "via a turnaround within formalism, from a strict *apriorism* to a juridical positivism, where the question of the foundation outruns [Kantian] practical reason and falls under the control of empirically and historically constituted legislating authorities."[23] The problem, Ricoeur continues, is that within this turnaround there is "no place either for the idea of the common good or for the idea of substantive goods that give content to the idea of justice in unequal shares."[24] Both procedural justice and legal positivism trust formalism to deliver equality by turning the interpersonal into an "everyone." But this "everyone" (anchored by law's expected impartiality) only delivers justice if it "subtracts nothing from solicitude,"[25] which it presupposes because people are "irreplaceable," an idea that extends to "the historical community governed by the state and, ideally, the whole of humanity."[26]

The second text we republish is "The Plurality of Instances of Justice" which Ricoeur first delivered as a talk at the *Institut des hautes études sur la justice*, where it was followed by a critical reply by Ronald Dworkin, the most eminent legal scholar at the time. We are pleased to include Dworkin's reply.[27] Ricoeur starts his lecture with the observation that the "transfer of competence" from the nation-state to the European Union is by many perceived as a loss of sovereignty. Sovereign power, seen as "indivisible" and "inalienable" aims to unify the "juridical power of the state" with the collective of "we, the people." How, though, can law and sovereign power be monistic if whom it represents is fundamentally pluralistic? To examine this "asymmetrical problem," Ricoeur turns to Michael Walzer's *Spheres of Justice*[28] and *De la justification*[29] by Luc Boltanski and Laurent Thévenot. Both works challenge Rawls's *Theory of Justice* by asking whether substantive justice, reformulated as the need to establish distributive *fairness*, can indeed be realized by juridical proceduralism only, for example, by creating equal opportunity through equal rights, or instead requires the redistribution of economic goods. While Walzer focuses on the manifestation of *domination*, as the suppression of equality of social goods, Boltanski and Thévenot examine the processes of *dissent* as the search for justification regarding the "economies of scale."[30] To avoid violence, we need to respond to both domination by "complex equality" and dissent by "'tested judgment.'"[31] These works clarify the "previously unrecognized situation," Ricoeur argues, "that the State, as the source of right, finds itself today placed in the uncomfortable situation of an entity called upon to behave at the same time as the whole and as the part, as the container and the contained, as an inclusive agency and an included region."[32] The tension between the claim to an indivisible sovereign power and a strongly divided, even ruptured, plural "we" could hardly be more visible than in uncertain times in which political leadership in too many nations use current crises—such as a global public health pandemic—to further divide and dominate instead of to unify and cooperate to secure the survival of the "community of life" on Earth. Ricoeur concludes "The Plurality of Instances of Justice" with great foresight:

> It will be no easier in the coming decades to reconcile indivisible popular sovereignty with the blossoming of a multitude of centers of rights than to reconcile this same indivisible sovereignty with new postnational, if not suprastate, institutions, which themselves will give rise to rights. Just as we shall have to deal with a complex situation, stemming from the intertwining of several agencies of juridicity at the level of the state and the suprastate, so too we shall more and more have to deal with a symmetrical situation issuing from the intertwining of several sources of juridicity at the infrastate level. This situation is a result of the figure that clothes the political paradox.[33]

This prediction has, unfortunately, shown its political accuracy. Political populism, illiberal democracy, and new geopolitical uncertainties trigger new authoritarianism in liberal states, revealing the unresolved and ongoing effects of the political and legal paradox between sovereign power and pluralism.

READING RICOEUR ON LAW

The authors gathered in this volume offer insights on Ricoeur's *direct* and *indirect* engagement with juridical questions, his *critical dialogues* on law with other thinkers, his renewal of a *phenomenology* and *hermeneutics* of law, the complex *intertwining* of law with ethics, politics, and religion, and, finally, the *liminality* of law as demarcated by law's others: evil, love, and forgiveness. As the following chapters show, re-reading Ricoeur's philosophical anthropology through a legal lens not only reveals his original views on key aspects of law such as rights, responsibility, judging, legal reasoning, judicial argumentation, punishment, and authority, but also demonstrates how Ricoeur's philosophical reconceptualization of symbolism, action, ideology, narrative, selfhood, testimony, history, reconciliation, justice, and forgiveness are made productive for our understanding of law and legal institutions.

Roger Savage investigates the political paradox of the State symbolized by its claim simultaneously to legitimate the violence of State action and also promise social peace. To examine how this paradox applies to law and justice, Savage takes up a well-known legal problem: how to find a just verdict in so-called hard cases where no precedents are available and, thus, a legitimate verdict must be (re-)invented. Ronald Dworkin famously resolves this scenario by perceiving law as a "chain novel" into which each new verdict needs to be integrated by fitting in an overall narrative anchored in core legal principles. Savage reads Ricoeur's interpretation of this scenario to show how it rather is the productive imagination that, beyond just establishing differences and semblances between cases, allows us to recognize how each case summons its own rule. Combining the active creation of meaningful action with our will to live together, law ideally represents an ethico-political aspiration, as well as the reasonable form through which its authority can be justified by legal institutions and the State.

In an essay on legal responsibility, Guido Gorgoni offers a cross-reading between H. L. A. Hart's famous article, "The Ascription of Responsibility and Rights," and Ricoeur's notion of rights and responsibility as developed in *The Just*. As Gorgoni sets out to show, Ricoeur rethinks the subject of rights within his theory of action and the capable human offering a *prospective* concept of responsibility in contrast to the juridically formalized *retrospective* ascription and imputation of acts to legal persons. If we perceive our responsiveness also as a moral commitment to others (like the obligation to keep a promise), responsibility is more than legal accountability or liability and reflects an ethics of care anchored in a mutual recognition of vulnerability. Hence, rights and responsibility are fundamentally intersubjective and not merely legally defined forms of causality between acts and sanctions entirely detached from capable humans.

In his contribution, Antoine Garapon[34] focuses on the "generativity" of justice. How does our initial "cry of indignation" lead to a desire for vengeance, a formal complaint, and a demand for legal justice? To explain law's generativity, Garapon returns to Ricoeur's early work in *The Symbolism of Evil* to show how law is "amputated from its symbolic part." For Garapon, following Ricoeur, symbols and myths are not merely historical but very much "alive" and still connect an eschatological vision of judgment—*The Last Judgment!*—with parts of the legal process—the final verdict! Law appears as a search for justice through action while mediated by symbols whereby the courtroom appears, Garapon explains, as a cosmic scene through which the history of humanity (as destiny) and the "relation to oneself through guilt" become articulated. In contrast to Foucault, Levinas, and Derrida, Ricoeur does *not* accept that justice is a priori impossible but, as Garapon argues, rather shows that justice ought to be perceived as an attempt to restore both the social bond and the authentic human beyond the convicted person. Garapon's application of Ricoeur's anthropology of symbolism ends with his frustration about the enormous, yet unrecognized, promise of Ricoeur's work for our legal understanding. This is a frustration that this volume seeks to alleviate a least a little.

For George Taylor's essay on narrative and legal contingency, Rev. Martin Luther King Jr.'s famous proclamation, "The arc of the moral universe is long, but it bends towards justice," forms the critical starting point. If we understand humanity not as a given but as a "task," we must acknowledge, contra Hegel and King, that the development of our humanity will never be complete but remains in constant flux, open and beset with unpredictable and unlikely "black swan" events such as the lone shooter who killed eleven congregants in a synagogue close to Taylor's Pittsburgh home. In times of radical populism in established democracies and an unprecedented global health crisis, Taylor's employment of Ricoeur's philosophy of narrative to examine how we integrate radical contingencies in the "task" of humanity seems very timely and urgent. But while Ricoeur perceives narrative as a reestablishing of the concordant through the discordant, unity through difference, and tradition through innovation, Taylor emphasizes the often insolvable depth of discordance and fracture as a more accurate reflection of the human condition setting out its task. In a way similar to how narratives integrate contingencies to create a retrospective logic, the law uses legal interpretation, judgment, and imagination to overcome the multiplicity of potential paths towards a logical verdict, allowing closure, but the logic chosen is not inherent but one of multiple potential paths. Further, legal closure is not permanent. Particular decisions in fundamental legal questions—such as abortion, migration, or partisan gerrymandering—trigger strong political responses that aim to change key legal arguments and decision makers in the legislative and judicial arenas, hoping to overturn the established law. Sometimes this works, sometimes it does not. Taylor's reading of Ricoeur clarifies that contingencies in life and law are inevitable factors that must be addressed as part of our ongoing search for a more just society, factors that inform the task to understand and imagine our own humanity.

Marc de Leeuw's chapter examines how Ricoeur's writings on the juridical system reflect his philosophical anthropological perspective on the fragile *and* capable nature of our being. In presupposing the subject's a priori autonomy, in concert with the expectation that we remain imputable over time, law conceals the actual, more complex, and delicate condition of *who* we are or can be. Ricoeur's essay on vulnerability and autonomy in law adds an anthropological, phenomenological, and hermeneutic understanding of the subject to the Kantian notion of autonomy and Hegelian concept of ethical life which shapes our philosophical understanding of the subject of law as a person who can give itself the law, or as a citizen who actualizes the shared values of the community through constitutive self-affirmation.

If we perceive law as a field taking place in *between* practice and theory, norms and facts, or morality and politics, the question becomes how this "betweenness" affects our understanding of law. Jay Mootz takes up this question in his chapter on Gadamer, Habermas, and Ricoeur. In Gadamer's philosophy, law becomes an exemplary model for hermeneutical understanding as the *application* of practical reasoning, defined as situated knowledge, to the case at hand. For Gadamer, to understand a legal text and to know how to apply this understanding is inseparable from any correct legal interpretation, placing hermeneutics in-between knowledge and practice. But, Mootz argues, drawing upon Habermas, this faith in legal reasoning is misplaced, because it does not sufficiently account for fundamental shifts in the social organization of pluralistic societies. To integrate these shifts in our legal institutions, law must resolve the tension between normative universality and social context, between enforcing behavioral rules and the values that represent democratic deliberation and legitimacy. The hinge position of law functions as a "transmission belt" enabling emancipatory social integration. For Ricoeur as well, law exists between morality, ethics, and politics on the one hand, and interpretation, understanding, and argumentation on the other. Yet, Mootz claims, it is particularly the "middle zone" between rhetoric, poetics, and hermeneutics where creative arguments regarding the probable come to guide law and social action. For Mootz, Ricoeur's contribution to legal thinking comes most to fruition in clarifying what is at stake in this middle zone.

Geoffrey Dierckxsens's essay focuses on how Ricoeur's work can help surpass the overformalization of the ascription of rights in pragmatist approaches to democracy. General rules and principles often exclude the most vulnerable or those lacking a voice, such as refugees or excluded minorities. How can a substantial recognition of otherness be included in rights and law? Dierckxsens shows how Ricoeur offers an alternative path between formalism and personalism: beyond pure pragmatic norms and intersubjective relations, we need a "third person" representing the natural dignity, need for respect, and recognition of each capable human, as protected by "just institutions." While the formal ascription of rights depends on our ability to speak, act, and take responsibility, it is our ability to recognize, befriend, love, or care for others that informs the respect and dignity we aim to uphold with rights. For Dierckxsens, Ricoeur's notion of rights finds its shape by shifting between formalism and personalism, combining principles with an understanding of concrete situations and a "metaphysics of otherness," allowing those who are not yet citizens, such as refugees, to be granted rights due to being recognized as capable humans, being another like oneself.

Although testimony and the retelling of events, experiences, and facts form a key part of any trial, the narrative aspects of law and justice need greater development. In her chapter on storytelling in the legal process, Marie-Hélène Desmeules examines Ricoeur's narrative theory to understand how stories shape and affect the epistemological challenges within the legal process. Desmeules focuses on three phases of the trial to test the usefulness of Ricoeur's narrative theory in law: 1) the truth assessment of facts in dispute, 2) the search for the applicable rule of law, and 3) the application of the rule of law to the facts in dispute. In narrative, heterogeneous events are given intelligibility by the creation of a meaningful unity. But *meaningfulness* does not equal *truthfulness*, in the sense of the law where rules and principles, legal reasoning, and argumentation determine the definition of a just outcome. Although storytelling is central for effective testimonials or the pursuit of judges and juries to accepts the "facts," it is the tension between the function of narrative as documenting (reconstruction) and the dialectical dynamic between *interpretation/argumentation* and *explaining/understanding* (to find, understand, apply, and argue for the right rules and legal principles) that needs to be resolved *before* any verdict can be proclaimed. Desmeules's original reading of Ricoeur's work on narrative reveals the highly complex entanglements of the aims of truth, meaning, and justice in the stories we tell.

Hans Lindahl's contribution to our volume revives a phenomenological understanding of law through the lens of Ricoeur's interpretation of the act of judging. By bringing Ricoeur's conceptualization of judging back into dialogue with Husserl's phenomenology, Lindahl shows how Ricoeur moves from a solitary to an intersubjective notion of judging, because perception itself is "intersubjective through and through." Although otherness and negation evoke self-affirmation (I am me because I am *not* you), this *mine/thine* duality also creates a fundamental tension, experienced as uncertainty, with the "we" symbolizing the presupposed unity of the legal order. It is the "we" of an intentional collective self-affirmation, Lindahl argues, that the judge represents while judging. But just as in Ricoeur's notion of selfhood, the collective "we" forms through its external and internal Other. Although by granting rights the collective can overcome indefensible exclusions of otherness, as happened in the Australian *Mabo* case dealing with Aboriginal rights, rights cannot overcome "the non-reciprocal emergence of legal reciprocity." Rights are granted only to those *already* recognized as equal legal subjects, just like impartial treatment is promised only to those already within the legal circle. Hence, Aboriginals receiving inclusion within the Australian "us" does not offer real equality. It merely subsumes *ipseity* (selfhood) under sameness, resulting in an additional form of legal imperialism. Lindahl's chapter, simultaneously arguing with and against Ricoeur, shows that ultimately no real passage exists from "ourselves as others" to "ourselves as strange." Only a constrained self-affirmation of the "we" (as represented by law and the judge) allows the reflection of a non-reciprocal equality, evoked by the *suspension* of law instead of its actual application. Only this suspension offers otherness—such as Aboriginal otherness—true equality through, for example, the constitution of a co-imperium. The radicalness of Lindahl's reading and the extension of Ricoeur's phenomenology of legal reciprocity cannot be underestimated, in particular regarding Australia's unsettled colonial legacy.

Stephanie Arel's chapter on the "crisis of witnessing" examines the complex dynamic between memory and mourning, truth and belief, and the theological or juridical perception of justice. Arel's starting point is the observation that the process of recollection and retelling of traumatic experiences often fails the legal notion of testimony aiming to find evidential "truth." Three examples of trauma narrative reveal the legal-ethical difficulties of victim testimonials within a legal setting: the story of a Holocaust survivor, of a 9/11 survivor, and of a witness on the stand in the trial of Ted Bundy, questioned by the suspect himself. Legal testimony can liberate or re-traumatize the victim. If a victim's fragmentary testimony—fragmentary due to the trauma experienced—frustrates a courtroom's expectation of linear coherence and consistency, it also undermines the credibility of the witness and, subsequently, her notion of self. This leads Arel, deploying Ricoeur's model of the *horizontal* dialogical constitution of the self combined with the *vertical* pursuit for the good and justice, to ask how law can better account for the victim as suffering other. How can we avoid that the law's success (finding truth and justice) does not simultaneously evoke its failure (causing more trauma, undermining the self-constitution of the victim)? Ultimately, the law's obligation to justice can only be met by a similar obligation to the "good life" of the testifying victim. As Arel aptly recalls from Ricoeur, it is the "duty of justice to legitimate the duty of memory."

Ricoeur's writings on love and justice form the departure point for Walter Salles's chapter probing how elements of love can be incorporated in law, while law can also help to preserve the possibility of love in society. How do acts of gratuity, compassion, and mercy relate to the operative rational of commercial, contract, or penal law? How does love relate to pure utilitarian reciprocity, a distribution of rights based on mutual obligations, or a justice determined by the logic of to "each its due"? Can we ever give (love) without expecting something in return? Unlike Ricoeur, who mostly focuses on the *theological* aspects of the relation between love and justice, the latter perceived as operating along the logic of *equivalence*, Salles stresses the "*anthropological optimism*" that love brings to law, for example, by seeing how the guilty are more than their faults and wrongdoing. For Salles love can lead us to be just—to treat others justly is intrinsic to acts of love and empathy—and, in reverse, justice can be perceived as an expression of love through gratuity, recognition of human dignity, restorative justice, and the creation of just institutions. Love also symbolizes the desire to live life in common with others in a just world, which reflects the paradigm statement of Ricoeur's ethics—to live "with and for others in just institutions." Following Ricoeur's "optimistic anthropology," Salles shows that love, beyond its Biblical or sentimental meaning, can inform law and justice through its intrinsic focus on countering evil and looking beyond the criminal act to the person, with regard for the dignity and otherness of others, and in this way can inform our legal institutions and daily legal practices.

How and when does law allow forgiveness to resolve its punitive verdicts? Building upon his own writings on the topic,[35] Oliver Abel offers both a genealogical and systematic overview of Ricoeur's thinking about forgiveness. Although the theme comes late in Ricoeur's work, Abel convincingly shows how forgiveness is clearly present in Ricoeur's earlier reflections on punishment, the tension between love and justice, the idea of compromise and, in particular, in his examination of the tragic condition. Abel emphasizes the dialectical aspect Ricoeur projects, following Arendt, into forgiveness. To be able to bind oneself through the promise creates the mirror image for the way one can be untied through forgiveness. As singular exception, forgiveness cannot be institutionalized in law because, as Abel argues, forgiveness simultaneously shows the law's "intention from within" and its "limits from without." Ultimately, forgiveness points back to the epic scale of tragedy in the *Iliad*, *Oedipus Rex*, *Antigone*, or the *Oresteia*, exemplifying the conversion of vengeful divinities into divinities of civic justice, of pain into tragic wisdom, or of fate into the need for reconciliation. It is also at this point that the tension in Ricoeur's work between a theological and humanistic understanding of forgiveness resurfaces.

Bertrand Mazabraud concludes our volume by returning to Ricoeur's early work on the symbolism of evil to explore the difference between moral law and juridical law. According to Mazabraud, Ricoeur at once thinks that law is necessary to oppose the evil of violence, the power of one person over another, and at the same time he views the law as inflicting evil in the administration of punishment. In the first case, the law constitutes the deontological moment that is essential for preventing the ethics of self-affirmation from turning into bad faith and abuses that could ensue in our relations with others. In the second case, the law, which should prevent or contain evil, oversees inflicting evil, which for Ricoeur constitutes an aporia. In both cases, Mazabraud states, the relation of law to evil is focused on the figure of radical evil. Thus, on the one hand, the law is in danger of itself succumbing to this kind of evil and, on the other hand, it obscures the figure of tragic evil, recalling the limits of law and requiring correctives in the law's concrete application. Following Ricoeur, Mazabraud concludes that the "law needs thought, a thought that is oriented by justice, to apply itself, correct itself, and avoid evil."

This echo of Ricoeur's famous statement that "the symbol gives rise to thought"[36] offers an appropriate ending to the impressive re-readings by our contributors of Ricoeur's overall philosophy through law. What all of the chapters in this volume prove is that although Ricoeur never wrote a separate treatise on law, many fundamental legal and philosophical questions are from the very beginning interlaced in Ricoeur's thinking. Through the themes of human willing and evil, language and meaning, identity and otherness, ethics and politics, history and forgetting, and, finally, recognition and giving, Ricoeur attends to the ethical-legal aspects of our human condition, revealing how law as a "practice of justice stems from the fragility, the vulnerability, of all the enterprises of that capable human being whom I have characterized as an acting and suffering being."[37]

NOTES

1. H. L. A. Hart, *The Concept of Law* (Oxford: Oxford University Press, 1961), 1.

2. Paul Ricoeur, *The Just*, trans. David Pellauer (Chicago: University of Chicago Press, 2000), viii.

3. Ricoeur, *The Just*, viii.

4. Ricoeur, *The Just*, viii.

5. Ricoeur, *The Just*, viii.

6. Ricoeur, *The Just*, viii.

7. Paul Ricoeur, "The Political Paradox," in *History and Truth*, trans. Charles A. Kelbley (Evanston: Northwestern University Press, 1965), 247–70.

8. Ricoeur, *The Just*, ix.

9. Ricoeur, *The Just*, ix.

10. Critical Legal Scholars will happily disagree with this point. Law is not only used to solidify the power of authoritarian rulers but also of political and financial elites in well-working democracies. In addition, "lawfare" is a normalized aspect of the "judiciary" in most societies.

11. Ricoeur, *The Just*, x.

12. Ricoeur, *The Just*, xii.

13. Ricoeur, *The Just*, x.

14. Ricoeur, *The Just*, xi.

15. Ricoeur, *The Just*, xi.

16. Paul Ricoeur, *Reflections on the Just*, trans. David Pellauer (Chicago: Chicago University Press, 2007), 2.

17. Ricoeur, *Reflections on the Just*, 2.

18. Ricoeur, *Reflections on the Just*, 2.

19. Ricoeur, *Reflections on the Just*, 3.

20. Ricoeur, *Reflections on the Just*, 4, quoting Aristotle, *Nichomachean Ethics*, Book V, 1129b.

21. Ricoeur, *The Just*, viii (emphasis added).

22. Paul Ricoeur, *Oneself as Another*, trans. Kathleen Blamey (Chicago: University of Chicago Press, 1992), 172.

23. Paul Ricoeur, "The Just between the Legal and the Good," trans. Eileen Brennan, in *Reading Ricoeur through Law*, ed. Marc de Leeuw, George H. Taylor, and Eileen Brennan (Lanham: Lexington, 2022), 26.

24. Ricoeur, "The Just between the Legal and the Good," 26.

25. Ricoeur, "The Just between the Legal and the Good," 36n3.

26. Ricoeur, "The Just between the Legal and the Good," 36n3.

27. Both the talk by Ricoeur as well as Dworkin's reply were first published in the legal journal *Ratio Juris* (Vol. 7, no. 3, 1994). Ricoeur's text was later included in *The Just* in a new translation by David Pellauer and with a revised title: "The Plurality of Instances of Justice," *The Just*, 76–94. It is this new translation that we republish here.

28. Michael Walzer, *Spheres of Justice: A Defense of Pluralism and Equality* (New York: Basic Books, 1983).

29. Luc Boltanski and Laurent Thévenot, *De la justification: les économies de la grandeur* (Paris: Gallimard, 1991).

30. Ricoeur, "The Plurality of Instances of Justice."

31. Ricoeur, "The Plurality of Instances of Justice" (quoting Boltanski and Thévenot on the latter term), 37.

32. Ricoeur, "The Plurality of Instances of Justice," 51.

33. Ricoeur, "The Plurality of Instances of Justice," 51.

34. Garapon is the current Secretary General of the *Institut des hautes études sur la justice* where, as previously noted, Ricoeur delivered several of his most important lectures on law and justice. Ricoeur wrote an important "Preface" to Garapon's book *Le gardien des promesses* (1996) which Ricoeur included in his *Reflections on the Just*, 156–168.

35. Oliver Abel, ed. *Le pardon, briser la dette et l'oubli* (Paris: Autrement, 1991).

36. Paul Ricoeur, *The Symbolism of Evil*, trans. Emerson Buchanan (New York: Harper and Row, 1967), 347.

37. Ricoeur, *Reflections on the Just*, 39.

BIBLIOGRAPHY

Abel, Oliver, ed. *Le pardon, briser la dette et l'oubli.* Paris: Autrement, 1991.

Aristotle. *Nichomachean Ethics*. Translated by Terence Irwin. Indianapolis: Hackett, 1985.

Austin, John. *The Providence of Jurisprudence Determined*. Cambridge: Cambridge University Press, 1995.

Boltanski, Luc and Laurent Thévenot. *De la justification: les économies de la grandeur*. Paris: Gallimard, 1991.

Hart, H. L. A. "The Ascription of Responsibility and Rights." *Proceedings of the Aristotelian Society*, New Series, no. 49 (1948): 171–94.

Hart, H. L. A. *The Concept of Law*. Oxford: Oxford University Press, 1961.

Hegel, G. W. F. *Philosophy of Right*. Translated by T. M. Knox. New York: Oxford University Press, 1967.

Rawls, John. *A Theory of Justice*. Cambridge, MA: Harvard University Press, 1971.

Ricoeur, Paul. *The Just*. Translated by David Pellauer. Chicago: University of Chicago Press, 2000.

Ricoeur, Paul. *Oneself as Another*. Translated by Kathleen Blamey. Chicago: University of Chicago Press, 1992.

Ricoeur, Paul. "The Political Paradox." In *History and Truth*, Translated by Charles A. Kelbley, 247–70. Evanston: Northwestern University Press, 1965.

Ricoeur, Paul. *Reflections on the Just*. Translated by David Pellauer. Chicago: Chicago University Press, 2007.

Ricoeur, Paul. *The Symbolism of Evil*. Translated by Emerson Buchanan. New York: Harper and Row, 1967.

Walzer, Michael Walzer. *Spheres of Justice: A Defense of Pluralism and Equality*. New York: Basic Books, 1983.

Part I

RICOEUR ON LAW, JUSTICE, AND PLURALITY

Introduction to Paul Ricoeur's "The Just Between the Legal and the Good"

Eileen Brennan

Paul Ricoeur wrote "The Just Between the Legal and the Good" for the inaugural lecture of the Institut des hautes études sur la justice (IHEJ), which he delivered in 1991. The IHEJ was created with the aim of "developing exchanges between legal professionals and academics in order to promote reflection and research on standards, legal regulation, missions and the functioning of justice and to contribute to the development of the values of justice" (Article 2 of the Statutes). One of the contributors to this volume, the magistrate Antoine Garapon, is a founding member and currently Secretary General of the IHEJ. In the period leading up to the inaugural lecture, Ricoeur and Garapon met several times at Ricoeur's home in Châtenay-Malabry to work on the text. Writing for members of a professional body whose interest in justice was decidedly practical represented an interesting challenge for the philosopher and he wanted to be sure that he had got it right. When, in *The Just,* Ricoeur looks back on this period, he sees it as a time when, thanks to his collaboration with Garapon and his work with the IHEJ, he was finally able to pay attention to the "juridical problematic." Ricoeur also acknowledges his debt to the École nationale de la magistrature, the nearby training school for public prosecutors and judges. He recalls that it was there that he met the question of the juridical in the figure of the judiciary, with its written laws, its tribunals, its judges, its ceremonial processes, all culminating in the pronouncement of a sentence where the law is stated in the circumstances of a trial, an eminently singular affair. Ricoeur came to believe that the juridical, comprehended through the features of the judiciary, provided philosophy with an opportunity to reflect upon the distinctiveness of right and the law in its proper setting, that is midway between moral philosophy or ethics and politics.

Chapter One

The Just Between the Legal and the Good

Paul Ricoeur

The reflections that I propose here lie at the level of the principles of justice as formulated and discussed in moral and political philosophy. However, before going down this path, I want to remind you of the practical context to which those principles belong. The idea of justice—whatever the meaning or the content—regulates a social practice, the occasions and circumstances of which it is important to remember first, followed by its paths or channels at the institutional level, and finally its arguments at the level of discourse. In speaking of the circumstances of justice, we must remember that we are dealing with justice whenever a higher authority is asked to decide between claims that are underpinned by competing interests or rights. As regards the channels of justice, it is a question of the judicial system itself, which comprises several things: a body of written laws; tribunals or courts of justice responsible for stating the law; judges, that is to say, individuals like us, who are supposed to be independent and who are responsible for rendering a judgment that is meant to be just in a particular circumstance; and we must not forget to add the monopoly on coercion, namely, the power to impose a court decision through the use of law enforcement authorities. As regards the arguments of justice, they remind us that justice is a part of our communicative activity, the confrontation between arguments before a court offering a remarkable example of the dialogical employment of language. I will come back to this sequence: occasions of justice—channels of justice—arguments of justice when I take the journey back from the principles to the practice of justice. That will be the third part of my lecture.

Having said that, the concept of justice, to which we will now devote the first two parts of this lecture, constitutes the regulative idea behind this complex practice, comprising familiar disputes, codified procedures, the set confrontation of arguments, and finally, rendering a judgment. As such, the idea of justice may be considered the reflexive moment of this practice.

But how are we to conduct the reflection?

It must be said straightaway that the two paths that we will explore do not exhaust the resources of what can be described as the "idea of justice." This idea is a conquest of reason, halfway between everyday practice, whose obligations we just recalled, and the mythic root from which the idea slowly emerges—as we see in the Greek Pre-Socratics, in Aeschylus's and Sophocles's tragedies, and in the pleas of the great Athenian orators. These sacred connotations are so strong that they persist within secularized societies, in that way demonstrating that the sense of justice is not exhausted in the construction of the juridical systems that they continue to generate. That is why I am now speaking about the sense rather than the idea of justice, so as to indicate its emergence from the immemorial past. In this regard, it must be said that we are sensitive first to injustice: "Unjust!" and "What injustice!," we exclaim. It is in the mode of complaining that we enter the field of the unjust and the just. And even at the level of instituted justice, before the courts of justice, we continue to act as a "complainant" and to "lodge a complaint." Now, the sense of injustice is not only more poignant, but more perspicacious than the sense of justice, because justice is more often what is missing and injustice what prevails, and human beings have a clearer vision of what is missing in human relations than they have of the right way in which to organize them. So, even among philosophers, it is injustice that first sets thought in motion. This is evidenced by Plato's dialogues and Aristotelian ethics, and their similar concern to name the unjust and the just at the same time. Our idea of justice is thus doubly reflexive: on the one hand, with regard to the social practice that it regulates; on the other hand, with regard to its almost immemorial origin. As I said a moment ago, that idea has two paths open to it, leading to two rival conceptions of justice, and whose opposition, as I would like to demonstrate, is no invention of philosophers but is constitutive of the very idea of justice. The predicate "just" certainly appears to be pulled alternately from the "good" side and the "legal" side, as the title of my lecture suggests. What does this opposition signify? Does it mark the indistinctness of a concept or, on the contrary, does it represent dialectical structure, something that it is important to respect? According to this second interpretation, the one I will adopt, the dialectic of the "good" and the "legal" would be inherent in the role of a regulative idea, which can be assigned to the idea of justice in respect of the social practice that is reflected in it. This is the working hypothesis that I now intend to develop.

THE JUST AND THE GOOD

At first sight, the two orientations placed under the headings of the "good" and the "legal" appear to be diametrically opposed. In academic language, one of them falls within the province of a *teleological* conception, the other within the province of a *deontological* conception of the moral and political life generally considered.

Where the dominant theme is the *good*, justice looks like one of the virtues, in the sense that the Greeks gave to the term *aretê*, which we could translate as "excellence," and which the Romans (Cicero, Seneca, and Marcus Aurelius) translated as *virtus*. To consider justice a virtue, alongside prudence, temperance, and courage—to recall the great medieval square of the cardinal virtues—is to acknowledge that it helps orient human action toward a fulfilment or perfection, an approximate idea of which is to be found in the popular notion of happiness. This aim of a *good life* gives the particular virtue of justice the teleological character that I mentioned. To live well is its *telos*. But we see straightaway that this conception is both appealing and troubling. On the one hand, human action acquires a meaning from this aim—by that I mean not only significance but also direction, two things that the French word *sens* brings to mind. On the other hand, the lack of consensus about what the Good truly and absolutely is means that the significance attached to the predicate "good" is stricken with uncertainty. Even though Aristotle was very close to Plato, he did not hold back from ridiculing the "Platonic Good," which he considered a nebulous idea, choosing instead to refer only to the human good. But what can we say about the human good? We are acquainted with the debates that were still ongoing in the Hellenistic period among the Platonists, Aristotelians, Epicureans, and Stoics, etc., regarding the relationships between pleasure and happiness and between the active and the contemplative life. But there is more to the teleological approach to justice than having this particular presupposition in common with the analysis of all the virtues. Justice has always been a separate chapter in the treatises on virtues because of a particular trait that prefigures the reversal from a teleological perspective to a deontological one, a move that will give priority to the ideas of obligation and duty, but also to the idea of being in conformity with the law. The trait in question is formalism, which we can think of as imperfect by comparison with the perfect formalism that is found only in the modern, purely procedural conceptions. By "imperfect formalism" I mean this: like every virtue, according to Aristotle's *Nicomachean Ethics*, justice is defined by the delicate balance it establishes between excess and insufficiency—a too much and a not enough—which is deemed "a mean," a middle term between two extremes. Now in the case of the virtue of justice, this equilibrium point is quite remarkable: it is the great *isotês*, extolled by Solon and Pericles, namely, that "equality" which reigns halfway between the excess of taking-too-much, of wanting-to-always-have-more—the great *pleonexia*, the vice of greed or envy—and the insufficiency of not contributing enough toward the city's expenses.

To what quantities and in accordance with what procedures does this equality apply? Two new difficulties await us here. To the first question, the answer has to be that justice regulates the distribution of all sorts of goods, external and precarious, respecting prosperity and adversity, which look like goods to share and expenses to apportion. Let us focus for the moment on these verbs: "distribute," "share out," and "apportion." They can only concern institutions, mainly political, which allow themselves to be defined by this distribution, sharing out, and apportionment function. This idea is of great significance and has lost none of its strength as the discussion of the second conception of justice will confirm. Might we venture to say that every society, as instituted, shares out roles, jobs, benefits, disadvantages, honors, and expenses? The idea of justice would then require us to take as our starting point the image of a society that was not only characterized by a will to live together, a wish for cooperation, but also by rules of distribution—distributed shares making each citizen a partner in the true sense of the word.

Two corollaries of this idea of society as a distribution system are worth commenting on. First, in passing through the institution, as a body for the distribution of roles, the virtue of justice is distinguished from the virtue of friendship, which is practiced directly between equals in a one-to-one situation, without institutional mediation. Friendship has a fellow human being as a counterpart, justice, a third party. Thus, the other of justice is not the other of friendship, but the *everyone* of a just distribution: *suum cuique tribuere*, as the well-known Latin saying goes. The second corollary: this concept of distribution that, from Aristotle to the Medieval philosophers and to John Rawls,[1] is closely related to the idea of justice, allows us to dismiss the protagonists of a false debate on the relationship between individuals and society. In line with a sociologism like Durkheim's, society is always more than the sum of its members; the individual and society are not in continuity with one another. Conversely, in line with the methodological individualism of a Max Weber, the key concepts of sociology indicate nothing more than the probability that individuals will behave in a certain way. The idea of society as a distribution system transcends the terms of that opposition. The institution as regulation of the distribution of roles is so much more and other than the sum of individuals who have designated roles; in other words, the social relationship cannot be reduced to the terms of the relationship. But the relationship is not an additional entity. An institution considered as a distribution rule exists only for as long as individuals are involved. And that participation—in the sense of taking part—lends itself to probabilistic analyses that have no application other than to individual behaviors. But the answer given to the first question, namely, the nature of the quantities to which the idea of justice as *isotês* applies, raises a specific difficulty that will also contribute to the substitution of a deontological conception for a teleological one. The difficulty is this: what allows us to characterize as *good* both the participation of the beneficiaries of sharing and the nature of the things to be shared? Might a formal procedure for sharing avoid the need for a substantive definition of the goods at issue?

But let us turn to the second question. In accordance with what procedures should such a distribution of shares be implemented? This is where a new problem awaits us, one which modern societies can only exacerbate. Aristotle is the first to have seen that the real stumbling block is the question posed by unequal shares. The idea of a numerically equal share is easily understood, and besides, it has applications even in ancient societies, for example, in the form of rotating public offices. As for modern societies, they have continued to extend the field of application of numerical equality: equality before the law; equal rights to freedom of expression, of assembly, and of publication; equal voting rights for all citizens; and, at least as a promise, equal opportunity, that is to say, equal starting points for assuming positions of authority, command, and influence. Tocqueville wants to persuade us that modern democracies tend towards this equality. However, in reality no society functions, and perhaps cannot function effectively, in the numerical equality mode—that is, using an egalitarian distribution—particularly when it comes to the production of wealth, but this applies to the whole range of goods to be shared.[2] The only thing worth considering is proportional equality, which delimits that form of justice that the medieval philosophers will call "distributive." It is called "proportional" because, as in the theory of mathematical proportions, equality is not between things, but between relationships: the relationship between the contribution of that person and that share, and the relationship between the contribution of some other person and some other share. The idea of *isotês* is saved, but at the price of an artifice; that of a four-term relationship: two people and two shares.

Thus, Aristotle poses the formidable problem, which the Social Contract theorists and Rawls in their wake will take up again: that of justifying a certain idea of equality, without endorsing a strict egalitarianism.[3]

THE JUST AND THE LEGAL

At the end of this first series of analyses, the question is whether the transition from an imperfect formalism to a perfect formalism, as happens in a purely procedural conception of justice, will help us surmount the difficulties created by the idea of proportional equality.

To go from an imperfect formalism to a perfect formalism is to break the link between the ancient and medieval philosophers' virtue of justice and the idea of the Good, whether it be the Good in general, the idea of the good life, the good of a particular historical community, or the substantive goods that give content to the idea of justice in unequal shares.

It was through the impetus given by Kantian philosophy that the theory of justice was pulled over to the deontological side, that is, to a conception in which all moral, juridical and political relations are placed under the idea of legality, of conformity with the law. But this conception is far from homogeneous. According to the orthodox Kantian line, it is only juridical provisions, which can be derived from a supreme, wholly *aprioristic* imperative, that merit the name "law." Kant formulates this imperative as follows: "Act in such a way that you always treat humanity, whether in your own person or in the person of any other, never merely as a means but always at the same time as an end."[4] But as his theory of law in *The Metaphysics of Morals* shows, only a very small number of laws may be regarded as indisputable corollaries of the formal imperative. For the rest, conformity with the law means conformity with the laws that are developed through the legislative activity of the body politic. We go then, via a turnaround within formalism, from a strict *apriorism* to a juridical positivism, where the question of the foundation outruns practical reason and falls under the control of empirically and historically constituted legislating authorities.

What these two branches of juridical legalism have in common, however, is the transition from the imperfect formalism, characteristic of the teleological conception, to a complete formalism, where there can be no place either for the idea of the common good or for the idea of substantive goods that give content to the idea of justice in unequal shares. We can say that it is in a procedural conception of justice that such a formalization achieves its purpose. Anticipating further discussion, one might ask whether such a reduction to procedure does not leave a residue that requires some kind of return to a teleological perspective, not at the price of a repudiation of formalizing procedures, as I will try to demonstrate, but in the name of a claim to which these very procedures give a voice. How they do so will be revealed in due course. But we must win the right to this critique by following as far as is practicable the process of formalizing the idea of justice, through which the deontological perspective earns its fame.

It is noteworthy that the deontological approach could expand into the institutional field, where the idea of justice is applied, only by uniting with the contractualist tradition—more precisely with the fiction of a social contract thanks to which a certain group of individuals successfully rises above a supposedly primitive state of nature in order to arrive at the rule of law. There is nothing contingent in this encounter between a perspective that is deliberately deontological in its moral claims and the contractualist current. The purpose and function of the fictional contract is to separate the just from the good by substituting the procedure of an imaginary deliberation for any prior commitment concerning an alleged common good. According to this hypothesis, it is the contractual procedure that is supposed to generate the principle or principles of justice. But this successful union between the deontological perspective and the contractualist approach does not just have a polemical purpose. One could say that the contract occupies at the level of institutions the place that autonomy occupies at the fundamental level of morality. That is, a freedom sufficiently extricated from the straitjacket of inclinations gives itself a law, which is the very law of freedom. But whereas the autonomy of the individual can be called a "fact of reason," attested to by consciousness, the contract can only be a fiction—a founding fiction certainly, but a fiction nevertheless—because the republic is not a fact as consciousness is a fact, but is always still to be founded, and will probably never be definitively founded. So, the fiction of the contract lives on in order to coordinate a deontological conception of justice with the moral principle of autonomy and the person as an end in itself.

There is an element of the unresolved enigma of the foundation of the republic in the formulation of the contract both in Rousseau and in Kant. In the former, we must resort to a legislator to exit the labyrinth of politics. In the latter, the connection between autonomy or self-regulation and the social contract, whereby each member of a multitude gives up his or her natural liberty in order to regain it in the form of civil liberty as a member of a republic, is presupposed but not justified.

It is to this unresolved problem that Rawls attempted to provide a solution, one of the best offered in the contemporary era. If the term *fairness* (which can be translated as *équité*) is proposed as the key to the concept of justice, it is because *fairness* characterizes the original situation of the contract from which the justice of the basic institutions is supposed to derive. Rawls thus fully assumes the idea of an original contract between free and rational persons, concerned with promoting their individual interests. Contractualism and individualism thus move forward hand in hand. Had the attempt been successful, a purely procedural conception of justice would not only have freed itself from every presupposition concerning the good, but it would have definitively liberated the just from the tutelage of the good—first at the institutional level, then, by extension, at the levels of individuals and of nation states, regarded as individuals on the grand scale. Rawls's project is best understood if we keep in mind the paradox generated by Kant himself, namely, that because it is not possible to derive a body of laws from a principle as abstract as respect for the human person, we rely on the *de facto* legislative power to give a content to this void of formalism, and we switch then from an abstract formalism to the most radical juridical positivism. This danger internal to the deontological approach would be addressed if, in the unreal situation of deliberation, it was possible to produce principles of justice that were sufficiently complex and clear to set up the law as a real organizer of the social sphere.

From Rawls's vast work I have retained only his contribution to solving the following problem. Are the principles of justice, which are supposed to derive from deliberation in an unreal, imaginary, ahistorical, so-called original situation, sufficient to articulate a *real* historical community's desire to live together in a network of juridical relations that would rescue that desire to live together from fusional indistinction, without endlessly moving subjects reduced to juridical atoms apart from one another ad infinitum? The answer that I present for your consideration and further discussion is highly nuanced. I do not doubt that this unreal deliberation, conducted under the veil of ignorance, leads to principles that are more precise, and so more socially fecund, than the empty imperative of respect for persons. But the gap between these still very formal principles of justice and the juridical practice mentioned in the opening lines of my lecture prompts us to think about the *mediators* (*les relais*) that the principles of justice must find in a discussion that is no longer *unreal*, conducted under the veil of ignorance, but *real* and conducted at the level of what Hannah Arendt calls the public "space of appearance." Let us say straightaway that it is at the level of these mediators, to be used for entrenching the idea of justice in an effective judicial practice, that a certain recourse to a transformed idea of the good or goods will be necessary, contrary to the asceticism of a purely procedural conception of justice.

I will retain from Rawls's analyses of the principles of justice those parts that put the principles on the path to arbitrating between conflicting social demands. *Three* points are worth highlighting.

First key point: the principles we will set out are principles of distribution. The brief summary devoted above to the Aristotelian and then medieval idea of distributive justice familiarized us with this notion of distribution. Justice as distributive is applicable to all sorts of benefits that can be treated as shares to be distributed: rights and duties on the one hand, benefits and burdens on the other. It is clear that for Rawls, the focus should not be on the peculiar character of the things to be shared, on their valuation as distinct goods, under penalty of reintroducing a teleological principle and, following that, opening the door to the idea of a diversity of goods, even to the idea of an insurmountable conflict among goods. The formalism of the contract has the effect of neutralizing the diversity of goods for the benefit of the sharing rule. We will have to return to this working hypothesis when we discuss the transition from the original situation under the veil of ignorance to the real conflict situations of a society as complex as ours. Insofar as society allows itself to be recognized as a distribution system, any sharing appears problematic and open to equally reasonable alternatives. Since there are many plausible ways of distributing advantages and disadvantages, society proves to be a consensual-conflictual phenomenon. On the one hand, any allocation of shares can be contested, especially (as we will see) in the context of unequal distribution. When, on the other hand, it comes to stability, distribution requires consensus on the procedures for arbitrating between competing claims. The problems of priority, which we will discuss later, stem very precisely from the *problematic* nature of the sharing rule.

Second key point: Rawls offers us not one, but two principles of justice, the second one taking up again the thorny issue of unequal shares, which Aristotle had already discussed under the heading of "proportional equality." It is important, however, that a first, egalitarian principle be formulated, which is said to have lexical priority over the second one. This first principle ensures that all citizens are treated equally under the law.[5] This principle formalizes the major achievement of advanced democratic societies and the freedoms they have won of expression, assembly, the vote, and the right to stand for election to public office. This is the modern triumph of Solon's *isotês* in a considerably wider sphere of action. However, one part of the debates that we will discuss later has to do with the breadth of the sphere of equal citizenship, it being the case that any system that specifies membership also specifies exclusions. Thus, from the first principle, there is an open debate which calls for the *mediators* mentioned above. But one point is to be excluded from the debate: this first principle must be satisfied as a priority, without the unequal sharing rule, included in the second principle, giving license to infringe the right to equality before the law. In other words, the serial or lexical order means that "infringements of the basic equal liberties protected by the first principle cannot be justified, or compensated for, by greater social and economic advantages."[6]

I come to the third key point, the most crucial and the most controversial in the entire book. It has to do with the second principle of justice, which, as already mentioned, takes over inequality principles regarding differences in income and wealth, certainly, but also differences in levels of authority and responsibility in all kinds of organizations. The principle states that, among all the unequal shares, there is one that is more just than any other. It is the one where any increase in benefits for the most advantaged is offset by a reduction in disadvantages for the least advantaged. A formula sums up the principle: "maximize the minimum," hence the name, the maximin principle. I am not concerned here with the highly sophisticated demonstration of that principle that is given on the basis of decision theory under conditions of uncertainty. The essential thing for us is the idea that there is a point of equilibrium in unequal shares, such that certain inequalities must be preferred to greater inequalities, but also to an equal distribution. In a sense, something of the first principle of justice is preserved within the second, in the form of equality of opportunity or, in Rawls's vocabulary, "starting positions," but equality of opportunity remains an aspiration and unfulfilled requirement, as it is only to economic and social inequalities, recognized as just, that the aforementioned open positions provide access. Rawls's formulation betrays this embarrassment at the intersection point of the two principles, one of which is egalitarian and the other not: "social and economic inequalities are to be arranged so that they are both (a) reasonably expected to be to everyone's advantage, and (b) attached to positions and offices open to all."[7]

This ambiguity raises a substantive question: to what extent can the principles of justice—and particularly the second—play the role of the *regulative idea* that we presupposed in our introduction for justice as a social practice? Is it not an uninterrupted public debate that can guide the *mediators* that are required between those still too abstract principles and an effective judicial practice?

FROM THE PRINCIPLES OF JUSTICE TO LEGAL PRACTICE

What we will now try to explore in this third part is the *gap* that remains between principles of justice supposed to stem from merely procedural discussion in an original situation under the veil of ignorance, and a practice characterized, as we saw at beginning, by its occasions, its ways and means, and its mode of argumentation.

The exploration of this gap can be done from both ends—the formal idea on the one hand, the concrete practice on the other—by going back and forth in pursuit of the sort of mutual adjustment that Rawls himself calls "reflective equilibrium," but which he applies only to the way the theory relates to what he calls "considered convictions."

Let us start with the *circumstances*, or *occasions* of justice. They all take the form of a conflict between purported rights, real interests, and even acquired privileges. In all subdivisions of law—criminal, civil, social, and international—the demand for justice arises in situations of conflict that the law shapes into the trial. It is at this point that considerations borrowed from the teleological conception of justice are first revitalized. The demands which justice is called upon to decide between—or, more precisely, and we will come back to this, to which justice is asked to give their fair share—carry values, evaluations in terms of goods. Here a purely procedural theory requires the mediator of an ethics of values, which is itself laden with difficulties and weighed down with unanswered questions. Yet, even in Rawls, the furtive evocation of "considered convictions" already implies that it is not possible to stick to a simple calculation of maximum and minimum, without overlooking the major difficulty presented by *the real heterogeneity of goods* invested in the things to be shared. This problem is the inescapable counterpart of the conception of society as a system of distribution. The very notion of a share changes meaning according to whether it is a question of market goods—such as revenues, common properties, services—or non-market goods—such as security, health, education, and citizenship, to say nothing of positions of authority, responsibility, and influence, which are connected to the hierarchical structures of all the institutions which, like political institutions, know the distinction between governors and the governed, leaders and the led, and directors and employees. The company, the family unit, the hospital, and the prison environment are familiar with these problems of the division of authority among unequal partners. It is therefore not enough to have a very broad idea of the notion of the distribution of shares and the division of roles. We must still be attentive to the real heterogeneity of what we can call, with Rawls again (although he does not offer a theory of them), "primary social goods," which are what is at issue in a concrete way in shares likely to be considered just. It is upon this heterogeneity that some critics of Rawls insist, among them Michael Walzer, who goes so far as to break up the unitary idea of justice, based on the procedural schema and supposedly free of any reference to the quality of the goods to be distributed. Indeed, the procedural scheme leading to the *maximin* principle derives its universality only from the unreal character of the original situation, on the threshold of which those contracting are stripped not only of their characteristics, their interests, but also of their convictions concerning the good or goods. However, in a real historical situation, these goods make a return with the concreteness of things to be shared. The problem of justice then becomes that of the priorities to be established, within a historical community, among goods that encroach on one another where each one claims the whole area. We rediscover here a problem previously posed by Max Weber in his Nietzschean phase, concerning the polytheism of values.

Anticipating the discussion on the channels of justice and especially its argumentation, it must be said that the mediator of a theory of values, required at least by a purely procedural conception of justice, operates with considerable difficulty in a society like ours, which lacks a strong consensus when it comes to ethics. I would nevertheless like to make three brief comments here. First, the conditions for consensus are not lost. They depend on the capacity that our fellow citizens have retained to intertwine, in a thriving secularism, legacies as diverse as those received from the Judeo-Christian past, the Greco-Roman culture, the Renaissance and the Enlightenment, and the nineteenth century of nations and socialisms. Second comment: it has to be acknowledged that such a consensus is itself involved in a history. If the idea of value suffers from a certain conceptual weakness, because it cannot take the place of a principle, its historical strength is to perform the function of *interchange* between an abstract level where the consensus remains very strong (everyone has always known that people are not things, even if this high principle has always been violated) and the level of everyday life, where new situations arise, calling for a decision. That is why a Platonism of values in the style of Max Scheler's can no longer convince. But thirdly, it depends on the quality of the public discussion, which we are now going to discuss, to give life to the *overlapping consensus* mentioned in my first comment and to the exchange between very slowly evolving "background" convictions and more rapidly evolving "foreground" convictions.

That being said about the interface between the idea of justice and the circumstances of justice, what then about the intersection with what we have called the *ways and means* of justice? I would like to remind you of the way I spoke about it in my introduction. As regards the channels of justice, I said, that is a question of the judicial system itself, which comprises several things: a body of written laws; tribunals and courts of justice whose function it is to state the law; judges, that is to say, individuals like us, who are supposed to be independent and are responsible for rendering the judgment of what is just in a particular circumstance. How does the idea of justice apply to this institutional context? And which mediators should be introduced between the principles of justice and ordinary judicial practice? It seems to me that here we must reposition the judicial system, even as broadly defined by the sequence laws-tribunals-judges-judgment, *between* a higher authority and a carrier base (*une base porteuse*).

The higher authority is the state, and the judicial system expects two things of it: that it guarantee the proper functioning of justice in a protected space, delimited within the public space; but also that it decide through a legislative process on the order of priority, in the medium term, between the major categories of primary social goods, both market goods and non-market goods. The urgency of setting such an order of priority arises from the above description of society as a distribution system in which the demands arising from the different "spheres of justice" cannot all be met, either at the same time or to the same extent. The real heterogeneity of those goods corresponding to the shares and the roles to be distributed underlines the random and always revocable character of the chosen order of priority. Ensuring this global framing of the law is, then, dependent upon *political* discussion and *political* decision-making. It is in this sense and to this extent that the idea of justice requires *political mediation* in order to connect with the practice of justice and its own institutions.

But another mediation is required on the lower edge of the judiciary, as it were. That is to say, there is a floor for debate at the level of what is nowadays called "civil society." It is certainly up to the state to set an order of priority among competing primary social goods in order to provide a political line, but it is at the level of that larger public space, in which the legal space is carved out, that the values mentioned a bit earlier confront one another. It is in this public space that evaluations, which give the meaning "goods" to those shares and roles that society distributes and assigns to rights-holders, are weighed up against one another. It is during this public discussion that (as we said above) the ambiguous status of values is confirmed, values which rise in tiers from "background" values, as close as possible to the stable principles of justice, and "foreground" values, affected to a greater degree by the harsh dynamics of tradition and innovation—as is the case in the new fields of the environment and the applied life sciences. Without placing greater emphasis on those dynamics of evaluation in the context of public discussion, let us say that the judicial institution would not function either in a society without the rule of law or in a civil society where we did not learn to debate, where we had no idea of the unwritten rules that trace the boundary between speech and violence, and where exercising oral judgment—whose formalized manner is the judicial system—were missing. So, at the top and above, the state; below and at the base, the public discussion space; and, *between the two*, the procedural as such, taken out of the mediation of the state and situated in its instituted space.

Let us be clear: by "procedural" we do not mean here the unreal proceduralism of the contractualists, but rather the established and operative procedures that govern the sequence laws—courts and tribunals—judgment and judges. Let us say a word about each of the constitutive moments of judicial *praxis*. Subject to the jurisdiction of the law, conflicts are placed at a good distance from passions, interests, and fanaticism. As for the trial itself, it establishes between the parties what Antoine Garapon calls a "just distance," halfway between a clash, which is a type of misunderstanding, and contempt, which backs away from discussion. As for the judgment, it can be interpreted as a way of putting the parties themselves in their rightful place, primarily through unequal shares of all kinds, which in the end becomes the rule. As for the judge, the judge appears as the figure appointed to maintain all of the following distances: between the judicial system and politics, between the judicial system and open conflict, and between the parties themselves.

If we retain the idea of the just distance in the juridical space, the whole process can be defined as regulating and modulating proximity and distance in the public sphere. Thus, unexpectedly I retrieve Aristotle's idea of a midpoint between *too much* and *not enough*, whereby he defined the virtue of justice. In quasi-topological terms, "just distance" is the mean between too much and not enough distance. Of course, this search for the just distance should be particularized in the penal order, in the civil order, in the social order, and in the international order. At least, the great mediation of proceduralism is warranted in outline, from which the state derives legitimacy as much as it exercises the guarantee, while the conflicts that tear civil society to shreds assume the codified and distanced form of the trial.

But I hasten to my conclusion, which will deal with the last component of what, in my introduction, I called "justice as a social practice," namely, the *arguments* of justice (which I mentioned following the *circumstances* and *channels* of justice). Indeed, it is only fitting that our concluding words should be reserved for the *discourse of justice*. We were, in a sense, continually dealing with it, without saying so explicitly, under the two previous headings. On the one hand, the discourse of justice is at work in the public debate regarding the order of priority to be established among the primary social goods and the values underlying those goods. On the other hand, the entire procedure, from the law and then via the trial to rendering the judgment, is only a long discourse. Nevertheless, emphasis must be placed on that discursive and argumentative character of justice, for itself and in itself, lest we retain from the trial only its conclusion, and mainly its implementation, and, in the latter, only the use of public force—as if the monopoly on violence summed up the work of justice, the gavel eclipsing the scales. That is why I want to emphasize strongly the argumentative dimension of justice, in its circumstances and in its ways and means. Before constraining, the judgment aims to *state the law*, that is to say, to situate the parties in their rightful place. That is undoubtedly the most important meaning that should be attached to the *judgment* as arrived at in a particular circumstance. If that is the case, it is because this judgment provisionally concludes the acrimonious part of the *trial*, which is none other than a *ruled exchange of arguments*, that is to say, of reasons *for* and *against*, supposed as plausible and worthy of consideration by the other party. Taken from this angle, the trial is a segment of the communicative activity of a society, the confrontation between arguments in front of a tribunal constituting a remarkable case of the dialogical use of language.

However, this use of language has its logic and its ethics, one inseparable from the other.

From a logical standpoint, the discourse of justice beautifully illustrates the place that argumentation occupies, halfway—at a just distance, dare we say—between intellectually compelling evidence, as in mathematics, and the rhetorical use of language. Certainly, in a trial one is asked to provide evidence—material evidence and credible testimony; but, taken as a whole the trial does not have the order of proof, that is to say, logical necessity. Although failing as a way of proof in that rigorous sense, juridical argumentation is not condemned to sophistry, to that kind of discourse that wins favor through its power to please and seduce in collusion with bad and partisan passions. Here we touch upon the *fragility* that judicial discourse has in common with other types of discourse: political discourse, of course, but also that of the historian and the columnist, the historian of the present. Fragility, then, of a discourse that though failing to prove, still aspires to persuade, without being just a matter of pleasing. Its epistemological status, if you will permit this rather technical expression, is that of the *logic of the probable*, whereby Aristotle defined "dialectic" and to which he related rhetoric, *or the art of using probable arguments in public speaking*. A remarkable feature of this argumentative structure of justice should be given some thought. The onslaught of arguments is, in a sense, infinite since in the order of the probable there is always room for a "but"—in the form, for example, of appeals and avenues of appeal to a higher court. In another sense, it is finite, insofar as the exchange of arguments ends with a decision, namely the *judgment* made in a particular situation. But, in order not to be arbitrary, it must draw its justification from the deliberation that it ends and the argumentative quality of that deliberation.

However, that quality depends on the link between *logic* and *ethics* in the argument. That ethics is none other than the ethics of the *better* argument, the one that the *other* can hear. What better formula is there for summing up this ethics of argumentation than the adage: *Audi alteram partem* [*Listen to the other side*]?

Translated by Eileen Brennan

NOTES

1. See John Rawls, *A Theory of Justice* (Cambridge, MA: Belknap Press of Harvard University Press, 1971).

2. That was clearly the case with the ancient city, even reduced to the circle of its citizens by right. Aristotle admits that the numerical equality rule is not suitable for the nature of people and shared things.

3. Regardless of the difficulties that we will consider further on, it is worth retaining the convincing and durable strength of the link between justice and equality. Equality, however one may choose to delineate it, is to life in institutions what friendship—or others would say pity, solicitude—is to interpersonal relationships. Friendship, we have already said, gives the self as a counterpart another who has a face, in the strong sense that Emmanuel Levinas taught us to recognize her. Justice, thought of as equality, gives the self as a counterpart another who is everybody. This way, the meaning of justice subtracts nothing from solicitude; it supposes it, insofar as it holds people to be irreplaceable. On the other hand, insofar as the field of application of equality is the city, justice broadens friendship to include the historical community governed by the state and, ideally, the whole of humanity.

4. Immanuel Kant, *Groundwork of the Metaphysics of Morals*, trans. H. J. Paton (New York: Harper and Row, 1965), 96.

5. More precisely, "Each person is to have an equal right to the most extensive scheme of equal basic liberties compatible with a similar scheme of liberties for others." Rawls, *A Theory of Justice*, 53.

6. Rawls, *A Theory of Justice*, 53–54.

7. Rawls, *A Theory of Justice*, 53.

BIBLIOGRAPHY

Kant, Immanuel. *Groundwork of the Metaphysics of Morals*. Translated by H. J. Paton. New York: Harper and Row, 1965.

Rawls, John. *A Theory of Justice*. Cambridge, MA: Belknap Press of Harvard University Press, 1971.

Chapter Two

The Plurality of Instances of Justice
Paul Ricoeur

The theme of this lecture might appear inopportune, even untimely, in the precise sense of the word. At a time when public opinion and the public powers are questioning the nature of the transfers that our nation-state must yield to the present European institutions and those to come, and are asking if it is a question of a simple transfer of competence or a real transfer of sovereignty, which is reputed to be indivisible and, owing to this fact, inalienable—it is at this very time that I want to attempt to take the measure of asymmetrical problem, although one pointing in the opposite direction. Here it is no longer a question of a limitation from on high of what we can call the juridical power of the State, but of the limitation in a sense from below of this very juridical power. It is a question about a historical force, operating within a particular state, for which various authors are at work trying to formulate the theory. I propose examining two of these pleas in favor of an intrastate differentiation of generative instances of right. The first, that of Michael Walzer, in his *Spheres of Justice*,[1] has been taken as one of the most brilliant rebuttals yet offered of John Rawls and of his abstract, formal, and strictly procedural concept of justice. The second is that which Luc Boltanski and Laurent Thévenot present in their *De la justification: les économies de la grandeur*.[2] In this book it is the idea of justification and not directly that of justice that provides the focus, while it is the cities and worlds governed by what the subtitle calls economies of scale or standing that introduce plurality at the very heart of the demand for justification. The target is no longer Rawls's procedural abstraction, but rather the apparent antinomy between the holism of Durkheimian sociologists and the methodological individualism professed by economic theory. It remains true, however, that these two works, despite their differences (which I shall discuss below), both deal with a pluralism that takes up—in an inverted fashion, so to speak—the unitary focus on the judicial that the nation-state constitutes in our Western and more precisely our republican tradition.

There is one pitfall I wish to avoid: that of a term-by-term comparison ending up with a mere juxtaposition of these two short monographs.

Beyond the difference in the way of dividing what are here called spheres and cities, I want to consider two questions. The first has to do with the different nature of these projects and the criteria of distinction that result from this. The second, and more important, question, although governed by the first, concerns the new possibilities for regrouping the political community and its justice left open by these two enterprises of what we can call juridical pluralism. Indeed, if these two works invert our republican conception of the oneness of the source of juridicity, summed up by the concept of the sovereignty of the people, do they not invite us to take them in turn in an inverted manner by asking what there is to say, in the last analysis, about justice or justification as singular terms at the end of the long detour through multiplicity and the diversity of sources of right.

TWO PROJECTS OF PLURALIZATION

Approaching these two works beginning from the projects that set them on their way and the criteria of distinction that flow from these projects, we must first attend to the differences expressed in their subtitles: on the one side, "defense of pluralism and equality"; on the other, "the economies of *grandeur*." What does this say?

Walzer's project has to do with equality. But the criterion of differentiation is provided by the notion of social goods. Thus it is necessary to examine the nature of this connection. Ever since Solon, Pericles, Isocrates, and Aristotle, equality has been a synonym of justice, once justice is held to govern the distribution of equal or unequal shares, in the varying senses I shall speak of as qualitative. Let us say that justice, in a distributive sense, identifies the idea of equality with that of a fair share. Difficulties begin when one sets aside simple equality—arithmetic equality, Aristotle said—following the formula, the same share to everyone. Only a repressive society, it is said, could impose such equality, and it would be to everyone's detriment. So what then of complex equality? The demand for such equality turns out to be essentially reactive or corrective, not to say abolitionist. What one wants to abolish is domination. Whence Walzer's project: "The aim of political egalitarianism is a society free from domination."[3] The same applies, as we shall see, for Boltanski and Thévenot. But how does domination manifest itself in our societies? Essentially in the way social goods are distributed. What can we do so that no social good serves as a means of domination? With this question we tie the project to its criterion, namely, the principle of differentiation of social goods. Three interconnected assertions serve as a guide here:

1. social goods are irreducibly multiple;
2. each one rests on some symbolism (Walzer calls it a shared understanding); and
3. each develops an internal logic, on the basis of the shared understanding of the groups in question, that is, the reasons that govern both the extent of its validity and the limit of the claim it makes.

These three assertions give us a threefold criterion for identifying the goods at issue, differentiating the implied symbolism in each case, and delimiting the concerned spheres.

Thus we can see how the project—to counteract domination—and the threefold criterion bound to the notion of social goods are articulated in terms of each other. The notion of complex equality then appears as the concept resulting from the intersection between the project of combating domination and the program of differentiating spheres of justice. Like the idea of simple equality, that of complex equality is a concept of protest, of abolition. From this, we can already presume that the concern for differentiation will win out over that of integration. But this will be the theme of the next section of this chapter.

If we now look at the open-ended list of social goods Walzer proposes, we are struck by several surprising features. My first impression is one of bric-a-brac—of *bricolage* in the sense made famous by Claude Lévi-Strauss. This effect is undeniably the one sought. If it is true that social goods are heterogeneous, the reasons that govern their evaluation are themselves incommensurable. A rapid glance at the list confirms this. We begin with membership. How is the inside and outside of a political community to be assigned between members and strangers? We continue with social provision, essentially security and assistance to those most in need, with the question what needs entail an obligation that they be provided for, along with a corresponding right to such provision? From there we pass on to money and commodities, with the question what can and cannot be bought with money? As complete a list as possible of what is not commercial answers this question. Therefore it is by considering the legitimate meanings attached to the notion of saleable goods that the limits attached to the notion of the market and to that of a market economy are decided. Next considered are offices open to rule-governed competitions, with a cluster of questions: What tests? Who judges? And above all: is every job to be considered an office? The whole question of a "right to" and the limits of the notion of public service in office are at issue here. This, curiously, is followed by the question of hard, degrading, or dangerous work, all taken to be negative values that need to be fairly distributed without regimenting the whole world. From here we pass to leisure activities, which, as positive, do not reduce to idleness, or vacations, but preside over the distribution of social time and the rhythms of activity in the city. It is not surprising next to read many pages devoted to education, which is a social good inasmuch as the transmission of knowledge and the formation of personal autonomy are traceable back to social symbolism. A string of questions touching on justice flows from the understanding of this good: Who teaches? To whom? Under the control of what offices? And above all, how to assure equality of opportunity, without falling once again into repressive systems through an excess of pedagogical zeal? The reader, educated in political philosophy, will be astonished to turn next to three chapters devoted to kinship and love, divine grace, and the struggle for recognition. This is another occasion to say that the list of social goods is long and open-ended, as soon as one takes into account the amplitude of shared symbolisms, the internal logic of the goods considered, and above all the delimitation that results from their spheres of validity. Who can deny that kinship, marriage, and the equality of the sexes pose questions of distribution? Or that the quarrel between Church and State calls for the curbing of rival pretensions, raised in turn by one side or the other across a line of demarcation bought at a high price? Finally, recognition itself is a social good in the form of titles, honors, compensations, and prizes, but also punishments: "What we distribute to one another is esteem, not self-esteem; respect, not self-respect; defeat, not the sense of defeat; and the relation of the first to the second term in each of these pairs is indirect and uncertain."[4] We see that the notion of social goods extends far, even to the sphere of intimacy, and the problems of a just distribution pursue us to the very core of our conscience.

But we come to the last chapter, whose place in the whole edifice, or rather in its enumeration, will be at the center of our critical reflections when we come in the next section to ask ourselves about the resources for another grouping left open by one or the other of the juridical pluralisms we are considering. This last chapter is titled "Political Power." It is worth noting that in it we find no definition in the form of a State, even though we find enumerated (though not lingered over) sovereignty, authority, and the power of decision-making. It is as one good among goods, therefore as a distributed good, that political power is sought and feared and resisted. If this is the case, it is because no other good poses in such a critical manner the problem of boundaries. Sometimes it is colonized by money, by the competence of experts, even by sex; sometimes it invades all the other spheres, to the point of giving tyranny its most visible form. How is it to be kept within its boundaries? Well, by proceeding as in the case of money, where it was asked what cannot be bought thanks to the internal logic of commercial goods. In the same way, one makes a list of what we cannot do with political power: tolerate slavery, corrupt the system of justice, discriminate among plaintiffs, control religion, confiscate or abusively tax property, arrogate to ourselves the monopoly of education, restrain basic liberties. For Walzer, this question about what political power can and cannot do precedes and commands the question of who governs. Taking up the much-used metaphor of the captain of the ship, he forthrightly proclaims that it is up to the passengers, not the captain, to choose the destination and evaluate the risks. Here Walzer is close to Hannah Arendt, for whom power proceeds from the conjunction of wills and not from any higher agency.

In this regard, the most important peril for our societies comes from the coalition between property as power over things and political power as exercised over human beings. Whence the permanent urgency of a correct delimitation of spheres. Still the reader cannot fail to wonder: is political power a good like all the others? As the "crucial agency of distributive justice,"[5] is it not itself also the border guard? And, in this, does it not pose a quite specific problem of self-limitation, whether by constitutional or some other means? We touch here on what I shall call below the political paradox, namely that politics seems both to constitute one sphere of justice among others and to envelop all the other spheres.

Turning from Walzer to Boltanski and Thévenot, we are immediately struck by the difference not only at the level of their project but also in the criteriology that results from it. To the pair formed by the search for complex equality and the investigation of social goods corresponds another pairing: that between the search for justification and the investigation of orders of scale. These massive differences refer back to different initial situations. For Walzer, this is tyranny; the perverse form of domination; for Boltanski and Thévenot, it is conflict, disputes, differences of opinion, in short, discord. Domination calls for a curbing strategy, discord one of justification consisting of a battery of arguments intended to prevail in disputes or litigation. When so associated with the search for justification, the sense of injustice constitutes a motivation within the framework of disagreement no less strong than it does within that of domination. For it is violence that haunts discord once this fails to raise itself to the level of discourse. This then is the question from which this work proceeds: how to justify agreement and manage disagreement without succumbing to violence?

This project makes use of a methodology, or better a criteriology, consisting, as in the case of Walzer, of a work of differentiation. This is why an identical problem of redistribution will be considered below. However, differentiation does not bear here on social goods and shared understanding, but on principles of scale. The difference is not easy to make clear. Let us say that one starts by looking for forms of equivalence—and therefore generalities—among social actors, resulting from their recourse to final principles of legitimation in situations of agreement and disagreement. It is these principles that turn out in the end to be multiple.

It is necessary to stop somewhere in the regression toward always prior arguments. The necessity for such a halt in operations of justification cannot fail to interest the jurist reflecting on the relationship between judgment and stopping point: stop in deliberation, stop in the confrontation of claims, a final word pronounced in the debate of oneself with oneself or between oneself and another. But this is not all. We have not yet introduced the idea of scale or of an economy of scale. Orders of generality corresponding to forms of justification are not just a means of classification, but also scales of evaluation. Think of Pascal and his "established scales" [*grandeurs d'établissement*]— our authors have. That principles of justification govern relations of standing becomes obvious once the idea of justification takes over in determining what counts or does not count in qualifying tests.

Here is what for Boltanski and Thévenot occupies the place held for Walzer by the idea of a heterogeneity of social goods, namely, the plurality of principles of justification invoked when social actors undertake to plead for their cause or to uphold their criticism in situations of discord.

I do not want to push this opposition too far, for didactic reasons. There is a kinship between these two projects of pluralizing the idea of justice that brings them close together. We can show this by the implicit borrowings each makes from the other. For example, the notion of social goods develops an internal logical heavily freighted with a prescriptive load (for example, what one does or does not have the right to purchase). In this sense, the notion of a shared understanding links up with that of justification. In an opposite sense, we can say that scales of standing give rise to distributions just like that of social goods. Justification too then has to do with distributive justice. What is more, in both cases it is power, and therefore also satisfaction and enjoyment, that gets distributed. It is true, however, that the gap remains between a project aimed at equality, that is, at the limitation of domination, and one aimed at justification, that is, at a reasonable treatment of opposing claims.

This initial difference finds an echo on the plane of the models with which the two enterprises end up. It is not by chance that Boltanski and Thévenot call into question not spheres of justice but cities and worlds. Regimes of justified action can be called "cities" insofar as they give some sufficient coherence to an order of human transactions. They are "worlds" insofar as some things—objects or arrangements—serve as established referents, something like a "common world," for tests that occur within a given city. Thus, in the "inspired" city, the standing of persons is authorized by grace or a gift, with no relation to money, glory, or utility. In the "city of opinion" standing depends on renown, on the opinion of others. In the "commercial" city, it is rare goods, submitted to everyone's envy, that are negotiated, people being united only through the agreement they find in their desires. In the "domestic" city, which extends to include what Hannah Arendt called the household, the values of loyalty, fidelity, and reverence reign. The "civic" city rests on the subordination of one's own interest to the will of the whole, expressed in positive law. In the "industrial" city, which is not to be confused with the commercial city where the instantaneous fixing of prices is what is operative, what dominates are long-standing functional rules submitted to the higher principle of utility.

The first striking thing is the superficial resemblance between these two works. The chapter on the commercial city recalls that on money and commodities; the civic city evokes political power; and one could easily find equivalencies between what is said on the one hand about the inspired city, and on the other about divine grace, or between the domestic city and free time, recognition, and so on. But we can doubt whether such a term-by-term correlation gets us very far, given that the methodology used differs so profoundly. Walzer draws on a cultural anthropology in the eyes of which the evaluation of social goods presents an enduring relative stability. In this, he proceeds as does Clifford Geertz in his "understanding of cultures." He confines himself to telling examples as a way of presenting the profiles of relatively stable and enduring evaluations. It is the idea of shared understandings that allows this procedure to work, which, after all, was already that of Max Weber with his elaboration of ideal types. Boltanski and Thévenot's cities are not ideal types of shared evaluations but rather forms of argumentation in situations of agreement and disagreement. This is why their reconstruction has to be more complex than a mere redoubling of the understandings effectively at work over a sufficiently long period. They consist curiously and, may I say, happily in a direct confrontation, with a view to clarifying them in terms of one another, of, on the one hand, speculative works received from the philosophical and theological tradition, and, on the other hand, training manuals intended for the managers of enterprises and for union leaders.

This intersecting reading is first put into practice in the setting of the commercial city. Our authors extract from Adam Smith the elements that assure the establishment of a commercial bond. These elements constitute, as Smith expresses it, the outlines of a "grammar" it is possible to identify in the weakest, least articulated of arguments, like those in the already mentioned training manuals. In the same way, Augustine's *City of God* is asked to bring to an appropriate level the weaker discourse articulated by spiritual guidebook authors, popular artists, and other marginal talents who people the inspired city. Rousseau's *Social Contract* is, as might be expected, the major resource for the civic city. Hobbes's conception of honor helps make explicit the subtle rules of hierarchy for the city of renown, where standing depends entirely on others' opinion. Saint-Simon is the guide for making use of the discourse of those he was the first to call industrialists. Bossuet and other moralists provide a discourse appropriate to the domestic city. (And I note in passing that philosophy finds itself reintroduced into the heart of the social sciences as an argumentative tradition, which constitutes both an indirect justification of it and, for our two authors, a sociologist and an economist, recognition of their belonging to a long history concerned with meaning.)

The advantage of the methodology at work in *De la justification* is to push much further the conceptual analysis that in Walzer is taken for granted, once the symbolism governing a category of social goods has been established. I want to show this in regard to two subdivisions where these two works seem to overlap: the commercial and the political bonds.

As regards the commercial bond, Walzer, who is essentially concerned to prevent one sphere from reaching into another, confines himself to a brief summary of what sharing, buying and selling, and exchanging can signify. He counts on a kind of clarifying intuition, applied to the internal logic of the goods under consideration, in order to make up his list of what cannot be bought or sold. In the end, it is by composing the list of items having to do with other categories of goods that one specifies, in a negative sort of way, the commercial good itself. In *De la justification*, a work of constitution based on a type of argumentation that is more evaluative of the commercial bond itself corresponds to this operation of marking things. We can even speak of a veritable constitution of a common good that leads individuals to surpass their singularity. I shall return in the next part to the role played by this notion of a common good, which our authors specify in each case in terms of the city under consideration. Thus, in the case of the commercial city, the common good is figured by the price that concludes the negotiation sparked off by the free play of desire for coveted things: "The commercial bond unites persons through the intermediary of scarce goods open to the appetites of all and the competition of desires subordinates the price, attached to the possession of a good, to the desires of others."[6] It is clear therefore that it is the rules governing the market—rules, the authors say, similar to rules of grammar—that allow, secondarily, criticism of the pretension of the commercial sphere to contaminate all the other spheres. This example of the commercial city provides a good occasion for refining the difference between an evaluative approach and an argumentative one, whatever their undeniable kinship may be.

I would like now to consider the other register where the two analyses overlap: political power on the one hand, the civic city on the other. For Walzer, we have seen, the question of power touches closely on the major preoccupation of his book, namely, the fate of domination. We have equally seen that it is in discovering the list of what political power does not have the right to control that we outline the contours of the sphere of power. But this internal constitution is taken as already understood, whereas with Boltanski and Thévenot the social contract gives rise to a conceptual genesis, namely, the one that proceeds from the transference of sovereignty from the body of the king to the general will. This is the case of a kind of subordination where the common good is defined as a "public" good. Degrees of civic standing proceed from the reciprocal commitment between particular individuals and the general public, depending on whether the will that makes citizens act is singular or, on the contrary, turned toward the general interest. It is at this point that the analysis of the civic city leads to the same perplexities as does that of the sphere of political power. Is the civic city—the very oddness of this term ought already to alert us—a city like all others? Is its paradox not that it also envelops all the other cities? This perplexity will be at the center of the second part of this chapter.

But I want to say a few more words about the difference in strategy in these two books. This is all the more necessary once Boltanski and Thévenot complete their theory of "cities" with that of "worlds." Allow me to recall how our authors pass from the first to the second theme. The attention paid to the grammar that is constitutive of each city has to be accompanied (according to them) by attention to the ways in which the qualification of persons of this or that standing are tested. I will underline in passing the importance for jurists of the moment of judgment, which is the moment when a ruling that decides a dispute is given, ending any incertitude concerning the standing of the parties involved. What is important for our present analysis lies elsewhere, however. This is the use made of a basis in things, objects, states of affairs in those qualifying tests that authorize us to speak not just of cities but also of worlds. "From justice," say our authors, "the question of agreement thus leads to that of 'adjustment.'"[7] (Thévenot has spoken more recently of what he calls "fitting action.") It is perhaps this attention to material states of affairs, comparable to the judicial apparatus of the tribunal, that most distances our authors from the phenomenology of shared symbolism and commits them instead to a criteriology of judgment under the heading of "tested judgment."[8] This is the part of Boltanski and Thévenot's work that runs the greatest risk of being overlooked. Yet it is here that our authors' approach is most clearly distinguished from that of Walzer. The passage from the idea of a city to that of a world allows, in effect, for verifying the grammar of works of political philosophy with the aid of forms of discourse that come closest to the actual practice of those training manuals destined for managers and union leaders, as guidebooks for real worlds. However, rather than prolonging this confrontation on the plane of the realization of these two projects which differ so in where they begin, let us now turn toward the critical question posed at the beginning of this lecture.

TOWARD THE POLITICAL PARADOX

What resources for grouping the political body, and hence for unifying different foci of right, remain open when we come to the end of our reading of these books?

We cannot say that Walzer's book is completely lacking any encompassing aim. The theme of complex equality, a theme reckoned to be abolitionist and the polar opposite of domination, runs through every sphere. It is, if I may so put it, what holds everything together. This theme already appears in the subtitle, "a defense of plurality and equality." Let us understand this to mean pluralism at the service of complex equality. And let us recall the formula already quoted from *Spheres of Justice*: "The aim of political egalitarianism is a society free from domination."[9] With this theme, Walzer can enter into competition with Rawls at the level of Rawls's second principle of justice. More fundamentally, it is what authorizes preserving, in the very title of the book, the word "justice" in the singular. Everything that is subsequently said about domination stems from what we can call a minimal formalism, which is expressed in the working definitions of terms like monopoly, domination, dominance, or finally tyranny. This minimal formalism is further expressed in the correlation between the abolitionist project and the criteriology of social goods. In this respect, we can take as a formal feature the threefold criterion: heterogeneity of social goods, shared symbolism, and internal logic of the prescriptive import. But I want to emphasize a concept we have not yet considered, which is situated at the point of encounter between the project of differentiation and the criteriology drawn from the notion of social goods: the concept of *conversion*, and with it of *convertibility*. Conversion consists in the fact that a social good, let us say money, wealth, gets set up as a function of its value in another sphere of justice, say that of political power. Here is the ultimate secret of the phenomenon of dominance, defined as "a way of using social goods that isn't limited by their intrinsic meanings or that shape those meanings in its own image."[10]

Conversion can thus be characterized as a kind of symbolic violence. For as Walzer states: "A dominant good is converted into another good, into many others, in accordance with what often appears to be a natural process but is in fact magical, a kind of social alchemy."[11] This surprising text makes me think of the famous chapter in *Capital* devoted to the fetishism of merchandise, merchandise being given a kind of mystical grandeur thanks to a fusion of the economic and the religious. Walzer will refer to conversion a number of times, but leave it, without further reflection, its metaphorical status. But it is not nothing if we admit, with Walzer, that "we can characterize whole societies in terms of the patterns of conversion that are established within them."[12] And again: "History reveals no single dominant good and no naturally dominant good, but only different kinds of magic and competing bands of magicians."[13] Walzer's reticence to say more stems from the major stance in his book, which is vigilance over the frontiers, as though the concern to found or integrate the most far-reaching social bond blocked us from the task of combating monopolies and tyrannies, as though (but this is my personal interpretation) every foundational enterprise was condemned to play the perfidious magical game of conversion.

Yet can a theory exclusively concerned to differentiate spheres avoid the question of integration of these same spheres into a single political body? It is not that Walzer is unaware of this question. At the very moment he puts in place his argument, he declares, "the political community is the appropriate setting for this enterprise."[14] But nowhere does the status of this setting become the object of a distinct reflection. This reticence explains certain anomalies in the treatment of the first and last spheres of justice: nationality and political power.

As regards the first sphere of justice, we must observe that all the other distributions of goods unfold within it. Nationality is not a social good like the others: "we don't distribute it among ourselves; it is already ours. We give it out to strangers."[15] And again: "membership cannot be handed out by some external agency; its value depends upon an internal decision."[16] In other words, here we run up against a phenomenon of self-constitution that is difficult to place under the aegis of distribution, except through the bias of a pairing: citizen-foreigner. The unusual character of this phenomenon of self-constitution in relation to an idea of distributive justice is underscored again by the fact that almost all other social goods turn out to be goods that cross frontiers, for which the world constitutes the final distributive agency about which we say that it is "self-contained." In contrast, we have to say that "the political community is probably the closest we can come to a world of common meanings."[17]

Reading the last chapter, which in a way corresponds in a polar manner to the first one, reinforces our difficulty. As I said at the end of the first section of this chapter, political power is both a shared good like the others and—if we are careful to watch over it—the guardian of the frontiers. But it soon becomes clear that what interests Walzer is not the status of popular sovereignty and its eventual indivisibility, hence the foundation of the political body, which would touch the very question of the source of right, but the likelihood of what has appeared to us as the major perversion of the process of evaluating goods, namely, the unwarranted conversion of one good into another: of wealth into political power, of political power into religious power, and so on. In this way the question of the unitary ground of the political body is avoided. At the same time, this work also avoids confronting the political paradox that is constituted by treating the State in terms of distributive justice. As a good to be distributed, political power has to be given its place among all other goods. This is a way of contributing to demystifying it. But, insofar as it is not just one good among others, insofar as it is what regulates different distributions, including those having to do with such incorporeal commodities as affective, mystical, and ethico-juridical goods, political power seems to overflow the framework of distributive justice and to pose the specific problem of its self-constitution and, correlative to this, of its self-limitation. Why does Walzer avoid posing the problem of the State and of sovereignty in terms of this paradox? Undoubtedly he would say that this problem has been dealt with so often that today it covers over the one that seems more urgent to him, the problem of a limited government. Thus his argument is not really with Rawls, on the point of the principles of justice, but with Nozick, on the point of minimal government. He is like the firefighter who runs to where the fire is—where there is a transgression of some frontier. And the peril is greatest in his eyes with the question of political power. Yet we may suspect that there is a more basic reason at work here. A political philosophy constructed entirely around the theme of the heterogeneity of social goods is poorly armed to pose the problem of the self-constitution of the political body along with the connected problems of its self-limitation.

So the question arises whether a theory of justification, concerned for its part to differentiate cities and worlds, is better prepared to confront this figure of the political paradox. As a first approximation, one could say that Boltanski and Thévenot's book is better prepared than is Walzer's to take up such all-encompassing considerations. Long analyses devoted successively to the "figures of criticism" in situations of disagreement, then to that particular form of a return to agreement constituted by a compromise, can be seen as responding to the theme of complex equality. This order of succession is important. We do not go directly to the possibilities of agreement on the scale of a unified political community. First we make a long detour through the conflict between different worlds. The two works certainly resemble each other in this way. From both sides, pluralism can lead to the beginning of a tragic vision of action, agreement in one city having as its price disagreement between cities. But what Walzer treats as a conflict between shared symbolic systems, in the extension of the heterogeneity of goods, Boltanski and Thévenot deal with as a conflict between principles of justification, hence as an exercise in criticism. The transfer from one world to another is characterized by a transfer of arguments capable of sapping from within the principles of scale of this or that city, submitted in this way to the fire of a suspicious judgment. This capacity for mutual challenges is structural and not accidental. The common good of one city is vulnerable to the critique provided by the vision of another common good that accounts for the common bond of another city. In this way, our authors are led to lay out the map of intersecting critiques leading from one world toward each of the five other worlds. I shall not go into detail here about the crossfire that results, wherein there are many missed shots. Instead I shall dwell upon one remark that will lead us directly to the question of compromise, where the overall significance of the work is finally at issue: "There exists no overarching position, external to and above each of these worlds, from which the plurality of justices could be considered from on high, like a range of equally possible choices."[18] The absence of any overarching position is a major theme common to both these books. What is the result for a theory of compromise? Does this offer new openings for a recomposition of a unitary idea of justice?

Let us first observe, as a kind of transition, that the critique exercised starting from one world toward others is carried out by people capable of changing worlds, and therefore of transporting with them the internal vision of the world from which they come. An implicit trickster theory is thereby presumed. It is the defector, the traitor, that allows our authors to write: "The possibility of leaving the present situation and denouncing it by basing oneself on an external principle and, consequently; a plurality of worlds, constitutes therefore the condition for a justified action."[19] But is not this individual who goes over the wall, so to speak, moved by the vision of a common good that is not just that of one city, of one world?

This is the question that is finally at issue for this whole enterprise. And it is difficult to answer either yes or no to this question.

At the very beginning of the book, still at a very formal level—before we enter into the maze of cities, somewhat like when Walzer speaks of domination before beginning his tour of his spheres—our authors set out a series of axioms that directly anticipate the answer to our question. The first axiom is constituted by the principle of "the common humanity of all members of any city."[20] This equalizes every human being as human, excluding in particular any slavery or any category of subhumans. But in the absence of any differentiation, this bond remains nonpolitical inasmuch as it only brings onstage a single man, an Adam. Eden is not a political setting. The perpetual agreement of all with all proposes nothing other than a utopia, at the limit of any city. It is only with the second axiom, the principle of dissimilarity, that at least two possible states for the members of a city can be distinguished. We are no longer in Eden. The tests that attribute different states of affairs can begin. Therefore only a model of humanity in different states gives access to a political life. This is why it is necessary to add a supplementary axiom that defines the model of a "well-ordered humanity."[21] It is in terms of this polar status set over against the utopia of an undifferentiated Eden that we can talk about a common good, albeit in each case from the angle of some city or world.

Having made this reservation, we can return to the question of compromise, or rather compromises, between each city and the other five cities. All that ever exists are the figures of compromise. Thus it seems an improper use of the term when one of the last chapters is titled "Compromise for the Common Good."[22] How can there be a supercompromise at the scale of the undivided political body, once compromise is only the suspension of some difference of opinion by which violence is avoided? That this is what is meant is clear:

> The principle intended by a compromise remains fragile so long as it cannot be referred back to a form of common good constitutive of a city. Putting in place a compromise does not allow ordering people in terms of some universal scale.[23]

In reading the part of this book devoted to compromise, one gets the impression that compromises are always weaker than the internal bonds of the different cities. The result is that if some higher common good is affected by the compromise, as a general figure of interaction, it is just as indeterminate as the bond set up by the compromise is fragile. Outside the utopia of Eden there is only the possibility of dealing with disagreements in terms of compromises always threatened by turning into a compromising of principles, on a slippery slope that recalls the perverse effect denounced by Walzer under the heading of conversion.

I therefore want to ask whether, with Boltanski and Thévenot as with Walzer, one has not underestimated the paradox of the political, resulting from the fact that the civic city is not a city like all the others, in any case not in the sense that the market, the family, or the inspired city are. I see a reinforcement of my perplexity in the very choice these authors make of Rousseau's *Social Contract* as a model of the civic city. (And as regards the very term "civic city," our authors show some hesitation. Is it not a pleonasm?) If the *Social Contract* does work as a model, it is difficult to take it for the model of one city among others. It can only be the model of an inclusive city. To the extent that it is true that the general will tolerates no coalition within or outside itself, Rousseau would have called these other cities building "bricks."

Do these critical remarks undercut the analyses of Walzer and of Boltanski and Thévenot? I am more inclined to give credit to these two works for having helped us become aware of a previously unrecognized situation, or in any case one not thinkable in terms of our French republican and Jacobin tradition—that is, that the State, as the source of right, finds itself today placed in the uncomfortable situation of an entity called upon to behave at the same time as the whole and as the part, as the container and the contained, as an inclusive agency and an included region. It is in this sense that our authors' reticences, admitted or not, have become our own awkward position. This latter points to hard times for the question of rights. It will be no easier in the coming decades to reconcile indivisible popular sovereignty with the blossoming of a multitude of centers of rights than to reconcile this same indivisible sovereignty with new postnational, if not suprastate, institutions, which themselves will give rise to rights. Just as we shall have to deal with a complex situation, stemming from the intertwining of several agencies of juridicity at the level of the state and the suprastate, so too we shall more and more have to deal with a symmetrical situation issuing from the intertwining of several sources of juridicity at the infrastate level. This situation is a result of the figure that clothes the political paradox.

NOTES

1. Michael Walzer, *Spheres of Justice: A Defense of Pluralism and Equality* (New York: Basic Books, 1983).
2. Luc Boltanski and Laurent Thévenot, *De la justification: les économies de la grandeur* (Paris: Gallimard, 1991).
3. Walzer, *Spheres of Justice*, xiii.
4. Walzer, *Spheres of Justice*, 273.
5. Walzer, *Spheres of Justice*, 281.
6. Boltanski and Thévenot, *De la justification*, 61.
7. Boltanski and Thévenot, *De la justification*, p ?
8. For the kinship to judicial judgment, cf. Boltanski and Thévenot, *De la justification*, 175–76.
9. Walzer, *Spheres of Justice*, xiii.
10. Walzer, *Spheres of Justice*, 10–11.
11. Walzer, *Spheres of Justice*, 11.
12. Walzer, *Spheres of Justice*, 11.
13. Walzer, *Spheres of Justice*, 11.
14. Walzer, *Spheres of Justice*, 28.
15. Walzer, *Spheres of Justice*, 32.
16. Walzer, *Spheres of Justice*, 29.
17. Walzer, *Spheres of Justice*, 28.

18. Boltanski and Thévenot, *De la justification*, 285.
19. Boltanski and Thévenot, *De la justification*, 289.
20. Boltanski and Thévenot, *De la justification*, 96.
21. Boltanski and Thévenot, *De la justification*, 99.
22. Boltanski and Thévenot, *De la justification*, 337.
23. Boltanski and Thévenot, *De la justification*, 338.

BIBLIOGRAPHY

Boltanski, Luc and Laurent Thévenot. *De la justification: les économies de la grandeur*. Paris: Gallimard, 1991.

Walzer, Michael. *Spheres of Justice: A Defense of Pluralism and Equality*. New York: Basic Books, 1983.

Reply to Paul Ricoeur
Ronald Dworkin

1. What is pluralism?[1] It has a sociological sense: In that sense, it describes a political community in which a number of different moral communities co-exist. Pluralism, in that sociological sense, is a fact-of-life in many parts of the world, including Western democracies, and Rawls's political philosophy is motivated by the need to respond to it. But Professor Ricoeur, I believe, is using the idea of pluralism in a somewhat different, philosophical sense as referring to a kind of moral scheme: A single moral scheme an individual might embrace or a moral community might share. A pluralistic morality, in this sense, is compartmentalized: It includes different and independent goals or ideals or principles. Professor Ricoeur, as I understand him, discusses two examples of pluralistic moral attitudes.

2. The first splits morality between the political and the ethical: It draws a sharp line between the ideals of justice and of the good life. It is an ancient question in philosophy what the relation between these ideals actually is. Three views have been defended. The first argues that the two ideals are completely independent, and may be antagonistic. On that view, for the strong, justice consists in sacrifice. The second argues that justice is a component of the good life: Being just and living in a just state are part of what makes life good. Justice might be the most important part of the good life, but it is not all of it. So being just may not be an overall sacrifice, for those who would have more wealth if they were unjust, but it is a sacrifice relative to other goods. On the third view, justice is a condition of the good life: Living in a just state is a condition of other things being as good as they can be. So it is not in any sense a sacrifice to have less material wealth in a more just state, because having more than what justice allows is not even *pro tanto* good. The first of these three views is strongly pluralist, because it holds that justice and the good life are independent ideals that may pull in opposite directions.

3. The second example of a pluralistic moral scheme divides conceptions of justice and state. It announces, for example, that the virtues of justice and democracy are correspondingly independent, and holds that they, too, may pull in different directions, as they will if the majority votes for unjust laws. Once again, there are other, less pluralistic views; an opposing view might, for example, make the satisfaction of some minimal requirements of justice a condition of democracy, which would limit the degree of possible opposition between the two virtues. That alternative view would argue that even a majoritarian decision is not truly democratic if it subjects a minority to tyranny or gross unfairness.

4. My instincts are, I fear, anti-pluralist. I agree there was a time when philosophers were too committed to the premise that one big idea or assumption must explain everything, that everything is water or idea or liberty or equality, so that there cannot be genuine oppositions or paradoxes or necessary compromises. But the alternative of pluralism has now become too fashionable, and often serves as an excuse for giving up on analysis too soon.

5. I begin with the first example, with the question of the connection between justice and the good life. Professor Ricoeur opposes the first view I described, the strongly pluralistic view that these are independent ideals. He says that people think it is part of their good—part of what is good for them—that they live in just institutions. But I am not clear whether he prefers the second or third view: whether he believes that justice is a component or a condition of the good. It makes a difference which of those views of the connection we are assuming when we consider and compare strategies for deciding what is just. If we think justice is a component of the good life, we can proceed by stages. We agree that it is desirable to live in a just state, and then ask, as a further and independent question: What is just? We can answer that by ignoring ethics, and assuming, for the moment, the independence view of the connection between justice and the good life. We can make assumptions, for example, like Rawls's assumption that the more primary goods we have the better for us, all else equal, and so forth. In fact, Rawls's and other versions of contractualism depend on proceeding in this way. Then, once we have answered the question of what justice demands in this way, we return to our ethical reason for wanting to live in a society like *that*. But if just is a *condition* of the good, even in the weak sense I described, we cannot bracket ethics in the way I just described. Ethics must figure in the *substance* of the argument, and the argument must be different because, of course, it can no longer make use of assumptions like the idea that, all else equal, having more wealth is better.

6. We would then need a very different approach to ethics, one from *within* ethics. I have sketched out a possible approach under this hypothesis,

which uses ethical arguments not only to show the importance of living in a just state, but to help define what a just state is. Great art is great because it is a suitable response to the right challenge. There is no such thing as art in the abstract—we cannot make a sonnet a better sonnet by adding an extra line. We might say the same of athletic achievement: There is no such thing as the perfect athletic performance except with respect to some understood standard or set rules or restrictions. That seems to me the best place to start. The good life is the life that is the best response to the right circumstances, and that explains why it is easier to live well in a just society. I have developed that idea in other writing.[2] I have argued that we must think of justice and ethics after the model of art and discipline, or athletics and rules: that is, that living well is a response to the right conditions. But I can't go into this now.

7. Now turn to the second example of pluralism Professor Ricoeur discusses: justice and politics. Here the pluralism is very deep, but those who embrace it must answer an important question. If we do regard politics as a separate, independent sphere, then what are its distinctive regulative ideals? Many people assume that in politics equality reigns, and that that means democracy. But there are two difficulties. First, "democracy" is itself a contested concept. How do we choose among rival interpretations of what democracy is? If we say: choose that conception which really promotes equality, overall, then we face a difficulty. Is there a distinctive *procedural* sense of equality? If not, then both the pluralism and the independence of justice from politics or state collapses. If so, then what is it? What is the metric of procedural equality? We have two candidates: that political influence should be equal and that political impact should be equal. But as I have argued elsewhere neither of these candidates can provide a satisfactory metric for a purely procedural sense of equality.[3] Both fail.

8. We have, in fact, no option but to *integrate* justice and politics. Our question is: What provision will a just society make for its own governance so that people are overall treated with equal concern and respect? Of course, that standard is too abstract to be more than a beginning. We must develop appropriate conceptions of equal concern and respect. But when we do, we must take into account that one dimension of an appropriate procedure is consequentialist in the broad sense: We must design procedures that, among other things, promote substantive justice. That assumption provides the best defense of *constitutionalism*, but I cannot begin upon that large claim now.

NOTES

1. I did not prepare a text for my reply to Professor Ricoeur at the colloquium [on Consensus and Democracy: An Anglo-French Conference on John Rawls]. I was un-

able to write a text for publication, but I have tried to summarize the remarks I made in the following brief sketch.

2. Ronald Dworkin, "Foundations of Liberal Equality," *The Tanner Lectures on Human Values*, volume 11. Salt Lake City: University of Utah Press, 1990.

3. Ronald Dworkin, "Equality, Democracy and Constitution: We the People in Court," *Alberta Law Review*, 28 no. 2 (1990): 324–46.

BIBLIOGRAPHY

Dworkin, Ronald. "Equality, Democracy and Constitution: We the People in Court," *Alberta Law Review*, 28 no. 2 (1990): 324–46.

Dworkin, Ronald. "Foundations of Liberal Equality," *The Tanner Lectures on Human Values*, volume 11. Salt Lake City: University of Utah Press, 1990.

Part II

READING RICOEUR THROUGH LAW

Chapter Three

Juridical Precedents and Reflective Judgment

Roger W. H. Savage

The privilege granted to the State to enforce the rule of law sets the State's claim to the right to command obedience in relief. In the case of a trial where the court exercises its authority in sentencing the defendant, the court's power to try and punish the accused bears out the State's claim to a legitimate violence. This "privilege of *legitimate* violence,"[1] which is granted first to the State and then to the court as representative of the State's juridical arm, is the sign of the trust commanded by the State. As such, any privilege with regard to the right to the legitimate use of the means of violence to uphold the rule of law is caught up in an intractable paradox. By suggesting that the institution of a just distance, which in the case of the sentence pronounced "places the accused and the victim in distinct places,"[2] is the public manifestation of the fittingness of the solution achieved with the conclusion of the trial, I propose to set the difference between the political dimension of the privilege of legitimate violence and the authority of the judiciary against the backdrop of a consideration of the value of exemplary moral and political acts. Juridical precedents owe their significance to the way that in reflective judgment, the individual case summons the rule. Accordingly, I intend to explore how the exemplary value of juridical decisions that contribute to the institution of a just distance figures in the adequation of the rational and the real. To the degree that *stare decisis* is the fruit of the search for juridical solutions aimed at restoring the social peace, the value of the rule or norm established by juridical precedence counterpoints the State's recourse to a legitimate violence in maintaining the rule of law.

THE POLITICAL PARADOX AND JURIDICAL AUTHORITY

The legitimacy of the State's recourse to the means of violence seems at first inherently contradictory. How, we might wonder, could the rule of law be amenable to this recourse to the instruments of a coercive force in the interest of reestablishing the social peace? Furthermore, we could ask whether the authority of the juridical system and its representatives can truly operate independently of the ideological phenomenon's justificatory function, which the ideal of the fairness of a third party aims to guarantee. In view of the apparent contamination of the juridical by the political on which the partisan fight over Judge and now Justice Brett M. Kavanaugh's appointment to the United States Supreme Court has placed an indelible mark, we might even think that the political dimension of claims to authority has recast the belief in an impartial judiciary capable of, and responsible for, administering the law.

The paradox of a *legitimate* violence highlights the strange power that a ruling authority has to compel those subject to its rule to obey. This power, Paul Ricoeur explains, rests on the legitimacy of the claim to the right to exercise it. As such, the legitimacy of this claim is supported in part by the citizenry's belief in it. Authority, Ricoeur tells us, here borders on violence "as the power to impose obedience"[3] inasmuch as the structure of authority also institutes the vertical dissymmetry separating those who are subject to another's rule from those who command. Conversely, the recognition of a ruling authority's superiority tempers the impulse to identify the phenomenon of authority with that of domination by distinguishing this right to impose obedience from naked violence. For Ricoeur, the credibility attached to the character of authority with regard to its legitimacy thus distinguishes the claim to authority from the violence that ensues when one individual or group dominates or coerces another by force.

Yet if, as Ricoeur and Hannah Arendt remind us, power is irreducible to violence, the hierarchically dissymmetrical relation between those who command and those who obey lays bare the deficit of belief that threatens the legitimacy of the ruling order. This credibility gap, Ricoeur maintains, is the locus of the difference between the claim to legitimacy on the part of a ruling authority and the credit extended to it on the part of the citizenry. Attributing the "source of what Marx called surplus-value"[4] to this difference between the claim to legitimacy of a leader or system of rule and the belief in it frees the concept of surplus value from its rigidly economic determination. Reducing the political origins of the surplus value of an ideological system to the economic sphere, where "[a]ll the evil of life in society can [be regarded] only [as] result[ing] from surplus value, itself interpreted as the exploitation of labor from the perspective of profit alone,"[5] thus obviates eminently political problems that inhere in the exercise of, and deliberations over, the just sharing of power.

The legitimacy of the claim to the right to command is clearly distinguishable from the authority vested in the judiciary by reason of the latter's presumed impartiality, its representatives' knowledge of the law, and their jurisprudential wisdom. Like the right to command, the power exercised by a judge who presides over a trial rests in part on the recognition of her superiority with regard to these requisite conditions for administering the law in a fair and equitable manner. At the same time, this power in principle is separated formally and institutionally from the surplus value of an ideological system's justificatory function. Ricoeur reminds us that, when all is said and done, ideology "revolves around power."[6] At the same time he stresses that, with regard to legal authority, members of the group or citizenry "do not owe obedience to authorities as individuals but as representatives of the impersonal order"[7] as constituted by a legal system. He adds, however, that this legal type of authority can scarcely operate independently of two other types of authority, traditional authority and charismatic authority, with which it remains entwined. If, as Ricoeur says, we owe our obedience to those vested with legal authority as representatives of this allegedly, and ideally, impartial order, does the right to impose obedience within the juridical sphere at the same time then also rest on the way that the surplus value inhering in all structures of power fills the gap between the claim to authority and the belief in it?

We might therefore wonder if the authority of a purportedly impartial order operates independently of ideological justifications of the right to rule. Conversely, we could ask whether the intersection of the political and the juridical vis-à-vis the question of authority is indicative of an overlapping concern with fulfilling a common aim. Politics' genuinely distinct finality and the reestablishment of the social peace through the institution of a just distance are mutually implicated in a process that, following Ricoeur, I will say promotes the adequation of the rational and the real. Accordingly, I intend to take the adequation of the rational and the real as a critical touchstone for drawing out the connection between politics' privileged position with regard to the problem of power and the significance that juridical precedents have with regard to the judiciary's authority.

JURIDICAL HERMENEUTICS

The notion that the judgment rendered in an individual case establishes a rule or norm to be followed sets in motion a series of questions and reflections on juridical precedents. Ricoeur reminds us that where "none of the legal dispositions drawn from existing law seem to constitute the norm under which the affair in question might be placed,"[8] so-called hard cases prove to be a test for reflective judgment. Furthermore, he stresses that the meaning of a law results not from its pedigree but is instead "to be sought in the text and its intertextual connections."[9] Seeking the meaning of a law in the will of a legislator or that of the authors of a constitution is of a piece with the intentionalist fallacy. Conversely, leaving the judgment to the judge's discretionary power in instances where no response to the requirements presented by the case appears to be contained in the law proves to be fatal with respect to the juridical characterization of a decision. For, as Ricoeur points out, either this decision "is arbitrary, in the sense of being outside the law, or it enters the law thanks only to the legislative claim with which it cloaks itself."[10] Accordingly for him, "[o]nly the capacity to draw on a precedent preserves the juridical characterization of a decision stemming from any discretionary power."[11]

By appealing to the hermeneutical principle according to which the mutual fit of the parts and the whole is a result of the work of interpretation, Ricoeur highlights the symmetry between literary criticism and juridical practice. For him, the disjunction between the immanent meaning of a text and its author's intentions has a parallel in juridical theory with respect to the "disjunction in juridical practice between the meaning of a law and the instance of a decision that juridical positivism identifies as the source of a law."[12] The canonic character of the literary enterprise vis-à-vis juridical theory highlights the value of the narrative model. To the degree that the mutual adjustment of the parts and the whole governs the interpretation of a text, any evaluation of the reading of a difficult passage rests on the validity of that reading with respect to the passage's fit within the work as a whole. Claims regarding the rightness of the proposed interpretation of a difficult passage are open to dispute. Controversy is therefore not only possible, but it also invites, and even calls for, arguments in support of the plausibility and probability of an interpretation that claims to be more convincing and hence more acceptable than another.

Ricoeur's thesis that "a juridical hermeneutic centered on the thematic of argument requires a dialectical concept of the relation between interpretation and argumentation"[13] is strategically positioned with respect to the practical difficulty of arriving at a determination of the application of the law in difficult cases that cannot be placed easily under an existing rule or norm. In response to Ronald Dworkin's effort to "checkmate the positivist theory of law,"[14] which Ricoeur remarks is Dworkin's constant target, Ricoeur takes up the problem as he says Dworkin sees it, namely, "how to justify the idea that there is always a valid response [in every case calling for a decision], without falling into the arbitrary or into the judge's claim to make himself a legislator."[15] In Ricoeur's view, Dworkin overlooks how a theory of argumentation would escape the alternative either of a demonstrable proof of a judicial decision's rightness as a valid response or of the arbitrariness of judicial discretion. The too rigid connection that Ricoeur maintains is instituted between the solution of difficult cases as represented by particular juridical decisions and the thesis that juridical propositions that ostensibly support and justify these decisions are demonstrable is indicative of the gap in reasoning that for him calls for a dialectical rapprochement between the work of interpretation and the structure and processes of argumentation. By drawing a "general conception of law [that is] inseparable from 'a substantive political theory'"[16] from the distinction between principles of an ethico-juridical nature and univocal rules, Dworkin places the accent on these principles' ethico-political horizon. For Ricoeur, Dworkin thus owes a "conception of law freed from what he calls its pedigree"[17] to the model of the text, the understanding of which puts into play the dialectic of explanation and understanding.

By asking how the claim to correctness of the arguments advanced in favor of or against a particular interpretation of a case is to be defined, Ricoeur highlights the connection between the normative ideal of a universal consensus regarding the recognition and acceptance of a judgment and the openness of the process in which different interpretations of the law concerning the case in question are debated. The internal justification of the arguments supporting the judgment pronounced at the end of a trial rests on the narrative coherence of the evidentiary facts in question, premises regarding motives, circumstances, and consequences of the events set in motion by a particular act. Like narrative, where the reader draws incidents and events together as a coherently meaningful whole, the interpretation of these facts acquires an evaluative texture by virtue of the manner in which motives, circumstances, and the like are woven together in recounting the events that are said to have taken place. Ricoeur stresses that the judicial syllogism cannot be reduced to the subsumption of a case that is placed under a rule in this regard. Rather, in order to "satisfy a criterion of recognition"[18] with respect to this rule's appropriate application to the case in question, the interpretation of the facts and the interpretation of the norm must also meet the requirement of their mutual fit. The test of universalization "only provides a check on the process of mutual adjustment between the interpreted norm and the interpreted fact."[19] Consequently, even the question: "[U]nder which rule should a particular case be placed?"[20] calls for an interpretation that Ricoeur emphasizes constitutes the *organon* of juridical argumentation.

To what, then, should we attribute the evaluation of the relation of fittingness or mutual adjustment that Ricoeur maintains escapes the alternative between a logical demonstration and the arbitrariness of the judge's discretionary power? If for the juridical syllogism the legal norm or rule comprises the major premise and the facts of the case comprise the minor premise, this evaluation of the fit between the rule and the case seemingly breaches the limits of this syllogism's logical structure. Ricoeur points out that placing a case under one norm or rule rather than another based on precedent involves making "some selection in the *thesaurus* of legal rulings"[21] in which this relation of mutual adjustment is already at work. The respective weighing of resemblances and differences between this precedence and the case in question, together with the question of which resemblances and differences are relevant, thus puts into play the kind of judgment that Ricoeur, following Kant, identifies with the productive imagination's operative power. By risking the suggestion of another analogy besides, or in addition to, that of the symmetry between argumentation and interpretation and explanation and understanding, Ricoeur ties this operative power to the challenge and difficulty of finding the "rule *under* which it is appropriate to place a fact that itself must be interpreted."[22] Here, Ricoeur tells us, the "problem is no longer to apply a known rule to a presumably correctly described case,"[23] as in situations where determinative judgments suffice. Selecting a norm or rule from the *thesaurus* of prior legal rulings is therefore one instance where interpretation follows a different path in seeking the fit between the rule and the case in question. The analogy between explanation-understanding and augmentation-interpretation therefore does not exhaust the field in which judgments regarding the facts of the case and the rule or norm to be applied are in play.[24] In passing from this analogy to the instance in which, in a particular case, one seeks the appropriate norm or rule, reflective judgment in its Kantian sense therefore proves to be key to apprehending the fit between the case and the rule, the evaluation of which remains subject to the adversarial arguments advanced by the different parties.

PRECEDENTS

The question to which I now want to turn concerns the way that the precedent set by a judgment rendered in an individual case becomes part of the canon of established law. On what basis, we could ask, could such a precedent come to be regarded as "settled law"? From one vantage point, this question regarding the establishment of precedents based on an individual case finds its practical answer in the recognition of, and the appeal to, the authority of a particular ruling as establishing the norm to be followed in subsequent cases to which this precedent applies. Ricoeur stresses that a "precedent assures the stability, security, and confidence of a decision."[25] As such, the fit between the norm and the cases to which it subsequently applies gives rise to the historicity of the rule, which acquires its concrete specificity as "settled law" in the decisions that follow it. The first ruling's normative value acquires its accumulative legal force only through its continued application to subsequent cases that are judged to be similar and hence are governed by it. The legal and public recognition of the suitability of this legal norm thus ratifies the legitimacy and authority of the precedent set by this first ruling in each case to which it is appropriately applied.

By suggesting that reflective judgment is operative in the pairing of argumentation and interpretation, Ricoeur opens the door to a broader consideration of the productive imagination's operative role in decisions that play a constitutive role in establishing legal precedents. Why, we could ask, would reflective judgment be limited to weighing the resemblances and differences in selecting the legal norm or rule under which to place a particular case? To be sure, this weighing of resemblances and differences is critical to the mutual adjustment of the rule and the case when it comes to discerning the fit between them. As such, establishing this fit through legal arguments in effect augments, as it were, the initial ruling in much the same way that an ideology augments the energy of a founding event.[26] The "difficulty, even the impossibility of legitimating authority in the final instance"[27] therefore is indicative of the density of the enigma that is the spring, so to speak, of the historicity of an event extended and prolonged through the recognition of its singular significance and exemplary value.[28]

That the authority of the law itself seems to be caught up in the paradox or enigma that Ricoeur identifies with the tradition of sovereignty is indicative of how legal institutions are entangled in justificatory systems of power. We cannot avoid the fact that even the belief in the idea of an impartial judiciary is part of a system of thought that lends support to this impartial judiciary's legitimacy as a third party. That this impartiality and even alleged independence can be called into question is due to the gap between the claim to legitimacy and the credit extended to it that, like the surplus value of an ideological system, inheres in all structures of power, as I previously indicated. Conversely, the legal and public recognition of this impartial third party's authority in each case where the verdict in the trial and the judgment pronounced is appropriate or fitting enhances this third party's institutional legitimacy and credibility.

These few remarks on the connection between the judiciary's impartiality and the enigma of authority open the door to a broader consideration of the relation between a founding event and some ruling that subsequently is cited as a juridical precedent. In the case of a founding event, the energy transmitted by the belief in the State's just and necessary character has its source in the initiative taken by historical agents who, acting in concert, institute the beginning of something new. Similarly, juridical rulings subsequently accepted as precedents in case law stand as singular solutions to hard cases not adequately covered by existing norms and rules. To the degree that these initiatives and these legal rulings represent singular solutions to unique problems, challenges, or demands, the kinship between them is borne out by the way that the exemplary value of a response to a problem or challenge for which it constitutes the singular solution attests to the power of imagination at work.

By insisting that the individual case "engenders its normativity and not the reverse,"[29] Ricoeur underscores how the rule exemplified by the individual case acquires its significance and force. The injunction issuing from St. Francis of Assis's act of renunciation, to which Ricoeur refers as an instance where the effect of being drawn to follow [*Nachfolge*] arises from the example set by the act, passes by way of this injunction of one individual to another, "just as analogous acts, themselves just as singular, are inspired by it."[30] Ricoeur stresses that "in the sphere of reflective judgment . . . communicability does not lie in applying a rule to a case but in the fact that it is the case that summons its rule."[31] In this sphere, in rendering itself communicable, the case engenders its normativity in response to the demands of the situation to which it uniquely replies. Hence, like legal precedents, the act's normative value is borne out by the way that the rule summoned by the act augments the *thesaurus* of moral and political conduct.

Ricoeur's remarks concerning the Doctrine of Right at the end of his essay, "Aesthetic Judgment and Political Judgment according to Hannah Arendt," leads me to ask whether legal judgments subsequently recognized as precedents operate in a region that is unique vis-à-vis the value of exemplary works and acts. For him, extending constitutive features of the judgment of taste—distinctiveness, communicability, and after the factness—from aesthetic judgment to political judgment is convincing, because these features inhere in reflective judgment in its various applications. The opposition between taste and genius is comparable to the one between the historical spectator and the historical agent in that the spectator's judgment regarding the significance of past events stands in marked contrast to the risks taken and wagers made by historical actors. Moreover, Arendt's wager—that it is "more profitable to attempt to disengage a conception of political judgment from the theory of the judgment of taste than to bind this conception to the theory of teleological judgment *via* a philosophy of history"[32]—privileges the spectators' retrospective view over historical actors' prospective one. If, as Ricoeur maintains, Arendt dealt too severely with the Doctrine of Right, this Doctrine for him "lies at the turning point between the view of citizenship and that cosmopolitan point of view, stemming from a philosophy of history."[33] Hence for Ricoeur, the entire weight of the demand of a philosophy of right that would occupy "an intermediary position between those 'dispositions' arising from a natural finality and the *moral* requirement of a law-governed State, both in cities and among cities"[34] cannot be placed on reflective judgment alone. At the same time, reflective judgment, Ricoeur remarks, "prevents the Kantian philosophy of history from tipping over into a philosophy of a Hegelian type."[35] Accordingly, only the "exemplarity that gives a point of futurity to communicability, and in this way, a 'prophetic' dimension to reflective judgment"[36] offers an indication of how reflective judgment might be reconciled not only with the rule of practical reason but also with the place that juridical precedents have in promoting the rule of law.

REASON AND JUSTICE

The notion that reflective judgment places a critical check on a philosophical style of thought that dares to elevate itself to the level of the absolute invites some further consideration of the connection between reason and justice. When, earlier in this chapter, I related the question of the legitimacy of juridical rulings to the political paradox, I wanted to give the challenge posed by the enigma of a legitimate violence this broader extension. Juridical institutions, I suggested, are authorized by political bodies in which the surplus value intrinsic to all structures of power is in play. That a State in which the rule of law prevails exercises a legitimate violence in preserving the rule of law brings to the fore the tension between the State's rational form and this legitimate use of force in this regard. Ricoeur underscores the two directions taken by different styles of political philosophy that emphasize form or force. A reflection on force leads straightway to the enigma engendered by the phenomenon of power. Conversely, a reflection on form, which according to Ricoeur is "better suited to the concrete rational function of the state, leads to an emphasis on the constitutional aspect characteristic of a State of law."[37] In his view, the State fulfills this rational function through reconciling the techno-economic rationality governing the social order with the reasonable character of mores, customs, practices, and laws as accumulated within, and in that regard constitutive of, a concrete historical community.

To the degree that the administration of the law aims at upholding the State's reasonable form, the credit extended to the judiciary rests in part on the citizenry's confidence in the fiduciary relation established by the judiciary's institution as a third party, as previously outlined. In turn, the strength of this fiduciary relation depends to a large degree on the public recognition of the fairness of the application of the law to individual cases for which members of the citizenry demand credible—that is, fitting—resolutions. That justice must not only be done but also be seen to be done attests to the burden of responsibility weighing on the institutional response to some alleged misconduct or miscarriage of justice by the police, prosecutors, defense lawyers, jurors, and judges. To the extent that the suitability of this response with regard to the public trust stands as proof of the legitimacy and authority of the rule of justice, the appropriateness of the way the investigation is conducted, the alleged violation addressed, and the verdict handed down strengthens this bond of trust. Conversely, miscarriages of justice—perceived or real—undermine the public confidence in the institutions that are meant to serve it. This proof, or the lack of it, is therefore no mere formal demonstration or discreditation of the virtue of the law. It may be that from the vantage point of members of a group or political community in positions of authority and power, the reasonable character of the law appears to be self-evident. However, we need only recall how in the United States in 1869 the 15th Amendment extended the right to vote to African Americans (ratified in 1870) and how in 1920 the 19th Amendment extended this same right to women to recognize that the rights, liberties, and advantages enjoyed by some have not always been distributed equally among all. Social and political demands fueled by experiences of disesteem and disregard have their place in the quest for justice. The suitability or fittingness of the response to these demands accordingly takes its place among the signs of the State's reasonable character.

That the reasonable form of a State of law has a decidedly historical dimension evinces one, if not the principal staging ground for the interplay between reflective judgment and the rule of practical reason. By defining the State as the "decision-making organ of a historical community,"[38] Ricoeur emphasizes how the community's organization with respect to its institutions, the different functions and social roles adopted by its members, and the spheres of activity in which they participate constitutes the concrete expression of the will to live together. For him, the State's organization and its articulation of this diversity of institutions, functions, roles, and the like "make human action reasonable action."[39] If, with Ricoeur, we recognize that the task of political philosophy is to attend to "what, in political life, is the bearer of meaningful action in history,"[40] we cannot avoid the challenge posed by Hegel. Human action, Ricoeur reminds us, only "makes sense because we can discern in some places [an] adequation between rationality and reality."[41] In these instances, "the Hegelian axiom is true: what is rational is real, what is real is rational."[42] Yet, by equating freedom's actualization with Spirit's fulfillment of its rationally necessary plan, Hegel identifies the dimension of fulfilled accomplishment with a philosophical system in which reason creates the conditions for its own realization.

By asking whether Hegel destroys the spring of action through identifying Spirit's self-actualization as concluding the "reconciliation already at work in the successive phases of the philosophical process between certitude and truth,"[43] Ricoeur draws out the difference between the Hegelian style of thinking and a Kantian philosophy of limits. For the latter, the totality demanded by reason is the limit condition of the task of making freedom a reality within the history of humankind. For Ricoeur, the "impossibility and even the prohibition of achieving any given totality"[44] either in the field of knowledge or in the field of action brings to the fore the structure of action's two dimensions. As the most adequate philosophical approximation of the concept of the actualization of freedom, the projection of the task of making freedom a reality sets one dimension (that of fulfilled accomplishments) against the other (that of unfulfilled claims and demands). Ricoeur accordingly emphasizes the necessity of preserving the tension between the space of our experiences and the horizons of our expectations. The universal ambition of the metahistorical categories, "space of experience" and "horizon of expectation," stems from the implications that these metahistorical categories have with regard to the field of practical reason. In the final analysis, the unity of the problematic that Ricoeur identifies with these categories' significance for historical thought and for the problematic of politics as it concerns the subject of rights defines the task of practical reason by setting it within the field in which reflective judgment's retrospective and prospective dimensions are in play.

In view of these remarks concerning the State's organization, and in the light of the ethical intention inhering in the will to live together, which the political sphere aims at actualizing in a State of law, we could ask what role the administration of justice and the institution of a just distance have when it comes to the adequation of the rational and the real. The reality of evil, Ricoeur tells us, prevents us from equating our experiences in which our expectations are fulfilled with the entire field of human action. On the contrary, the reign of suffering begins when the power exercised by one will over another diminishes the other's power to act. For evil "affects the origin of action at its root."[45] The reality of evil cannot be divorced from the experience of unfulfilled claims regarding rights, liberties, and opportunities of socially marginalized and historically execrated individuals and groups. Equality before the law does not necessarily guarantee the equality of opportunities that would ensure a better and more equitable share in social goods such as health care, education, and food security. Furthermore, since a political community's ethical basis rests on values for which there is some consensus, "any examination [of] the justification, motivations, and deep sources"[46] of these values lies beyond, and hence can even be excluded in advance by, this consensus. The axiological diversity of values rooted in the symbolic constitutions of different groups' cultural traditions clearly gives rise to competing and conflicting claims and demands in this regard. The diverse foundations of values, demands, and aspirations in multicultural societies complicate the fact that "human beings have concrete duties, concrete virtues, only when they are capable of situating themselves within historical communities, in which they recognize the meaning of their existence."[47] In multicultural democratic States, the procedures for expressing conflicting views, demands, and claims is therefore all the more critical for the process of public will formation. The role of the judiciary is equally critical with respect to upholding the principle of rights and equality before the law. Dividing power against itself by separating the executive, legislative, and judicial branches of government constitutes one political experiment in holding at bay the enigma of legitimate violence exercised by the State. In the light of this enigma, and in view of the aim of a State of law, the power of an impartial judiciary in the end analysis is, or at least should be, "one of the least debatable criteria of democracy."[48]

In what way might we then say that the law contributes to the development of the State's reasonable form? To the extent that the reasonable form of the State actualizes the ethical intention inhering in the will to live together, the rule of law bears out this intention within the juridical domain. For Ricoeur, the set of alternatives that the process of a trial opposes to violence marks out the place of justice in a provisionary way. Justice, he insists, is "opposed not just to violence per se, or even to [subtly] concealed [forms of] violence . . . , but [also] to the simulation of justice constituted by vengeance, the act of procuring justice by oneself."[49] Accordingly, justice for him rests on the fundamental act whereby a society elevates each individual to the level of right and law by reason of the humanity in each. The public confiscation of the power to judge and to pronounce and impose the sentence expresses the force of the law. The legitimacy and ultimate justification of this force of the rule of law thus rests on the equitable restoration and reestablishment of the social peace. From this vantage point, the horizon of the State's reasonable form with regard to the juridical sphere takes shape in accordance with the way that the institution of a just distance promotes the reciprocal recognition of the plaintiff and the accused as subjects of rights.

By suggesting that the institution of a just distance is vital to the reasonable form to which a State of law aspires, I want *in fine* to recall how reflective judgment figures in the interpretation and the application of the law. Using Kantian language, Ricoeur maintains that the act of judging is one of reflective judgment inasmuch as this act consists in seeking the rule under which to place a new case in a trial. That the "established law, as a system of rules, does not exhaust the law as a political enterprise"[50] is indicative of the value of the precedents set by judgments in which argumentation and interpretation are vigorously in play. By exemplifying the rule appropriate to the individual case, each precedent stands as a testament to the ethico-juridical nature of its inspiriting principle. As such, judgments that in retrospect are cited as precedents concretize a State of law's inspiriting principles by reason of this institutionalized recognition of their normative value. That the tension between *stare decisis* and decisions that overrule prior judgments regarded as precedent in the end is insurmountable attests all the more to the place that that these inspiriting principles have in judgments that are intended to uphold the rule of law. The disparagement, discreditation, and delegitimization of legal norms predicated on democratic values places the rule of law at risk, as Arendt has warned us in her incisive analysis of the rise of totalitarianism.[51] Conversely, to the degree that the rule of law is the guardian of a State of law's reasonable form and a check on its use of force, the history—and historicity—of precedents, the singular value of which springs from the normative force of judgments that actualize this rule, bear out the State's ethico-juridical aspirations vis-à-vis the adequation of the rational and the real. An impartial judiciary safeguards the realm of action by upholding the principle of the equality of subjects of rights and by reestablishing the social peace in answer to the violence that disrupts and undermines it. In turn, the citizenry's confidence in this impartiality is borne out by the public recognition of the legal system's legitimacy and authority in each case where the judgment pronounced stands as a fitting response to the alleged violation of the law.

NOTES

1. Paul Ricoeur, *From Text to Action: Essays in Hermeneutics, II*, trans. John B. Thompson and Kathleen Blamey (Evanston: Northwestern University Press, 1991), 332; see Paul Ricoeur, "The Political Paradox," in *History and Truth*, trans. Charles A. Kelbley (Evanston: Northwestern University Press, 1965).

2. Paul Ricoeur, *Reflections on the Just*, trans. David Pellauer (Chicago: University of Chicago Press, 2007), 36.

3. Ricoeur, *Reflections on the Just*, 93.

4. Paul Ricoeur, *Lectures on Ideology and Utopia*, ed. George H. Taylor (New York: Columbia University Press, 1986), 14.

5. Ricoeur, *From Text to Action*, 327.

6. Paul Ricoeur, *Memory, History, Forgetting*, trans. Kathleen Blamey and David Pellauer (Chicago: University of Chicago Press, 2004), 83.

7. Ricoeur, *Lectures on Ideology and Utopia*, 204.

8. Paul Ricoeur, *The Just*, trans. David Pellauer (Chicago: University of Chicago Press, 2000), 110. While in this chapter I have not expressly addressed the question as to whether the idea that an existing law is determinate obfuscates the roles of

interpretation and argumentation, one could reasonably ask to what degree claims of determinacy mask their recourse to acts of interpretation and argumentation.

9. Ricoeur, *The Just*, 112.
10. Ricoeur, *The Just*, 112.
11. Ricoeur, *The Just*, 112.
12. Ricoeur, *The Just*, 112.
13. Ricoeur, *The Just*, 110.
14. Ricoeur, *The Just*, 111.
15. Ricoeur, *The Just*, 112.
16. Ricoeur, *The Just*, 115–16.
17. Ricoeur, *The Just*, 115. Dworkin's position with respect to the law is comparable to Ricoeur's, which has a corollary counterpart in his understanding of the semantic autonomy of the text. Ricoeur, *From Text to Action*, 298; cf. Ronald Dworkin, "Reply to Paul Ricoeur" (in this volume). According to Dworkin, Ricoeur opposes a pluralistic view that regards justice and the good life to be independent ideals. For Dworkin, it is an open question as to whether Ricoeur "believes that justice is a component or a condition of the good," 54. Dworkin believes that by asking "What is just?" we can assume, at least provisionally, "the independence view of the connection between justice and the good life," 54. For him, initially bracketing ethics leads to a different approach to it, according to which the good life is the "best response to the right circumstances," 54. However, one could ask in response whether the good life is one the exemplary value of which stems from the fitting response to those life demands and exigencies to which it replies.
18. Ricoeur, *The Just*, 121.
19. Ricoeur, *The Just*, 122.
20. Ricoeur, *The Just*, 122.
21. Ricoeur, *The Just*, 124.
22. Ricoeur, *The Just*, 126.
23. Ricoeur, *The Just*, 126.
24. See Ricoeur, *The Just*, 126. The dialectic between argumentation and interpretation is analogous to how, in reflective judgment, the case summons the rule. At the same time, there is an important difference between them, which turns on the respective ways in which the apprehension of the fit in question is secured. In a juridical situation, arguments advanced in support of a particular interpretation aim at justifying the fit between the facts, the case, and the rule. By contrast, as Ricoeur often points out, reflective judgment is aesthetic in the sense that there is a pre-reflexive, ante-predicative apprehension of the fit of the case with the rule exemplified by it.
25. Ricoeur, *The Just*, 125. The security of a legal ruling that follows precedent furthers the confidence in the stability of "settled law." In turn, this confidence that the law concerning a particular matter is settled offers some assurance that rulings in similar matters will be resolved in a comparable manner. Justice Brandeis opined that "in most matters it is more important that the applicable rule of law be settled than it be settled right." Burnet v. Coronado Oil and Gas Co., 285 U.S. 393, 406 (1932) (Brandeis, J., dissenting). That this opinion seemingly privileges settled expectations at the possible expense of the rightness of a judgment opens the door to challenges to

stare decisis that may hinder the security of the law on the basis of the discretionary preferences of individual justices. In dissenting from a recent Supreme Court 5–4 judgment that overruled a 40-year decision, Justice Breyer expressed the reservation that one can only "wonder which cases the court will overrule next." Franchise Tax Board of California v. Hyatt, 139 S. Ct. 1485, 1506 (2019) (Breyer, J., dissenting). To the extent that concerns over the Court's politization are inseparable from questions regarding the "correct" interpretation of the law, a ruling that either upholds precedent or overturns it both reflects and shapes a society's ethico-political landscape. See note 28 below.

26. See Ricoeur, *The Just*, 99.
27. Ricoeur, *The Just*, 91.
28. In the case of authority, the density of this enigma stems from the fact that authority cannot legitimate itself in the final instance. However, in the case of a legal ruling, the fittingness of the judgment in a particular case authorizes its legitimacy. Yet clearly, the authority of this judgment cannot be isolated from the ethical substance of the political community for which it holds true. In this regard, judgments that overturn "established law" are indicative of how the historical character of this ethical substance is bound up with a contested political terrain. The augmentation of an initial ruling by subsequent judgments that either follow or overturn precedent are therefore ideological in the sense that they are 1) rooted in a symbolic system that integrates values and beliefs, and 2) lay claim to their legitimacy by reason of the fit evinced by each. Following Ricoeur's analysis of the phenomenon of ideology, each can be accused by the other of distorting the application of the law.
29. Paul Ricoeur, François Azouvi, and Marc de Launay, *Critique and Conviction: Conversations with François Azouvi and Marc de Launay*, trans. Kathleen Blamey (New York: Columbia University Press, 1998), 183.
30. Ricoeur, *Critique and Conviction*, 183.
31. Ricoeur, *Critique and Conviction*, 183.
32. Ricoeur, *The Just*, 101.
33. Ricoeur, *The Just*, 108.
34. Ricoeur, *The Just*, 108.
35. Ricoeur, *The Just*, 108.
36. Ricoeur, *The Just*, 108.
37. Ricoeur, *From Text to Action*, 331.
38. Ricoeur, *From Text to Action*, 330.
39. Ricoeur, *From Text to Action*, 330.
40. Ricoeur, *From Text to Action*, 330.
41. Paul Ricoeur, *Figuring the Sacred: Religion, Narrative, and Imagination*, trans. David Pellauer (Fortress Press, Minneapolis, 1995), 210.
42. Ricoeur, *Figuring the Sacred*, 210.
43. Ricoeur, *Figuring the Sacred*, 208.
44. Ricoeur, *Figuring the Sacred*, 209.
45. Ricoeur, *Figuring the Sacred*, 211.
46. Ricoeur, *From Text to Action*, 335.

47. Paul Ricoeur, *Philosophical Anthropology: Writings and Lectures*, Volume 3, ed. Johann Michel and Jérôme Porée, trans. David Pellauer (Cambridge: Polity Press, 2016), 141.
48. Ricoeur, *From Text to Action*, 335.
49. Ricoeur, *The Just*, 130–31.
50. Ricoeur, *The Just*, 114.
51. Hannah Arendt, *The Rise of Totalitarianism* (New York: Harcourt Brace and Co., 1973).

BIBLIOGRAPHY

Arendt, Hannah. *The Origins of Totalitarianism*. New York: Harcourt Brace and Co., 1973.
Burnet v. Coronado Oil and Gas Co., 285 U.S. 393, 406 (1932) (Brandeis, J., dissenting).
Dworkin, Ronald. "Reply to Paul Ricoeur," in this volume, 53–56.
Franchise Tax Board of California v. Hyatt, 139 S. Ct. 1485, 1506 (2019) (Breyer, J., dissenting).
Ricoeur, Paul. "The Political Paradox." In *History and Truth*. Translated by Charles A. Kelbley, 247–70. Evanston: Northwestern University Press, 1965.
Ricoeur, Paul. *Lectures on Ideology and Utopia*. Edited by George H. Taylor. New York: Columbia University Press, 1986.
Ricoeur, Paul. *From Text to Action: Essays in Hermeneutics, II*. Translated by Kathleen Blamey and John B. Thompson. Evanston, IL: Northwestern University Press, 1991.
Ricoeur, Paul. *Figuring the Sacred: Religion, Narrative, and Imagination*. Translated by David Pellauer. Minneapolis: Fortress Press, 1995.
Ricoeur, Paul. *The Just*. Translated by David Pellauer. Chicago: University of Chicago Press, 2000.
Ricoeur, Paul. *Memory, History, Forgetting*. Translated by Kathleen Blamey and David Pellauer. Chicago: University of Chicago Press, 2004.
Ricoeur, Paul. *Reflections on the Just*. Translated by David Pellauer. Chicago: University of Chicago Press, 2007.
Ricoeur, Paul. *Philosophical Anthropology: Writings and Lectures*, Volume 3. Edited by Johann Michel and Jérôme Porée. Translated by David Pellauer. Cambridge: Polity Press, 2016.
Ricoeur, Paul, François Azouvi, and Marc de Launay. *Critique and Conviction: Conversations with François Azouvi and Marc de Launay*. Translated by Kathleen Blamey. New York: Columbia University Press, 1998.

Chapter Four

The Subject of Rights and Responsibility in Ricoeur's Legal Philosophy

Toward a Prospective Idea of Responsibility

Guido Gorgoni

In the opening essay of *The Just*, Paul Ricoeur analyzes the subject of legal rights according to a fundamental anthropology of the self-defined by the ideas of capacity and attestation, claiming that the subject of rights should not be distinguished from the self at the moral level:

> I want to show that the question with a juridical form "Who is the subject of rights?" is not to be distinguished in the final analysis from the question with a moral form "Who is the subject worthy of esteem and respect?" . . . Furthermore, the question with a moral form refers in turn to a question of an anthropological nature: "What are the fundamental features that make the self (*soi, Selbst. ipse*) *capable* of esteem and respect?"[1]

Ricoeur's epistemological stance questions at its very roots the separation between the idea of a person and that of a "legal personality/subjectivity" that marks the orientation of Western legal systems, where the subject of rights is considered as an abstract reference for the imputation of rights and duties.[2] The pivotal role of this traditional theoretical framing is meaningfully contested in the opening study of Ricoeur's first book explicitly consecrated entirely to law and justice. A similar contestation of the tradition is evident in the book's second essay, dedicated to the semantic analysis of the concept of responsibility, which has to be read in strict conjunction with the first study as part of a single line of argumentation, in this way opening the possibility for an innovative reading of the ideas of both rights and responsibility.

While the legal concept of a subject of rights is eminently an abstraction, Ricoeur's philosophical challenge seeks to rethink its identity within the philosophy of action, in correlation with the ideas of capacity, attestation, and recognition. The terminology Ricoeur employs presents some significant marks of this theoretical stance, as he speaks of a "veritable" or a "real" subject of rights[3] as distinguished from the purely formal one. I argue that Ricoeur's approach to the legal subject attains its highest meaning in connection with the renewal of the semantics of responsibility in a prospective sense. In particular, I contend that Ricoeur's idea of a "veritable" subject of rights deploys its full theoretical potential in relation to a prospective idea of responsibility in contrast to the "static" perspective of the ascription of rights and duties. Reciprocally, a prospective idea of responsibility deploys its full meaning in relation to a subject of rights not reduced to a legal abstraction since, as far as narrative identity is implied, this subject is and *has to be* an embodied one.[4] I shall show that the thesis advocating a projection of responsibility towards the future may have some significant theoretical implications, in particular in relation to the effect of techno-scientific development[5] in areas such as Artificial Intelligence.[6]

THE ROLE OF RECOGNITION

As noted below, Ricoeur's change of perspective requires a switch from, in his terms, the "fundamental" to the "historical" to consider responsibility and the subject of rights from the perspective of the philosophy of action, blending the autonomy and the vulnerability of the subject of rights, so that both its identity and the idea of responsibility are to be thought through the idea of recognition, with the historical dynamics it implies, more than through that of imputation of rights and duties. Speaking about the paradox of autonomy and vulnerability Ricoeur writes:

> It is not one of the least aspects of this paradox that there is more of the fundamental on the side of autonomy, at least in what it proposes, whose contemporary indications are precisely what disturb us and press us to shift autonomy from the plane of the fundamental toward that of the historical.[7]

This change in perspective characterizes both the subject of rights and the notion of responsibility in intersubjective terms. In *Oneself as Another* Ricoeur stresses the crucial relevance of the dynamics of recognition for the constitution of the self in the juridical sphere:

> Recognition is a structure of the self-reflecting on the movement that carries self-esteem toward solicitude and solicitude toward justice. Recognition introduces the dyad and plurality in the very constitution of the self. Reciprocity in friendship and proportional equality in justice, when they are reflected in self-consciousness, make self-esteem a figure of recognition.[8]

Later, in *The Course of Recognition*, in particular in the section dedicated to "The Struggle for Recognition on the Juridical Plane,"[9] Ricoeur considers more explicitly the role of the idea of recognition for the constitution of the self as a subject of rights:

> [R]ecognition intends two things: the other person and the norm. As regards the norm, it signifies, in the lexical sense of the word, to take as valid, to assert validity; as regards the person, recognition means identifying each person as free and equal to every other person. Thus juridical recognition adds to self-recognition . . . new capacities stemming from the conjunction between the universal validity of the norm and the singularity of persons.[10]

These dynamics of recognition on the juridical plane generate new capacities, as the formal enlargement of the plane of rights awarded by the legal system enriches the capacities that the subjects recognize in themselves and, reciprocally, in others. A different concept of legal personhood is engaged, with the formal legal recognition of the subject as a pole of imputation of rights and duties being only a part, albeit a crucial one. From this perspective, the legal subject cannot be reduced to an abstraction of the legal system, since the triadic relation "I-you-third person," which is mediated by different "orders of recognition,"[11] gives the subject of rights, in Ricoeur's words, a "dialogical and institutional structure."[12]

As Ricoeur explicitly states in *The Just*, in order to become a "veritable" subject of rights, the capacities of the self-need to be actualized through the "continual mediation of interpersonal forms of otherness and of institutional forms of association in order to become real powers to which correspond real rights."[13] The connection between universal rights and the capacities of the subject of rights is the product of a concrete "struggle for recognition,"[14] which is mobilized by the indignation subsequent to misrecognition ("humiliation" in Ricoeur's terms[15]). Here it emerges clearly how responsibility is to be understood primarily in terms of a capacity of the self, which is both reflexive and intersubjective, rather than in the purely legal terms of imputation:

> [I]ndignation can disarm as well as mobilize people. In this regard, the idea of responsibility draws one of its meanings from this passage from humiliation, felt as a blow to self-respect, passing through indignation as moral riposte to this hurt, to choosing to participate in the process of enlarging the sphere of personal rights. Responsibility can be taken in this regard as the capacity recognized by both society and oneself that "a subject is capable of acting autonomously on the basis of rational insight." Responsibility as a capacity to take responsibility for oneself is inseparable from responsibility as the capacity to participate in a rational discussion concerning the enlarging of the sphere of rights, whether they are civil, political, or social. The term *responsibility* therefore covers self-assertion

and the recognition of the equal right of others to contribute to advances in the rule of law and of rights.[16]

At the end of this route, responsibility appears as a form of capacity characterizing the "veritable" subject of rights, and it is characterized in active more than in reactive terms. This progression reconnects the thematic of the subject of rights to Ricoeur's parallel revision of the legal idea of responsibility, the subject of the next section, which will add more crucial elements to Ricoeur's theoretical architecture.

REVISING THE SEMANTICS OF RESPONSIBILITY: FROM RETROSPECTIVE TO PROSPECTIVE

In discussing the semantics of responsibility in *The Just*'s second essay,[17] Ricoeur has in mind the developments of continental legal positivism—exemplified in Hans Kelsen's neo-Kantian *Pure Theory of Law*[18]—that are dominated by the perspective of imputation, in which the concepts of legal subject and responsibility are presented as purely formal constructions. Indeed, Kelsen completely disconnects legal responsibility from moral imputation, so that responsibility is a purely formal concept entirely defined within the legal concepts of imputation and sanction: "Imputation, which expresses itself in the concept of responsibility, is therefore not the connection between a certain behavior and an individual who thus behaves. . . . Imputation, implied in the concept of responsibility, is the connection between a certain behavior, namely a delict, with a sanction."[19] This contention leads Kelsen to state that the idea of a "legal subject" is a purely artificial notion, something that may be useful as a descriptor within a legal system but which is not necessary for grasping the essence of the law,[20] since ultimately a "legal person" is a metaphor referring to a complex of rights and obligations:

> "to be a person" or "to have legal personality" is identical with having legal obligations and subjective rights. The person as a holder of obligations and rights is not something different from the obligations and rights . . . . The physical or juristic person who "has" obligations and rights as their holder, *is* these obligations and rights—a complex of legal obligations and rights whose totality is expressed figuratively in the concept of "person." "Person" is merely the personification of this totality.[21]

In contrast, Ricoeur proposes to recover the idea of imputation as the primary root of the idea of responsibility: "It is outside the semantic field of the verb "to respond," whether it be a question of answering for or responding to, that we have to seek the founding concept; in fact, we must look in the semantic field of the verb 'to impute.'"[22] This theoretical approach stresses the essential connection of responsibility with its subject beyond the idea of its retrospective ascription, since it emphasizes the role of the subject as agent: "Let me emphasize this again: to attribute an action to someone as its actual author. We must not lose sight of this reference to an agent."[23] In this renewal of the semantics of responsibility, Ricoeur recognizes the merits of the philosophical theory of ascription[24] in freeing the discourse of responsibility from the exclusive reference to the idea of obligation, but at the same time he stresses how the reference to an agent's self-designation as responsible requires more resources than those offered by the philosophy of language.[25] As Geoffrey Dierckxsens argues of Ricoeur, "[T]he idea of moral imputation implicates the hermeneutical and phenomenological idea of self."[26] Moreover, notes Ricoeur, we have to face the uncertainties that mark the recent evolution of the idea of responsibility in the moral and in the legal fields, namely those of identifying the author of the action, of determining the extents of the effects for which one is made responsible, and of assessing reparation if faced with the loss of reciprocity between the agent and the victim of the action.[27] As Ricoeur states, these issues require a paradigm shift, in particular with a more deliberate orientation of responsibility towards the future: "For the retrospective orientation that the moral idea of responsibility has in common with the juridical idea, an orientation thanks to which we are eminently responsible for what we *have done*, must be substituted an orientation that is more deliberately prospective, as a function of which the idea of prevention of future harm will be added to that of reparation for harm already done."[28]

In order to fully grasp the relevance of this shifting of perspective, it is necessary to consider it in light of the differences between retrospective and prospective responsibility. In the traditional legal perspective, these are considered symmetrical, with prospective responsibility being merely a synonym for the retrospective one. In order to disentangle these concepts, I would maintain with some unavoidable simplification that the different meanings of responsibility can be referred to two different semantic poles, namely a passive one, that of imputation and sanction, typical of the traditional moral-legal concept, and an active one, that of assuming responsibility implied by the idea of responsibility as a reflexive capacity of the self. As Peter Cane argues:

> In a temporal sense, responsibility looks in two directions. Ideas such as accountability, answerability and liability look backwards to conduct and events in the past. They form the core of what I shall call "historic responsibility." By contrast, the ideas of roles and tasks look to the future, and establish obligations and duties—"prospective responsibilities," as I shall call them. Accounts

of legal responsibility tend to focus on historic responsibility at the expense of prospective responsibility.[29]

Retrospective responsibility, or "historic responsibility," is backward-looking and is essentially linked to the idea of an ex post facto evaluation of a situation and a subsequent judgment in terms of imputation of the consequences. It is characterized by the ideas of sanction (liability), compensation (damage), and justification (accountability), which shape responsibility essentially as a reaction to a certain state of affairs. In contrast, prospective responsibility is forward-looking and is connected to the idea of spontaneously assuming responsibility, not only in the sense of complying with some pre-established duties, but also in proactively assuming responsibilities for a certain state of activities even when specific duties are not (or cannot) be established in advance. Therefore, prospective responsibility is more freely assumed by the subject than imputed as an obligation,[30] and it is related to the fundamental anthropology of the self.

In order to understand the place of prospective responsibility in the legal field, Ricoeur's reflections on the subject of rights and responsibility can be fruitfully cross-read with H. L. A. Hart's analysis of responsibility,[31] which is still quite influential within jurisprudence.[32] I suggest that Ricoeur complements Hart's analysis by offering a way to detach responsibility from a (still prevailing) retrospective account. In turn, Hart's analysis offers a theoretical grid that helps to locate the place for prospective responsibility to emerge within jurisprudence,[33] regardless of the fact that Ricoeur does not directly discuss Hart's writing on the concept of responsibility.[34] (In *The Just*, Ricoeur refers to Hart's work in his discussion of the *ascription* of responsibility and rights rather than Hart's concept of responsibility itself.[35])

Hart highlights different meanings of the legal idea of responsibility (role, capacity, cause, liability), among which I shall consider closely the idea of *role-responsibility,* which he defines as "the duties of a relatively complex or extensive kind, defining a 'sphere of responsibility' requiring care and attention over a protracted period of time."[36] In particular, Hart links role-responsibility to the idea of a "responsible person," who is characterized as "one who is disposed to take his duties seriously; to think about them and to make serious efforts to fulfil them."[37] This element of strong personal commitment goes beyond the strict boundaries of law.[38] Haydon calls this commitment "virtue-responsibility."[39] Virtue-responsibility refers to some personal quality of the agent, intended as a capacity or a disposition.[40] In the context of Hart's analysis of responsibility, this implies the idea of "taking role-responsibility seriously,"[41] which is therefore marked by an ethics of excellence going beyond the "morality of duty" characterizing the law (in contrast with the "morality of aspiration" distinguishing ethics),[42] as it makes reference to a proactive engagement that extends further than simple compliance with an obligation.

I suggest that the prospective idea of responsibility evoked by Ricoeur fits within the idea of role-responsibility developed by Hart, since it connects legal obligations and non-legal elements, notably personal commitment. It cannot be exhausted by the pole of juridical imputation, precisely because it implies a distinctive personal element as a qualifying feature of this sense of responsibility: "To be responsible, in this sense, it is not simply to be able to designate oneself as the agent of an action already accomplished but to be in charge of a certain zone of efficacy where the capacity to keep one's word is put to the test."[43] Ricoeur's analysis of responsibility, then, finds an echo in the character of role-responsibility and, in turn, the latter can be characterized as a prospective form of responsibility in that its relevant features are connected to personal qualities (capacities) to be exercised in the present.

The theoretical contribution of Ricoeur's analysis is particularly relevant for a theory of legal responsibility, and especially for grasping the distinctive elements characterizing prospective responsibility.[44] Considered as a specific form of capacity of the subject of rights, responsibility is engaged in an active or even proactive manner, more than being conceived in a reactive manner as the product of a retroactive ascription. In contrast with emphases on liability or accountability, prospective responsibility implies behavior and practice that extend over and above legal requirements. Prospective responsibility takes responsibility far from the logic of responding to a charge—linked to legal duties and obligations—to action motivated by the care for the other, which is implied in the dynamics of recognition. This capacity for recognizing the other as fragile, and therefore as an object of responsibility and care, is an essential attribute of the constitution of the self as a subject of rights.[45] The crucial role of this essentially personal element in the "veritable" subject of rights, which may be termed *responsiveness*, gives to responsibility more of a constructive rather than a reactive connotation, as the *motivation* to take care of the other is part of the idea of being responsible.[46]

Deploying the potential of Ricoeur's analysis demonstrates that the distinction between retrospective and prospective responsibility is not merely a matter of a shifting of a temporal perspective that is reciprocal backward and forward, nor can it assume an inherent interrelation between the two forms. Contrary to what is often maintained within legal theory,[47] the two dimensions are not fully symmetrical. There are indeed crucial differences between them. Where the central dimension of retrospective responsibility is that of imputation, prospective responsibility has to be read not simply in terms of an anticipated ascription (as is sometimes suggested in theoretical legal analysis[48]) but as linked to the capacity of the self implicated as a subject of rights in a concrete situation. Thinking of responsibility as a reflexive and intersubjective capacity implies that—contrary to Kelsen's stance—the connection with the subject is an essential element of prospective responsibility, and in this way disconnects the semantics roots of responsibility from the exclusive reference to the idea of obligation.

RESONANCES OF RICOEUR'S THEORETICAL ANALYSIS WITHIN LEGAL THEORY

Despite the doctrinal persistence of a fundamentally retrospective theoretical framing, in recent years the idea of responsibility has gained new interest in the legal philosophical literature, with a growing attention to its prospective declination. This has arisen in particular in relation to the development, dating to the late 1970s, of the precautionary principle. A pioneering definition of the principle states: "Where there are threats of serious or irreversible damage, lack of full scientific certainty shall not be used as a reason for postponing cost-effective measures to prevent environmental degradation."[49] The precautionary principle represents a novelty since, in situations of scientific uncertainty, it introduces a logic of anticipation of events that have not yet occurred and may never occur, based on a case-by-case evaluation analogous to the ethical judgment in situation, in this way disconnecting legal responsibility from the idea of an existing liability.[50] The principle represents a novelty not simply as a normative instrument, but more radically for its fundamental epistemological value, which may explain its expansion in other fields of application beyond the environmental: "Precaution tends to defy standard or classical legal assumptions. It is in essence a meta-legal principle, allowing legal provisions to incorporate considerations beyond those resulting from strictly positive law."[51] Ricoeur's contribution to the theory of prospective responsibility may help better consider the proper cognitive stance of precaution, by helping to distinguish it from the logic of liability or risk management which characterize traditional forms of legal responsibility.

Ricoeur's theory may also be pertinent in the context of the increasing relevance of so-called "soft-law" and voluntary self-regulatory instruments. Soft-law refers to texts which, despite not being legally binding in the ordinary legal sense, nonetheless are not completely devoid of legal effects,[52] and voluntary self-regulatory instruments are similar, as self-imposed codes of conduct.[53] These two concurring phenomena share a similar approach to responsibility, which they do not construct as a form of reaction (in particular through a judgment by the judiciary) but rather as a form of anticipation of responsibility intended in a prospective manner.[54] We are indeed witnessing the development of "soft" regimes of regulation, especially in fields whose societal impacts pose relevant issues of responsibility, such as technological innovation. The "softness" of these regulatory regimes puts into question precisely the traditional dynamics of responsibility based on the ascription of rights and duties. These alternatives to formal regulation are becoming increasingly pertinent, which may help explain, at least partially, the recent revisions of the concept of responsibility giving weight to the distinction between retrospective and prospective responsibilities.[55] Ricoeur's theoretical approach offers a way for reading these phenomena within a more articulated idea of responsibility, refining how we characterize them and assess their merits and their limits, for instance by assessing whether these initiatives are purely unilateral or possess an authentic dialogical nature.

The connection between an embodied subject and prospective responsibility may be of even greater relevance today in connection with the evolution of so-called Artificial Intelligence, given the fact of the pervasive role of technology in increasingly mediating both our face-to-face and institutional relations, where "humans are confronted with computational 'others' that supposedly 'outperform' human experts."[56] The supposed (out)performance and alleged greater accuracy of these systems implies an increasing computational reduction of the self and the self's determinations and is obtained through the automation of decision-making, included in the legal field, mainly based on profiling techniques, in particular with a preventive aim.[57] By directly putting into question the bodily and hermeneutical identity of the self, this contemporary evolution may have a crucial effect on the autonomy of the individual (representing a new form of vulnerability), on the construction of individual identity, and on the articulation (both theoretical and practical) of responsibility.

Facing these technological and social developments, Ricoeur's theoretical reconstruction of the subject of rights as an embodied self, coupled with his parallel revision of the semantics of responsibility that had been offered under the original idea of imputation, offers a contribution of paramount relevance to the theoretical struggle for preserving a human character in the structures mediating relations to ourselves and with others.

SOME FINAL CONSIDERATIONS

Ricoeur's contribution to the theory of the legal subject is relevant both within Ricoeur's own philosophical route as well as in relation to the contemporary evolution of the law. The idea of responsibility is the place where the two different meaning of autonomy highlighted by Ricoeur, that of being both a presupposition and a task for the subject,[58] coexist. The inscription within the legal sphere does expand the capacities of the self, and this explains why Ricoeur considers the self-imputation of responsibility as being at the same time constitutive of the subject of rights and the highest level of capacity of the self: "[W]ith imputability the notion of a capable subject reaches its highest meaning, and the form of self-designation it implies includes and, in a way, recapitulates the preceding forms of self-reference."[59]

Reconsidering the subject of rights within this perspective implies a crucial theoretical shift, that of framing this subject not primarily in relation to a reactive and retrospective idea of responsibility, which engages a subject to which it is ascribed, but to a prospective and proactive one, which engages a subject capable of assuming it by virtue of a disposition to take responsibility for the other. At the end of this traverse, the subject of rights becomes an essential component of the constitution of the self elaborated in *Oneself as Another*, bringing justice—in multiple senses—to the "neglect of the juridical" highlighted by Ricoeur.[60] Indeed, the self and the legal subject are strictly intertwined in Ricoeur's later reflections. On the one side he makes reference to a *subject* of rights, and on the other side he affirms that imputation represents a higher level of capacity of the self. In other words, the formal legal identity of the subject of rights is an essential part of the identity of the self, and vice versa the legal self is not constituted exclusively within the legal system as its identity stands also, and crucially, on non-juridical grounds.[61] It is through their virtuous intertwining that the self becomes a "full" subject of rights, or even we could term it a "subject of the law" (*sujet du droit*), this expression implying a central and active role of the subject within the law and not a mere subordination.

Within this perspective, framing responsibility prospectively does not imply simply altering the conditions for its ascription, but more radically revisiting its fundamental semantics. Re-centering the semantics of responsibility on the role of the agent opens two parallel but interconnected streams of reflection, namely, that of the redefinition of the agent as a subject of rights and that of the temporal articulation of responsibility. Once reconnected to the revised idea of the legal subject, more than to the idea of obligation, responsibility is connected to the ideas of *care* and *responsiveness*, both of which characterize responsibility more in prospective and proactive terms rather than in reactive ones. These features make the idea of prospective responsibility far more complex than being identified as symmetrical to the idea of obligation. Ricoeur's renewal of the semantics of responsibility under the sign of the idea of capacity and imputation and his parallel revision of a fundamental legal anthropology under the sign of attestation may have a crucial theoretical relevance in articulating the legal idea of responsibility beyond the idea of obligation, as he suggests:

It is in the end this appeal to judgment that constitutes the strongest plea in favor of maintaining the idea of imputability in the face of the assaults from those of solidarity and of risk. If this last suggestion makes sense, then the theoreticians of the law of responsibility, careful to preserve a just distance among the three ideas of imputability, solidarity, and shared risk, will find support and encouragement in those developments that seem at first sight to derive from an idea of responsibility quite far removed from the initial concept of an obligation to make compensation or suffer a penalty.[62]

The prospective idea of responsibility is not a reaction to a certain state of affairs but a projection ahead which requires that a capable subject recognize its responsibility towards the other. The dimension of prospective responsibility, thus, links the abstract subject of rights and the *responsive* self.

With the interrelation between Ricoeur's concept of responsibility and his revised fundamental anthropology of the subject of rights deepening the meaning of them both, the subject of responsibility is now the "veritable" subject of rights, a subject assumed in its ethical and phenomenological constitution and not confined to a pure legal abstraction.

NOTES

1. Paul Ricoeur, "Who Is the Subject of Rights?," in *The Just*, trans. David Pellauer (Chicago: University of Chicago Press, 2000), 1.

2. Yan Thomas, "Le sujet de droit, la personne et la nature," *Le Débat* 1998, no. 3 (2011): 85–107; Francois Xavier Druet and Etienne Ganty, *Rendre Justice Au Droit: En Lisant Le Juste de Paul Ricoeur* (Namur, Belgium: Presses universitaires de Namur, 1999).

3. Ricoeur, "Who is the Subject of Rights?," 5.

4. Ricoeur's approach to law and ethics is marked by the unicity of the body and by the theme of vulnerability. See Theo L. Hettema, "Autonomy and Its Vulnerability: Ricoeur's View on Justice as a Contribution to Care Ethics," *Medicine, Health Care and Philosophy* 17, no. 4 (November 1, 2014): 493–98, https://doi.org/10.1007/s11019-013-9532-y; Geoffrey Dierckxsens, "Responsibility and the Physical Body: Paul Ricoeur on Analytical Philosophy of Language, Cognitive Science, and the Task of Phenomenological Hermeneutics," *Philosophy Today* 61, no. 3 (2017): 573–93.

5. Hans Jonas, *The Imperative of Responsibility* (Chicago, IL: University of Chicago Press, 1984).

6. Tomasz Pietrzykowski, "The Idea of Non-Personal Subjects of Law," in *Legal Personhood: Animals, Artificial Intelligence and the Unborn*, ed. Visa A.J. Kurki and Tomasz Pietrzykowski (Cham, Switzerland: Springer International Publishing, 2017), 49–67, https://doi.org/10.1007/978-3-319-53462-6_4.

7. Paul Ricoeur, "Autonomy and Vulnerability," in *Reflections on the Just*, trans. David Pellauer (Chicago: University of Chicago Press, 2007), 74.

8. Paul Ricoeur, *Oneself as Another*, trans. Kathleen Blamey (Chicago: University of Chicago Press, 1992), 296.

9. Paul Ricoeur, *The Course of Recognition*, trans. David Pellauer (Cambridge, Harvard University Press, 2005), 196–201.

10. Ricoeur, *The Course of Recognition*, 197.

11. Ricoeur, "Who is the Subject of Rights?," 6.

12. Ricoeur, "Who is the Subject of Rights?," 5.

13. Ricoeur, "Who is the Subject of Rights?," 5.

14. Ricoeur, *The Course of Recognition*, 152–53. Ricoeur closely follows Axel Honneth's analysis. Ricoeur, *The Course of Recognition*, 186. See Axel Honneth, *The Struggle for Recognition: The Moral Grammar of Social Conflicts* (Cambridge, Mass: MIT Press, 1996).

15. Ricoeur, *The Course of Recognition*, 200.

16. Ricoeur, *The Course of Recognition*, 200, quoting Honneth, *Struggle for Recognition*, 114.

17. Ricoeur, "The Concept of Responsibility: An Essay in Semantic Analysis," in *The Just*, 11–35.

18. Hans Kelsen, *Pure Theory of Law*, trans. by Max Knight (Berkeley: University of California Press, 1967). For a long time Kelsen's legal philosophy was considered the *de facto* "standard" doctrine of continental European legal culture.

19. Hans Kelsen, *Pure Theory of Law*, trans. by Max Knight (Clark, NJ: Lawbook Exchange, 5th ed., 2009), 81.

20. Kelsen, *Pure Theory of Law* (2009), 169.

21. Kelsen, *Pure Theory of Law* (2009), 172–73.

22. Ricoeur, "The Concept of Responsibility," 13.

23. Ricoeur, "The Concept of Responsibility," 14.

24. H. L. A. Hart, "The Ascription of Responsibility and Rights," *Proceedings of the Aristotelian Society, New Series*, 49 (1948): 171–94.

25. Ricoeur, "The Concept of Responsibility," 19–24.

26. Dierckxsens, "Responsibility and the Physical Body," 584.

27. Ricoeur, "The Concept of Responsibility," 28–31.

28. Ricoeur, "The Concept of Responsibility," 31.

29. Peter Cane, *Responsibility in Law and Morality* (Portland, OR: Hart Publishing, 2002), 31. See also Mark Bovens, *The Quest for Responsibility. Accountability and Citizenship in Complex Organisations* (Cambridge: Cambridge University Press, 1998).

30. Cane, *Responsibility in Law and Morality*, 48.

31. H. L. A. Hart, *Punishment and Responsibility: Essays in the Philosophy of Law* (Oxford University Press, 1968).

32. Ibo van de Poel, "The Relation Between Forward-Looking and Backward-Looking Responsibility," in *Moral Responsibility. Beyond Free Will and Determinism*, ed. Nicole A. Vincent, Ibo van de Poel, and Jeroen van den Hoven (Dordrecht, Netherlands: Springer, 2011), 37–52; Nicole A. Vincent, "A Structured Taxonomy of Responsibility Concepts," in *Moral Responsibility*, 15–35, https://doi.org/10.1007/978-94-007-1878-4_2.

33. Cane, *Responsibility in Law and Morality*, 34.
34. Hart, *Punishment and Responsibility*, in particular the Postscript dedicated to "Responsibility and Retribution."
35. Ricoeur, "The Concept of Responsibility," 20–21, citing Hart, "The Ascription of Responsibility and Rights."
36. Hart, *Punishment and Responsibility*, 213.
37. Hart, *Punishment and Responsibility*, 212.
38. Lon L. Fuller, *The Morality of Law*, Revised Ed. (Yale University Press, 1969).
39. Graham Haydon, "On Being Responsible," *The Philosophical Quarterly* 28, no. 110 (1978): 46–57.
40. Haydon, "On Being Responsible," 46.
41. Cane, *Responsibility in Law and Morality*, 32.
42. Fuller, *The Morality of Law*.
43. Paul Ricoeur, "Un Entretien" in Éthique et *responsabilité: Paul Ricoeur*, ed. Jean-Christophe Aeschlimann (Neuchâtel: La Baçonnière, 1994), 30–31.
44. Ricoeur's analysis is centered on the role of the agent and considers responsibility on the plane of the capacities of the self. By contrast, Peter Cane's approach, which is very relevant for disentangling prospective responsibility from retrospective responsibility, grasps this aspect only partially.
45. Paul Ricoeur, "Autonomy and Vulnerability," 72–90.
46. Dierckxsens, "Responsibility and the Physical Body," 589.
47. Ernesto Garzón Valdés, "El enunciado de responsabilidad," *DOXA, Cuadernos de Filosofía del Derecho* 19 (1996): 259–86; Joel Feinberg, "Responsibility for the Future," *Philosophy Research Archives* 14 (1988): 93–113; Hart, *Punishment and Responsibility*; Michel Villey, "Esquisse historique sur le mot responsable," *Archives de philosophie du droit, La responsabilité*, XXII (1977): 45–58.
48. Feinberg, "Responsibility for the Future."
49. Principle 15 of the Rio Declaration on Environment and Development (Rio de Janeiro, 3–14 June 1992). UN Doc. A/CONF.151/26, vol. I, annex I, 1992. Subsequently, the principle acquired a strong legal status within European Union law and is now enshrined in Article 191 of the Treaty on the Functioning of the European Union.
50. François Ewald, "Philosophie Politique Du Principe de Précaution," *Le Principe de Précaution*, 2001, 29 ff.
51. Laurence Boisson de Chazournes, "New Technologies, the Precautionary Principle, and Public Participation," in *New Technologies and Human Rights*, ed. Thérèse Murphy (Oxford: Oxford University Press, 2009), 163.
52. Jaap Hage, "What Is Legal Validity? Lessons from Soft Law," in *Legal Validity and Soft Law*, ed. Pauline Westerman et al., Law and Philosophy Library (Cham, Switzerland: Springer International Publishing, 2018), 19–45, https://doi.org/10.1007/978-3-319-77522-7_2.
53. John J. Kirton and Michael J. Trebilcock, *Hard Choices, Soft Law: Voluntary Standards in Global Trade, Environment and Social Governance* (Routledge, 2017).
54. Gregory C. Shaffer and Mark A. Pollack, "Hard vs. Soft Law: Alternatives, Complements, and Antagonists in International Governance," *Minnesota Law Review* 94 (2009): 712.

55. Cane, *Responsibility in Law and Morality*; van de Poel, "The Relation Between Forward-Looking and Backward-Looking Responsibility"; Luigi Pellizzoni, "Responsibility and Environmental Governance," *Environmental Politics* 13, no. 3 (September 2004): 541–65, https://doi.org/10.1080/0964401042000229034; Bovens, *The Quest for Responsibility*.

56. Mireille Hildebrandt, "Privacy as Protection of the Incomputable Self: From Agnostic to Agonistic Machine Learning," *Theoretical Inquiries in Law* 20, no. 1 (January 23, 2019): 84, http://www7.tau.ac.il/ojs/index.php/til/article/view/1622.

57. Mireille Hildebrandt and Bert-Jaap Koops, "The Challenges of Ambient Law and Legal Protection in the Profiling Era," *The Modern Law Review* 73, no. 3 (2010), https://works.bepress.com/mireille_hildebrandt/32/.

58. Ricoeur, "Autonomy and Vulnerability."

59. Ricoeur, *The Course of Recognition*, 106.

60. Ricoeur, *The Just*, vii.

61. Johann Michel, *Paul Ricoeur, Une Philosophie de l'agir Humain* (Paris: Cerf, 2006), 424.

62. Ricoeur, "The Concept of Responsibility," 35.

BIBLIOGRAPHY

Boisson de Chazournes, Laurence. "New Technologies, the Precautionary Principle, and Public Participation." In *New Technologies and Human Rights*, edited by Thérèse Murphy, 161–94. Oxford: Oxford University Press, 2009.

Bovens, Mark. *The Quest for Responsibility. Accountability and Citizenship in Complex Organisations*. Cambridge: Cambridge University Press, 1998.

Cane, Peter. *Responsibility in Law and Morality*. Portland, OR: Hart Publishing, 2002.

Dierckxsens, Geoffrey. "Responsibility and the Physical Body: Paul Ricoeur on Analytical Philosophy of Language, Cognitive Science, and the Task of Phenomenological Hermeneutics." *Philosophy Today* 61, no. 3 (2017): 573–93.

Ewald, François, "Philosophie de La Précaution." *L'Année Sociologique* (1996): 383–412.

Feinberg, Joel. "Responsibility for the Future." *Philosophy Research Archives* 14 (1988): 93–113.

Fuller, Lon L. *The Morality of Law*. Revised Ed. Yale University Press, 1969.

Garzón Valdés, Ernesto. "El enunciado de responsabilidad." *DOXA. Cuadernos de Filosofía del Derecho* 19 (1996): 259–86.

Hage, Jaap Hage. "What Is Legal Validity? Lessons from Soft Law." In *Legal Validity and Soft Law*, edited by Pauline Westerman et al., 19–45. Cham, Switzerland: Springer International Publishing, 2018. https://doi.org/10.1007/978-3-319-77522-7_2.

Hart, H. L. A. "The Ascription of Responsibility and Rights." *Proceedings of the Aristotelian Society, New Series*, 49 (1948): 171–94.

Hart, H. L. A. *Punishment and Responsibility: Essays in the Philosophy of Law*. Oxford University Press, 1968.
Haydon, Graham. "On Being Responsible." *The Philosophical Quarterly* 28, no. 110 (1978): 46–57.
Hettema, Theo L. "Autonomy and Its Vulnerability: Ricoeur's View on Justice as a Contribution to Care Ethics." *Medicine, Health Care and Philosophy* 17, no. 4 (November 1, 2014): 493–98. https://doi.org/10.1007/s11019-013-9532-y.
Hildebrandt, Mireille. "Privacy as Protection of the Incomputable Self: From Agnostic to Agonistic Machine Learning." *Theoretical Inquiries in Law* 20, no. 1 (January 23, 2019). http://www7.tau.ac.il/ojs/index.php/til/article/view/1622.
Hildebrandt, Mireille, and Bert-Jaap Koops. "The Challenges of Ambient Law and Legal Protection in the Profiling Era." *The Modern Law Review* 73, no. 3 (2010). https://works.bepress.com/mireille_hildebrandt/32/.
Honneth, Axel. *The Struggle for Recognition: The Moral Grammar of Social Conflicts*. Cambridge, Mass: MIT Press, 1996.
Jonas, Hans. *The Imperative of Responsibility*. Chicago, IL: University of Chicago Press, 1984.
Kelsen, Hans. *Pure Theory of Law*. Translated by Max Knight. Berkeley: University of California Press, 1967.
Kelsen, Hans. *Pure Theory of Law*. Translated by Max Knight. Clark, NJ: Lawbook Exchange, 5th ed., 2009.
Kirton, John J., and Michael J. Trebilcock. *Hard Choices, Soft Law: Voluntary Standards in Global Trade, Environment and Social Governance*. New York: Routledge, 2017.
Michel, Johann. *Paul Ricoeur, Une Philosophie de l'agir Humain*. Paris: Cerf, 2006.
Pellizzoni, Luigi. "Responsibility and Environmental Governance." *Environmental Politics* 13, no. 3 (September 2004): 541–65. https://doi.org/10.1080/0964401042000229034.
Pietrzykowski, Tomasz. "The Idea of Non-Personal Subjects of Law." In *Legal Personhood: Animals, Artificial Intelligence and the Unborn*, edited by Visa A. J. Kurki and Tomasz Pietrzykowski, 49–67. Cham, Switzerland: Springer International Publishing, 2017. https://doi.org/10.1007/978-3-319-53462-6_4.
Poel, Ibo van de. "The Relation Between Forward-Looking and Backward-Looking Responsibility." In *Moral Responsibility. Beyond Free Will and Determinism*, 37–52. Cham, Switzerland: Springer, 2011.
Ricoeur, Paul. "Autonomy and Vulnerability." In *Reflections on the Just*. Translated by David Pellauer, 72–90. Chicago, University of Chicago Press, 2007.
Ricoeur, Paul. "The Concept of Responsibility: An Essay in Semantic Analysis." In *The Just*. Translated by David Pellauer, 11–35. Chicago: University of Chicago Press, 2000.
Ricoeur, Paul. *The Course of Recognition*. Translated by David Pellauer. Cambridge, MA: Harvard University Press, 2005.
Ricoeur, Paul. "Un Entretien. " In *Éthique et responsabilité: Paul Ricoeur*, edited by Jean-Christophe Aeschlimann. Neuchâtel: La Baçonnière, 1994.
Ricoeur, Paul. *The Just*. Chicago: University of Chicago Press, 2000.

Ricoeur, Paul. *Oneself as Another*. Translated by Kathleen Blamey. Chicago: University of Chicago Press, 1992.

Ricoeur, Paul. "Who is the Subject of Rights." In *The Just*. Translated by David Pellauer, 1–10. Chicago: University of Chicago Press, 2000.

Shaffer, Gregory C., and Mark A. Pollack. "Hard vs. Soft Law: Alternatives, Complements, and Antagonists in International Governance." *Minnesota Law Review* 94 (2009): 706–99.

Thomas, Yan. "Le sujet de droit, la personne et la nature." *Le Débat* 1998, no. 3 (2011): 85–107.

United Nations Conference on Environment and Development. "Rio Declaration on Environment and Development." Report of The United Nations Conference on Environment And Development (Rio de Janeiro, 3–14 June 1992). UN Doc. A/CONF.151/26, vol. I, annex I, 1992.

Villey, Michel. "Esquisse historique sur le mot responsable." *Archives de philosophie du droit*, XXII (1977): 45–58.

Vincent, Nicole A. "A Structured Taxonomy of Responsibility Concepts." In *Moral Responsibility*, edited by Nicole A. Vincent, Ibo van de Poel, and Jeroen van den Hoven, 15–35. Dordrecht, Netherlands: Springer, 2011. https://doi.org/10.1007/978-94-007-1878-4_2.

Xavier Druet, Francois, and Etienne Ganty. *Rendre Justice Au Droit: En Lisant* Le Juste *de Paul Ricoeur*. Namur, Belgium: Presses Universitaires de Namur, 1999.

Chapter Five

Symbolism and the Generativity of Justice

Antoine Garapon

Ricoeur's thought on law is most often studied in his works that explicitly focus on justice, that is to say in the late writings from 1990 onward, which have been collected in the two volumes *The Just* and *Reflections on the Just*. But there are other underused resources in his early works, which are less interested in the dilemmas of the just than in the *generativity* of justice, that is to say, in its ritual, procedural and legal engendering, the three levels being intimately connected. How do we go from the cry of indignation to the drafting of a complaint, from the desire for vengeance to an argument before a court? Obviously there has to be a right and institutions before which to appeal, but these institutions themselves rely on more profound representations of evil and its remedies. There can be no action on the side of the institutions of justice without the mobilization of myths. The symbolism of evil, understood in a broad sense (because Ricoeur invites us to distinguish between myths and symbols), is required in order to allow the institution of justice to deal with the enigma of violence and the scandal of crime.

Ricoeur takes on the task of identifying and classifying those symbols and myths in his *Philosophy of the Will*, Vol. II, whose title is *Finitude and Guilt*, and, more particularly, in its second part, *The Symbolism of Evil*.[1] He provides us with extremely rich material that combines erudition and philosophical depth. This early work appears to be seminal in many respects, as it is here that we find the seeds of themes that he will develop in his later work.[2] Neither lawyers nor legal anthropologists have taken hold of this material. Yet, it raises a fundamental question, suppressed while remaining a burning issue (especially in the digital era): how can we conceive the law *with* its symbolism and not by *abstracting from* it as is so often the case today? Work on the symbolic foundations of justice is all the more indispensable, since justice has now taken over from religion in dealing with the question of the evil that torments society.

Such an evaluation of myths and symbols, which does not limit them to a mere historical curiosity but gives them an active role in justice, attests to the deeply dynamic and open character of Ricoeur's thought. Myths are always "alive," an adjective that he was particularly fond of.[3] At the end of *The Symbolism of Evil* he affirms that "the symbol gives rise to thought,"[4] inviting lawyers to take hold of symbols so as to render justice with them, that is to say, in full awareness of what they are doing. It is this work that we would like to sketch out with due modesty, as it is monumental,[5] by demonstrating that Ricoeur's original position, which distinguishes him from other French philosophers (I), explores reciprocal borrowings between the eschatological vision of the Last Judgment and early forms of the legal process (II), and thereby opens up an expanded vision of justice (III).

MYTH, MATERIAL TO DECONSTRUCT, AND THE ACTIVE PRINCIPLE OF THE INSTITUTION

For many years, training for lawyers has concentrated on the study of texts: texts that can be used directly by practitioners or texts furnishing philosophers and historians with their material. Legal theory is thus amputated from its symbolic part, perhaps because we do not know what to do with it. If literature is easy to handle, exploitable through interpretation and transmissible (it is one of the many virtues of writing), the same cannot be said of myths and symbols that are more difficult to interpret but no less active for all that. Myths and symbols do not have a directly readable form. As a matter of fact, they have a latent existence; they lie concealed in images, are present in representations, and are implied by texts rather than being made explicit. They never do better than when they are present without revealing themselves, as if they were comfortable with this clandestine presence in the life of institutions. Furthermore, Ricoeur writes that his project in *The Symbolism of Evil* is to "surprise penal conceptualization in its inchoate state";[6] to "surprise," as if he wanted to intercept a communication that was directly addressed to us over and above the level of consciousness. Symbols and myths thus constitute a particular type of knowledge of the world that we use without knowing what the codes are and that we have but without realizing that we have it, albeit intuitively. Ricoeur wants to write this grammar that we use without ever having formulated it,[7] and to do so through work of clarification and formulation that is both *critical* and *constructive*, critical so as to liberate the discourse that is cognizant of its implicit connections, and constructive so as to ensure that institutions are equal to the task.

This dual perspective was an exception in the French intellectual debate of his era. The French school of sociology had substituted the notion of the symbolic for the sacred, but it came up against the problem of the status to accord to the symbolic. Marcel Mauss, in particular, ended up explaining "mana" (this is what a Melanesian tribe called the mysterious force attached to certain things) . . . through mana![8] Claude Lévi-Strauss would reproach him for this tautology because it sought "the origin of the notion of mana in *an order of reality other than* that of the relationships it helps to build, that is to say, in the order of feelings, volitions and beliefs, which are, from the point of view of the sociological explanation, epiphenomena or mysteries, in any case objects extrinsic to the field of investigation."[9] For the father of structuralism, "a law forbids science to find in its field of investigation anything other than what it should find in virtue of its principles and its method, namely that which can be calculated."[10] This imperative to not leave social rationality to explain the social drove him to distance himself from experience and to embark on a systematization or even a progressive mathematization of the social. Positive law and the social sciences would drive everyone in their path in that direction: for Bourdieu,[11] it is "social science" and for positivist lawyers, it is the pyramid of social norms.[12] These two trends come together in our time thanks to digital analysis, which would have us believe that it will objectify social or judicial practices by going beyond language.

This process of the rationalization and internalization (what this means is not clear to me) of the symbol, which began with structuralism and has since been sanctioned by the digital, confuses two meanings of the word "symbol." The mathematical symbol and the social symbol do not, in fact, have the same sense.

> The symbol is effective only where it introduces something more than life, something like an oath, a pact or a sacred law that makes death, finitude, and the consciousness of fault appear essential to the dignity or elective singularity of human destiny, and not merely incidental to it. While the methodological symbols, such as the algorithm, are the *result* of a prior agreement, the traditional symbols are the *source* that engenders any possible agreement, any formative bond of properly human societies, because the very function of speech requires that the reference to the departed (the ancestor, the god, the absent) be integrated into the pact that ties the relation to the living.[13]

Ricoeur escapes this aporia of the symbolic—explaining "mana" through "mana" or searching for the cornerstone of a systemization of social functioning there—by positioning himself both inside and outside the symbolic, that is to say, by juggling demythization work, similar to the deconstruction work favoured by the social sciences, and demythologization work proper to the hermeneutic approach. He summarizes his conception of the dual intellectual work that myth imposes as follows:

> On the one hand, demythization recognizes myth as myth but with the purpose of renouncing it. In this sense we must speak of demystification. The result of this renunciation is the gaining of a thought and a will which are no longer alienated. The positive side of this destruction is the manifestation of man as maker of his own human existence. It is an anthropogenesis. On the other hand, demythization is recognizing myth as myth but with the purpose of freeing its symbolic basis. In this sense we must speak of demythologization. What is deconstructed here is not so much myth as the secondary rationalization that holds it captive, the pseudo-logos of myth. The result of this discovery is the gaining of the revealing power that myth conceals under the mask of objectification. The positive side of this destruction is the establishing of human existence on the basis of an origin which it does not have at its command but which is announced to it symbolically in a word which founds it.[14]

This perspective on myths also distinguishes Ricoeur's approach from that of Michel Foucault, who aims to produce an archaeology of penal institutions.[15] Foucault refuses to think about punishment, for example, believing that the only alternative to prison is the non-prison. Unlike Ricoeur, he never confronts the difficulty to which that abolitionist position gives rise. Ricoeur does not reduce symbolic forms to the effects of power, which is perhaps a way of evading the serious difficulty they pose. On the contrary, he tackles head on the difficulty of thinking about punishment, which philosophy considers a scandal.[16] Two irreconcilable schools divide French intellectuals: supporters of a political origin of the symbolic, like Bourdieu or Foucault, and those who postulate, on the contrary, the symbolic origin of the social, like Ricoeur.

The preoccupation with thinking about justice as something practicable also distinguishes Ricoeur from Emmanuel Levinas, to whom he was close. For Levinas, justice is an infinite requirement, without limit and so necessarily aporetic. The latter develops a hyperbolic conception where the goodness of justice is an impossibility that is forever repeated.[17] Ricoeur's determination to hold on to the two perspectives, critical and constructive, concurrently also distinguishes him from Derrida, who endeavoured to deconstruct the conditions of possibility, the roots of justice. Derrida writes in "Force of Law: The 'Mystical Foundation of Authority,'" "I think that there is no justice without this experience, however impossible it may be, of aporia. Justice is an experience of the impossible."[18]

Opposing these "radical" visions of justice in Derrida and Levinas, Ricoeur concentrates on the experience of justice. He does not assume the point of view of Sirius as though he were a social physicist (a position that a Bourdieu advocates), but he feels part of the drama of the human condition tormented by violence and fault, and wants to contribute to its denouement through just action. Ricoeur is acutely conscious of the inevitability of the violence that he discusses in *History and Truth*.[19] Violence is neither the best available tool to hurry the end of history, nor the sign of a form of alienation destined to disappear with it. Rather, it should be seen as part of the political condition of humanity. Ricoeur refuses to get around this difficulty through "an eschatology of innocence, which takes the place of an ethics of limited violence," as he claims Marxists do.[20] Nor does he seek the redemption of justice in the affirmation of limitlessness, as Levinas does, or in the radicalism of deconstruction, as Derrida does. His objective is to think about the generativity of justice by using imperfect mediations and representations of evil and its resolution.

Ricoeur analyzes that generativity both on the historical level (the transition from defilement to sin and then guilt) and on the level of philosophical anthropology. Justice must be understood as action articulated and mediated by symbols.[21] The court is considered less as an institution and more as a cosmic scene that articulates the history of humanity, individual destiny, and relation to oneself, through guilt.[22]

MYTHIC ORIGINS OF FORMS OF JUSTICE, THE LEGAL FORM OF MYTHS

When we apply the approach that Ricoeur developed in *The Symbolism of Evil* to the contemporary judicial institution, we come up against a methodological obstacle. How do we go about extending to a secular institution like the court demythologization work that is of a hermeneutic nature and refers ultimately to a religious text? Does this not amount to a power grab on the part of religious figures against civil institutions in a secularized world? We do not think so, and Ricoeur provides us with arguments to that effect. First, the Bible, and the same holds for the other mythic narratives, does not have a monopoly on the story of evil. Ricoeur relies equally on Greek tragedy and other foundation myths. He brings another strong argument in the central place he gives to the trial.

For Ricoeur, the specific form of the court serves as a bridge between the reality of current or past judicial practices and their religious counterpart: the Last Judgment. Indeed, he makes a philosophical choice very early on whose scope becomes apparent as his work proceeds: the question of justice is approached not from legal texts, but from its effective exercise, from the proper place of its fulfilment, that is to say, from the trial. Far from being reduced to the status of a mere instrument for ensuring rights and a tool for settling disputes, the trial is analysed as "a paradigmatic case,"[23] that is to say, both as an historical matrix *institution* that has provided the consciousness of evil with its vocabulary and as a *metaphor* for universal justice.

The trial is the interface between exteriority and interiority, between history and the present, between the religious and the civil. Legal proceedings and the consciousness of evil are, in Ricoeur's opinion, two coextensive phenomena: "The metaphor of the tribunal . . . invades all registers of the consciousness of guilt. But before being a metaphor of the moral consciousness, the tribunal is a real institution of the city."[24] The appearance of the penalty and so, the desire to measure it, provides guilt with its basic vocabulary. The setting of the trial allows us to "fix" evil, to provide a framework for capturing it in words and in categories, both procedural and legal.

The trial can thus be described as the *first form* of justice in that it is not derivable from any other, not even from the law. A first form that is inclusive of the law—while today we think that it is the law that institutes the trial and the procedure. Thus, the legal mysticism of John the Evangelist is not centered on the law (unlike justification in Saint Paul, which revolves around the law and sin) but around the ideas of "testimony," "witness," "truth," "falsehood," and "paraclete," that is to say, a witness for the defense.[25] These are organized according to the core functions: charge, defense, and judgment. The biblical account represents the eschatological judgment starting from this dividing up of roles between prosecutor, witness, counsel for the defense, and judge.

Such borrowing of the conventions of the court by the biblical myth of the Last Judgment is not an isolated case. The structure of the Agon of Greek tragedy, that is to say, the confrontation between symmetrical and opposing discourses, also takes its form from the archaic trial.[26] This suggests that if there is a mythical origin of the forms of justice, and particularly of the trial, there is also a legal form of myths. The borrowings are reciprocal. This leads one to assume that there have always coexisted a right and a strictly functional justice to deal with current business and to resolve conflicts,[27] and a symbolic overdetermination of this activity which sustains mythical narratives about adjudicating between good and evil (just like *Themis* and *Dikē*).[28]

"The 'juridical' symbolism conveys some fundamental significations without which the 'mystical' symbolism itself would lose its force."[29] Such reliance on a legal vocabulary is as old as the religious, biblical narrative: "It can be traced very far back, to the archaic theme of retribution as well as to the contractual aspects of the 'Covenant.'"[30] The Hebrew Bible has multiple references to debt and forgiveness. The consciousness of guilt proceeds from an ethical-legal experience.

The Primary Symbolism Developed Through Law, the First Foundation of Meaning

According to Ricoeur and extending a prior quotation, "The metaphor of the tribunal . . . invades all registers of the consciousness of guilt. But before being a metaphor of the moral consciousness, the tribunal is a real institution of the city, and this institution was the channel by which the religious consciousness of sin was reformed."[31] For Ricoeur, everything begins in Greece with a division between Cosmos and City, with a separation between, on the one hand, what is sacred and is thus not subject to the political capacity of the city, and on the other, what is more prosaic and is subject to "the activity by which the city is defined."[32] "Private offenses," that is, those that affect the relationships between individuals, give the jurisdictions the opportunity to more objectively define the various reprehensible acts that can be perpetrated by human beings on other human beings (homicide, accidental injury during games, for example, and mistakes in war (*méprise à la guerre*)). The establishment of a variation in the gravity of the fault is expressed through the penalty measure. The birth of the court in Greece is concurrent with the birth of money and that of writing.

"The tribunal goes before, psychology follows after," writes Ricoeur in a lapidary phrase.[33] "Whereas sin is a qualitative situation—it is or it is not—guilt designates an intensive quantity, capable of more and less."[34] The variations permitted by currency as a standard of measurement or by the length of the period of exile allow the issue of guilt to be taken up again. It is the judicial organization that raises a number of legal arguments, because the jurisdictions competent to judge voluntary and involuntary crimes are not the same (the Areopagus for the former, the Palladion for the latter). "The *Dikē* ceases to denote the cosmic order and becomes identified with the proceedings of the tribunal."[35]

The city must establish this hierarchy so as to appease social anger, on the one hand, and to buy out the victim's desire for revenge, on the other. It is no longer a question of a metaphysical punishment but a concern for what one would describe in modern terms as the preservation of public order, through a decommissioning of vengeance, that is, of the natural right of the victim to claim his or her share. The Greeks distinguish according to whether the crime is purely accidental, intentional but driven by interest or greed, or intentional but animated by the desire to deliberately provoke the power of the city (*hubris*). "[T]he sacredness of the city reconstructs *in* the criminal, but beyond his acts, a will to evil for the sake of evil which is the analogue of the spirit of perdition that, according to tragedy, blows where it will."[36] This danger undermines the sacred in the city.

The delimitation of a space specific to the trial and the separate procedural roles give a certain concreteness to the injustice that goes hand in hand with its formulation. As long as sin enveloped an entire people, justice did not need to have space allocated to it. It was born very prosaically with the political imperative to rule on cases that can degenerate and introduce discord, due to the practical necessity to gather in a place to deliberate, to define roles to organize debates. Then the accusation arises that isolates a person from the group so that he or she may be charged with wrongdoing. The ritual part of justice (which is also one of the characteristics it shares with other non-Western traditions) is a way of localizing evil and its solution, of fixing them in space and time for the purpose of driving them out.

The "Swollen" Sense of Ordinary Justice

The Last Judgment is a "second-degree symbolism," which is thus supported by a first, strictly secular register of sense, whose significance it will, in return, cause to "swell."[37] The relations between real institution and symbolic figure are made of reciprocal borrowings: the eschatological figure draws on a first foundation of significance and will enduringly permeate the judicial institution in multiple ways.

The tension that the eschatological figure of the Last Judgment introduces into judicial institutions is indeed an essential element for understanding the far-reaching institution of justice in the West, and especially, the particular respect—even reverence—that is given to it, and the desire to export it around the world[38] in a sort of messianism of human rights. In Chinese culture, for example, justice is a distinguished field of activity, but it does not have this sacred character. It is not clearly distinguishable from the activity of government[39] and finds its legitimacy in effectiveness rather than in the scrupulous respect for a procedure and a specific ritual. The corruption of a judge is ruthlessly pursued, but while it represents the ultimate evil in Christian cultures, in China it is likened to a simple dysfunction, just like a bad doctor or an ignorant professor, nothing more.[40]

Justice's investment in the symbolic introduces a *temporal tension* between human beings' justice, their fragile institutions—Ricoeur would say "perishable" institutions[41]—and God's justice. As Robert Jacob demonstrates, that temporal tension first occurred in the Trial by Ordeal, a trial which is found only in the West. He explains that the thing that seems peculiar to the Christian world is, however, the oath that judges take.[42] It refers to the sentence from the Scriptures, "For in the same way you judge others, you will be judged"; in other words: you have the right to judge only on the condition that you submit to the judgment of God. It is definitely a reference to the Last

Judgment that establishes the modern judge's power to judge, a reference that will gradually become secularized.[43]

MYTH AND THE PLENITUDE OF THE EXPERIENCE OF JUSTICE

The tension that Ricoeur explores between the real institution and the symbolic representations that sustain it restores to the experience of justice its dimension of bringing humanity to fulfillment. The penalty and the strictly legal provisions of the trial are not sufficient to fulfil all the aspirations of justice. "The symbolism of the Judgment says, finally, that the fulfilment of humanity is mysteriously linked to a redemption of bodies and of the whole Cosmos: the soul cannot be saved without the body, the inner cannot be saved without the outer, the subjective cannot be saved without the totality."[44] The contemporary judicial process has liberated itself from this cosmic dimension. While this can be considered fortunate, the fact remains that the detached state of the contemporary judicial process prevents it from fulfilling all the aspirations of justice. It is as if justice were only truly done, in the minds of the public, when the condition of being detached from the cosmos, which as we have seen was the driving force behind justice in Greece, has been satisfied anew. And at further expense of course.

Ricoeur informs us about the multiple ways in which our contemporary institutions will treat the link with the totality. He identifies four main myths, assigning us the task of discovering "the latent life of the myths and the play of their latent affinities" that "must prepare the way for a philosophic recapture of the myth."[45] It would take too long, though it would be exciting, to identify the traces of these myths in the contemporary trial. That is why we will confine ourselves to pointing out only a few features.

A Ritual of Termination and Regeneration

The first myth that Ricoeur identifies is the drama of creation for which the origin of evil is coextensive with the creative act of the god. The struggle consists of a ritual repetition of battles that took place at the beginning of the world. The judicial ritual multiplies traits with this myth: in the kinship between the myth of the regeneration of democracy through the ballot and the selection of jurors, but we could also consider the ritual, agonistic confrontation between two versions of the facts, between two arguments. The trial re-enacts the crime and so re-enacts the exiting of evil after work that will always be called for again. Justice is not a perfect order; the just is not the direct result of justice, of the spirit of justice, but is rather the result of a constant struggle.

> [O]rder is not something tranquil and absolutely stable; order vibrates; "order" is a "power." The mythical dimension of power makes the rational dimension of order distressing. Throughout the pretended explication by demons, the State appears as an unstable, dangerous reality: not merely instituted but destituted-restituted, at once transcended and retained.[46]

Late modernity does not escape this imperative of restoring the order of the world, by re-enacting the crime and staging its resolution, and by filing lawsuits against murderous sovereignties following genocides; including in particular the Nuremberg, Arusha, or Phnom Penh trials. But is it sufficient to convict the offenders after a mass atrocity? The question was raised at the end of the Second World War by philosophers like Karl Jaspers[47] and theologians like Paul Tillich,[48] who distinguished several registers of guilt. Both say that the penal is not enough, because these crimes refer to a metaphysical guilt. There is still a mysterious but nonetheless perceptible link between the fulfillment of the duty of justice and the order of the world. It is perhaps the function of ritual (whose etymology recalls the link with the cosmic order[49]) to take charge of it. The trial but also the different forms of transitional justice demonstrate the need for symbolically fencing off an era as well as the need for regenerating the world.

The Tragedy as an Aesthetic Deliverance of Injustice

Another myth that Ricoeur identifies—that of the evil god—can be described as "'tragic,' because it attains its full manifestation all at once in Greek tragedy."[50] Through the idea of the tragic, Ricoeur most closely approximates the experience and its inexpressible, the dual experience of the actor: the coryphaeus and the spectator. The surpassing of the aporia of a hero who is partly a toy in a quarrel of the gods proceeds via an "aesthetic deliverance issuing from the tragic spectacle itself."[51] The spectacle is neglected by the actors in the trial and frequently by its analysts too, while, as Ricoeur understands it, it is essential. It restores to their rightful place the conscious operations of the law, which favor the written word, and helps us to understand that the efficacy of justice lies equally in the spectacle. This is evidenced by post-conflict, transitional justice, which attaches great importance to it, or by the issue of filming trials. The spectacle of the trial allows us to contemplate the tragedy of the human condition and provides us with the nourishment we need to maintain hope in the world. Aesthetics saves the drama of human finitude, something that will be a major theme in Camus.

Evil and fault are no longer formulated reflexively but are shown "by means of the characters in a spectacle, in the vestments of poetry, and through the specific emotions of terror and pity."[52] In other words, everything takes place in the immediacy of the gaze, that is to say, in space. Time having been abolished (a characteristic of contemplating a work of art), the tragic spectacle is the counterpoint to the temporal tension, which is characteristic of eschatological judgment. The tragic hero is struggling with forces that transcend him or her, and even when the gods have deserted Olympus, he or she will continue to do so. At the end of the Oresteian trilogy, the Erinyes become the Eumenides, who will keep the laws of the city, but if the transition is permanent, their stay in the cave is in fact a back and forth: if the decision of the court is final as far as the law is concerned, the society well knows that other conflicts will arise, that the Eumenides will have to leave their caves. . . .

The last, more solitary myth is that of "the soul exiled in the body." It is not difficult to see a basic structuring there that is still current in today's outreach programs for juvenile offenders: its strategy consists of helping them control their impulses, awakening what on Rousseau's reading is the citizen depository of the public good. But attaching reintegration measures to the punishment, measures whose content varies according to country and culture, is something that points to a deeper dialectic that Ricoeur outlines in *The Symbolism of Evil*.

Love and Justice

The Last Judgment introduces a tension into the Bible between two theories of justice or, more precisely, between two moments of justice: equivalence and superabundance, separation and reunion. Equivalence is a spatial idea; it is even anti-temporal, since its goal is to negate the effects of time and "wipe the slate clean." These two modalities of justice are called *justitia passiva* and *justitia activa*,[53] the search for reparation for harm and positive action in favor of reconciliation. Paul Tillich writes:

> But there is another definition of the concept of justice. It does not deny the proportional element but transcends it: I am thinking of the Old and New Testament concepts of justice. It recognizes the violation of justice and the consequences of the injustice that follow. But this is not the final word. The goal of justice is the reunion of that which has been separated through injustice, God and human beings, one human being and another human being, one group and another group. The point of this idea of justice is the justification of the unjust man.[54]

Later, Ricoeur will develop this dialectic between love and justice to the full. I propose to name this dynamic vision an "expanded" conception of justice (*une conception élargie*), taking advantage of the polysemy of the French word *élargissement*, which means both "to extend" and "to release." We talk about extending a field of vision and also of releasing a prisoner. Ricoeur's conception of justice does not cross boundaries surreptitiously, fraudulently. He does not "saw the prison bars" as if by magic or advocate removing them, but he repositions justice with a view to liberation; he reintroduces hope within the limits of the law and the institution.

This, in my opinion, is what gives Ricoeur preeminence over Foucault but also over Levinas's and Derrida's radical thoughts on justice: he confronts the difficulty of thinking about the penalty in its most unpleasant aspects, namely, the felt need to respond to evil with evil. He makes the idea of justice the product not of an absolute but unattainable imperative nor of a regression *ad infinitum* to conditions of possibility, but of a tension between, on the one hand, the search for a just measure by justice's third party (the court) and, on the other, the aim of a positive dimension oriented towards a longer-term goal. Justice is not only the fruit of *ars aequi et boni*, a strict division between competing claims, the process of rendering to each his or her own, it also looks at the restoration of the social bond on the strength of the convicted person and on the part of his or her person not affected by the crime, with the aim of rendering it authentically human.

Ricoeur thus touches on one of the shortcomings of our democracies which are more ready to exclude than to reintegrate; and clasping a wealth of safeguards against liability claims does not change this observation. Hence Ricoeur's subsequent criticisms of the coldness of the proceedings, its dearth of symbols and its lack of a shared life. Our institutions rely on the kind of evidence of reintegration that actually hides evidence of stigmatization. Should we not find positive forms of reconciliation? Hence, the interest that the author of *Oneself as Another* has in non-violent forms of justice, which means at one and the same time exclusion and reintegration, and bringing together in the same testimonial (*une même cérémonie de parole*) the short and longer term purposes of justice as was the case in South Africa's Truth and Reconciliation Commission.

* * *

This quick overview of the theoretical potentialities that Ricoeur's work contains for thinking about the generativity of justice from an anthropological point of view appears to be very promising, but it is also very frustrating because it is limited to indicating paths of inquiry, stopping when faced with the difficulty of submitting the insights that they provide to an in-depth scientific analysis. We have not had the time—nor the skills—to do that analysis here, but it is certainly worth doing!

Translated by Eileen Brennan

NOTES

1. Paul Ricoeur, *The Symbolism of Evil*, trans. Emerson Buchanan (Boston: Beacon Press, 1967).
2. Notably in Paul Ricoeur, "Love and Justice," in *Figuring the Sacred*, trans. David Pellauer, ed. Mark I. Wallace (Minneapolis: Fortress Press, 1995), 315–29.
3. Paul Ricoeur, *La métaphore vive*, Paris, Seuil, 1975, translated as *The Rule of Metaphor: Multi-disciplinary Studies of the Creation of Meaning*, trans. Robert Czerny, Kathleen McLaughlin, and John Costello, SJ (Toronto: University of Toronto Press, 1977).
4. This is the title given by Ricoeur to the conclusion of *The Symbolism of Evil*.
5. Ricoeur was very preoccupied with being received by professional circles (historians, literary figures, psychoanalysts, doctors and, at the end of his life, lawyers) who did him the honor of sharing their own concerns with him and that he modestly tried to shed light on through philosophy.
6. Ricoeur, *The Symbolism of Evil*, 109 (translation modified).
7. It is characteristic of mythical expression to be lacunal and hidden.
8. Marcel Mauss, *The Gift: The Form and Reason for Exchange in Archaic Societies* (London and New York: Routledge, 1990).
9. Claude Lévi-Strauss, *Introduction to the Work of Marcel Mauss*, trans. Felicity Baker (London: Routledge and Kegan Paul, 1987), [xlv French] (emphasis added).
10. Vincent Descombes, "L'équivoque du symbolique," *Revue du Mauss*, 34, no. 2 (2009): 446.
11. Pierre Bourdieu, Jean-Claude Chamboredon, and Jean-Claude Passeron, *Le métier de sociologue* (Paris: Mouton, 1983).
12. Hans Kelsen, *Pure Theory of Law* (New Jersey: The Lawbook Exchange, Ltd., 2005).
13. Edmond Ortigues, *Le discours et le symbole* (Paris: Aubier, 1962), 65–66.
14. Paul Ricoeur, *The Conflict of Interpretations*, ed. Don Ihde (Evanston, IL: Northwestern University Press, 2007), 335–36.
15. Michel Foucault, *Discipline and Punish: The Birth of the Prison* (New York and Toronto: Random House, Inc., 1995).
16. Paul Ricoeur, *Le juste, la justice et son échec* (Paris: L'Herne, 2005).
17. Bertrand Mazabraud, *De la juridicité. Le droit à l'*école de Paul *Ricoeur* (Rennes: Presses Universitaires de Rennes, 2017), 233.
18. Jacques Derrida, "Force of Law: The 'Mystical Foundation of Authority,'" in *Deconstruction and the Possibility of Justice*, eds. Drucilla Cornell, Michel Rosenfeld, and David Gray Carlson (New York: Routledge, 1992), 16.

19. Paul Ricoeur, *History and Truth*, ed. Charles A. Kelbley (Evanston: IL: Northwestern University Press, 1965).

20. Ricoeur, *History and Truth*, 262.

21. Paul Ricoeur, "The Symbolic Structure of Action," *Philosophical Anthropology*, eds. Johann Michel and Jérôme Porée, trans. David Pellauer (Cambridge: Polity Press, 2016), 176–94.

22. One thinks of Ricoeur, *The Conflict of Interpretations*, op. cit.

23. Paul Ricoeur, *The Just*, trans. David Pellauer (Chicago: University of Chicago Press, 2000), 119.

24. Ricoeur, *The Symbolism of Evil*, 108.

25. Ricoeur, *The Symbolism of Evil*, 277.

26. Jacqueline Duchemin, *L'Agôn dans la tragédie grecque* (Paris: Les Belles Lettres, 1968).

27. We could put this hypothesis side by side with the similar one that Marcel Hénaff puts forward on the economy. He notes that two forms of economy have always coexisted: one to exchange goods and the other for offerings and the sacred, and that it is therefore wrong to see the modern economy as representing the secularization of the symbolic economy. Marcel Hénaff, *The Price of Truth: Gift, Money, and Philosophy*, trans. Jean-Louis Morhange and Anne-Marie Feenberg-Dibon (Stanford, CA: Stanford University Press, 2010).

28. François Tricaud, *L'accusation. Recherche sur les figures de l'agression éthique* (Paris: Dalloz, 2000).

29. Ricoeur, *The Symbolism of Evil*, 276.

30. Ricoeur, *The Symbolism of Evil*, 276.

31. Ricoeur, *The Symbolism of Evil*, 108.

32. Ricoeur, *The Symbolism of Evil*, 111.

33. Ricoeur, *The Symbolism of Evil*, 112.

34. Ricoeur, *The Symbolism of Evil*, 107.

35. Ricoeur, *The Symbolism of Evil*, 112.

36. Ricoeur, *The Symbolism of Evil*, 117–18.

37. Ricoeur, *The Symbolism of Evil*, 276.

38. Prophetic monotheism is the monotheism of justice. The gods of space necessarily destroy justice. The unlimited claim of every spatial god unavoidably clashes with the unlimited claim of any other spatial god. The will to power of the one group cannot give justice to another group. This holds true of the powerful groups within a nation and of the nations themselves. Polytheism, the religion of space, is necessarily unjust. The unlimited claim of any god of space destroys the universalism implied in the idea of justice. This and this alone is the meaning of prophetic monotheism. God is one God because justice is one.

39. Robert Jacob, *La grâce des juges. L'institution judiciaire et le sacré en Occident* (Paris: Presses universitaires de France, 2014).

40. On this subject, see Antoine Garapon et al., *Le procès civil en version originale. Cultures judiciaires comparées: France, Chine, États-Unis* (Paris: Lexis-Nexis, 2014). The only dimension of the sacred in China has to do with the "Lord of the Place," that is to say, with a spatial reference.

41. "The city is fundamentally perishable. Its survival depends on us." Paul Ricoeur made this statement when interviewed by Roger-Pol Droit. See Roger-Pol Droit, *La compagnie des contemporains. Rencontres avec des penseurs d'aujourd'hui* (Paris: Odile Jacob, 2002), 33. The interview was published in *Le Monde* on October 29, 1991.

42. Jacob, *La grâce des juges*.

43. The Chinese judges never took an oath.

44. Ricoeur, *The Symbolism of Evil*, 277–78.

45. Ricoeur, *The Symbolism of Evil*, 174.

46. Ricoeur, *History and Truth*, 240.

47. Karl Jaspers, *The Question of German Guilt*, trans. E. B. Ashton (New York: Fordham University Press, 2001).

48. Tillich, *Theology of Culture*.

49. Antoine Garapon, *Bien juger, essai sur le rituel judiciaire* (Paris: Odile Jacob, 1996).

50. Ricoeur, *The Symbolism of Evil*, 173.

51. Ricoeur, *The Symbolism of Evil*, 173.

52. Ricoeur, *The Symbolism of Evil*, 225.

53. Théo Preiss, "La justification dans la pensée johannique," in *Hommage et reconnaissance: Recueil des travaux publiés à l'occasion du soixantième anniversaire de Karl Barth, Cahiers théologiques de l'"Actualité protestante"* (special issue, Neuchâtel, 1946), 115.

54. Paul Tillich, "The Jewish Question: A Christian and German Problem," in *Bulletin of the North American Paul Tillich Society*, trans. Marion Pauck and William Pauck, vol. 30, no. 3 (Summer 2003), 3–24.

BIBLIOGRAPHY

Bourdieu, Pierre, Jean-Claude Chamboredon, and Jean-Claude Passeron. *Le métier de sociologue*. Paris: Mouton, 1983.

Derrida, Jacques. "Force of Law: The 'Mystical Foundation of Authority.'" In *Deconstruction and the Possibility of Justice*, edited by Drucilla Cornell, Michel Rosenfeld, and David Gray, 3–67. Carlson, NY: Routledge, 1992.

Descombes, Vincent. "L'équivoque du symbolique." *Revue du Mauss* 34, no. 2 (2009): 438–66.

Droit, Roger-Pol. *La compagnie des contemporains. Rencontres avec des penseurs d'aujourd'hui*. Paris: Odile Jacob, 2002.

Duchemin, Jacqueline. *L'Agôn dans la tragédie grecque*. Paris: Les Belles Lettres, 1968.

Garapon, Antoine. *Bien juger, essai sur le rituel judiciaire*. Paris: Odile Jacob, 1996.

Garapon, Antoine et al., *Le procès civil en version originale. Cultures judiciaires comparées: France, Chine, États-Unis*. Paris: Lexis-Nexis, 2014.

Hénaff, Marcel. *The Price of Truth: Gift, Money, and Philosophy*. Translated by Jean-Louis Morhange and Anne-Marie Feenberg-Dibon. Stanford, CA: Stanford University Press, 2010.

Jacob, Robert. *La grâce des juges. L'institution judiciaire et le sacré en Occident.* Paris: Presses universitaires de France, 2014.

Jaspers, Karl. *The Question of German Guilt.* Translated by E. B. Ashton. New York: Fordham University Press, 2001.

Kelsen, Hans. *Pure Theory of Law.* New Jersey: The Lawbook Exchange, Ltd., 2005.

Lévi-Strauss, Claude. *Introduction to the Work of Marcel Mauss.* Translated by Felicity Baker. London: Routledge and Kegan Paul, 1987.

Mauss, Marcel. *The Gift: The Form and Reason for Exchange in Archaic Societies.* London and New York: Routledge, 1990.

Mazabraud, Bertrand. *De la juridicité. Le droit à l'école de Paul Ricoeur.* Rennes: Presses Universitaires de Rennes, 2017.

Ortigues, Edmond. *Le discours et le symbole.* Paris: Aubier, 1962.

Preiss, Théo. "La justification dans la pensée johannique." In *Hommage et reconnaissance: Recueil des travaux publiés à l'occasion du soixantième anniversaire de Karl Barth, Cahiers théologiques de l'"Actualité protestante,"* special issue, Neuchâtel, 1946.

Ricoeur, Paul. *The Conflict of Interpretations.* Edited by Don Ihde. Evanston, IL: Northwestern University Press, 2007.

Ricoeur, Paul. *History and Truth.* Edited by Charles A. Kelbley. Evanston: IL: Northwestern University Press, 1965.

Ricoeur, Paul. *The Just.* Translated by David Pellauer. Chicago: University of Chicago Press, 2000.

Ricoeur, Paul. *Le juste, la justice et son échec.* Paris: L'Herne, 2005.

Ricoeur, Paul. "Love and Justice." In *Figuring the Sacred*, translated by David Pellauer, edited by Mark I. Wallace, 315–29. Minneapolis: Fortress Press, 1995.

Ricoeur, Paul. *La métaphore vive.* Paris: Seuil, 1975.

Ricoeur, Paul. *The Rule of Metaphor: Multi-disciplinary Studies of the Creation of Meaning.* Translated by Robert Czerny, Kathleen McLaughlin, and John Costello, SJ. Toronto: University of Toronto Press, 1977.

Ricoeur, Paul Ricoeur. "The Symbolic Structure of Action." In *Philosophical Anthropology*, edited by Johann Michel and Jérôme Porée, translated by David Pellauer, 176–94. Cambridge: Polity Press, 2016.

Ricoeur, Paul. *The Symbolism of Evil.* Translated by Emerson Buchanan. Boston: Beacon Press, 1967.

Tillich, Paul. "The Jewish Question: A Christian and German Problem." In *Bulletin of the North American Paul Tillich Society*, translated by Marion Pauck and William Pauck 30, no. 3 (Summer 2003): 3–24.

Tillich, Paul. *Theology of Culture.* Edited by Robert C. Kimball. Oxford/New York: Oxford University Press, 1959.

Tricaud, François. *L'accusation. Recherche sur les figures de l'agression éthique.* Paris: Dalloz, 2000.

Chapter Six

Ricoeur, Narrative, and Legal Contingency

George H. Taylor

This chapter's thesis arises out of a contrast between the following two statements.[1] On the one hand, the Rev. Dr. Martin Luther King, Jr. issued the famous contention, "The arc of the moral universe is long, but it bends towards justice."[2] On the other hand, Paul Ricoeur has argued, "We speak of humanity not only as a species but as in fact a task, since humanity is given nowhere."[3] My claim is that the statement by Dr. King is incorrect while Ricoeur's is accurate. I shall employ Ricoeur's theory of narrative, in particular of the interrelation between narrative concordance and discordance, to develop this argument. The pursuit of a just legal system is a persisting task, an ongoing struggle, and not the result of some overarching historical trajectory. I begin by signifying the nature of the thesis in broader social and political terms and move over time toward narrowing the focus toward the law. Along the way I integrate Ricoeur's more specific work in legal hermeneutics into his larger theory of narrative, and I close with more extended application of my argument to the contemporary legal problematic of partisan gerrymandering.

I offer Dr. King's statement as a vivid and memorable representation of a wider train of thought against which I argue. According to this broader conception, whether due to the natural law of reason, the role of providence, or the logic of history, justice is claimed inevitably to fall on the side for which one is contending. History is ineluctably a march of progress. Truth is with us in the end. In the 1960s, when Dr. King's work was bearing fruition, some might have assumed in the United States greater assurance of history's arc. Yet even then, the war in Vietnam and the difficulty of establishing national support for a war on urban poverty brought King himself pause. The great resilience of King's Christianity that helped ground his pursuit of civil rights had to face the objection of Christianity's invocation on behalf of racist tenets.[4] And King's assassination gave pause to the confidence in others. The

1960s also saw a rising liberal political confidence in the sweeping 1964 election of Democrat Lyndon Johnson to the presidency, defeating Republican Barry Goldwater. But the 1960s also saw the seeds of a conservative counter-revolution in the beginning rise of Ronald Reagan, who eventually became United States President in 1981. More recently, the more liberal presidency of Barack Obama was followed by a populist revolt that led to the presidency of conservative Donald Trump. I do not intend to focus on these American moments. Indeed, we are witnessing the rise of conservative forms of populism in many countries, including on their courts. Nor would I contend that the arc of justice and law is bending in a conservative direction. It may be that this conservative ascendancy is itself facing the threat of challenge by a younger, more diverse population—nationally and internationally—that will replace an aging, white majority. But in my view the coming ascendancy of a more liberal youth movement is not inevitable either.

As I will develop, the course of history depends instead on multiple variables that affect its unpredictable trajectory: the larger pushes and pulls between competing political interests domestically and internationally, whose course remains both unpredictable and in flux; political machinations, which may disrupt seeming majoritarian trends; the "butterfly effect," where apparently small changes lead to a wide divergence in trajectory over time; and "black swan" events,[5] highly unanticipated incisions in history whose effects are significant. While the basic definitions of most of the variables I have mentioned are likely familiar, the ascription of events as black swans may be less well known, so let me offer some greater explication there.[6] The black swan event is one that at the time of its occurrence is highly unlikely. It may operate at a macro or micro level, and the local event may have spreading ramifications: the advent of World War I; the plane attacks in the United States on September 11, 2001; the 2008 financial crisis. At the time of this writing, memory is still fresh of the October 2018 shooting by a lone gunman at a Pittsburgh synagogue, less than a mile from my home, that killed eleven congregants. The tearing of the community fabric caused by this one individual has been deep, as fortunately have been the positive efforts of local, national, and international solidarity seeking to repair the scar. But the scarring has changed our history. It is of the moment that many readers—wherever they are located internationally—will be able to relate to the Pittsburgh black swan event upon the basis of unforeseen shootings within their locale. Again, I do not want to concentrate on the present events either of United States or international history, both of which new events will supersede. The evidence is suggestive both that historical inevitability does not exist and that the pursuit of elemental values within the structures of a legal system depend instead on continuing social, political, and legal struggle. As noted in Ricoeur's words quoted at the outset, humanity is a task; it is given nowhere.

To develop the chapter's theme, I draw on the work of Ricoeur to relate together the perhaps seemingly disparate themes of narrative and the quest for a just legal system. Narrative helps us incorporate the call for justice with that call being a struggle. While we may frequently think of narrative, justice, and law from the perspective of their terms being established—a completed story or an existing principle that we attempt to apply—I want to interrelate narrative and the pursuit of a just legal system precisely as tasks, as terms not established but open, incomplete, and subject to ongoing human struggle and creativity.

NARRATIVE AND CONTINGENCY

It is perhaps appropriate that I situate my thesis with an opening narrative. I want to analogize from a story told about human evolution to the relation between narrative and a just legal system. The evolutionary biologist Steven Jay Gould argues that evolution on the earth is subject to significant contingency. The earth's history is witness to periods of mass extinction, where a high percentage of species do not survive due to the extreme circumstances. Perhaps the best known of such occurrences is the evidence that an asteroid hit the earth sixty-five million years ago, and the resulting dust and ash caused severe environmental disruption that led both to the extinction of dinosaurs and the environmental space for vertebrates to flourish, eventually including humans.[7] Contingencies in numerous prior events led to the asteroid hitting the earth, and absent those contingencies, vertebrates might not have flourished and humans might not have come into being. Gould argues that any replay of the earth's history would, because of the impact of changed contingent events, "lead evolution down a pathway radically different from the road actually taken."[8] The existence of humans on Earth is a contingent event in the earth's story. Gould does not reject the existence of design constraints on this process: the obedience of life to physical principles, the probable limits on biological design and construction, and so forth.[9] But Gould distinguishes between "laws in the background" and "contingency in the details" and maintains that the great potential variations in the earth's history—including the appearance of humans within this history—depend on the contingent details.[10] Evolution is not senseless or without meaningful pattern, but the pattern is ascertainable only after the fact. If contingent events are altered, the evolutionary pattern alters too.[11]

We do not need to witness these contingencies only at the scale of the Earth's evolution, for they are perceivable also at the human scale. Within the past seventy-five or so years we have faced numerous times where the threat of nuclear war—and the potential devastation of the human race—has seemed very real. Gould wonders too, for example, how human history might have changed if Chinese naval expeditions, which reached eastern Africa in the early 1400s, had not been curtailed by subsequent Chinese leaders. Would the combination of naval skills and China's invention of gunpowder have led to Chinese domination of Europe?[12]

I want to develop Ricoeur's philosophy to argue for a similar contingency—a similar story of a contingent narrative—in the nature of what we humans have determined to be the law. As with Gould on evolution, we can look back on the evolution of human notions of law and see logic in the development, but the logic could have developed quite differently. And the trajectory of the law may assume different logics in the future. The law is not a matter of an arc toward some inherent notion of justice but instead a product of human choice, human judgment, and human creativity, for better or ill.

In turning to Ricoeur's reflections on narrative, I draw on his three-volume work, *Time and Narrative*. What I find particularly distinctive in those texts is Ricoeur's emphasis that a narrative is not a seamless whole, a playing out of a story with an inevitable conclusion. As in Gould's views on biological evolution, we may look back on a narrative we have read and appreciate the logic in its development, but in the midst of the story, the logic is unsure and unsettled. The narrative's logic is contingent on events. Ricoeur encapsulates the narrative act as that which seeks the concordant through the discordant or acts as a "synthesis of the heterogeneous."[13] The narrative is not pre-given in either human or individual history but must be constructed. It is an act. The character of narrative as something that seeks the concordant through the discordant is reinforced when we recall Ricoeur's parallel discussion of metaphor in his book, *The Rule of Metaphor*. In the metaphoric creation of resemblance, Ricoeur says, "the 'similar' is perceived despite difference, in spite of contradiction. . . . '[T]he same' operates in spite of 'the different.'"[14] The action of metaphor makes more precise the narrative function of seeking the concordant across the discordant. It is of course not surprising to ascertain this similarity between metaphor and narrative. Ricoeur's two books on these topics were "conceived together."[15] In both narrative and metaphor, a comparable act of productive imagination bridges across discordance and difference.[16] The narrative is a creative act.

Bringing us closer to our discussion of law, it is revealing that Ricoeur's characterization of narrative as that which seeks the concordant through the discordant applies not only to literary narratives but to social and political narratives as well. Ricoeur situates tradition as a form of narrative. A tradition is not a manifestation simply of continuity. A tradition is not, Ricoeur says, "the inert transmission of some already dead deposit of material but the living transmission of an innovation always capable of being reactivated by a return to the most creative moments of poetic activity."[17] Tradition consists of an interplay between innovation and sedimentation. Narrative incorporates innovation; it remains open to change; it is plastic. Ricoeur extends the point by identifying innovation as an act of productive imagination. The narrative is not inherent, not fixed; it entails acts of imagination to establish coherence across disparity as the narrative is extended to new situations.

A second bridge to our discussion of law lies in the recognition that Ricoeur's treatment of narrative is very similar to his larger theory of hermeneutics. For hermeneutics, it is insufficient to describe understanding as applying what has come before (a sedimentary notion of narrative) to the instance at hand. Instead, the existing narrative is informed by the new instance (the instance of application), and understanding of the part is informed by the whole.[18] The new particular is not understood on the basis of its adequation to the existing narrative, for the narrative may be informed and transformed by the manifestation and incorporation of the particular.[19]

Before turning more directly to the relation Ricoeur provides between narrative and the search for a just legal system, let me offer two concluding comments on Ricoeur's theory of narrative itself, one very positive and one more critical. The positive comment is that Ricoeur's theory, in its negotiation of the tension between concordance and discordance, in its ambition—always partial, never certain—to achieve concordance across discordance, meets the challenge to narrative posed by postmodernist critiques such as Lyotard's. Indeed, I would claim that Ricoeur's theory of narrative demonstrates the postmodernist side of Ricoeur's work. As well known, Lyotard defines the postmodern on the basis of "incredulity toward metanarratives."[20] Although he does not mention Ricoeur by name, Lyotard criticizes as "modern" any science legitimating itself by "an explicit appeal to some grand narrative," such as Hegel's "dialectics of Spirit" or "the hermeneutics of meaning."[21] By contrast, Lyotard argues, the loss of metanarratives leaves the "postmodern condition" as one of the "heterogeneity of language games," of only "local determinism." The postmodern "refines our sensitivity to differences and reinforces our ability to tolerate the incommensurable."[22] Lyotard also characterizes justice as succumbing to the "grand narrative" in the same way as does truth.[23] For Lyotard, our choices are two: between unity—the overarching narrative, such as Dr. King's—and difference, and for him, the postmodern condition must acknowledge difference. What I find remarkable about Ricoeur's theory of narrative is that it mediates between these choices.

We seek for concordance, but we seek for it not in denial or derogation of discordance, but across discordance, across difference. Any concordance attained is always fractured, always limited, always threatened by existing or new situations of discordance that require us to take up the narrative again. Humanity is a continuing task, not something given. In the next section, I shall argue that the same is true of law. It is regrettable that Ricoeur's more modulated portrayal of narrative is not better appreciated and that he is often, as apparently in Lyotard, reduced to a stance endorsing metanarrative.

My critique is that at the same time that Ricoeur's theory of narrative can be defended against Lyotard's challenge, it is also susceptible to it. As I have developed elsewhere,[24] a significant portion of Ricoeur's work exhibits two sides. One side maintains the tension between concordance and discordance. On this first side, concordance seeks to bridge discordance, while recognizing that this act is a perpetual challenge; distance remains. The other side appears to locate itself more at one end, with concordance. My reservation with Ricoeur's theory of narrative is that for him the act of narrative configuration mediates, integrates,[25] grasps the manifold of events and brings them together in one story, one narrative, one whole. Ricoeur's description of narrative as concordant discordance gives predominance to concordance. Narrative is a "*synthesis* of the heterogeneous."[26] Ricoeur claims that the synthesis of the heterogeneous in narrative brings it "close" to metaphor, in the sense that metaphor too is perceptive of resemblance and similarity.[27] My concern is that the vocabulary of mediation, integration, concordance, synthesis, and similarity gives priority to the resolution of difference and not instead to the depths of discordance—new, contested possibilities—nor to the fractured narrative that may result or be in repeated need of a new, transformed telling. As evident from my argument, I find the side of Ricoeur attentive to the narrative tension between concordance and discordance more valuable as more descriptively accurate about the nature of the human condition and to the side of his larger reflections ascribing humanity as a task.

NARRATIVE AND LAW

It is this tensive side of narrative that I retain as I turn to develop the relation between narrative and the pursuit of a just legal system. Lyotard has already alerted us that as must be the question of truth, so also the question of justice must be located in response to the postmodern challenge. Law too is encompassed by the struggle to attain and maintain a narrative, a narrative that pursues justice. The meaning and application of the just are not something defined by anything pre-given. I have already anticipated two bridges between narrative, justice, and law in Ricoeur's characterization of tradition within a narrative framework and in the juxtaposition between narrative and Ricoeur's larger hermeneutics. In the application of a narrative tradition and its principles to a new situation, the new situation is not judged on the basis of whether it falls within or outside the existing narrative—the existing norms—because the incorporation of the new situation into the narrative may transform the narrative and the principles it represents.

Let me use this relationship between narrative and hermeneutic application as a point of entry into legal hermeneutics and the questions of legal justice it raises. Before developing Ricoeur's theory of legal judgment, I briefly contextualize the issue by reference to Gadamer's appraisal of legal hermeneutics. Legal hermeneutics does indeed have, in Gadamer's phrase, "exemplary significance"[28] for hermeneutics more largely. The law is replete with case after case where existing meanings must be extended to new situations of application. The relationship between meaning and application is not one of subsumption. Rather, as Gadamer famously maintains, application involves "co-determining, supplementing, and correcting [a] principle."[29] Meaning is not determined once and for all at the moment of origin but must be reassessed as new circumstances arise. Meaning can change as it is applied; the determination of meaning requires judgment. It is at the point of judgment that I want to unfold the dimensions of poetics—of imagination—in the creation of a narrative in legal and general hermeneutics.

I was much taken in the chapter on "Interpretation and/or Argumentation" in Ricoeur's book, *The Just*, with his extremely insightful elaboration of what the process of legal application entails. Ricoeur's precision here goes far beyond Gadamer. "The application of a rule," Ricoeur says, "is in fact a very complex operation where the interpretation of the facts and the interpretation of the norm mutually condition each other."[30] As his chapter title suggests, Ricoeur argues that legal application includes both interpretation and argumentation, and he draws a parallel between these two and his earlier interplay between explanation and understanding.[31] Argumentation is necessary, because the extension of law to a new application is not a mere intuitive leap but requires a judgment of fitness, something that mandates analysis—explanation.[32] As Ricoeur relates, this analysis includes such factors as empirical investigation, interpretation of facts, employment of canons of interpretation, and assessment of precedent.[33] But determination of fit requires both the logical face of argumentation and the inventive side of interpretation.[34] Ricoeur's turn to Kant's theory of reflective judgment in the *Critique of Judgment* is particularly useful in clarifying, and in fact expanding, the nature of the interplay between argumentation and interpretation. Ricoeur relates that we find in the *Critique of Judgment* a play between the poles of "the understanding (that is, an ordering function) and the imagination (that is, a function of invention, creativity, fantasy)."[35] Ricoeur calls this play the "judicatory imaginary."[36] Interpretation in law is the path that "the productive imagination follows once the problem is no longer to apply a known rule to a presumably correctly described case, as with determinative judgment, but to 'find' a rule *under* which it is appropriate to place a fact that itself must be interpreted."[37] Let me delineate the implications of this sentence. In a number of cases, legal judgment is a "determinative judgment" in the sense that the case of application falls quite squarely within the boundaries of an existing legal rule. By contrast, "reflective judgment" arises where the existing applicable legal rules do not directly encompass the facts of a new case. The facts of this case must be interpreted to relate them to legal categories, but the legal categories must themselves undergo transformation in order to accommodate the facts presented. In such cases, the ordering function requires supplementation by the productive imagination in order to extend and transform a rule to a new context. Imagination is thus not extraneous to argumentation but part of the argumentation process.[38] The legal imagination is at one level, then, the creativity and invention that lies at the heart of legal application. It is a form of productive imagination—a matter of reflective judgment—in its creation of new linkages that transform prior understandings and rules.

The reflective judgment in legal imagination can be readily related to our prior discussion of metaphor and narrative. A brief return to metaphor will set the stage for elaboration of the interrelation between narrative and law. As we have seen, Ricoeur contends that the ground for metaphoric predication arises when customary meaning is no longer sufficient; a gap appears between our present understanding and a new set of facts or conditions. Metaphor can cross this gap. "In metaphor," Ricoeur writes, "'the similar' is perceived despite difference."[39] In this sense legal application is metaphoric, because it acts to transcend and transform existing legal categories. Application creates resemblance where previously there was simply difference. Similarly, the act of reflective judgment in legal imagination is also an act of narrative. A legal actor must transform the existing legal narrative to seek concordance across the discordance created by the new factual situation. The new factual situation does not fit the existing narrative, and so a larger concordance—a transformed narrative—must be created.[40] To express the point in the vocabulary of tradition, the existing legal tradition—the doctrine—has been sedimented, and innovation in the tradition must occur to address the new situation. Tradition is renovated. The legal imagination transforms the existing narrative through a metaphoric act that creates concordance where it did not exist before. "Imagination," says Ricoeur, "is this ability to produce new kinds of assimilation and to produce them not above the differences, as in [the nature of] the concept, but in spite of and through the differences."[41] Imaginative interrelation of existing rules and new particularities can create some new metaphoric resemblance—a transfigured narrative—across an initial divide.

The analysis of reflective judgment in legal imagination in turn deepens and extends our understanding of narrative. In Ricoeur's vocabulary, if an initial legal actor such as a court *configures* the narrative—emplots it into a legal story—subsequent legal interpretation of the narrative in a new case acts as a reader of the narrative and *refigures* it at the point of application.[42] Indeed, consistent with my general thesis, legal application of a line of precedent allows a court not only to receive and refigure as a reader a prior author's (court's) narrative but also to act as a new author and so *reconfigure* the narrative in a direction it chooses to take. The claim here finds that Ricoeur's vocabulary both recalls and enhances Ronald Dworkin's argument that judicial opinions in a line of cases serve as a chain novel, with new authors (courts) writing new chapters that build on but do not simply track prior chapters.[43] The role of the court acting as a new author takes the theory of narrative further than does Ricoeur himself.

If we recall my beginning example from Gould, just as many historical and biological contingencies have affected the course of human evolution and history, so too the course of the law is continuously affected by contingencies as well. At every step where new facts require the law to incorporate reflective judgment, legal imagination may argue for or create new law that can extend in a variety of directions. The meaning of legal principles and legal precedents is not predetermined but unfolds in the process of application. A legal narrative's direction is not foretold but a product of human judgment. In retrospect, the logic of the narrative may make sense, but the logic could have been otherwise, and at the time of judgment the logic is potentially open to multiple paths. At any juncture of reflective judgment, the productive imagination may lead the legal narrative in diverse trajectories.

Let me take one final consequence for law of my argument before concluding, in the final section, with an exemplification of the thesis as applied to partisan gerrymandering. We often think of the establishment of a legal right as a precedent that creates a firm legal foundation moving forward. Under this view, the flexibility of the legal imagination is constrained by the existing rules that have been laid down. In an incisive article, law professor Mark Tushnet shows that the trajectory of the law is not that simple.[44] Tushnet's message returns us to the interrelation between social, political, and legal struggle. The development of legal doctrine is subject not only to the legal hermeneutic critique demonstrating the plasticity of legal interpretation on its own terms. Doctrinal development is subject to social and political factors as well. Importantly, Tushnet shows also that the correlation between legal victory and political victory may not be positive. He develops a fourfold analysis of the interrelation between legal and political victories: there may be (1) legal and political victory, (2) legal and political loss, (3) legal victory and political loss, or (4) legal loss and political victory. The easiest cases to understand occur when the legal victory leads to a political victory or a legal loss leads to a political loss. Of greater interest, particularly for our purposes, are cases where a legal victory leads over time to a political loss, or, for those on the other side, a legal loss leads eventually to a political victory. Tushnet offers as a primary example the United States law governing abortion. In *Roe v. Wade*,[45] the U.S. Supreme Court granted a constitutional right to abortion as a matter of privacy. As a result of the legal victory, Tushnet observes,[46] advocates for the right to abortion moved to other issues, while those fervent in their opposition turned to the vehicle of political change: to elect members of Congress more responsive to restrictions on abortion; to impose statutory and regulatory restrictions on the right to abortion (e.g., waiting periods; onerous health requirements imposed upon providers); and ultimately to effectuate constitutional change, including the nomination of more conservative judges to the federal judiciary.[47] The legal victory on behalf of abortion led to a political loss that in turn has led to legal restrictions on abortion and, with the ascension of new conservative majority on the U.S. Supreme Court (discussed more below) to the threat of the Court's reversal of *Roe v. Wade*, eliminating the federal constitutional protection or, more extremely, to a ruling that abortion is unconstitutional and so legally prohibited. Our argument drawing upon Ricoeur helps us frame the larger implications of Tushnet's argument. Despite often its pretenses, the law does not invoke an ineluctable logic leading to one true form of justice. The law is a product of concordance and discordance due to competing logics, values, and pressures. No legal victory is inherently permanent. Legal victory (or legal change) is the result of social and political struggle, and that struggle may continue to persist. The creation of a just legal system remains an ongoing task.

THE CONTINGENCY OF LEGAL NARRATIVE: THE EXAMPLE OF PARTISAN GERRYMANDERING

I conclude by offering the example of partisan gerrymandering in the United States as a useful illustration of the vagaries of the quest for a just legal system and the struggle over what legal justice means. The example offers all the variables I mentioned earlier: the pushes and pulls of competing political interests; political machinations; the butterfly effect of small changes over time; the effect of unexpected, black swan events; and the uncertain ties between legal and political success. The example reflects a continuing political and legal battle over congruence and discordance and what the resulting narrative will be.

United States law requires that seats in both the federal House of Representatives and in State legislative branches must be based on "one person, one vote,"[48] so internal to a State, districts must be divided equally in population. Redistricting is constitutionally required every ten years[49] to ensure equal populations across districts within a State, for example, due to population changes. Many States permit their State legislatures to redraw the district lines. Gerrymandering refers to arguable skews in the redistricting process so that even though districts are of equal size, representation is claimed to be unequal on the basis of other measures.[50] I will concentrate here on partisan gerrymandering (in contrast to racial gerrymandering). While in the United States partisan gerrymandering has been undertaken at the State level by both of the two major political parties—the Republicans and the Democrats—I will restrict my example to a 2016 case out of the State of Wisconsin, *Whitford v. Gill*,[51] where the gerrymandering was the product of Republican effort, and I will further restrict discussion to the question raised in the case of the election of representatives to the State Assembly.

In Wisconsin, the Republican State legislature controlled the redistricting plan enacted in 2011. Through the use of computerized drafting of alternative district maps, the Republican drafters were able to assess the likely partisan success of various alternatives, and they contoured and subsequently enacted a redistricting plan that would significantly enhance their chance of electoral success. The Republican plan sought to restrict the political ability of Wisconsin Democratic voters to elect representatives on a basis equal to their percentage in the State population by means of the two main types of gerrymandering: cracking and packing. Through cracking, a population that might have a particular set of legislative interests (such as being Democratic) is dispersed across legislative districts so that its chance of gaining electoral victory and hence State representation and policy is significantly diminished. Through packing, a population with a distinct set of legislative interests is intentionally gathered into one or more districts, which allows electoral victory in the district(s) but a more minimal political voice than if the group's votes had been distributed across multiple districts with multiple chances of electoral victory.

In a case brought by opponents of the plan, the federal trial court evaluated the 2012 and 2014 State Assembly election results in relation to the plan. In 2012, Republicans received just under forty-nine percent of the statewide vote for State Assembly seats but won sixty of the ninety-nine seats (sixty-one percent). In 2014, Republicans garnered fifty-two percent of the statewide votes and won sixty-three assembly seats (sixty-four percent). The federal trial court held that the redistricting plan was an unconstitutional partisan gerrymander in violation of the U.S. Constitution's Equal Protection clause and the First Amendment (right of association). More recently, in 2018, Republicans again won sixty-three Assembly seats, while Democrats won thirty-six, yet the statewide vote for Governor was nearly evenly split, with the Democratic candidate eking out a slight victory over the Republican incumbent.[52]

In itself the alleged gerrymandering is instructive. Political machinations have skewed what would seem a just legal result as to Wisconsin State representation. But provision of a larger context to the gerrymandering undertaken situates the larger differing views on legal congruence and discordance, on the legal narrative being told. The 1960s saw the ascension not only of a more liberal political order, as described in this chapter's beginning, but of a more liberal legal order as well. The Supreme Court's *Roe v. Wade* decision in 1973 is just one example of the Court's protection of civil rights during that period. The conservative political counter-revolution also led to a legal counter-revolution. A very dedicated organizing effort by Republicans since the mid 1960s has led to an emphasis, increasingly successful, on the nomination of federal judges of a conservative legal orientation. The conservative majority on the U.S. Supreme Court was finally assured with the controversial elevation of Brett Kavanagh to this body in the fall of 2018. There is no inherency to the logic or merits of this conservative trend. Butterfly effects and black swan effects both played a role. A black swan event—highly unexpected—was the 2016 refusal of the U.S. Senate to review the nomination to the Supreme Court by then President Obama of a judicial moderate, judge Merrick Garland, to replace the very conservative justice Antonin Scalia, who died earlier in the year. Garland's presence on the Supreme Court would have likely meant that when the Wisconsin gerrymandering case was appealed to the Court, the Court would have affirmed the substance of the lower court's ruling. When in fact the case did reach the Court, a butterfly effect occurred. Swing vote Justice Anthony Kennedy did not rule on the substance of the case but remanded on a technicality (on the basis of the contesting litigants' standing—their right to bring an action).[53] A subsequent butterfly effect was Justice Kennedy's decision to step down at the end of the 2017–2018 term. With the ascension of Justice Kavanagh to replace him, commentators anticipated that when a partisan gerrymandering case returned to the Court, a conservative majority would decline to uphold such a claim in this or any case, ruling that it is a political question beyond the scope of judicial authority.[54] In a case decided in June 2019, those prognostications proved to be accurate. In a 5–4 decision on a bitterly divided Court, the Court majority held that partisan gerrymandering claims were nonjusticiable.[55] Whether such a legal victory for those protecting partisan gerrymandering will lead over time to a legal loss (the overturning of the decision) or a political loss is still to be seen and subject to future contingencies.

Different forms of reflective legal judgment seek to create concordance across discordance—congruent narratives—in diverse ways. The course toward a just legal system is not a progressive arc. Ricoeur helps us to understand that this course remains an ongoing political and legal task.

NOTES

1. For an earlier, much briefer version of this chapter, see George H. Taylor, "Ricoeur, Narrative, and the Just," *Universitas* [Taiwan] 40, no. 7 (2013): 145–58.

2. Rev. Dr. Martin Luther King, Jr., "Out of the Long Night," *The Gospel Messenger*, February 8, 1958, 14; John Craig, "Wesleyan Baccalaureate Is Delivered by Dr. King," *Hartford Courant*, June 8, 1964, 4 (quoting King). The statement by King is a well-known part of his legacy and has appeared in his writings on various occasions, as in the sources cited. In the first it is noteworthy that it appears in quotations, indicating an (unattributed) source elsewhere. It appears that the original source of the sentiment is the nineteenth century minister and abolitionist, Theodore Parker. Theodore Parker, "Of Justice and the Conscience," in *Ten Sermons of Religion* (Boston: Crosby, Nichols and Company, 1853), 84–85. For a discussion, see Quoteinvestigator, "The Arc of the Moral Universe is Long, But It Bends Towards Justice," November 15, 2012.

3. Paul Ricoeur, *Lectures on Ideology and Utopia*, ed. George H. Taylor (New York: Columbia University Press, 1986), 253.

4. The use of Christianity for racist ends was a particular concern of critical race scholar Derrick Bell. See George H. Taylor, "The Last Decade of Derrick Bell's Thought," in *Racism and Resistance: Essays on Derrick Bell's Racial Realism*, ed. Timothy Joseph Golden (New York: SUNY Press, (forthcoming) 2021). Particular to our present concerns, Bell described as a "fantasy" the liberal assumption that the path of the law inextricably moved toward equality. Derrick Bell, "The Role of Fantasy in Politics and School Desegregation Policy-Setting," Penn State Mitstifer Lecture, University Council for Educational Administration, Kansas City, Missouri, Nov. 12, 2004 (2d revised version, Nov. 18, 2004), 10, 11 (unpublished; on file with author).

5. Nassim Nicholas Taleb, *The Black Swan: The Impact of the Highly Improbable* (New York: Random House, 2007).

6. The black swan metaphor originated at a time when it was assumed that black swans did not exist. (Black swans are now known to exist in Australia.) The notion was that the existence of one black swan would undo the logic of a system of thought that claimed, on the basis of a multiplicity of existing examples, that all swans are white. An unexpected event could disrupt the existing logic derived from previously available evidence. Taleb, *Black Swan*, xvi.

7. Stephen Jay Gould, *Wonderful Life: The Burgess Shale and the Nature of History* (New York: W. W. Norton and Co., 1989), 45–55, 280.

8. Gould, *Wonderful Life*, 51.
9. Gould, *Wonderful Life*, 289.
10. Gould, *Wonderful Life*, 290.
11. Gould, *Wonderful Life*, 51.
12. Stephen Jay Gould, "Second-Guessing the Future," in *The Lying Stones of Marrakech: Penultimate Reflections in Natural History* (New York: Harmony Books, 2000), 214–16.
13. As evidence of the proliferation of Ricoeur's reference to these terms, consider the citations in volume 1 of *Time and Narrative* to concordance/discordance (4, 21, 31, 38, 42, 43, 44, 50, 66, 69, 70, 73, 161, 168, 229) and to the synthesis of the heterogeneous (83, 142, 179, 197, 216, 229).
14. Paul Ricoeur, *The Rule of Metaphor*, trans. Robert Czerny (Toronto: University of Toronto Press, 1977), 96.
15. Paul Ricoeur, *Time and Narrative* (vol. 1), trans. Kathleen McLaughlin and David Pellauer (Chicago: University of Chicago Press, 1984), ix.
16. Ricoeur, *Time and Narrative* (vol. 1), x.
17. Ricoeur, *Time and Narrative* (vol. 1), 68.
18. I understand that in *Time and Narrative* Ricoeur separates the productive imagination as a form of narrative configuration from the moment of refigurative application.
19. For Ricoeur's differentiation between adequation and manifestation, see Paul Ricoeur, *Figuring the Sacred*, trans. David Pellauer, ed. Mark I. Wallace (Minneapolis: Fortress Press, 1995), 36.
20. Jean-François Lyotard, *The Postmodern Condition: A Report on Knowledge*, trans. Geoff Bennington and Brian Massumi (Minneapolis: University of Minnesota Press, 1984), xxiv.
21. Lyotard, *Postmodern Condition*, xxiii.
22. Lyotard, *Postmodern Condition*, xxiv–xxv.
23. Lyotard, *Postmodern Condition*, xxiv.
24. See George H. Taylor, "Prospective Political Identity," in *Paul Ricoeur in the Age of Hermeneutical Reason*, ed. Roger W. H. Savage (Lanham, MD: Lexington Books, 2015), 123–37; "Ricoeur versus Ricoeur? Between the Universal and the Contextual," in *From Ricoeur to Action: The Socio-Political Significance of Ricoeur's Thinking*, ed. Todd S. Mei and David Lewin (London: Continuum, 2012), 136–54.
25. Ricoeur, *Time and Narrative* (vol. 1), 65.
26. Ricoeur, *Time and Narrative* (vol. 1), 66 (emphasis added).
27. Ricoeur, *Time and Narrative* (vol. 1), x.
28. Hans-Georg Gadamer, *Truth and Method* (2d revised edition), trans. Joel Weinsheimer and Donald G. Marshall (New York: Crossroads, 1989), 324.
29. Gadamer, *Truth and Method*, 39.
30. Paul Ricoeur, "Interpretation and/or Argumentation," in *The Just*, trans. David Pellauer (Chicago: University of Chicago Press, 2000), 121.
31. Ricoeur, "Interpretation and/or Argumentation," 110, 126. For Ricoeur's earlier work, see Paul Ricoeur, "Explanation and Understanding: On Some Remarkable Connections Between the Theory of Texts, Action Theory, and the Theory of

History," in *From Text to Action*, trans. Kathleen Blamey and John B. Thompson (Evanston: Northwestern University Press, 1991), 125–43.

32. Ricoeur, "Interpretation and/or Argumentation," 121.

33. Ricoeur, "Interpretation and/or Argumentation," 121–25.

34. See Paul Ricoeur, *Reflections on the Just*, trans. David Pellauer (Chicago: University of Chicago Press, 2007), 70: "Establishing this fit that makes up the application of the norm to the case presents . . . an inventive and a logical face."

35. Ricoeur, *The Just*, 97.

36. Ricoeur, *The Just*, 98.

37. Ricoeur, "Interpretation and/or Argumentation," 126.

38. Ricoeur, "Interpretation and/or Argumentation," 122.

39. Ricoeur, *Rule of Metaphor*, 196.

40. For a comparison to the argument of Ronald Dworkin, see the next paragraph.

41. Paul Ricoeur, "The Metaphorical Process as Cognition, Imagination, and Feeling," in *On Metaphor*, ed. Sheldon Sacks (Chicago: University of Chicago Press, 1979), 146.

42. Ricoeur, *Time and Narrative* (vol. 1), 64–65, 70–71.

43. Ronald Dworkin, *Law's Empire* (Cambridge, MA: Harvard University Press, 1986), 229.

44. Mark Tushnet, "The Critique of Rights," *Southern Methodist University Law Review* 42 (1993): 23–34.

45. 410 U.S. 113 (1973).

46. Tushnet, "Critique of Rights," 30–31.

47. As I shall return to, note also that the significant increase in more conservative legislators and judges has had ramifications far beyond abortion.

48. Reynolds v. Sims, 377 U.S. 533, 568 (1964).

49. U.S. Const., art. I, § 2, cl. 3; amend. XIV, § 2.

50. The term "gerrymander" dates to the early 1800s and is named after a Massachusetts Governor, Elbridge Gerry, who urged passage of and signed a bill that redrew the boundaries of State senate election districts to favor his political party. One of the changed districts was so contorted that it looked like a salamander, and the ascription of a gerrymander entered the political lexicon.

51. 218 F. Supp. 3d 837 (W.D. Wis. 2016).

52. "Wisconsin Election Results," *New York Times*, January 14, 2019.

53. Gill v. Whitford, 138 S. Ct. 1916 (June 18, 2018).

54. Michael Wines, "Kennedy's Retirement Could Threaten Efforts to End Partisan Gerrymandering," *New York Times*, June 30, 2018.

55. Rucho v. Common Cause, 139 S. Ct. 2484 (2019).

BIBLIOGRAPHY

Craig, John. "Wesleyan Baccalaureate Is Delivered by Dr. King." *Hartford Courant*, June 8, 1984.

Dworkin, Ronald. *Law's Empire*. Cambridge, MA: Harvard University Press, 1986.

Gadamer, Hans-Georg. *Truth and Method* (2d revised edition). Translated by Joel Weinsheimer and Donald G. Marshall. New York: Crossroads, 1989.

Gould, Stephen Jay. "Second-Guessing the Future." In *The Lying Stones of Marrakech: Penultimate Reflections in Natural History*, 201–16. New York: Harmony Books, 2000.

Gould, Stephen Jay. *Wonderful Life: The Burgess Shale and the Nature of History*. New York: W. W. Norton and Co., 1989.

Kant, Immanuel. *Critique of Judgement*. Translated by J. H. Bernard. New York: Hafner Press, 1951.

King, Rev. Dr. Martin Luther. "Out of the Long Night." *The Gospel Messenger* [Official Organ of the Church of the Brethren] February 8, 1958, 3–4, 13–15. https://ia800304.us.archive.org/12/items/gospelmessengerv107mors/gospelmessengerv107mors.pdf.

Lyotard, Jean-François. *The Postmodern Condition: A Report on Knowledge*. Translated by Geoff Bennington and Brian Massumi. Minneapolis: University of Minnesota Press, 1984.

Parker, Theodore. "Of Justice and the Conscience." In *Ten Sermons of Religion*, 66–101. Boston: Crosby, Nichols, and Company, 1853. https://books.google.com/books?id=sUUQAAAAYAAJ&printsec=frontcover&source=gbs_ge_summary_r&cad=0#v=onepage&q&f=false.

Quoteinvestigator. "The Arc of the Moral Universe is Long, But It Bends Toward Justice." November 15, 2012. https://quoteinvestigator.com/2012/11/15/arc-of-universe/.

Ricoeur, Paul. "Explanation and Understanding: On Some Remarkable Connections Between the Theory of Texts, Action Theory, and the Theory of History." In *From Text to Action*, translated by Kathleen Blamey and John B. Thompson, 125–43. Evanston: Northwestern University Press, 1991.

Ricoeur, Paul. *Figuring the Sacred*. Translated by David Pellauer, edited by Mark I. Wallace. Minneapolis: Fortress Press, 1995.

Ricoeur, Paul. "Interpretation and/or Argumentation." In *The Just*, translated by David Pellauer, 109–26. Chicago: University of Chicago Press, 2000.

Ricoeur, Paul. *The Just*. Translated by David Pellauer. Chicago: University of Chicago Press, 2000.

Ricoeur, Paul. "The Metaphorical Process as Cognition, Imagination, and Feeling." In *On Metaphor*, edited by Sheldon Sacks, 141–57. Chicago: University of Chicago Press, 1979.

Ricoeur, Paul. *Reflections on the Just*. Translated by David Pellauer. Chicago: University of Chicago Press, 2007.

Ricoeur, Paul. *The Rule of Metaphor*. Translated by Robert Czerny. Toronto: University of Toronto Press, 1977.

Ricoeur, Paul. *Time and Narrative* (vol. 1). Translated by Kathleen McLaughlin and David Pellauer. Chicago: University of Chicago Press, 1984.

Ricoeur, Paul. *Time and Narrative* (vol. 2). Translated by Kathleen McLaughlin and David Pellauer. Chicago: University of Chicago Press, 1985.

Ricoeur, Paul. *Time and Narrative* (vol. 3). Translated by Kathleen Blamey and David Pellauer. Chicago: University of Chicago Press, 1988.

Taleb, Nassim Nicholas. *The Black Swan: The Impact of the Highly Improbable*. New York: Random House, 2007.

Taylor, George H. "Prospective Political Identity." In *Paul Ricoeur in the Age of Hermeneutical Reason*, edited by Roger W. H. Savage, 123–37. Lanham, MD: Lexington Books, 2015.

Taylor, George H. "Ricoeur, Narrative, and the Just." *Universitas* [Taiwan] 40, no. 7 (2013): 145–58.

Taylor, George H. "Ricoeur versus Ricoeur? Between the Universal and the Contextual." In *From Ricoeur to Action: The Socio-Political Significance of Ricoeur's Thinking*, edited by Todd S. Mei and David Lewin, 136–54. London: Continuum, 2012.

Tushnet, Mark. "The Critique of Rights," *Southern Methodist University Law Review* 42 (1993): 23–34.

Wines, Michael. "Kennedy's Retirement Could Threaten Efforts to End Partisan Gerrymandering." *New York Times*, June 30, 2018.

"Wisconsin Election Results." *New York Times*, January 14, 2019. https://www.nytimes.com/interactive/2018/11/06/us/elections/results-wisconsin-elections.html.

Chapter Seven

Paul Ricoeur's Juridical Anthropology
Law, Autonomy, and a Life Lived-in-Common

Marc de Leeuw

In the mid-nineteenth century, philosophers Jeremy Bentham and John Austin, the iconic founders of the "science of law," argue that to properly understand the practice and function of law we should perceive its utility solely by detaching it from the speculative realms of moral and political philosophy. This assault on the connection between legal, moral, and political thinking led to the "neglect of the juridical"[1] in philosophy and the dominance of an empirical, pragmatic Jurisprudence (placed under the umbrella of a utilitarian "economy of law"). For Paul Ricoeur, however, as he recalls in the introduction of *The Just,* it was Hegel's *Philosophy of Right* that "served professional philosophers of my generation as the only basis for reflections on the sequence ethics-law-politics."[2] But due to the horrors of the Holocaust, ethics and politics became the "principal object of concern" leaving the "*impasse* over the specific status of the juridical"[3] unresolved. This impasse, concerning the place of the legal within the political and ethical, forms the starting point for Ricoeur's critical exploration of law and justice.

Ricoeur's early analysis of the subject's phenomenological, ontological, and religious self-constitution through the experience of willing, fallibility and evil, show how liminal and legal questions indeed belong to Ricoeur's "oldest preoccupations"[4]. But more concrete reflections on our juridical practices (such as court proceedings, legal reasoning, the act of judging, legal authority, rights, punishment, and pardoning) also follow, Ricoeur admits, from the need to add a new element to the "the table of capacities" and the "phenomenology of the I can"[5] he formulated in *Oneself as Another.*[6] Besides the capacity to speak, act, and narrate which form the "hermeneutics of selfhood," there is the fundamental capacity to *ascribe* acts to ourselves. In law, this act marks the subject's ability to be *imputable,* that, indeed, "I can take myself to be the true author of acts assigned to my account."[7] Ricoeur now perceives this act of self-attribution as the omitted *legal* dimension of the capable *moral* self (arising from the triad: ethical aim, the moral norm, and practical wisdom). Against this background Ricoeur applies his post-Hegelian Kantianism, phenomenology of moral experience, and hermeneutics of the symbolic order to the Hegelian "impasse" in order to explore the subject of rights and law. For Ricoeur, examining the "*subject* of law" means reframing this theme in an anthropological register by asking *what* (an identifiable body?), or *who* (a culpable person?) the legal subject is or can be? This leads to the question how the subject becomes the subject "*of* law," "*of* rights": how do we *attach to* or *detach* ourselves *from* law as symbolic order? How can the excluded be included? Why, and when do we feel or have an obligation to obey authority? What do we perceive as legitimate power? How do power and community align? What is the function of law for our desire to live together with others? How can law represent a "power-in-common" in a pluralistic, fragmented society? And finally, how do we *actualize* the aspiration of law to be just? This chapter "reads" Ricoeur's response to these questions through his exploration of autonomy and vulnerability in law. I will argue that Ricoeur's reflections on law show that our modern juridical notion of autonomy and accountability must be perceived and mediated through the lens of our prior ontological, social, and legal vulnerabilities (to realistically reflect *who* the subject is that stands before the law). This reveals that Ricoeur's original contribution to Jurisprudence consist of the application of his philosophical anthropological perspective on the human condition to the legal sphere. By taking "the question of the human" as the starting point to resolve the Hegelian "impasse" concerning the meaning of the legal (as connecting the ethical and political), Ricoeur offers an alternative understanding of legal autonomy and accountability. Concretely this means that the subject of law is a fragile, fallible, and capable human *who* shares a life "with and for others"—this anthropological diagnosis needs to be inscribed in our legal institutions so they can act as *just* institutions. The role of the juridical is to represent and protect our life as vulnerable and shared, and our self as fragile and capable. Our sense of attachment and accountability to the law, as a religious or secular symbolic order, needs to be "read," ultimately, as a phenomenology of ethical-juridical liminality.

To set the stage for Ricoeur's reconfiguration of autonomy through vulnerability (explored through the notions of identity, time, authority, and otherness), I first sketch Ricoeur's early work on the liminal condition of our willing and the religious-juridical evocation of sacred obligations, which leads into his examination of our capacity to recognize ourselves as accountable. In the second section, I identify the emergence of the problem of legitimate authority and mutual recognition in and through Ricoeur's analyses of the symbolic order. As the last section shows, it is our ability to constitute a "power-in-common," to take an impartial position, and to create a "just distance" between conflicting parties, that allows a resolution to the "impasse" over the status of the juridical (by thinking ethics and politics through the juridical, and vice versa).

FROM SACRED OBLIGATIONS TO AUTONOMOUS ACCOUNTABILITY

For Ricoeur the "subject of law" stands "at the junction of a self that posits itself and a rule that imposes itself."[8] This tension between freedom and constraint recalls Ricoeur's earliest phenomenological studies in *Freedom and Nature*,[9] the first volume of the *Philosophy of the Will*, where the imposition of an "invincible involuntary" includes both the *"bodily necessity"*[10] (character, the unconscious and the heart "the day it fails us"), and "the factual position of other wills, of history, of men, and the structure of life."[11] Confronted with these fundamental and historical limitations, Ricoeur concludes that the voluntary and involuntary elements of our willing can only reconcile through the act of *consent*: "Consent is the movement of freedom towards nature in order to become reunited with its necessity and convert it into itself."[12] Put more directly, *"the yes of consent is always won from the no."*[13] But it is in Ricoeur's diagnosis of human fallibility, evoked by the "non-coincidence of self with self,"[14] that the susceptibility to evil emerges.

In *The Symbolism of Evil*, Ricoeur offers a complex and original analysis of the expressions of evil as formulated in the Jewish-Christian religions, and Hellenistic myths and tragedies.[15] Through the confession of sin, defilement, and guilt, and the redemptive, tragic or eschatological vision of history, a juridical-religious and juridical-ethical thinking far beyond the interpretation of sacred scripture or human drama crystallizes within Western notions of law. The Pharisees' teaching of the Torah offer, as Ricoeur explains, "an irreducible *type* of moral experience, in whom every man can recognize one of the fundamental possibilities of his own humanity."[16] To submit to the absolute guidance of the Torah symbolizes a voluntary surrender to an heteronomy for which "the abdication of freedom of choice becomes the supreme assertion of the will."[17] For the laws of the Torah, our ultimate willing becomes the will to give up "willing" and, for this reason, it is a "blessing to have the Law" because "the obedient man is 'happy,'"—"he has 'found life.'"[18] Several centuries later Immanuel Kant reverses this logic, in a secular mode, by replacing the religious heteronomy with the "supreme assertion" of reasoning: my willing now stands as a symbol for freedom from tutelage, allowing an autonomy that gives itself, and is obliged to, the law.[19] This short overview of Ricoeur's early examination of the liminal experience (in regard to the involuntary), and the ethical-religious structure of subjection and obedience (in regard to the Jewish law) indicates how "Law" becomes the main source for our subjection to an external or internal authority. Through this religious-moral authority, perceived as an absolute symbolic order, we come to perceive ourselves as attached to and accountable to the Law. It is against this background—which can be summarized by the question "how does the human perceive itself as a subject accountable before the law?"—that Ricoeur further examines the relation between human vulnerability and autonomy. In "Autonomy and Vulnerability,"[20] a lecture delivered at the *Institutes des hautes études sur la justice*, Ricoeur states that the subject of rights forms "both the major *presupposition* of every juridical investigation and the *horizon* of judicial practice."[21] This means that autonomy in law simultaneously signifies a "condition of possibility" (as a capacity available to the subject) and a "task" (as what the subject must become).[22] A similar circularity between presupposition and task is at work in the classical Kantian understanding of autonomy (because we *can* think for ourselves, we *must!*), and the relation between the moral and legal imperative of freedom. For Kant freedom is "the *ratio essendi* of the law, while the law is the *ratio cognoscendi* of freedom."[23] Translated to the juridical sphere this amounts to a similar obliqueness: because you *can* follow the law you *ought* to do so; because you *can* be accountable for your acts, you *ought* to act accountably.[24]

Rather than start from a purely moral position, Ricoeur takes the subject's fundamental *vulnerability* as the "major presupposition" necessitating our return to the "question of the human" and, hence, move "as far away as possible from the ethico-juridical plane."[25] Why? Because the law no longer questions *what* or *who* the human is, but simply considers the subject as a priori autonomous, singular, and accountable. To counter this mistaken assumption, we must start with the question of the actual ontological pre-condition of autonomy: "What kind of being is a human being that he or she can give rise to the problematic of autonomy?"[26] The importance of this query is clear if we, for example, ask: what *kind* of subjects can law hold accountable? As we know, law ought to only hold accountable those who are *aware* of, and *capable* of, ascribing acts to "themselves" (and, hence, children, the intoxicated, or mentally incapacitated offenders are held to a different standard of culpability). For Ricoeur, the criteria set for how we define *imputability* stipulate what an autonomous subject in law is, whereby the actual content of legal autonomy refers both to the ability *to do* something (to speak, to act), and the actual performative *affirmation* of these abilities in the act itself ("I am the one *who* speaks, *who* acts"). The power to affirm our capabilities, Ricoeur asserts, "governs all the reflexive forms by which a subject can designate him- or herself as the one who can."[27]

Ultimately, the power "to do something"[28] signifies the innate desire to preserve life transpiring in our willing and acting (leading to my self-affirmation by stating "I did this!"). This existential drive (for which Spinoza's *conatus* is exemplary) informs our intentions and the fundamental ability to speak, to act or intervene, as well as how we express ourselves in symbols, metaphors, narratives, or testimonials. But these abilities are severely constrained by our vulnerabilities, fallibility, and incompleteness. Our "lack" of power is both historical and basic: the ability to speak depends on our present opportunities (to have a "voice," be heard, participate), and on the actual limits to expressing ourselves completely.[29] From a "juridical perspective" does not the law—Ricoeur asks rhetorically—"rest on the victory language gains over violence?"[30] Beyond language and our communicative abilities, it is "the incapacities humans inflict on one another," the incapacities "brought about by illness, old age," and, ultimately, "the way the world is" that demonstrate how our vulnerability weakens the affirmative capacities for autonomy. After this examination of the historical and fundamental presuppositions of autonomy and vulnerability, Ricoeur returns to his earlier work on time and singularity to propose an alternative concept of autonomy in narrative identity and attestation. In his trilogy on *Time and Narrative*,[31] Ricoeur explores how humans express their experience of temporality through a narrative retelling, creating an expressive, meaningful synthesis of dispersed events. At the end of his philosophical exploration of "human time," Ricoeur discovers an alternative concept of autonomy, which he coins *narrative identity*. Redefining autonomy through narrative highlights the importance of *change* for the way we narrativize and reconfigure personal experiences through time:

> The handling of one's own life, as a possible coherent narrative, represents a high-level competence that has to be taken as one of the major components of the autonomy of a subject of rights. In this regard, we can speak of an education of narrative coherence, an education leading to a narrative identity. To learn how to tell the same story in another way, how to allow our story to be told by others, how to submit the narrative of a life to the historian's critique, are all practises applicable to the paradox of autonomy and fragility. Let us say therefore that a subject capable of leading his or her life in agreement with the idea of narrative coherence is an autonomous subject.[32]

In short, our identity does not consist of what remains the same or identical, but of what emerges in the productive tension between sameness and change, both of which inform our notion of self. Sameness implies a "permanence in time," turning our bodies and notions of self into "immutable" things (as exemplified in forensic use of DNA or fingerprints).[33] Our temporal and ontological identity, though, appears more complex than the violent reduction of the body and the self to that which is *identical*. Law has little patience for the changes, ambivalences, and many pitfalls of identity; the juridical order simply demands that the subject remains the same identifiable and responsible person over time.

Ricoeur points to the act of *keeping a promise* as another form of personal consistency that produces an identity through the *commitments* we make towards others: it is our *trustworthiness* over time that constitutes "the basis for every contract, agreement, pact."[34] But our self-affirmation in promising can also reveal an ambivalence in attesting "what one stands for"; even if we "stand for" our personal history, we are not necessarily identical with this history; even if we have committed a harmful act, we must not be reduced to this act. What becomes clear is that for Ricoeur the notion of autonomy as perceived in law lacks a more fundamental inclusion of change and vulnerability. Ricoeur finds a more accurate description of the "self" in narrative identity, and the permanence of time as exemplified by acts of promising. It is, ultimately, our ability to "stand for" *who* we are which amounts to a more credible depiction of the subject who appears before the law. In the next section we will see how singularity and culpability inform the tension between vulnerability and autonomy.

SINGULARITY AND CULPABILITY

Besides the challenge of time and change, autonomy faces the challenge of *singularity* and *alterity*. While I experience my own uniqueness and develop a singular perspective on the world, I am always confronted with the singular viewpoint of all others. How can these singularities be reconciled? Otherness, extensively discussed in *Oneself as Another*,[35] signifies both the interior Other (like the body as flesh, or our conscience) that can evoke a "fracture" in the "reflexive relation of the self to itself,"[36] but also reveals the actual "unsubstitutability of persons."[37] These unique experiences create our memories, forming a sense of self on and through which we "act and designate ourselves"[38] as persons. But even this capacity for singular self-designation suffers from a "split at the interior"[39] of identification:

> On the one side, we identify ourselves by designating ourselves as the one who speaks, acts, remembers, imputes action to him- or herself, and so on; on the other, to identify oneself is to identify with heroes, emblematic characters, models, and teachers and also precepts, norms whose field extends from traditional

customs to utopian paradigms, which, emanating from the social imaginary, remodel our private imaginations. . . . [40]

While singularity strengthens my notion of a unique self, it is my identification with other persons and ideologies that both affirm and threaten my self-perception: external others can be "another me" (like my best friend), but also *strangers* we perceive as a threat, as "not me." The concept of the "stranger" also applies to how we experience nation-states, perceive social differences (like class, ethnicity, or gender), symbolic orders (ideological, religious), or a singular opponent like an abject authoritarian ruler.

It is here that Ricoeur's anthropological and phenomenological analysis of autonomy and vulnerability returns to the "properly ethic-juridical" domain by subsuming autonomy under the "aegis" of "imputability."[41] How do we, if our ontological, social, and political vulnerabilities so strongly determine who we can be and how we can act, define our accountability towards the law and others? Is accountability a human "capacity" enabling the law to make us imputable? According to Ricoeur, imputability is the "classical ancestor" of *responsibility*, but "richer"[42] than *obligation*. Reflecting on its Latin root—*putare, computare, imputabilitas*—Ricoeur stresses that to *impute* "is to assign to a person's account a blameable action, a fault,"[43] which the German legal notion of *Zurechnungsfähigkeit* and *Schuldfähigkeit*[44] (the ability to answer for my acts; the capability to be assigned blame) perfectly captures. Imputability connects Ricoeur's analysis of "autonomy" as capability, identity, or singularity to the *juridical* conceptualization of responsibility, blame and guilt: "Imputability is the capacity to be taken as responsible for one's acts as having been their actual author."[45] Hence, *how* we attribute actions to subjects determines if an act can be put "on my account": to be "imputable" simply means to be *accusable* by law. But there is a crucial difference between stating "I did this" and to "answer *for* my acts, that is, to admit that they belong on my account."[46] It is the "qualitative leap" from autonomy as *capacity* to autonomy as *imputability* which, Ricoeur argues, places human action "under the idea of obligation"[47]:

> [O]bligation is so pregnant that we willingly grant that subjects are responsible for, capable of answering for, their acts only insofar as they are capable of placing their action, first taken in the sense of an obligation to follow a rule, then in the sense of bearing the consequences of any infraction, tort, or offense.[48]

Obligation directly leads back to Kant's definition of imputation as a "judgment by which someone is held to be the *Urheber* (*causa libera*) of an action (*Handlung*) which is called a *Tat* (*factum*) and falls under the law."[49] In this way Kant conceptualizes autonomy as connecting *auto* with *nomos*—"oneself as author and the law that obliges"[50]—simultaneously inserting a moral and legal obligation into the subject of law. But for Ricoeur, the irreducibility of Kant's "Fact of Reason" (as an innate duty imposed upon us by reason), a true "ligature,"[51] needs to be pulled back into a *phenomenology of moral experience*. This phenomenology shows how the capacity to *bind* the "self to a norm" predetermines and shapes how we can fulfil "the requirements of a symbolic order."[52] The question of how the subject experiences and *attaches* itself to the authority of law, hence, how law constitutes itself as legitimate power, creates "the greatest difficulty for ethic-juridical philosophy"[53] because, Ricoeur asserts, the mode of delivery of authority remains opaque.[54] Hence, if we want to understand why the subject perceives itself as accountable to and bound by the law we need to explain in more concrete terms how our experience of law's authority emerges through its mode of inclusion or exclusion, its constitutive power as symbolic order, ability to resolve conflict, or, ideally, through the creation of a more just society. We focus on this in the next section.

CONSTITUTIVE POWER, IMPARTIALITY, AND A "JUST DISTANCE"

We assume secular liberal systems successfully contain and counter their opaque authority through democratic elections, the rule of law, and collective and transparent agreements about the principles and procedures constituting the legitimacy of state authority. But for Ricoeur the manner we recognize, in the sense of *recognizing as*, the "superiority of authority"[55] does not transcend the "phenomenological level"[56] because our concrete experiences with authority still indicate the existence of another legitimating foundation. What predates authority as superiority is the phenomenology of what Hannah Arendt defines as our "power-in-common" and John Rawls calls the "overlapping consensus."[57] Even in light of "reasonable disagreements," both represent a force "born in the present from the will to live together"[58] marking a constitutive affirmation of collective authority.[59] In short, Ricoeur suggests that instead of perceiving the authority of the symbolic order as originating in a presupposed archaic, ungraspable higher force, the actual affirmative power of authority originates in our will to live together. Our collective will, however, is—just like our autonomy—always hesitant, fragile, and threatened. For this reason, Ricoeur perceives the symbolic order as "both the very site of the strongest connection between the self and the norm and the very principle of its fragility."[60] This fragility refers not only to a potential *incapacity* to bind the self to a norm, or to bind the community to the symbolic order, but, in particular, to "those whom our sociopolitical order excludes."[61] Even if I *can* vote (I do have the *competence* to vote), I can be prevented from *performing* the act of voting (like refugees, the incarcerated, or other discriminated groups). If the community does not recognize my existence, the ability to use my "voice" and to be heard, cannot be actualized.

Hence, to be judged an accountable subject, we must first consider the "degree of the accused's capacity to situate him- or herself in relation to a symbolic order."[62] Put differently, if we do not have the same "founding narratives" we will not be seduced, for example, by the "heroes of the moral life"[63] we are meant to aspire to. Therefore, we experience the obligations and accountability this order imposes on us as merely arbitrary and involuntary, and demanding violent submission. This violence can be *internal* to the system: for example, same sex couples who accept the overall legal order but desire equal treatment within it. It can also be *external*: for example, the plight of Indigenous people whose own symbolic order and will "to-live-together" is upset by another, colonial one.[64]

To overcome such fundamental exclusions and this rejection of recognition, Ricoeur proposes reconstructing "the primary experience of entry into a symbolic order"[65]; if we cannot *enter* the symbolic order, we also cannot enact our capacities within that order. We need to understand the demand for rights as a call to be given *entry*, to be granted *access* to the symbolic order (enabling the potential flourishing of my capacities). But if we want to reconstruct the *legitimacy* of any symbolic order, Ricoeur argues, we need to return to its prime "dialogical dimension,"[66] and start from the notion that "the symbols of any ethico-juridical order stem from a shared understanding."[67] Ricoeur explains:

> To be capable of entering into a symbolic order is to be capable of entering into an order of recognition, of inscribing oneself in a "we" that distributes and apportions the authority of the symbolic order.[68]

Only a symbolic order that is dialogical and shared, reflects the "communalization of moral experience" upon which any legal-political system is built. After bringing together a phenomenology of moral experience with a hermeneutic of the symbolic order and authority, Ricoeur moves back to the anthropological level of the human condition. Thomas Nagel's notion of *impartiality* exemplifies our fundamental capacity to take the "perspective of the other person," and occupy "two points of view."[69] It is this human ability that establishes our sense "that every other life is worth as much as our own,"[70] which, Ricoeur concludes, is the "summit of ethical life."[71] It is through our capacity to imagine multiple points of view that impartiality becomes the "solitary face of moral effort" as a "victory over unilateralness."[72]

Thus, the imagination enables us to distance ourselves from our self and take an impartial position without which no just legal system can operate. But it is in the idea of a "just distance," borrowed from Antoine Garapon,[73] that Ricoeur discovers the intersection between *impartiality* and the *recognition* of a common symbolic order (beyond the outcome of a reasoned deontology):

> It is the complementarity between a shared understanding and the capacity of impartiality that gave me the idea to place these two practical modes of entry into the symbolic order at a point of intersection—the idea of a just distance between singular points of view against the backdrop of a shared understanding.[74]

To put conflicting parties at a spatial and communicative distance allows a recognized set of mutually agreed upon legal procedures, performances, and practices to step in and transfer the cycle of violence into a clash of legal argumentation and reasoning in court.[75] From Ricoeur's perspective, the conception of a "just distance"[76] signifies the most substantive aspiration of legal institutions: to overcome vengeance by pacifying conflicts through a "third" party, offering a "distanced" impartial view, and institutions for which all are equal under the law. Simultaneously, both victims and perpetrators share and recognize the same symbolic system of authority whose obligations and verdicts they accept, even if it amounts to violence (penal sanctions) against them.

CONCLUSION

Ricoeur's writings on the juridical system reflect his philosophically anthropological perspective on the fragile *and* affirmative nature of our being. In presupposing the subject's a priori autonomy, in concert with the expectation that we remain imputable over time, law conceals the actual, more complex, and delicate condition of *who* we are or can be. Ricoeur's essay on vulnerability and autonomy in law adds an anthropological, phenomenological, and hermeneutic understanding of the legal subject to the Kantian notion of autonomy and Hegelian concept of ethical life that shapes our philosophical understanding of the legal subject as a person who gives itself the law, or as a citizen who actualizes the shared values of the community by affirming the law. For Ricoeur though, beyond Kant and Hegel, it is the subject's fundamental vulnerability, in combination with the need to stay identifiable over time, that reveals not only our internal reflexive tensions, but also our dependence on the ability to speak, act, and attest to who we are and "what we stand for." We can only be subjects *of law* through the capacity to self-attribute and ascribe acts to ourselves. Without self-awareness guiding our acts we cannot be accountable. It is this ability which legitimizes law's authority to penalize us for violations. Only as the product of morally self-aware and participating subjects, can law set the normative rules for our partaking in the symbolic order and determine how we ought to act towards others.

Ultimately, it is the capacity to *distance* us from our own position which facilitates an *impartial* point of view. The possibility and aspiration of impartial judgment—even if rarely realized because we always remain contextual beings—stands for a just and equitable legal order, treating everyone as equal. For Ricoeur law connects to *politics* through the legitimacy of a "power-in-common"; law adheres to *ethics* through the threefold dynamic between the good, the obligatory, and phronesis. The subject of law is simultaneously singular, historical, and universal, but also always mediated by and dependent upon concrete others and political and legal institutions. According to Ricoeur's reflections on law, the ignored Hegelian "impasse" can ultimately only be resolved by affirming our *"desire to live well with and for others in just institutions."*[77]

NOTES

1. Paul Ricoeur, "Preface," *The Just*, trans. David Pellauer (Chicago: University of Chicago Press, 2000), vii.

2. Ricoeur, "Preface," viii.

3. Ricoeur, "Preface," viii. Emphasis added.

4. Ricoeur, "Preface," viii.

5. Ricoeur, "Introduction," 17.

6. Paul Ricoeur, *Oneself as Another,* trans. Kathleen Blamey (Chicago: University of Chicago Press, 1992).

7. Ricoeur, "Introduction," 17.

8. Paul Ricoeur, *Reflections on the Just*, trans. David Pellauer (Chicago: University of Chicago Press, 2007), 16.

9. Paul Ricoeur, *Freedom and Nature: The Voluntary and Involuntary,* trans. Erazim V. Kohák (Evanston IL: Northwestern University Press, 1966).

10. Ricoeur, *Freedom and Nature*, 243.

11. Ricoeur, *Freedom and Nature*, 243.

12. Ricoeur, *Freedom and Nature*, 347.

13. Ricoeur, *Freedom and Nature*, 354.

14. Paul Ricoeur, *Fallible Man*, trans. Charles A. Kelbley (Chicago: Henry Regnery, 1965), 24.

15. Paul Ricoeur, *The Symbolism of Evil*, trans. Emerson Buchanan (Boston: Beacon Press, 1967).

16. Ricoeur, *The Symbolism of Evil*, 122.

17. Ricoeur, *The Symbolism of Evil*, 123.

18. Ricoeur, *The Symbolism of Evil*, 130.

19. Immanuel Kant, *Grounding for the Metaphysics of Morals*, trans. Lewis White Beck (Indianapolis: Bobbs-Merrill, 1956).

20. Paul Ricoeur, "Autonomy and Vulnerability," *Reflections on the Just*, trans. David Pellauer (Chicago: University of Chicago Press, 2007), 72–91.

21. Ricoeur, "Autonomy and Vulnerability," 72.

22. Ricoeur, "Autonomy and Vulnerability," 72.

23. Ricoeur, "Autonomy and Vulnerability," 72.

24. In Kant's logic we have the duty to follow the outcome of our moral reasoning which are based on the three Kantian maxims. Law must simply follow these maxims whereby humans only claim one innate fundamental legal Right: the right to be free. If free, we are thus free to follow the moral, legal, and political categorical imperatives and, thus, it is our duty to do so.

25. Ricoeur, "Autonomy and Vulnerability," 74.

26. Ricoeur, "Autonomy and Vulnerability," 74.

27. Ricoeur, "Autonomy and Vulnerability," 75.

28. Ricoeur, "Autonomy and Vulnerability," 75.

29. Ricoeur further elaborates, "to believe oneself unable to speak is already to be linguistically disabled, to be excommunicated to speak." Ricoeur, "Autonomy and Vulnerability," 77.

30. Ricoeur, "Autonomy and Vulnerability," 76.

31. Paul Ricoeur, *Time and Narrative* Vol 1., trans. Kathleen Blamey and David Pellauer (Chicago: Chicago University Press, 1984).

32. Ricoeur, "Autonomy and Vulnerability," 80.

33. Ricoeur, "Autonomy and Vulnerability," 78.

34. Ricoeur, "Autonomy and Vulnerability," 79.

35. Ricoeur, *Oneself as Another*, 317–356.

36. Ricoeur, "Autonomy and Vulnerability," 80.

37. Ricoeur, "Autonomy and Vulnerability," 81.

38. Ricoeur, "Autonomy and Vulnerability," 81.

39. Ricoeur, "Autonomy and Vulnerability," 81.

40. Ricoeur, "Autonomy and Vulnerability," 81. Ricoeur concludes here that we "need to follow to its extreme form the protestation of singularity, of solitude, of autonomy, of self-esteem, that is raised by the I/me and confront it with the claims of alterity pushed to the point of the domination of the stranger over one's own self."

41. Ricoeur, "Autonomy and Vulnerability," 82. Ricoeur further explains, "The idea of obligation is so pregnant that we willingly grant that subjects are responsible for, capable of answering for, their acts only insofar as they are capable of placing their action, first taken in the sense of obligation to follow a rule, then in the sense of bearing the consequences of any infraction, tort, or offense."

42. Cf. Ricoeur, "Autonomy and Vulnerability," 82.

43. Ricoeur, "Autonomy and Vulnerability," 82.

44. Ricoeur, "Autonomy and Vulnerability," 82.

45. Ricoeur, "Autonomy and Vulnerability," 82.

46. Ricoeur, "Autonomy and Vulnerability," 83.

47. Ricoeur, "Autonomy and Vulnerability," 82.

48. Ricoeur, "Autonomy and Vulnerability," 82.
49. Cited in: Ricoeur, "Autonomy and Vulnerability," 83.
50. Ricoeur, "Autonomy and Vulnerability," 83.
51. Ricoeur, "Autonomy and Vulnerability," 83.
52. Ricoeur, "Autonomy and Vulnerability," 84.
53. Ricoeur, "Autonomy and Vulnerability," 84.
54. Ricoeur, "Autonomy and Vulnerability," 85. Ricoeur explains that authority appears as *antecedence* (as an order that precedes us), as *superiority* (as an order which is above and stronger than us), or as *exteriority* (as an order coming from outside to us). Our *experience* of authority presents it as *something* "that is always already there," arriving "from further off," coming "from the ancients," thus, authority cloths itself with a mythical, distanced force enhanced by the idea that all authority "proceeds from a prior authority." This mythical opaqueness of legal authority motivated the Austrian philosopher Hans Kelsen to formulate a "pure" theory of law built on the fundamental presupposition that all legal-normative authority assumes the existence of a prior, higher level of authority authorizing the lower-level authority. Considering the absence of absolute authority (God, the Queen), the need to "back up" all authority by other authority leads to infinite regress. To avoid this scenario, law necessitates a transcendental a priori category, which Kelsen coined the Basic Norm. The positing of the Basic Norm constitutes an artificial but foundational endpoint for all authority. See Hans Kelsen, *Pure Theory of Law*, trans. Max Knight (Berkeley: University of California Press, 1967).
55. Ricoeur, "Autonomy and Vulnerability," 85.
56. Ricoeur, "Autonomy and Vulnerability," 85.
57. Ricoeur, "Autonomy and Vulnerability," 85.
58. Ricoeur, "Autonomy and Vulnerability," 85.
59. Ricoeur, "Autonomy and Vulnerability," 85.
60. Ricoeur, "Autonomy and Vulnerability," 85.
61. Ricoeur, "Autonomy and Vulnerability," 86.
62. Ricoeur, "Autonomy and Vulnerability," 86.
63. Ricoeur, "Autonomy and Vulnerability," 86.
64. Hans Lindahl's chapter in this volume offers a detailed analysis of the complexity of indigenous recognition/ reconciliation.
65. Ricoeur, "Autonomy and Vulnerability," 87.
66. Ricoeur, "Autonomy and Vulnerability," 88.
67. Ricoeur, "Autonomy and Vulnerability," 88.
68. Ricoeur, "Autonomy and Vulnerability," 89.
69. Ricoeur, "Autonomy and Vulnerability," 88.
70. Ricoeur, "Autonomy and Vulnerability," 88. Nagel defines impartiality, Ricoeur summarizes, "by the capacity to take two points of view, that of our interest and that of the higher point of view that allows us to adopt in our imagination the perspective of the other person and to affirm that every other life is worth as much as our own."
71. Ricoeur, "Autonomy and Vulnerability," 88.
72. Ricoeur, "Autonomy and Vulnerability," 89.

73. Antoine Garapon, *Le Gardien des promesses: Le juge et la démocratie* (Paris: Odile Jacob, 1996).
74. Ricoeur, "Autonomy and Vulnerability," 89.
75. Ricoeur's description of the legal process as overcoming violence by replacing it with a conflict of interpretation and argumentation ignores the increasing occurrence of "lawfare" which although restraining from physical violence, uses law to destroy the opposing party by legal intimidation, financial burdens, and psychological pressure.
76. Ricoeur, "Preface," xi.
77. Ricoeur, *Oneself as Another,* 239.

BIBLIOGRAPHY

Garapon, Antoine. *Le Gardien des promesses: Le juge et la démocratie.* Paris: Odile Jacob, 1996.

Hegel, G. W. F. *Philosophy of Right.* Translated by T. M. N. Knox. New York: Oxford University Press, 1990.

Kant, Immanuel. *Grounding for the Metaphysics of Morals.* Translated by Lewis White Beck, Indianapolis: Bobbs-Merrill, 1956.

Kelsen, Hans. *Pure Theory of Law.* Translated by Max Knight. Berkeley: University of California Press, 1967.

Ricoeur, Paul. *Fallible Man.* Trans. Charles Kelbley. Chicago: Henry Regnery, 1965.

Ricoeur, Paul. *Freedom and Nature: The Voluntary and Involuntary.* Translated by Erazim V. Kohák. Evanston IL: Northwestern University Press, 1966.

Ricoeur, Paul. *The Just.* Translated by David Pellauer. Chicago: University of Chicago Press, 2000.

Ricoeur, Paul. *Oneself as Another.* Translated by Kathleen Blamey. Chicago: University of Chicago Press, 1992.

Ricoeur, Paul. *Reflections on the Just.* Translated by David Pellauer. Chicago: University of Chicago Press, 2007.

Ricoeur, Paul. *The Symbolism of Evil.* Translated by Emerson Buchanan. New York: Harper and Row, 1967.

Ricoeur, Paul. *Time and Narrative* (Vol. 1–3). Translated by Kathleen Blamey and David Pellauer. Chicago: University of Chicago Press, 1984–88.

Ricoeur, Paul. "Vulnerability and Autonomy." In *Reflections on the Just.* Translated by David Pellauer, 72–91. Chicago: University of Chicago Press, 2007.

Chapter Eight

The Unbearable Between-ness of Law

Francis J. Mootz III

Paul Ricoeur is remembered for many philosophical accomplishments.[1] Perhaps his signature achievement was steadfastly refusing to accept the necessity of designating one of two dueling conceptual antinomies as foundational. His insistence that understanding and explanation interpenetrate each other is the most well-known example of this lesson. The great debate between Gadamer's hermeneutics (the art of understanding) and Habermas's critical theory (the discipline of explaining the world that subtends naive understandings) was, for Ricoeur, a misguided contest.[2] He famously argued that we must resist the tendency to elevate one of these traditions as the master narrative, going so far as to insist on using a single (complex) term to refer to a dimension of historical inquiry: "explanation/understanding."[3]

In this chapter I recount Ricoeur's extension of his mediating approach to questions of law and justice. Law is quintessentially "between" our ordinary categories and methodologies, and so Ricoeur's investigations are particularly illuminating. Moreover, his interlocutors in the debate over the role of critical social theory strike a similar chord. Gadamer argues that law is an exemplary hermeneutical practice that embodies practical reasoning, charting a path between a rigorous and determinant *episteme* and a practical and creative *techne*. Habermas famously characterizes law as "between facts and norms," by which he means that law cannot be viewed solely as a sociological reality nor simply as a set of universalizing moral precepts. In this same vein, Ricoeur argues that law is between morality and politics. However, Ricoeur offers a more complex account that addresses other perceived polarities, insisting that law operates between interpretation and argumentation, and that legal discourse participates equally in rhetoric, hermeneutics, and poetics.

My thesis is that these three theorists acknowledge in different but related ways the unbearable between-ness of law that precludes a flattening inquiry guided by a singular focus. Ricoeur's careful observations can best be highlighted by comparing them with the similar positions adopted by Gadamer and Habermas. I do not argue that Ricoeur provides the superior methodological account, as that would undermine Ricoeur's essential insight. Rather, I conclude that the between-ness of law is best captured by philosophical commitments expressed as Gadamer/Ricoeur/Habermas.

GADAMER: LAW IS BETWEEN *EPISTEME* AND *TECHNE*

Law is the product of coordinated action designed to direct behavior, but it also is a normative system that claims validity. Reflecting this complexity, political scientists regard law as a social practice subject to empirical study, whereas legal philosophers assess law as a justified system of norms. Gadamer's philosophical hermeneutics provides a distinctive approach to law that rejects the sharp opposition of practice and theory. Building on Heidegger's *destruktion* of metaphysics and recuperation of the Aristotelian intellectual virtues, Gadamer locates law in the practical engagement of actors who rely on both theoretical knowledge and practical skill.

Heidegger famously argued against the reductionism of modern scientific consciousness that posits scientific theory as the only true knowledge and reduces practical engagement to calculative and manipulative technology. He recalls Aristotle's distinctions between theory (*theoria* grounded in *episteme*), practical making (*poiesis* grounded in *techne*) and wise deliberations (*praxis* grounded in *phronesis*) to critique modernity's equation of *theoria* with philosophical abstraction and *poiesis* with instrumentalism. Heidegger credits Aristotle with understanding the necessity of recognizing these distinctive ways of being in the world without casting them as wholly separate modes of being that can be ranked hierarchically. Heidegger contends that the modern separation of theory, practice, and making from each other conceals the "originary rootedness of *theoria, praxis,* and *poiesis* in the unitary and worldly being of Dasein."[4] Heidegger reclaimed *techne* and *phronesis* as comportments that are no less significant than *episteme*. His achievement was not to invert modernity's hierarchy, but rather to subvert it by acknowledging different dispersions of an originary being-in-the-world.[5]

Gadamer's philosophical hermeneutics continues this line of thinking and expressly describes law as an exemplary site of hermeneutical understanding. Gadamer first carefully distinguishes *poiesis* and *praxis* from each other to refine Heidegger's higher level distinction between deliberative knowing (*phronesis* and *techne*) and scientific knowing (*episteme* and *sophia*), and then he fully develops the contours of practical wisdom at the heart of understanding.[6] Gadamer often is misunderstood as rejecting theory in favor of practical engagement, but in truth he sought to recover the significance of practical wisdom against the overbearing claims of scientific knowing rather than to discredit scientific thought. As he explains, "the one-sidedness of hermeneutic universalism has the truth of a corrective."[7] Gadamer emphasizes the distinctive character of practical reasoning because it is uniquely experiential, in which ends and means are simultaneously determined within a circumscribed context.[8] Indeed, he characterizes Aristotle's activity in developing the theses of the *Nicomachean Ethics* as an example of the complete interpenetration of theory and practice.[9]

Gadamer reclaims the deep relationship of theory and practice by looking to the legal system as a "true model" for hermeneutical understanding generally.[10] Legal practice exemplifies the lesson that application is fundamental to all understanding.[11] There is no aimless and context-free knowing that is gained theoretically and then only later interpreted to address a practical concern. To the contrary, legal practice illustrates the universal condition that interpretation "is not an occasional, post facto supplement to understanding; rather, understanding is always interpretation, and hence interpretation is the explicit form of understanding."[12] Discovering "the meaning of a legal text and discovering how to apply it in a particular legal instance are not two separate actions, but one unitary process."[13] Gadamer thus rejects the traditional hermeneutical separation of *subtilitas intelligendi* (understanding), *subtilitas explicandi* (interpretation), and *subtilitas applicandi* (application). Understanding always requires interpretation, which only occurs in application,[14] and this is "one unified process."[15]

Gadamer explains his point by comparing the judge to a legal historian,[16] a particularly pertinent illustration in light of the recent ascendency of "originalist" theories of legal interpretation in American conservative circles. At a superficial level, Gadamer agrees that the roles are distinct in that a historian seeks meaning as it was understood in the past, whereas a judge must interpret the law to apply to the case at hand, thereby inevitably "updating" the meaning of the legal text to some extent. In truth, though, the quest for historical meaning involves an application no less than determining the meaning of the law for present case.[17] Thus, "the *problem of application . . . also characterizes the more complicated situation of historical understanding.*"[18] He concludes that the idea of a perfect legal dogmatics in which one first can discover the applicable rules through historical reconstruction and then later subsume individual cases under the determinant rules is absolutely "untenable."[19] By seeking a meaning that has been fixed in the past, originalist legal scholars attempt the impossible.[20]

Philosophical hermeneutics identifies the "between-ness" of law as an illustration of our hermeneutical nature. Following Heidegger, Gadamer rejects the belief that legal norms can be settled before applying them in cases. Understanding the norm, interpreting it in context, and applying it to resolve a case are not distinct activities. As a unified hermeneutical event, these features can never be fully separable into distinct domains of theory and practice. "To distinguish between a normative function and a cognitive one is to separate what clearly belong together. The meaning of a law that emerges in its normative application is fundamentally no different from the meaning reached in understanding a text."[21]

HABERMAS: LAW IS BETWEEN FACTS AND NORMS

Jürgen Habermas famously critiqued Gadamer's celebration of a hermeneutically self-sustaining lifeworld capable of providing the resources to overcome the reductionist scientism of modernity. Habermas agrees with Gadamer's rejection of a secure knowing subject able to discern philosophically valid legal rules, but he rejects Gadamer's faith that valid legal norms emerge simply as the product of "the fortuitous resources of successful histories and traditions."[22] Against the corrosive skepticism of "a false realism that underestimates the empirical impact of the normative presuppositions of existing legal practices," Habermas insists that democracy—and the legal system particularly—evidence the inseparability of facts and norms.[23]

Habermas argues that Gadamer's recuperation of Aristotelian practical reason is thwarted by the emergence in modernity of autopoietic systems with insular imperatives. We have moved from an unthinking lifeworld premised on "a massive background consensus," to the authority of archaic institutions that utilize ritual and myth to assert authority, to the disenchantment of modernity that requires a legal system to integrate social life by securing individual liberties through the force of the state.[24] The interpretive and argumentative resources of the lifeworld are unable to constrain or influence systems of power and money, leading to the rise of the modern legal state. In Habermas's estimation, Gadamer looks back to the tradition of practical reasoning without accounting for the fundamental changes in social organization. In our pluralistic society, what "counts for one person as a historically proven topos is for others ideology and shared prejudice," and so Gadamer's faith in the power of practical reason is misplaced.[25]

Habermas develops this critique along several different axes, all of which emphasize the between-ness of law. He agrees with Gadamer's description of legal argumentation as a unified process of identifying the norm and the rule for the case in application. In Habermas's terms, law is Janus-faced because it always appeals to universality but only from within a particular context.[26] As William Rehg summarizes, Habermas accepts the challenge to maintain the constructive "tension between the strongly idealizing, context-transcending claims of reason and the always limited contexts in which human reason must ply its trade."[27]

Habermas extends his analysis with a phenomenological account of legal practice that uncovers a deep tension between law as a social fact that organizes and compels behavior, on one hand, and law as a norm that has democratic legitimacy on the other hand. "Law borrows its binding force . . . from the alliance that the facticity of law forms with the claim to legitimacy," resulting in "the relation between the coercive force of law, which secures average rule acceptance, and the idea of self-legislation."[28] This tension is mirrored in the opposed traditions of inquiry that focus either on the facticity of law, culminating in a skeptical legal realism, or on the normative dimension of law, culminating in a sterile morality disconnected from practical affairs. David Rasmussen explains the challenge undertaken by Habermas: "From the sociological perspective, law must be authoritative enough to force social integration after the great religious traditions have lost their normative authority. From the philosophical perspective law must have some kind of basis in justice which will enable, particularly in a burgeoning democratic society, willful assent to its legitimacy."[29]

At the level of a sociological account of the legal system, Habermas emphasizes that law plays a fundamental role as the bridge between the ordinary discourse of the lifeworld and the complex systems that comprise the economy and political bureaucracy. He uses a variety of metaphors to make this point: "law is a hinge between system and lifeworld," such that it "functions as the 'transformer' that first guarantees that the socially integrating network of communication stretched across society as a whole holds together."[30] Thus, the

> legal code not only keeps one foot in the medium of ordinary language, through which everyday communication achieves social integration in the lifeworld; it also accepts messages that originate there and puts these into a form that is comprehensible to the special codes of the power-steered administration and the money-steered economy. To this extent, the language of law, unlike the moral communication restricted to the lifeworld, can function as a transformer in the society-wide communication circulating between system and lifeworld.[31]

Law is not only inherently "between," it is the active "transmission belt" that connects the solidarity achieved through mutual recognition in the lifeworld to "the anonymous and systematically mediated relationships of a complex society."[32]

The philosophical claim that law is between facts and norms might appear to be a transcendental claim in the tradition of the Enlightenment, but, as a postmetaphysical philosopher, Habermas claims only quasi-transcendental status for his discourse theory of communicative action. Language is constitutively idealizing, and so our very ability to communicate arises from the tension of fact and norm. Habermas has written extensively about the principles of communicative reason that he derives from discourse theory, but he eschews the hubris of attempting to provide a blueprint of substantive solutions to problems of social organization. The philosopher is rooted in the lifeworld no less than the law judge, and so philosophical understanding occurs only in the context of practical engagements. Nevertheless, Habermas insists that critical theory can reconstruct networks of discourses in a manner that can serve as a "critical standard, against which actual practices—the opaque and perplexing reality of the constitutional state—could be evaluated."[33]

It might appear that Habermas has shunted Gadamer's hermeneutics to the side as a quaint and antiquarian inquiry into the politics of the polis that have long since disappeared. Gadamer reclaimed the ontology of understanding in the face of the overblown claims of the Enlightenment's faith in the power of explanation, while Habermas argues that a distinct human interest in emancipation subtends critical theory and must be fostered.[34] And yet Habermas agrees that the philosopher-critic claims no special capacity for making policy determinations, raising the question of the degree to which Habermas can escape Gadamer's account of situated understanding. From Gadamer's perspective, Habermas's critical theory is just another (socially contingent) resource that emerges from lifeworld understandings.

RICOEUR: EMBRACING THE UNBEARABLE BETWEEN-NESS OF LAW

Gadamer and Habermas are in violent agreement that law resides between logical principles and facts on one hand, and social norms and interpretive techniques on the other. However, each thinker remains strongly identified with a distinct philosophical tradition even as both acknowledge the need to move beyond the traditional boundaries of hermeneutics and critical theory. The tension of Gadamer/Habermas appears to elevate the tension of understanding/explanation to a new level of sophistication without pretending to resolve the tension. It is at this juncture that Ricoeur intervenes as a mediator between mediated discourses, a role that he adopts with subtlety and precision.

Ricoeur turned his thinking to the legal system in the last decade of his life after having engaged with judges and legal theorists at a number of academic symposia.[35] Noting that philosophers have long neglected law and instead focused on ethics or politics, Ricoeur addresses law in an effort "to do justice to justice."[36] He regards law as a vital feature of modern society because it contributes to social cohesion and peace by replacing violence and domination with procedures that establish a cooperative framework.[37] The law is not just an extension of interpersonal relationships, but instead is a delimited forum in which the parties confront each other in their roles as citizens beholden to the generalized efforts to achieve justice through the oversight of a neutral judge.[38] Ricoeur undertakes his study by drawing on the previous work of Gadamer and Habermas, and then pushing beyond their seeming opposition to capture the full breadth of the role and operation of law in modern society.

Ricoeur deploys three distinct traditions of thought to understand the legal system. First, moral reasoning engages in teleological inquiry to identify the good. Second, deductive (rule-based) reasoning engages in deontological inquiry to identify obligations. Third, practical reasoning engages in hermeneutical inquiry to identify the wise course of action with regard to a particular case. Although these traditions are distinct, they are not autonomous. The legal system performs its vital functions by establishing a space in which we may simultaneously take into account the good, the obligatory, and the wise.[39]

Gadamer and Habermas each mediate these traditions, with different emphases. Gadamer argues that hermeneutic understanding is the ontological foundation of knowledge, and he regards law as a signature expression of practical reasoning in action. On the other hand, Gadamer understands that law is oriented around rules and the need for stability. Gadamer famously positions his account between the obligatory and the wise by focusing on the phenomenology of application, in which both the rule and the decision are articulated in the course of deciding a particular case.

For his part, Habermas regards the tension between law and morality as a foundational expression of the post-metaphysical constraints on knowledge. Without access to an unproblematic and universally shared vision of the good (as previously articulated through the great religious traditions), we must rely on legal relations that reduce the cognitive load on citizens by providing democratically-derived rules of behavior that do not require a full moral judgment in each case. Positing himself between a chastened gesture to the good and a reliance on the obligatory, Habermas provides an account of the institutional means of engaging in productive practical reasoning.

Gadamer and Habermas work at the intersections of the traditions identified by Ricoeur, although they each criticize the other for embracing too narrow a position. Habermas's claims for a vigorous critical social theory in his debate with Gadamer reach too far, according to Ricoeur, by remaining lodged in the hubris of enlightenment. Habermas's human interest in emancipation remains beholden to a structural analysis that is too easily reified as being beyond hermeneutical understanding, which leads to a false opposition with Gadamer's philosophical hermeneutics. As Ricoeur reminds us, "Hermeneutics without a project of liberation is blind, but a project of emancipation without historical experience is empty."[40] Ricoeur agrees with Gadamer that the social theorist is unable to replicate the physician-patient model of psychoanalytic critique, because "no one identifies himself or herself as the ill, as the patient, and no one is entitled to be the physician."[41] And yet Ricoeur agrees that critique must be fostered within hermeneutical exchanges to avoid the warping effects of social systems on human self-consciousness.

Ricoeur deepens the issues raised in Gadamer/Habermas by inviting us to consider a "middle zone" in which the traditions of rhetoric, poetics and hermeneutics are deployed to explore the nature of law as a space within which creative arguments about the probable can be fashioned to provide guidance for social action. This project mediates our longing for determinant knowledge and our tendency to manipulate, charting a course for legal theory that cuts across multiple planes.

> The whole problem, which I will risk qualifying with the adjective *phronetic*, lies in exploring the *middle* zone where the judgment is formed, halfway between proof, defined by the constraints of logic, and sophism, motivated by the desire to seduce or the temptation to intimidate. This middle zone can be designated by many names, depending on the strategy used: rhetoric, to the extent that *rhetoric*, following Aristotle's definition, consists in giving a "rejoinder" to dialectic, itself understood as a doctrine of probable reasoning; *hermeneutic*, to the extent that this joins application to understanding or explanation; *poetic*, to the extent that the invention of an appropriate solution to the unique situation stems from what, since Kant, we have called the productive imagination, in order to distinguish it from the merely reproductive imagination.
>
> [Adjudication offers a context in which] "*argumentation*," where the logic of the probable predominates, and *interpretation*, where the innovative power of the imagination acts on the very productions of arguments, meet and become entangled with each other.
>
> It remains to give a name to the just on the plane of practical reasoning, the one where judgment occurs in a situation. I propose that the just is no longer either the good or the legal, but the *equitable*. The equitable is the figure that clothes the idea of the just in situations of incertitude and conflict, or, to put it a better way, in the ordinary—or extraordinary—realm of the tragic dimension of action.[42]

This rich and complex account of law requires careful unpacking.

Ricoeur invokes a dialogic understanding of interpretation and argumentation in law. Lawyers do not first interpret the law, and then seek to persuade others of this meaning. Rather, interpretation is always in the service of some argument, and argumentation is always interpretive in character. Ricoeur expressly analogizes this feature of law to his treatment of explanation/understanding.[43] He assesses the hermeneutical legal theory of Ronald Dworkin and the critical theory of Robert Alexy as extensions of work by Gadamer and Habermas, concluding that legal argumentation involves interpretation rather than logical subsumption of a distinct case under a defined rule. The Frankfurt School productively moves beyond its Hegelian roots by insisting that universalization can occur only in actual dialogues oriented toward concrete problems involving conflicting interests.[44] Similarly, hermeneutical philosophy embraces legal practice as an historically unfolding narrative theory of law, even if Dworkin fails to appreciate the role of rhetoric in defining this activity.[45]

Interpretation and argumentation are not distinct activities: interpretation is always motivated by a question calling for resolution, and argumentation always rests on hermeneutical assessment. Put differently, one does not first interpret the law and then develop an argument about the application of the law. In legal practice, determining the norm and finding the facts "mutually condition each other."[46] The posture of a judge is different from that of the advocate. In this instance, the "argument" is a just resolution of the case by means of practical reasoning that rises above the tendency of litigants to engage in sophistic—the art of sophistry—and eristic—the art of disputation. "To use Kantian language again, we can say that the act of judging stems from a reflective judgment, itself consisting in seeking a rule for the new case."[47] The judge demarcates a space that is beyond vengeance and brute violence.

> With the institution of the tribunal, the trial brings into confrontation parties who are constituted as "others" by the judicial procedure. What is more, the institution is incarnated in the person of the judge, who, as a third party between the two parties, takes on the figure of a second-order third party. The judge marks out the just distance the trial establishes between the parties in conflict.[48]

The judicial role makes clear that legal argumentation and interpretation are not simply strategic or instrumental, but rather represent an effort to convey understanding in the form of rhetorical knowledge. Ricoeur's lesson is much broader, however. He investigates the legal system as a model of how discourse works generally. His account of explanation/understanding provides the basis for concluding that an interpreter can "follow the path of thought opened by the text" with integrity.[49] "Appropriation loses its arbitrariness insofar as it is the recovery of that which is at work, in labour, within the text. What the interpreter says is a re-saying which reactivates what is said by the text. . . . It is at the very heart of reading that explanation and interpretation are indefinitely opposed and reconciled."[50]

In the essay, "Rhetoric-Poetics-Hermeneutics," Ricoeur summarizes his philosophy of discourse in a manner that provides depth and detail to his account of the legal system.[51] We must begin with an understanding of discourse and the generation of meaning. Language is not a code comprised of words, each of which has a settled meaning. The basic unit of meaning is the sentence, which are combined creatively to create a text. Conservative legal theorists who urge a simplistic approach to legal texts premised on individual words having fixed meanings that persist through time are fundamentally confused about discourse. Even sophisticated theorists seeking to illuminate sentence meaning tend to use a single lens, drawing on hermeneutics, rhetoric, or poetics as the key to meaning. Because of the complexity posed by sentence meaning, Ricoeur emphasizes that none of these elements alone can provide a full account; instead, one must pursue all of these complementary access points.[52] Hence the title of Ricoeur's essay, which brings all three elements together in a non-reductive, tensive relationship.

In the essay, Ricoeur begins with rhetoric, the oldest of the disciplines. Rhetoric has ancient roots as the study of practical engagement in specific venues, but more recently has been extrapolated to claim authority over all dialogue engaging in practical reasoning.[53] On one hand, rhetoric is deeply connected to sophistic and eristic, and threatens to collapse into achieving persuasion through any available means. On the other hand, rhetoric aspires to be the equal of, or even to supplant, philosophy as the arbiter of reason and discourse. Chaïm Perelman's adoption of the "universal audience" as a means to infuse rhetoric with a claim to truth reveals this monopolizing tendency.[54] Rhetoric alone is unable to suppress the fundamental tension between discourse as strategic behavior and discourse as the practical engagement with truth. It is the same complexity that is at the center of legal discourse, which oscillates between crude manipulative argumentation and claims about the demands of justice.

Rhetoric focuses on the production of discourse to serve the ends of persuasion, but poetics more broadly is the art of creatively extending previous meanings. Rhetoric deploys arguments built on conventions—loci, or commonplaces—whereas poetics provides new resources to understand the world.

> Whereas the ambitions of rhetoric find their limit in its attention to the listener and its respect for conventional ideas, poetics points to the breach of newness that the creative imagination opens in this field. . . . [P]oetics stirs up the sedimented universe of conventional ideas which are the premises of rhetorical

argumentation. At the same time, this same breakthrough of the imaginary shakes up the order of persuasion.[55]

Poetics is beyond the scope of rhetorical "invention" of arguments for the case at hand, inasmuch as poetics creates new resources from which the rhetor may draw.

Discourse requires poetic creation and rhetorical argumentation, and neither may be reduced to the other. In legal discourse this complexity is found in the idea of "judicial craft," which oscillates between "schemes of conventional ideas appropriated to typical situations" and "an imaginative reconstruction of the field."[56] Neither poetics nor rhetoric can fully explore the idea of "making" legal arguments fully, and so the result is much like the relationship that Ricoeur explores between ideology (in this case, rhetoric) and utopia (in this case, poetics).[57]

Finally, Ricoeur acknowledges the critical role of the hermeneutical tradition in understanding discourse. In many respects, hermeneutics is similar to poetics because it creatively addresses potential meaning from among multiple understandings of a given text.[58] And yet interpretation operates as a reinterpretation of a living tradition from which the text emerges in an effort to come to a single meaning, more similar to the conventional rhetorical goal of inventing arguments based on established commonplaces.[59] Hermeneutical theorists argue that hermeneutics is the ultimate authority for understanding meaning, but they cannot subsume rhetoric and poetics completely in this effort. And, ultimately, hermeneutical inquiry must submit to an interrogation by critical theorists who seek to expose the hubris of its utopian gestures and the false consciousness of its ideological instantiation.

Ricoeur concludes that discourse is inextricably located between these schools of thought, each of which contributes to our understanding:

> In conclusion, it seems to me that one must leave each of these three disciplines undisturbed in their three respective birthplaces, which are irreducible one to another. And there is no super-discipline which would totalize the whole field covered by rhetoric, poetics, and hermeneutics. Lacking this impossible totalization, one can only locate the noticeable points of intersection between the three disciplines. But each discipline speaks for itself. Rhetoric remains the art of arguing with a view to persuading an audience that one opinion is preferable to its rival. Poetics remains the art of constructing plots with a view to broadening the individual and collective imaginary. Hermeneutics remains the art of interpreting texts within a context distinct from that of the author and from that of the texts' original audience with a view to discovering new dimensions to reality. Arguing, fashioning [*configurer*], redescribing; such are the three major operations whose respective totalizing aims are mutually exclusive, but the finiteness of whose original sites condemns them to complementarity.[60]

This conclusion is particularly true of legal discourse, whose procedures and practices sharpen the distinctions and similarities that Ricoeur describes. Ricoeur proves himself to be an important legal theorist who challenges us to rethink the reductive impulse to find that one or another disciplinary tradition is the foundational key to understanding legal meaning.

In an essay translated for this volume, Ricoeur concretizes his thinking about the medial character of law.[61] Law bridges the gap between competing conceptions of justice (teleological norms versus deontological positivism) and everyday social practices.[62] The gap is filled by a literal "space" between the political authority and everyday discussions, a courtroom where conflicts are recast into procedurally arranged trials. Ricoeur contends that the argumentative structure of the trial is a "remarkable" model of dialogic exchange, one that is shaped by the entwinement of a logic and an ethics.[63] The "logic" is the rhetorical logic of verisimilitude outlined by Aristotle. There is no certainty in these cases, but instead only plausible arguments about the probable.[64] The "ethic" is giving oneself over to the better argument by the hermeneutical principle—most consistently championed by Gadamer—of holding oneself open to the claims of the other side.[65] In this medial space emerges a contest of rhetorical-hermeneutical principles that connect with our overriding concern with justice.

This is not to say that we must end in a muddle. The insight that law is unbearably between various disciplinary investigations into meaning does not mean that there is no basis for claiming that a particular constellation of disciplines might better capture the reality of legal discourse. For example, in response to Ricoeur's insights I strive to check my tendency to prioritize philosophical hermeneutics as the master discipline for law, enabling and empowering me to see that Gadamer's philosophical hermeneutics is best read as having been deeply informed by rhetoric. And yet I contend that my concept of "rhetorical knowledge" is a more productive mediating approach than the structuralist legacy of Ricoeur's approach, even as I acknowledge a deep debt to Ricoeur for shaping my thinking.[66] There is need for deep work in hermeneutics, rhetoric, poetics, and critical theory to explore legal understanding, but all such projects must in the end acknowledge the between-ness of law that subverts all claims to have fashioned a master narrative. We are left with Ricoeur's summary that we are addressing the "equitable," a condition of between-ness that is unavoidable and whose resolution would mean the end of law.

CONCLUSION

We must remain vigilant in our effort not to subordinate law to a simple approach. For every sophisticated account of practical reasoning about indeterminate norms, we risk losing sight of the system imperatives of modern complex societies. For every refusal to reduce law judging to subsuming cases under rules, we risk underestimating the importance of judicial craft as a *techne*. Intellectual trends can productively offer a strong critique in the manner of a corrective, but in doing so we must acknowledge the ontological between-ness of law. It is an unbearable situation, but Paul Ricoeur serves as an experienced and trusted guide in this vital task.

NOTES

1. I dedicate this chapter to George Taylor in scholarly friendship. I have greatly benefitted from our ongoing conversation stretching back over three decades.

2. Paul Ricoeur, "What is a Text? Explanation and Understanding," in *Hermeneutics and the Human Sciences: Essays on Language, Action and Interpretation*, ed. John B. Thompson (Cambridge: Cambridge University Press, 1981), 145–64; Paul Ricoeur, *Freud and Philosophy: An Essay on Interpretation*, trans. Denis Savage (New Haven: Yale University Press, 1970), 27.

3. Paul Ricoeur, *Memory, History, Forgetting*, trans. Kathleen Blamey and David Pellauer (Chicago: University of Chicago Press, 2004), 182–233. In addition to the "documentary phase" of gathering historical data and the "representation phase" of articulating one's findings, Ricoeur contends that the historian engages in "explanation/understanding." He explains the term thus: "The double term 'explanation/understanding' is indicative of my refusing the opposition between explanation and understanding that all too often has prevented grasping the treatment of the historical "because" in its full amplitude and complexity." Ricoeur, *Memory, History, Forgetting*, 136. He qualifies the description as methodological rather than chronological, such that the three phases are never wholly distinct from each other. Ricoeur, *Memory, History, Forgetting*, 137.

> In truth, this new phase of the historiographical operation was already implied in the [documentary phase] insofar as there is no document without some question, nor some question without an explanatory project. It is in relations to explanation that the document is proof. Nevertheless, what explanation/understanding adds that is new in relation to the documentary treatment of the historical fact has to do with the modes of interconnectedness of the documented facts.

Memory, History, Forgetting, 182. For explications of Ricoeur's thesis that understanding and explanation are deeply entwined, see Willis F. Overton, "Understanding, Explanation, and Reductionism: Finding a Cure for the Cartesian Anxiety," in

Reductionism and the Development of Knowledge, eds. Terrance Brown and Leslie Smith (Mahwah, NJ: Lawrence Erlbaum Associates, 2002), 29–51; George H. Taylor, "Critical Hermeneutics: The Intertwining of Explanation and Understanding as Exemplified in Legal Analysis," *Chicago-Kent Law Review* 76, no. 2 (2000): 1101–23; and David E. Klemm, *The Hermeneutical Theory of Paul Ricoeur: A Constructive Analysis* (Lewisburg: Bucknell University Press, 1983), 90–108, 140–63.

4. William McNeill, *The Glance of the Eye: Heidegger, Aristotle and the Ends of Theory* (Albany: SUNY Press, 1999), 281.

5. McNeil, *The Glance of the Eye*, 61, 67–68.

6. Hans-Georg Gadamer, *Truth and Method*, trans. rev. by Joel Weinsheimer and Donald G. Marshall (New York: Crossroad Publishing, 1989), 314–24.

7. Gadamer, *Truth and Method*, xxvii.

8. Rod Coltman, *The Language of Hermeneutics: Gadamer and Heidegger in Dialogue* (Albany: SUNY Press, 1998), 22.

9. Francis J. Mootz III, "A Future Foretold: Neo-Aristotelian Praise of Postmodern Legal Theory," *Brooklyn Law Review* 68, no. 3 (2003): 699.

10. Gadamer, *Truth and Method*, 311.

11. Gadamer, *Truth and Method*, 324–41.

12. Gadamer, *Truth and Method*, 307.

13. Gadamer, *Truth and Method*, 310.

14. Gadamer, *Truth and Method*, 307.

15. Gadamer, *Truth and Method*, 308.

16. Gadamer, *Truth and Method*, 325–28.

17. Gadamer, *Truth and Method*, 327–28.

18. Gadamer, *Truth and Method*, 339 (emphasis in original).

19. Gadamer, *Truth and Method*, 330.

20. Francis J. Mootz III, "Getting Beyond the Fixation Thesis," in *The Nature of Legal Interpretation: What Jurists Can Learn about Legal Interpretation from Linguistics and Philosophy*, ed. Brian G. Slocum (Chicago: University of Chicago Press, 2017), 156–90.

21. Gadamer, *Truth and Method*, 311. In a complementary vein, Rodolphe Gasché assesses the activities of persuasion (through Aristotle), reflection (through Heidegger) and judgment (through Arendt) not for the purpose of championing the practical over the theoretical, but as a means to reveal the theoretical dimension of everyday life. His study is intended "to suggest that another front needs to be opened up in the weary debate between theory and praxis by acknowledging that there is a 'theoretical' dimension intrinsic to the practical, broadly speaking, to ordinary everyday life. Ordinary life is never just mere, immediate life. It is always inhabited by some form of thought and, thus, inherently 'theoretical.'" Rodolphe Gasché, *Persuasion, Reflection, Judgment: Ancillae Vitae* (Bloomington: Indiana Press, 2017), 7.

22. Jürgen Habermas, *Between Facts and Norms: Contributions to a Discourse Theory of Law and Democracy*, trans. William Rehg (Cambridge, MA: The MIT Press, 1996), 3.

23. Habermas, *Between Facts and Norms*, xl. Habermas follows a similar path in his recent efforts to mediate the increasing opposition of the two primary traditions

(radical naturalism and orthodox religiosity) in the fractured post-Enlightenment era. Habermas 2008.

24. Habermas, *Between Facts and Norms*, 22–27.
25. Habermas, *Between Facts and Norms*, 200–03.
26. Habermas, *Between Facts and Norms*, 21.
27. William Rehg, "Translator's Introduction," in *Between Facts and Norms*, xiii–xiv.
28. Habermas, *Between Facts and Norms*, 38–39.
29. David M. Rasmussen, "How is Valid Law Possible?," in *Habermas, Modernity and Law*, ed. Mathieu Deflem (London: Sage Publications, 1996), 21–44.
30. Habermas, *Between Facts and Norms*, 56.
31. Habermas, *Between Facts and Norms*, 81.
32. Habermas, *Between Facts and Norms*, 76.
33. Habermas, *Between Facts and Norms*, 5.
34. Jürgen Habermas, *Knowledge and Human Interests*, trans. Jeremy J. Shapiro (Boston: Beacon Press, 1971), 189–317.
35. David Pellauer, *Ricoeur: A Guide for the Perplexed* (London: Continuum Publishing, 2007), 134.
36. Paul Ricoeur, *The Just*, trans. David Pellauer (Chicago: University of Chicago Press, 2000), ix.
37. Ricoeur, *The Just*, ix–x.
38. Ricoeur, *The Just*, x–xiv.
39. Ricoeur, *The Just*, xvi–xxiv.
40. Paul Ricoeur, *Lectures on Ideology and Utopia*, ed. George H. Taylor (New York: Columbia University Press, 1986), 237.
41. Ricoeur, *Lectures on Ideology and Utopia*, 248.
42. Ricoeur, *The Just*, xxii–xxiv.
43. Ricoeur, *The Just*, 110, 125.
44. Ricoeur, *The Just*, 118.
45. Ricoeur, *The Just*, 113–16.
46. Ricoeur, *The Just*, 121.
47. Ricoeur, *The Just*, 129.
48. Ricoeur, *The Just*, xiv.
49. Ricoeur, "What is a Text?," 162.
50. Ricoeur, "What is a Text?," 164.
51. Paul Ricoeur, "Rhetoric-Poetics-Hermeneutics," in *Rhetoric and Hermeneutics in Our Time*, eds. Walter Jost and Michael J. Hyde, trans. Robert Harvey (New Haven: Yale University Press, 1997), 60–72.
52. Ricoeur, "Rhetoric-Poetics-Hermeneutics," 60.
53. Ricoeur, "Rhetoric-Poetics-Hermeneutics," 61–62.
54. Ricoeur, "Rhetoric-Poetics-Hermeneutics," 64.
55. Ricoeur, "Rhetoric-Poetics-Hermeneutics," 65–66.
56. Ricoeur, "Rhetoric-Poetics-Hermeneutics," 65.
57. Ricoeur, "Rhetoric-Poetics-Hermeneutics," 65. See Ricoeur, *Lectures on Ideology and Utopia*.

58. Ricoeur, "Rhetoric-Poetics-Hermeneutics," 65.
59. Ricoeur, "Rhetoric-Poetics-Hermeneutics," 69.
60. Ricoeur, "Rhetoric-Poetics-Hermeneutics," 71.
61. Paul Ricoeur, "The Just Between the Legal and the Good," in this volume: 21–36.
62. Ricoeur, "The Just Between the Legal and the Good," 23.
63. Ricoeur, "The Just Between the Legal and the Good," [translation draft 20].
64. Ricoeur, "The Just Between the Legal and the Good," in this volume: 34–35.
65. Ricoeur, "The Just Between the Legal and the Good," in this volume: 35.
66. Francis J. Mootz III, "Gadamer's Rhetorical Conception of Hermeneutics as the Key to Developing a Critical Hermeneutics," in *Gadamer and Ricoeur: Critical Horizons for Contemporary Hermeneutics*, eds. Francis J. Mootz III and George H. Taylor (London: Continuum Int'l Publishing Group, 2011), 83–103. I argue that Gadamer's deeply rhetorical approach to understanding blunts the criticism that his philosophical hermeneutics is quiescent, and that Ricoeur's concept of "critical distanciation" is best achieved rhetorically. As a matter of style and emphasis, Gadamer begins with actual dialogue and then extends his thoughts to other forms of understanding, whereas Ricoeur begins with the structure of the text. As John Arthos aptly summarizes, Gadamer is a "pub-crawler" seeking conversation, whereas Ricoeur is a "scholar" seeking philosophical clarity. John Arthos, "The Scholar and the Pub Crawler: Revisiting the Debate Between Ricoeur and Gadamer," *Journal of French and Francophone Philosophy* 16, nos. 1–2 (2006): 71–81. It is not so much that Gadamer, Ricoeur or Habermas has found a uniquely correct approach to legal understanding, but that they provide different complementary points of access that serve better or worse in different contexts and for different purposes. I have learned much from Ricoeur's exploration of explanation/understanding (Mootz, "Gadamer's Rhetorical Conception," 94–95), but I primarily follow Gadamer's path:

> If we are to make good on Ricoeur's project and extend Gadamer's insights, we must reorient the project of critical hermeneutics to the rhetorical realm and continually attend to the rhetorical limits of philosophy.
>
> Ricoeur emphasizes the "world of the text" because it provides the basis for an explanatory intervention that is not lodged in ordinary dialogue, and he then extends this model to social interaction by construing social action as a "text." In sharp contrast, Gadamer begins with dialogue and looks to the experience of textual interpretation in order to highlight the distanciating features of dialogic engagement. Ricoeur interjects philosophical critique into hermeneutics, whereas Gadamer philosophically recovers the critical features of understanding. I contend that Gadamer's path is more productive because the goal of a critical hermeneutics is to foster *rhetorical experience*, not to deliver *philosophical truths*.

Mootz, "Gadamer's Rhetorical Conception," 91.

BIBLIOGRAPHY

Arthos, John. "The Scholar and the Pub Crawler: Revisiting the Debate Between Ricoeur and Gadamer." *Journal of French and Francophone Philosophy* 16, nos. 1–2 (2006): 71–81.

Coltman, Rod. *The Language of Hermeneutics: Gadamer and Heidegger in Dialogue*. Albany: SUNY Press, 1998.

Gadamer, Hans-Georg. *Truth and Method*. Translation revised by Joel Weinsheimer and Donald G. Marshall. New York: Crossroad Publishing, 1998.

Gasché, Rodolphe. *Persuasion, Reflection, Judgment: Ancillae Vitae*. Bloomington: Indiana Press, 2017.

Habermas, Jürgen. *Between Facts and Norms: Contributions to a Discourse Theory of Law and Democracy*. Translation by William Rehg. Cambridge, MA: The MIT Press, 1996.

Habermas, Jürgen. *Between Naturalism and Religion*. Translated by Cairan Cronin. Cambridge: Polity Press, 2008.

Habermas, Jürgen. *Knowledge and Human Interests*. Translated by Jeremy J. Shapiro. Boston: Beacon Press, 1971.

Klemm, David E. *The Hermeneutical Theory of Paul Ricoeur: A Constructive Analysis*. Lewisburg: Bucknell University Press, 1983.

McNeill, William. *The Glance of the Eye: Heidegger, Aristotle and the Ends of Theory*. Albany: SUNY Press, 1999.

Mootz III, Francis J. "A Future Foretold: Neo-Aristotelian Praise of Postmodern Legal Theory." *Brooklyn Law Review* 68, no. 3 (2003): 683–719.

Mootz III, Francis J. "Gadamer's Rhetorical Conception of Hermeneutics as the Key to Developing a Critical Hermeneutics." In *Gadamer and Ricoeur: Critical Horizons for Contemporary Hermeneutics*, edited by Francis J. Mootz III and George H. Taylor, 83–103. London: Continuum International Publishing Group, 2011.

Mootz III, Francis J. "Getting Beyond the Fixation Thesis." In *The Nature of Legal Interpretation: What Jurists Can Learn about Legal Interpretation from Linguistics and Philosophy*, edited by Brian G. Slocum, 156–90. Chicago: University of Chicago Press, 2017.

Overton, Willis F. "Understanding, Explanation, and Reductionism: Finding a Cure for the Cartesian Anxiety." In *Reductionism and the Development of Knowledge*, edited by Terrance Brown and Leslie Smith, 29–51. Mahwah, NJ: Lawrence Erlbaum Associates, 2002.

Pellauer, David. *Ricoeur: A Guide for the Perplexed*. London: Continuum Publishing, 2007.

Rasmussen, David M. "How is Valid Law Possible?" In *Habermas, Modernity and Law*, edited by Mathieu Deflem, 21–44. London: Sage Publications, 1996.

Rehg, William. "Translator's Introduction." In *Jürgen Habermas, Between Facts and Norms: Contributions to a Discourse Theory of Law and Democracy*, ix–xxxviii. Translated by William Rehg. Cambridge, MA: The MIT Press, 1996.

Ricoeur, Paul. *Freud and Philosophy: An Essay on Interpretation*. Translated by Denis Savage. New Haven: Yale University Press, 1970.

Ricoeur, Paul. *The Just*. Translated by David Pellauer. Chicago: University of Chicago Press, 2000.

Ricoeur, Paul. "The Just Between the Legal and the Good." In *Reading Ricoeur through Law*, edited by Marc de Leeuw, George H. Taylor, and Eileen Brennan, 21–36. Lanham, MD: Lexington Books, 2022.

Ricoeur, Paul. *Lectures on Ideology and Utopia*, edited by George H. Taylor. New York: Columbia University Press, 1986.

Ricoeur, Paul. *Memory, History, Forgetting*. Translated by Kathleen Blamey and David Pellauer. Chicago: University of Chicago Press, 2004.

Ricoeur, Paul. "Rhetoric-Poetics-Hermeneutics." In *Rhetoric and Hermeneutics in Our Time*, edited by Walter Jost and Michael J. Hyde. Translated by Robert Harvey, 60–72. New Haven: Yale University Press, 1997.

Ricoeur, Paul. "What is a Text? Explanation and Understanding." In *Hermeneutics and the Human Sciences: Essays on Language, Action and Interpretation*, edited by John B. Thompson, 145–64. Cambridge: Cambridge University Press, 1981.

Taylor, George H. "Critical Hermeneutics: The Intertwining of Explanation and Understanding as Exemplified in Legal Analysis." *Chicago-Kent Law Review* 76, no. 2 (2000): 1101–23.

Chapter Nine

Law and Metadiscourse

Ricoeur on Metaphysics and the Ascription of Rights

Geoffrey Dierckxsens

In this chapter, I will draw on Ricoeur's work in order to take a position in the debate whether the ascription of rights in a democracy should be understood on the basis of pragmatism.[1] By doing so, this chapter aims at investigating the extent to which pragmatic and formal systems, understood as ethical, political, and legal systems, are significant for law. More exactly, I will argue that Ricoeur's conception of rights, as understood in his article, "Who is the Subject of Rights?,"[2] offers a pragmatic understanding of the ascription of rights based on the power to act and the promotion of democratic principles such as the freedom of speech. In this respect, Ricoeur's understanding of rights should be understood in line with recent pragmatic theories of democracy, according to which the ascription of rights is best maintained by self-promoting democratic principles that govern a just distribution of rights.

Yet at the same time, so I will assert, Ricoeur's understanding of rights can overcome one of the major pitfalls of a pragmatic approach to rights, namely the risk, despite its practical approach, of overformalizing the distribution of rights and thus the risk of overlooking the potential neglect, by self-governing formal systems, of minorities who are not part of "the system." Ricoeur underscores the importance of connecting rights to the ethical principle of the recognition of others, which in turn has a metaphysical connotation in that the ascription of rights implies a discourse on a *meta* level, in which there is attention to others in the sense of minorities who are not protected by the formalizations of a democratic society. Ricoeur shows, then, why rights are not reducible to legal rights but are intertwined with ethical principles. Similarly, formalizations of rights, such as in legal systems, are not sufficient but must be counterbalanced by an ethical notion of rights as forms of recognition.

This chapter is divided into four parts. In the first part, I will sketch the background of the discussion by briefly discussing the debate whether and to what extent the ascription of rights should be understood on the basis of a pragmatic theory of democracy. I will argue that by choosing a pragmatic approach, one avoids abstract metaphysical speculation about what a democracy ought to be. Yet, despite this emphasis on the practical, non-theoretical side of democracy, pragmatism runs the risk of overformalizing the principles of the ascription of rights, i.e., of focusing primarily on the formal conditions of the ascription of rights. In the second and third parts, I will argue that Ricoeur's understanding of the ascription of rights shows that the ascription of rights is not merely formal but based on natural ethical and anthropological principles of the recognition of others (e.g., care, friendship, love), which are therefore significant for law. Finally, in the fourth and last part, I will refer to Ricoeur's metaphysics of otherness and argue that an understanding of the ascription of rights should be complemented by a metaphysical discourse of otherness nonetheless, even though pragmatism remains important. This discourse of otherness has consequences for societal regard for minorities, such as political refugees, who cannot be understood as fully capable participants in a democratic society as citizens, yet still should be granted rights within this society.

PRAGMATISM AND THE ASCRIPTION OF RIGHTS

In recent years, several theories have emerged that take a pragmatic approach to the understanding of democracy.[3] These theories argue that, in order to cope with issues of institutional power and domination, democracies should continuously be revised and reconstructed. Instead of metaphysical speculation about the conditions of democracy (e.g., a priori legal theory), a pragmatic approach implies practical reasoning in order to find concrete solutions to problems that turn up in democratic societies, such as authoritarian power abuse.

Pragmatism thus offers a direct approach to thinking about democracy, rather than the implementation of theoretical principles to political reality. It aims to avoid an excess of rationalization at the risk of the theory losing touch with the reality of power abuse. The implementation instead of practical formal principles, such as the principle of free speech, is a salient part in the process of maintaining a democracy. Rather than a theoretical description of how an ideal democratic system would look like, a pragmatic approach to democracy implies a description of principles that directly promote the functioning of the democracy itself.

The need for these kind of principles in a democracy is immediately apparent, since any just democracy that aims for the recognition of all of its participants should function to guard this recognition by promoting freedom of speech, the protection of minorities (although not absolutely, as we will see), and the application of a just legal system. This is not only true in theory, as a matter of ethics, but also on the levels of politics (as a matter of policy) and that of law (as a matter of legal practice). The claim is that democracies that *do not* have pragmatic protection mechanisms on all of these levels are more prone to transformation into authoritarian or even violent ideological regimes.

Pragmatic theories of democracy stress the importance of the critical potential of pragmatism, and by doing so these theories aim to address some of the problems of the original version of pragmatism. Initial forms of pragmatism, Dewey's in particular, received criticism for endorsing an unfounded faith in science and for not assessing whether these measures would redress the authoritarian implementation of formal principles, which on their own are designed as rules and in that sense exercise power over those who have to comply with them.[4] For example, it is easy to think of historical and recent cases in which institutions or individuals refer to the principle of the freedom of speech while spreading violent and oppressive messages (e.g., racist ideological discourse). Several scholars have responded to this criticism in defense of Dewey.[5] They point out that the intention of pragmatism is not to turn away from the reality of power and violence but to turn toward the political problems themselves. They are skeptical about overtheorizing metaphysical speculations about justice. Hence, their pragmatic approach.

It is neither my intention to criticize pragmatism directly nor to defend it entirely. Yet one immediate problem of a pragmatic approach to democracy is that, despite its critical attitude toward rationalization, it risks overformalizing the principles of the ascription of rights. This risk can be understood in two ways. First, formal principles designed for an equal distribution of rights can have the opposite effect, or can even be abused for corrupt reasons (e.g., as in the use of one right of the freedom of speech for violent discourse). The formalization of law does not suffice as a focus of analysis; content and application must be analyzed as well. Secondly, the formal character of any kind of system, even a pragmatic one, implies an exclusion of otherness to some extent, because it uses general rules. The ascription of certain rights as a general rule can be at odds with the protection of minorities. For example, the freedom of speech does not take into account the most vulnerable, those who are most easily the victims of violent discourse or whose voice is simply not heard.

On social media, freedom of speech is often used to endorse the exclusion of others or of those whose traits do not accord with the "norm." This occurs not only as a result of emotional reactions but also on a political-practical level. Former president Trump's infamous comments in his presidential announcement speech about Mexican people[6] are one clear example of how the principle of the freedom of speech can be used to promote a political agenda that excludes minorities. It is surely the case that pragmatism defends that democratic principles should be continuously revised, exactly to better avoid these kinds of practices. Yet, this response alone is insufficient, because it leads to an increasingly complex legal system designed to account for as many particular situations as possible. And because such systems consists of general, formal principles, they cannot consider every particularity, any minority or any other. What is apparently missing is a reference to otherness in the practice of the ascription of rights, in particular in relation to law.

In order to search for this reference to otherness, I will focus in the next sections on Ricoeur's work, primarily on his article, "Who is the Subject of Rights?," and argue that it offers a middle way between a pragmatic and a metaphysical understanding of democracy. I will argue that for Ricoeur, democracy is based on a pragmatic principle, namely the equal distribution of rights, and not only on the formulation of theoretical principles. This distribution implies concrete actions of both individuals and institutions.[7] Yet at the same time, a theory of rights would have little sense for Ricoeur if it were detached from a metaphysics of otherness.[8] In fact, the principles of the distribution of rights are principles of justice for Ricoeur, yet justice only makes sense when it includes relations with others. The main point I will aim to make is that Ricoeur shows that referring to the other on a *meta* level—that is, the other who cannot immediately be calculated into a pragmatic or practical logic—is important for a theory of democracy, especially today, because of the increasing need for the protection of minorities.

RICOEUR ON RIGHTS

Although Ricoeur never wrote a separate book on law or justice,[9] he authored several articles on these topics, which have been published particularly in *The Just* and in *Reflections on the Just*.[10] One of these articles, which has an immediately apparent significance for a theory of law, is "Who is the Subject of Rights?"[11] Ricoeur offers an unusual perspective on a theory of rights in that he contests both formalist and personalist understandings of rights. According to Ricoeur, a purely formalistic understanding of rights would exclude the possibility of critically assessing the formal legal and political structure, of attaining justice from "outside" the system. A formalistic conception of rights amounts to a "systematic abstraction that would banish consideration of those initiatives and interventions by which persons posit themselves over against such systems."[12] That is to say, what a formalistic understanding of rights fails to account for is that a legal and political system may itself possibly fail to attain justice, either because its formal structures fail to consider particular cases that require an exception or interpretation of the rules, or because of an abuse of power or authority within the system (e.g., political corruption). As concerns this critique, Ricoeur's understanding of rights aligns with the newer versions of pragmatism, which, as noted above, aims to address these kinds of problems regarding power abuse.

Simultaneously, however, Ricoeur questions a personalist approach to a theory of rights, even though he also supported personalism in his earlier years, as Dries Deweer has argued.[13] In Ricoeur's own words, he contests a purely "personalist communitarianism that might dream of reconstructing the political bond on the model of the personal bond illustrated by friendship and love."[14] A purely personalist approach to rights overlooks the necessity of institutional intervention for recognition through the ascription of rights (e.g., as reflected in a legal system).

It would be wrong to assert that Ricoeur radically discharges both of these understanding of rights, that is, both formalism and personalism. Rather, he apparently wants to mediate between both of these positions or to connect one with the other. Indeed, as is well-known, for Ricoeur justice requires going beyond friendship and ethical care for others,[15] since these intersubjective relations exclude the recognition of the third person, which can only take place in the context of "just institutions."[16] Institutional justice has the function to "guard over" communities and to ensure that recognition takes place, not only through personal exchange but also on a formal, communal level.[17]

Ricoeur's strategy, to connect formalism with personalism, is twofold. In "Who is the Subject of Rights?" he first argues that the ascription of rights is based on the ethical/moral value of the recognition of persons out of respect for the person: "[T]he question with a juridical form 'Who is the subject of rights?' is not to be distinguished in the final analysis from the question with a moral form 'Who is the subject worthy of esteem and respect?'"[18] Secondly, Ricoeur's intention is to demonstrate that the ethico-moral principle of esteem/respect for persons has an "anthropological" root as well, insofar that humans respect each other, not exclusively because it is a general rule, but because they recognize in each other certain human capacities (to speak, to act, to narrate, and to be responsible) that demand esteem and respect.[19]

In short, we have rights, not only because this is written down by democratic law, but also because we are human—the moral principle of respect for humanity—which implies that we are capable persons—moral principles result from our anthropological nature. The ascription of rights is thus for Ricoeur a process that requires formal procedures (institutions, laws, norms, etc.), yet that can also be traced back to the ethical/moral nature of human beings, i.e., their natural capacity to recognize each other as persons (speaking, acting, narrating, and being responsible).

BEING A PERSON IS ALL TOO HUMAN: RICOEUR'S ETHICO-ANTHROPOLOGICAL UNDERSTANDING OF RIGHTS

Yet what does the ascription of rights on the basis of both formal procedures and ethical principles mean concretely? How do our capacities to speak, act, narrate, and be responsible lead to ethical and moral principles and ultimately to the ascription of rights in law? In order to answer this question, I will elaborate in this section on Ricoeur's understanding of these four capacities that, as will become clear, are interconnected: speech, action, the capacity to narrate, and responsibility.

As for the first capacity—speech—Ricoeur explains that it is a necessary condition for the ascription of human rights to persons: the ascription of rights implies a formulation and understanding of these rights, that is, a "reference to the very institution of language."[20] One can only ascribe rights to persons, if one knows what these rights are. Justice, law, and right require language. That is obvious. Yet, Ricoeur also means something else. He derives the ethical principle that we should ascribe rights to persons from the anthropological capacity that persons are capable of speaking. The ascription of rights is a "recognition [that] does not reduce to just the adoption of the same rules by everyone; it also requires the confidence each one of them places in the rule of sincerity, without which any linguistic exchange would be impossible."[21]

In other words, this means that the capacity to speak, and in particular to make and keep promises, is required in order to be responsible, and therefore to be entitled with particular rights that come with this responsibility. Someone who has no clear idea of what he or she is doing, who is incapable of expressing himself or herself as the author of *intentional* actions that one plans, promises to execute, beliefs in, etc., is not fully responsible for his or her actions. Such a person would not *know* what he or she is doing, and the ascription of rights is for that reason problematic. This does not mean, of course, that a person literally incapable of speaking or without a full consciousness of his or her actions would have no rights at all. That would be an inhumane way of excluding people with a disability out of society, and this is clearly not what Ricoeur has in mind. His approach is foremost descriptive or anthropological. Keeping in mind the different capacities people can have, as well as the possibility of fallibility within these capacities, in principle we ascribe equal rights to persons who also control their actions to a certain extent. Individual freedom and responsibility comes with the capacity to speak for oneself, at least that is how we humans naturally look at it.

In a similar sense this is the case for action as well because action and speech are connected.[22] As Ricoeur asserts: "The capacity to designate oneself as the author of one's own actions is inscribed in a context of interaction where the other figures as my antagonist or my helper, in relations that vary between conflict and interaction."[23] In other words, the capacity to act is a second anthropological principle that supports the ascription of rights. It is only through action that interaction can take place and thus that we ascribe rights to each other. That is to say, through interaction we are able to communicate, cooperate, or possibly create conflict. Therefore, any kind of recognition of others, including the recognition of others as subjects of rights, implies interaction with others.

This occurs on an intersubjective level, when, for example, I explain to a friend the right of the freedom of speech. Yet, obviously, the ascription of rights occurs also on a social level, within the context of "large-scale organizations that structure interaction: technical systems, monetary and fiscal systems, juridical systems, bureaucratic systems, pedagogical systems, scientific systems, media systems, and so on."[24] A democratic society cannot do without these kinds of social structures, which organize the ascription of rights, ultimately through legal systems. Moreover, recognizing each other as persons capable of acting is an important condition for the ascription of rights, just as is the recognition of each other as speaking subjects, because in order to be responsible and to have rights as a responsible citizen we need to able to act for ourselves.

Having a narrative identity is the third anthropological feature that is a condition for the ascription of rights according to Ricoeur. As Ricoeur explains, institutions and social relations have their own events and histories, which can be told in stories, which are intertwined with each other: "Life stories are so intertwined with one another that the narrative anyone tells or hears of his own life becomes a segment of those other stories that are the narratives of others' lives. We may thus consider nations, peoples, classes, communities of every sort as institutions that recognize themselves as well as others through narrative identity."[25]

Put differently, given that democracies can only exist in the context of social relations, they also imply narratives, because narratives are created in social relations. People tell stories about their lives and the lives of others. That is how they interact and recognize each other as persons capable of speaking, acting and of living a personal life. People are not "person-machines" with a series of ready-made capacities to which correspond a series of rights. We become human persons more organically, by growing up and becoming a capable human being by living through a series of life events (education, family relations, friendship, etc.). Moreover, on the legal level, narratives play a significant role in that any verdict implies hearing the stories of the parties involved.

Finally, a democracy in which rights are attributed to its citizens requires a distribution of responsibility: "The other is implicated here [in relations of responsibility] in multiple ways: as beneficiary, as witness, as judge, and, more fundamentally, as the one who, in counting on me, on my capacity to keep my word, calls me to responsibility, renders me responsible."[26]

Just as it requires communication (speech and narrative) and organization (action), the ascription of rights implies assigning people responsibility to execute these tasks. Conversely, responsibility clearly is an important condition for being a subject of human rights. In order to be recognized as a person, capable of participating in the social relations that are part of a democratic society, and to be ascribed the rights that come with that, one is held responsible for one's actions in the society.

This responsibility has an ethical sense: recognition already occurs in natural human relations such as friendship, yet our actions have consequences for others and can potentially harm them. It also has a moral sense (and here is the difference between ethics and morals), because it relates to systems of written and unwritten codes and norms, such as respect for others. Finally, responsibility should be understood in a juridical sense: whatever one does in a democratic society has to comply with the rules of justice of that community, and one can be juridically prosecuted in case of a violation of those rules.

In sum, Ricoeur's understanding of the conditions for democracy and for the ascription of rights is, from a certain perspective, pragmatic. It is pragmatic first of all, because Ricoeur puts the accent on concrete *action* (as related to speech, narrativity and responsibility). Ricoeur's point is not so much that we should ascribe rights on the basis of an abstract metaphysical theory about the potential conditions of the ascription of rights, such as subjectivity or agency. Rather the opposite seems to be Ricoeur's point, namely that in a natural way we ascribe rights to each other while living our lives, and by interacting with each other. For example, to ascertain that a person is capable of particular responsibilities, one needs to communicate with this person, have a conversation, and perhaps hear some of the person's life story.

Secondly, Ricoeur's understanding of the ascription of rights is pragmatic also in that it is critical with regard to the risks of overformalization. Ricoeur of course recognizes the need for formal principles and rules; any just democracy would need institutions and formal structures in order to arrange the distribution of rights. However, the application of formal rules should consider concrete situations and problems. For example, mitigating factors imply the hearing of the defendant's story. Recognition of the autonomy and freedom of speech, to give another example, is an important aspect in the struggle against potential power abuse. By shifting between personalism (the natural understanding of others as persons) and formalism (the need for formal organizing principles for the ascription of rights), Ricoeur's pragmatic approach to rights thus assumes its shape. However, an important part of this understanding is, so I will argue in the final section of this chapter, a "detour" or reference to metaphysics, by which Ricoeur understands a consideration of the relation between the self and the other on a *meta* level, i.e., in a non-formalistic, non-personalistic, and non-pragmatic sense.

THE METAPHYSICAL OTHER

I have argued that Ricoeur's understanding of the ascription of rights is not primarily based on metaphysical speculation. Yet metaphysics is important as well for Ricoeur. How are both of these assertions reconcilable? We find a clue in Ricoeur's article on his metaphysics of otherness, "Uncanniness Many Times Over."[27] In this article Ricoeur defines metaphysics in line with Plato and Aristotle as "a second-order discourse" that aims for "hierarchization and differentiation stemming from the meta-function of metaphysics."[28] This means that metaphysics opens another discourse, a discourse that differs from the "standard" categorization of being, of how things are. For Ricoeur this means concretely that his "phenomenology of action" is better understood when complemented by a "phenomenology of alterity."[29] Understanding the capacities of the self (speech, action, narrativity, and responsibility) implies a discourse of otherness or a reference to that which is other than the self (e.g., speaking also implies listening to other people). In the remainder of this chapter I will argue that this phenomenology of otherness is also important for the understanding of the ascription of rights in legal systems, because this ascription implies an ascription of rights to minorities, who are different from the "standard" capable selves that participate in a democracy.

I have already suggested the significance of a reference to otherness for an understanding of the ascription of rights. Certain minorities are vulnerable even in a democratic context, because there is a risk that they are excluded or stigmatized in the context of democracies, insofar as formal democratic principles are misused for political reasons of power (e.g., the exclusion of international political refugees on the grounds of nationalist discourse). Moreover, a pragmatic description of democratic principles—even if it has the greatest possible attention to detail and concrete situations—cannot take into account all situations and all others, since there can always be a particular situation or minority case that is not covered by the system.

In "Uncanniness Many Times Over," Ricoeur offers a triple understanding of otherness, which allows addressing some of the problems of pragmatism.[30] The other should be understood for Ricoeur as the other of "the flesh," as "the stranger," and in the sense of "the voice of conscience."[31] It would lead me too far here to elaborate in detail Ricoeur's triple understanding of otherness, which I have already done in another context.[32] Instead, I will briefly indicate how each of these three understandings of otherness according to Ricoeur, otherness of the flesh, of other people, and of conscience, underline the importance of the consideration of minorities for the ascription of rights.

First of all, Ricoeur's concept of the flesh indicates that sensibility is the condition of our contact with the world. This notion designates that in experiences of the outside world, the body feels a certain kind of strangeness or resistance, which it cannot completely dominate.[33] Talking, acting, narrating, and being responsible occur while being affected by the world, and while having a sensation of the strangeness felt in the contact of one's own body with the world. For example, while talking to other people in a noisy room, one is affected by the noise and acts differently accordingly (e.g., raising one's voice, leave the room, etc.). Important for our purposes here is the idea that there remains something "strange," "mysterious," "unsaid" or *meta* in our encounters with the world as capable selves. We cannot completely anticipate, or make our own, everything we experience. This is the case when we act, speak, take decisions, and so on. We possibly make mistakes, can suffer ourselves, or are sometimes ignorant. This is also true on an institutional level, within the context of the ascription of rights. No political or institutional system exists that can completely consider every situation or reach total justice. Therefore, it is important, for a theory of the ascription of rights, to make a reference to the metaphysical aspect of reality, to indicate the inherently fallible character of any system and the possibility of the neglect of otherness.

In order to make this idea more concrete, we can bring pragmatism back into the discussion. Consider an aspect of pragmatism that James Bohman has termed "practical verification."[34] The idea is that a pragmatic theory of democracy should not be limited to defining formal democratic principles, but also have principles that allow for the practical verification of the democracy itself, i.e., the verification of whether it works or not. Freedom of speech, for instance, would be a senseless and counterproductive principle when limited to angry tweets, threats, and insults between politicians. Successful communication should also be legitimized and be recognized by the persons who are affected by it, which is of course different from censorship in that the communication has also a sense on its own, without becoming only a means for a hidden political or ideological agenda. For these reasons, democracies consist of formal structures that are capable of problematizing and of targeting domination.[35] Yet here the necessity of practical verification itself recalls the significance of a reference to a *meta* level. Formal democratic principles should be guarded over at a different level. They are to a certain extent insufficient in themselves. There is something that escapes them, an otherness that resists them.

This otherness becomes more specific when understood in a second sense, as the otherness of other people. According to Ricoeur, otherness manifests itself not only within our sensible contact with the external world but also in encounters with other people. We cannot take the place of others. We can communicate with others, yet we do not live their lives, and in that sense "each life" contains "a secret."[36] In other words, understanding of other occurs through interpretation. There is no foolproof system for the understanding of others, and thus any formal system designed to ascribe rights to others can fail to take into account certain situations, others, or minorities.

Consider as an example the 2018 incidents at the United States border with Mexico, in which the United States separated children of refugee families from their parents. The incidents resulted largely from the implementation of a formal zero-tolerance policy to prosecute systematically all illegal refugees who cross the border.[37] One of the problems in these incidents is that United States policy did not allow for the consideration of the particular cases of these minorities, because they "fall out of the legal system." Whether or not they have grounded political and social reasons for leaving their countries is simply put aside, because they are excluded on "legal" grounds. Clearly, legal systems are not always perfectly designed for the recognition of other people and contain the possibility of the system ignoring minorities who are not part of it but nevertheless claim its justice (e.g., the "America first" system). My point is that a description of the conditions of democracy and the ascription of rights merits inclusion of a metaphysical reference to the otherness of other people, because the recognition of others may require an exception of the system or point to a failure of it.

To be sure, I am neither arguing in favor of an abrogation of the rule of law nor in favor of partiality. Rather, my point is that the rule of law, as well as legal pragmatic defense mechanisms that guard over these rules, are salient for the ascription of rights in a democracy. As I argued above, this is shown by pragmatic theories of law, as well as by Ricoeur.[38] Nonetheless, just as defense mechanisms are important for guarding over the fairness of the rule of law, attention to minorities is important for justice. At times, this kind of attention can require an exception to the rule of law, for example, in cases when mitigating factors apply in court because an accused was in a minority position because of certain circumstances. Yet on other occasions, attention to minorities demands enforcing certain rules of law. To give an example from the European context, when the former Belgian federal secretary for migration, Theo Francken, put pressure on the Belgian parliament to reinstate migration quota out of budgetary concerns (limiting the amount of asylum requests to 50 a day), his voice was overruled by Belgium's Council of State, which judged that the former rule was illegal because it promoted inequality and injustice.[39] One might contend that this example contradicts my argument, according to which there should be room for otherness in legal systems. Indeed, it might seem that Francken is pleading for another—a different—rule that would facilitate integration processes in Belgium. However, Francken's plea is in fact a good example of a tendency of overformalization, in this case on the basis of economic reasons. It aims to install purely formal criteria and rules that organize asylum requests, yet in doing so neglects the difficulty refugees encounter when seeking asylum in Western Europe.[40] In this case, the rule of law, based on the principle of respect for humanity, neatly complements attention for otherness. Thus, attention to otherness may require exceptions to rules, but, paradoxically, may also require reinforcing certain rules. Justice implies finding the right balance between individuality and equality; it implies finding "a just distance,"[41] to use a well-known expression of Ricoeur.

Ricoeur's notion of conscience can illuminate further where to look for this kind of just distance. Ricoeur defines otherness in relation to conscience. Conscience, for Ricoeur, should not be understood simply in terms of remorse or having a bad conscience. Rather, the voice of conscience can be stimulated by all possible others that the self encounters: "Listening to the voice of conscience would signify being-enjoined by the Other."[42] Further, Ricoeur understands this call as a call "to live well with and for others in just institutions."[43] This means that Ricoeur understands conscience more in a hermeneutical than in a theological sense, i.e., as practical wisdom or the capability of interpretation in order to make decisions in ethical and moral life. The process of the ascription of rights takes place in several different ethical and moral contexts, that is, values, norms, and institutions. There is no one universal set of values or one true institutional system that would do the trick here. Hence, pragmatism's idea of practical verification. Nonetheless, this kind of practical wisdom echoes the notion of otherness or an attention to minorities who risk being overlooked by the system.

To return to the example of the refugees at the borders between Mexico and the United States, the United States government only started questioning its separation policy after receiving domestic and international criticism that called attention to the vulnerability of the families who were put through inhumane treatment. It is insufficient to recognize refugees as individuals only on a formal basis and to ascribe rights and obligations in this regard on the basis of only formal and economic criteria, without the consideration of the otherness of their specific situations as well as consideration of rules that promote respect of humanity. These considerations include taking into account the particular contexts in which the refugees' circumstances (the otherness of the world), their specific situations and life stories (the otherness of each person), and a fair judgment based on interpretation of their circumstances, such as respect for humanity or compassion (the otherness of conscience). This insufficiency shows the fallibility of legal systems, insofar as they are formal and therefore risk excluding otherness. Yet, more importantly, it also shows that law should inherently include a reference to otherness or take otherness into account. Legal discourse should be complemented by metadiscourse.

In conclusion, Ricoeur shows that the ascription of rights in democracy should be understood in a practical sense, i.e., based on the recognition of each citizen as a capable human being and therefore entitled to the rights of a capable human being (e.g., freedom of speech). In this sense, Ricoeur's understanding of rights aligns well with a pragmatic understanding of rights. However, Ricoeur also shows that practical democratic principles find their roots in ethico-anthropological relations. For example, justice as a principle is related to the recognition of others in more natural and basic relations such as love or friendship. In this respect, Ricoeur combines pragmatism with personalism, even though he also seems to reject each of these principles when understood on its own.

Yet democracy also has a metaphysical side for Ricoeur. Hence, he writes in his discussion of Rawls's theory of democracy that democracy requires not only a formal consensus but also "'metaphysical' conceptions of the good."[44] This does not mean that democracies should return to unpractical metaphysical beliefs. Instead, the metaphysical can be understood to be more in touch with reality as that which transcends the sphere of explicit formal rules and implies an aim for living well with others, a reference to otherness, which is important for each democracy, because of the risk of the exclusion of minorities through the system. *Meta* therefore does not refer to the category of the unreal, while the practical side of democracy should be reminded of its fallibility, of its own shortcomings, yet also its strong points, to consider all possible others, and therefore of the importance, within legal systems, of a constant reference to the *meta* level of the otherness that escapes institutional democracy.

NOTES

1. For example, Brendan Hogan, "Pragmatism, Power and the Situation of Democracy," *The Journal of Speculative Philosophy* 30, no. 1 (2016): 64–74; James Bohman, *Democracy Across Borders: From* Dêmos *to* Dêmoi (Boston: MIT Press, 2007).

2. Paul Ricoeur, "Who is the Subject of Rights?," in *The Just*, ed. David Pellauer (Chicago: University of Chicago Press, 2000), 1–10.

3. See, e.g., Hogan, "Pragmatism, Power and the Situation of Democracy."

4. Hogan, "Pragmatism, Power, and the Situation of Democracy," 66.

5. See, for examples, Alison Kadlec, *Dewey's Critical Pragmatism* (Lanham, Md.: Lexington Press, 2007); and Melvin Rogers, *The Undiscovered Dewey: Religion, Morality, and the Ethos of Democracy* (New York: Columbia University Press, 2012).

6. "Here's Donald Trump's Presidential Announcement Speech," *Time*, June 16, 2015, https://time.com/3923128/donald-trump-announcement-speech/ (describing Mexicans as drug dealers, criminals, and rapists).

7. Hence, he defends the idea in *Oneself as Another* that ethical life implies acting in "just institutions." Paul Ricoeur, *Oneself as Another*, trans. Kathleen Blamey (Chicago: University of Chicago Press, 1992), 172. His theory of the self as a person (capable of responsibility (and thus entitled to recognition)) is also based on a pragmatic theory of speech acts, according to which, being a person implies being capable of speaking and in that sense of performing and acting within the context of a linguistic community. Ricoeur, *Oneself as Another*, 40 ff.

8. Paul Ricoeur, "Uncanniness Many Times Over," in *Philosophical Anthropology*, eds. Johann Michel and Jérôme Porée, trans. David Pellauer (Cambridge, UK: Polity Press).

9. Marc de Leeuw, "Paul Ricœur's Search for a Just Community. The Phenomenological Presupposition of a Life 'with and for others,'" *Études Ricœuriennes/Ricœur Studies* 8, no. 2 (2017): 46–54.

10. Paul Ricoeur, *The Just*, trans. David Pellauer (Chicago and London: The University of Chicago Press, 2000); Paul Ricoeur, *Reflections on the Just* (Chicago and London: The University of Chicago Press, 2007).

11. Ricoeur, *The Just*, 1–10.

12. Ricoeur, *The Just*, 7.

13. Dries Deweer, *Ricoeur's Personalist Republicanism: Personhood and Citizenship* (London and New York: Lexington Books, 2017).

14. Ricoeur, *The Just*, 7.

15. Friendship and care for others are concepts that are part of his ethics. See Ricoeur, *Oneself as Another*, 169.

16. Ricoeur, *Oneself as Another*, 171.

17. A longer study would incorporate Ricoeur's separate attention to the subject of recognition, which I will not attempt to do here. See Paul Ricoeur, *The Course of Recognition*, trans. David Pellauer (Cambridge: Harvard University Press, 2005).

18. Ricoeur, *The Just*, 1. I will come back later to the difference Ricoeur makes between ethics and morality.

19. Ricoeur, *The Just*, 1.

20. Ricoeur, *The Just*, 6.

21. Ricoeur, *The Just*, 6.

22. Cf. Ricoeur's theory of speech acts in *Oneself as Another*.

23. Ricoeur, *The Just*, 6.

24. Ricoeur, *The Just*, 6–7.

25. Ricoeur, *The Just*, 7.

26. Ricoeur, *The Just*, 7.

27. Ricoeur, "Uncanniness Many Times Over," 254–68.

28. Ricoeur, "Uncanniness Many Times Over," 255.
29. Ricoeur, "Uncanniness Many Times Over," 265.
30. For Ricoeur's metaphysics of otherness, see also Ricoeur, *Oneself as Another*, 297–356.
31. Ricoeur, "Uncanniness Many Times Over," 259.
32. See Geoffrey Dierckxsens, *Paul Ricoeur's Moral Anthropology: Singularity, Responsibility and Justice* (London and New York: Lexington Books), 130–42.
33. Ricoeur, "Uncanniness Many Times Over," 259 ff.
34. See James Bohman, "Theories, Practices, and Pluralism: A Pragmatic Interpretation of Critical Social Science," *Philosophy of the Social Sciences* 29, no. 4 (1999): 466.
35. Hogan, "Pragmatism, Power and the Situation of Democracy," 73.
36. Ricoeur, "Uncanniness Many Times Over," 265.
37. "Why Are Families Being Separated at the US Border?," *The Guardian*, June 18, 2018, https://www.theguardian.com/us-news/2018/jun/18/why-are-families-being-separated-at-the-us-border-explainer.
38. One can stress here once more Ricoeur's emphasis on the need of moral as well as legal obligations and rules to complement ethics. See Ricoeur, *Oneself as Another*, 203 ff.
39. See "Flemish Nationalist Pushes for Reinstatement of Asylum Quotas," *The Brussels Times*, July 10, 2019, https://www.brusselstimes.com/belgium/61756/europes-largest-public-artwork-to-be-unveiled-in-belgium/.
40. See the following article in Dutch, "Raad van State: 'Asielquotum dat Theo Francken Invoerde, is Onwettig,'" *Knack*, December 20, 2018, https://www.knack.be/nieuws/belgie/raad-van-state-asielquotum-dat-theo-francken-invoerde-is-onwettig/article-normal-1409441.html.
41. Ricoeur, *The Just*, 134–40.
42. Ricoeur, *Oneself as Another*, 351.
43. Ricoeur, *Oneself as Another*, 351.
44. Ricoeur, *The Just*, 73.

BIBLIOGRAPHY

"Flemish Nationalist Pushes for Reinstatement of Asylum Quotas." *The Brussels Times*, July 10, 2019. https://www.brusselstimes.com/belgium/61756/europes-largest-public-artwork-to-be-unveiled-in-belgium/.

"Here's Donald Trump's Presidential Announcement Speech." *Time*, June 16, 2015. https://time.com/3923128/donald-trump-announcement-speech/.

"Raad van State: 'Asielquotum dat Theo Francken Invoerde, is Onwettig.'" *Knack*, December 20, 2018. https://www.knack.be/nieuws/belgie/raad-van-state-asielquotum-dat-theo-francken-invoerde-is-onwettig/article-normal-1409441.html.

"Why Are Families Being Separated at the US Border?" *The Guardian*, June 18, 2018. https://www.theguardian.com/us-news/2018/jun/18/why-are-families-being-separated-at-the-us-border-explainer.

Bohman, James. *Democracy Across Borders: From* Dêmos *to* Dêmoi. Boston: MIT Press, 2007.
Bohman, James. "Theories, Practices, and Pluralism: A Pragmatic Interpretation of Critical Social Science." *Philosophy of the Social Sciences* 29, no. 4 (1999): 459–80.
De Leeuw, Marc. "Paul Ricoeur's Search for a Just Community. The Phenomenological Presupposition of a Life 'with and for Others.'" Études Ricœuriennes/Ricœur Studies 8, no. 2 (2017): 46–54.
Deweer, Dries. *Ricoeur's Personalist Republicanism: Personhood and Citizenship*. London and New York: Lexington Books, 2017.
Dierckxsens, Geoffrey. *Paul Ricoeur's Moral Anthropology: Singularity, Responsibility and Justice*. London and New York: Lexington Books, 2017.
Hogan, Brendan. "Pragmatism, Power and the Situation of Democracy." *The Journal of Speculative Philosophy* 30, no. 1 (2016): 64–74.
Kadlec, Alison. *Dewey's Critical Pragmatism*. Lanham, MD: Lexington Press, 2007.
Ricoeur, Paul. *The Course of Recognition*. Translated by David Pellauer. Cambridge: Harvard University Press, 2005.
Ricoeur, Paul. *The Just*. Translated by David Pellauer. Chicago and London: The University of Chicago Press, 2000.
Ricoeur, Paul. *Oneself as Another*. Translated by Kathleen Blamey. Chicago: University of Chicago Press, 1992.
Ricoeur, Paul. *Philosophical Anthropology*. Edited by Johann Michel and Jérôme Porée, translated by David Pellauer. Cambridge, UK: Polity Press, 2016.
Ricoeur, Paul. *Reflections on the Just*. Chicago and London: The University of Chicago Press, 2007.
Ricoeur, Paul. "Uncanniness Many Times Over." In *Philosophical Anthropology: Writings and Lectures*, vol. 3, edited by Johann Michel and Jérôme Porée, translated by David Pellauer 254–68. Cambridge (UK): Polity Press, 2015.
Ricoeur, Paul. "Who is the Subject of Rights?" In *The Just*, edited by David Pellauer 1–10. Chicago: University of Chicago Press, 2000.
Rogers, Melvin. *The Undiscovered Dewey: Religion, Morality, and the Ethos of Democracy*. New York: Columbia University Press, 2012.

Chapter Ten

Between Truth and Justice

Ricoeur on the Roles and Limits of Narrative in Legal Processes

Marie-Hélène Desmeules

Ricoeur is mainly known for his analyses of the narrative process and for the functions he attributed to it in his hermeneutic of the self.[1] In his work, however, he was a long way from limiting his methodological considerations to narrative or having blind faith in it. On the contrary, in order to counter potential misuses, Ricoeur constantly took care to link narrative to a set of other processes, and thus steered clear of any form of methodological reductionism.[2] We believe this is what grants strength and singularity to his methodological contributions in the domains of history, literature, and law.

What we would like to show is how Ricoeur justified the necessity of linking narrative in legal processes to various other methodological phases. The basic idea in the following pages is that both the furtherance of and competition between the two aims at work in legal processes (that is, the aim of truth and the aim of justice) justify our adding complexity to the methodological considerations that Ricoeur developed bearing in mind first and foremost the work of the historian. Thus, if Ricoeur explicitly proposed to apply to the judicial process the three methodological phases that must accompany the historian in his or her aim of truth, we will see that this schema valid for history cannot simply be transposed to the domain of law. For what was presented in history as solutions to resistances to its aim of truth is undermined by the introduction of an aim of justice.

We will examine this issue by reorganizing Ricoeur's thesis under three headings: assessment of the truth of the facts in dispute, the search for the applicable rule of law, and the application of the rule of law to the facts in dispute. We shall see that, according to Ricoeur, narrative brings a particular type of intelligibility to the facts in dispute, allowing us to form a cluster of disparate elements into a single meaningful unit—the story. However, narrative also comes with its dangers, including that of opposing, through the closing of the text, a resistance to the aim of truth (to judge what *really* happened) that runs through the trial. It is to address this resistance that Ricoeur appeals to the explanation/understanding and documentary phases. To these two phases he will also add the interpretation/argumentation phase, supposed to counterbalance certain discretionary powers held by the judge. But these phases will not come without opposing their own resistances, this time against the aim of justice pursued by legal processes. To explain, to argue, and to document further is, in a sense, to exonerate further.

However, we will suggest in the last section that the application of the rules of law will likely weaken these new resistances by demarcating and revealing precisely what components of past facts relate to justice properly speaking. The legal norm will thus acquire not only a practical function (that is, differentiating a legal action from an illegal action) but also an important epistemological function regarding narrative, explanation, argumentation and documentation.

NARRATIVE AND ASSESSMENT OF THE TRUTH OF THE FACTS IN DISPUTE

The first heading under which we would like to study the function performed by narrative in legal processes is the assessment of the truth of the facts presented by the parties in dispute. Here the judge must not only decide upon an applicable law and its application to the facts in dispute, but he or she must also make a decision in favor of a certain version of these facts. A truth intention is thus attached to his or her work.

However, anyone who wishes to examine the role that Ricoeur attributes to narrative in assessing the truth of the facts in dispute is faced with a first difficulty. When Ricoeur discusses the narration of past events, he mainly conceives the latter in relation to the role it plays for the historian. According to Ricoeur, to the extent that judges and historians face a similar intention—judging and telling *what really happened*—and that it is in relation to this intention that the narrative is necessary (i.e., to give a certain intelligibility to what really happened), then narrative developments in the work of the historian can be transposed to that of the judge.[3]

Ricoeur's central idea, whose strength we wish to restore as a first step, is that the narrative configuration of past facts enhances their intelligibility. Narrative and, more broadly, all scriptural forms of historiography "do not limit themselves to giving a linguistic covering to an understanding of the past that would already be wholly constituted and ready made."[4] They themselves provide past facts with a particular form of intelligibility. In that sense, Ricoeur does not subsume the contribution of narrative under another type of intelligibility; it is not a matter, for example, of making narrative a category of explanation/understanding. Nor is it a matter of dissolving the particularities of narrative within a broader genre, such as writing or literature. So, to narrate a story is not to describe a scene,[5] even if both gestures belong to what Ricoeur calls "scriptural representation."[6] Lastly, nor is it, as we will see, to exclude other types of intelligibility in favor of the narrative. Narrative participates in one of the three phases of reconstructing past facts in legal processes.[7]

What, then, is this intelligibility peculiar to the fact that past facts are not simply reported, explained, and proven but take place within a story that is being told? Ricoeur notes:

> What it itself brings is what I have called a synthesis of the heterogeneous, in order to speak of the coordination between multiple events, or between causes, intentions, and also accidents within a single meaningful unity. The plot is the literary form of this coordination. It consists in guiding a complex action from an initial situation to a terminal one by means of rule-governed transformations that lend themselves to an appropriate formulation within the framework of narratology.[8]

The function of narrative would therefore consist in bringing together and organizing under one sole and comprehensible unity of meaning disparate, or even discordant, elements.[9] The story that we tell and that we follow serves as a guiding thread in the organization of the heterogeneous.

Among these elements coordinated in order for us to be able to follow a story, Ricoeur first mentions events, causes, intentions and accidents. He also adds in a second step those that acted and suffered what happened in the story, that is, the characters. And since Ricoeur's concerns at this stage have to do with the place occupied by narrative *in the work of the historian*, he also mentions that all elements coming from the documentary phase and the explanation/understanding phase (to be discussed in our next section) can be coordinated, as this is precisely what is available to tell the story of what happened.[10] In that sense narrative can, for example, serve to coordinate structures, conjunctures and events,[11] or the interplays of history on a small scale (village, individuals, short time periods, etc.) with history on a grand scale (nation, long periods of time, etc.).[12] Historians "narrativize" these variations of scales peculiar to the explanation/understanding phase of the historiographical operation.

Would it then be possible to transpose the function performed by narration in the historiographical operation to the legal process itself?

In a sense, it is true that participants in a trial are not just facing a cluster or series of facts proven in court. They are linked in the form of a story, a narrative linkage traces of which we find especially when the parties present their versions of the facts during the pleadings,[13] in the narrative account of the facts produced by the judge when rendering his or her judgment, or during the testimonies—even if the witnesses are limited in their inclination to narrate what happened by the question-answer structure to which they are bound.

The enhanced intelligibility that facts acquire through these narratives is particularly significant in the context of the legal process. Indeed, the order of presentation of evidence does not necessarily follow an intelligible order. For instance, in the case of testimonies, the evidence presented follows the order of appearance of the witnesses and not the order of what happened. Several witnesses may testify to the same thing from different perspectives. One witness may repeat himself or herself several times during the examination and the cross-examination. Witnesses also on some occasions testify to events that are disparate and temporally disconnected, which do not seem at first sight to have links between them. Witnesses are also required to give their testimony in the form of answers to the questions that are directed to them; they cannot simply and freely tell the story of what they have witnessed. And if things are so, it is due to certain cardinal principles of justice, such as fairness. Thus, if every witness is required to answer twice—during examination and cross-examination—it is because we consider this a way of checking his or her credibility (will the witness contradict himself or herself?), but also because the right of each party to present his or her own evidence is essential to the fairness of the trial.

The capacity to pull all of these elements together—which are as we have suggested all the more disparate as they are presented according to the rules of legal procedure—and to give them an intelligible form therefore appears essential. It is for this reason that narrative plays such an important role in legal processes. Every element can be taken up and coordinated to advance the story, going from an initial situation to a final one. The story would thus serve as an Ariadne's thread for one to orient oneself in the various pieces of evidence presented during a trial.

RESISTANCES OF NARRATIVE
AGAINST THE AIM OF TRUTH

Yet despite the enhanced intelligibility it provides, Ricoeur also recognizes that there are limits to narrative. Unlike fiction, legal processes, like history, are characterized by Ricoeur as having a certain intentional aim: that of giving an account of what *really* happened. Ricoeur's developments regarding the role of narrative within historiography take place in a "progressive dramatization" of this intentional aim.[14] This is because narrative, just like rhetoric and the powerful images that are part of the representation of history, opposes a certain resistance to the intention of telling what really happened.[15]

The specific resistance of narrative to the intention of referring to what really happened stems from the fact that a narrative can easily, by virtue of its constitution as an intelligible unit, close in on itself and no longer refer to any extra-narrative reality. In this sense, Ricoeur repeatedly speaks of a true "tendency to closure" of the narrative, by virtue of which "the very act of recounting comes to split off from that 'real' thereby put in parentheses."[16]

In the weak sense, what this means is that the text does not need to refer to reality in order to make sense, which is what fiction tells us.[17] But in the strong sense, this can also mean that the narrative tends to recover everything for itself. By that we mean not only that everything can be incorporated into the narrative, but more importantly, that everything gains a new meaning in relation to its function in the narrative. Ricoeur insisted in this sense on the *narrative* redefinition of events: "On the narrative plane, the event is what, in happening, advances the action" whether the event is sudden or long-lasting.[18] What this means is that if, as Ricoeur has not specifically done, we transpose this idea to the level of the assessment of the facts in legal dispute, then the proven facts, which are now configured according to a storyline, will have the specific function of contributing to the *progression of a story,* and no longer that of determining the guilt or responsibility of an individual. In the same way, the "characters" are also redefined on the narrative level: if they "perform and suffer," Ricoeur tells us that it is "from the action recounted."[19] Transposed to the legal plane, what this means is that what we hold onto with regard to the parties to a trial is how they participate in the advancement of a story, and no longer exclusively the fact that they are litigants. If we extend the text's tendency to closure to the assessment of the facts in legal dispute, it means that unless we reduce the specifically legal features of both the events and the litigants to the function they perform in the advancing the story, these legal features will always be considered extra-textual references, which narrative (in so far as it forms a circle with itself) can and tends to leave aside.

These resistances to the closing of the text are intensified, or so it seems, by the fact that narrative comes with its own criteria of evaluation. Ricoeur speaks little of this, except when he addresses the question of rhetoric's power of persuasion: rhetoric persuades by revealing something plausible, something probable.[20] But narrative also has its own criteria of evaluation. We appeal here to research conducted by Pennington and Hastie, which allowed them to identify the criteria used by judges and juries in evaluating narratives of the facts in dispute. According to Pennington and Hastie's results, judges and juries usually choose the story offering the greatest coverage of proven facts and they are more confident in their choice if the story is the only one possible, if it is unique.[21] They also prefer the story that is the most coherent, that is, the one that is the most consistent, plausible, and complete.[22] Among these criteria, two of the components of the coherence criterion (consistency and completeness) appear to us to depend on what Ricoeur meant by "closure of the text."[23] Consistency means that a story will appear all the more likely "that it does not contain internal contradictions," namely, "with other parts of the explanation."[24] That is to say that it is all the more likely that it will stand on its own. Completeness means that the story will be all the more likely "when the expected structure of the story 'has all its parts.'"[25] Pennington and Hastie thus think that every narrative structure must integrate an initial situation, physical and mental states, motivations and goals, actions and consequences. Ricoeur would add that a story must contain all the events and characters necessary for the advancement of the story. But here again, this criterion of evaluation still does not imply any opening of the narrative onto what is exterior to itself. A narrative can very well have "all its parts" and contain no internal contradictions without referring to an extra-linguistic reality.

If we add to this the fact that judges and juries tend to infer facts that complete their narratives even if they have not been proven in court,[26] then we have managed, it seems to us, to make explicit the type of resistance that the closing of the text can oppose to the referential aim of legal processes, that is, to decide upon what really happened.

How does Ricoeur claim to respond to this resistance opposed by narrative in legal processes? His solution will be the same as the one suggested in the case of historiography: if "all the narratives are not equivalent" and there is always "a more plausible, more likely version,"[27] it is because in court, as in historiography, the most plausible story will be the one that best fits the documentary phase and the explanation/understanding phase of the trial.[28]

A first exit from the closure of the text would thus be made possible by the fact that the narrative must recount the facts proven in court through the testimonies and the material evidence presented. It is not simply a matter of freely following a storyline, but of following a storyline within the bounds of the evidence available. What Pennington and Hastie's research also illustrated through the criteria of coverage was that the more a narrative covers the whole of the facts proven in court, the more convincing it will be; the more a narrative closes in on itself without looking to cover the facts proven in court, the less convincing it will be.

The second exit from the text's tendency to closure could come from its linkage to the explanation/understanding phase, by which Ricoeur understands the form of intelligibility that is acquired when we try to explain "why things happened like that and not otherwise" giving answers that involve "multiple uses of the connective 'because.'"[29] In *From Text to Action*, Ricoeur says of explanation that it "is what allows us to continue to follow a story when spontaneous understanding is impeded," and that in explanation one does "not aim to place a case under a law but to interpose a law in a narrative, in an effort to set understanding in motion again."[30] In other words, it is a matter of overcoming our lack of understanding by explaining, notably through generalities and regularities, the action being recounted.[31] In *Memory, History, Forgetting*, Ricoeur will add that the answer "because" can refer not only to laws and general regularities, but also to an understanding of the motivations and intentions of another person:

> On the one side, the series of repeatable facts of quantitative history lend themselves to a causal analysis and to the establishing of regularities that draw the idea of a cause, in the sense of efficacy, toward that of lawfulness, toward the model of the "if . . . then" relation. On the other side, the behavior of social agents, responding to the pressure of social norms by diverse maneuvers of negotiation, justification, or denunciation, draw the idea of a cause toward the side of explanation in terms of "reasons for. . . ."[32]

Causal explanation and understanding of intentions and motives would thus both be part of the "the full range of modes of explanation likely to make human interactions intelligible."[33] But that means that these modes of explanation have the effect of limiting what we can recount. The narrative cannot make a circle with itself to the point of going against what can be explained and understood of human interactions. It must remain, to speak in terms of the criteria identified by Pennington and Hastie, plausible, that is, coherent with what we know about human interactions.

THE SEARCH FOR THE APPLICABLE RULE OF LAW

Unfortunately, Ricoeur elaborated very little on the way in which the documentary and explanation/understanding phases are linked to narrative *in the specific case of legal processes*. However, the latter includes a specific aim—the aim of justice—which undermines the pure and simple application of a solution to the resistance of narrative which applies first and foremost to history. For this reason, it must be remembered that unlike history, legal processes imply the application of a rule of law, which presents its own challenges. Above all, we think that this rule of law may provide an answer to some of the tensions raised by the application of the three phases of historiography to the legal processes and specifically related to the aim of justice that these three phases pursue.

Until now, we have examined only the function and the limits of the narrative with respect to the assessment of the truth of the facts in dispute. Ricoeur, then strongly influenced by Dworkin, attributed another function to narrative: that of participating in the determination of the rule of law applicable to a situation in dispute.

In fact, Ricoeur insists, thereby generalizing Dworkin's problem of *hard cases* to all legal processes (and rejecting any form of naïve legal positivism), that the rule of law according to which a case in dispute should be judged is not given in advance. According to Ricoeur, the answer to the question of what is the applicable and appropriate norm for a case in dispute—"under what rule should a particular case be placed?"[34]—is a real problem for the protagonists in a legal dispute. A portion of the judge's work is to search for the rule of law under which to subsume the situation in dispute, work that is listed under the Kantian reflective judgment.

As Ricoeur emphasizes, this problem is all the more pressing as he wishes to resolve it without the choice of the norm being based solely on the subjective power of the judge, whether arbitrary or legislative.[35] There exists, according to Ricoeur, a certain rule of law that is more suitable for a case in dispute.[36] The question is then one of knowing by which processes the judge and the protagonists ensure the *objectively* adequate character of the choice of the norm appropriate to a case in dispute. It is for this reason, we believe, that he rightfully qualifies this problem and its solution as "epistemological."[37]

It is within the framework of this search for the rule of law most appropriate to a case in dispute that Ricoeur deploys a phase that he calls the "interpretation/argumentation" phase. He then says that this phase is analogous to the "explanation/understanding" phase,[38] because it responds to resistances opposed by the judge's arbitrary or discretionary power to the aim of justice in much the same way as the "explanation/understanding" phase responded to resistances opposed to the referential aim of history. They both exercise a *critical* function.[39] However, this analogy should not mask the differences that remain between these two phases. For example, the "explanation/understanding" phase had to overcome the dangers linked to the narration of past events. Here narrative, thanks to the objectivity of the narrative text, comes to be included in the "interpretation/argumentation" phase, and thus itself participates in the criticism. And if this displacement is permitted, it is because it is not the narrative with its tendency to closure that here threatens the legal process and its aims, but the *subjective* power of the judge.

In this context, what does Ricoeur mean by "interpretation"? In *The Just*, Ricoeur (following Dworkin) puts interpretation into operation for the first time when it comes to determining *the meaning* of the applicable rule of law. This meaning would not be given in advance, especially because a certain equivocation would taint any rule of law.[40] But where legal positivism suggests determining this meaning either by referring to the intention of the legislator, or by leaving to the discretion of the judge the power to decide, Dworkin and Ricoeur, following in his footsteps, suggest that the interpretation of the meaning of the law is built on the connection of appropriateness between a particular rule of law and the whole historical development—past and future—of law, in short, between a part and the whole to which it belongs. It is at this stage that the idea of a narrative coherence of the historical development of law is deployed with Ricoeur recalling that "Dworkin has recourse to the fable of a chain of narrators, each one adding his chapter to the redaction of a story, where no one narrator determines the global meaning, which however each one must presume, if he adopts as a rule the search for maximal coherence."[41] Narrative would serve as a model for understanding the interpretive work of the judge, which is then linked, as was the case in *From Text to Action*, to the ability to follow but also to contribute to a story. Above all, the objectivity of the meaning accorded to the law would in this way be guaranteed by "a double surety: that of precedents, on the one hand, and that of the presumed aim of the juridical whole in the course of elaboration, on the other."[42] These are guarantees that are both—it is important to understand this—objective limits to the subjective power of the judge.

Yet, Ricoeur's strategy, surpassing that of Dworkin's, is not to be satisfied with the resources of interpretation, but also to deploy the resources that argumentation can oppose to the arbitrariness of the judge's discretionary power.[43] In "The Just Between the Legal and the Good," Ricoeur insists on the fact that during a trial, each party presents arguments *for* or *against* the different positions defended, and thanks to which they hope to justify their own position.[44] The recourse to arguments aims then to convince the judge, but without falling into sophistry and "its power to please and seduce."[45] Legal arguments are certainly not irrefutable or logically necessary pieces of evidence, nor are they compelling like mathematical proofs.[46] Yet, they are nevertheless more or less good—or to speak in Ricoeur's terms—more or less plausible and probable. Here Ricoeur is drawing legal arguments closer to the "*logic of the probable*" and Aristotelian rhetoric.[47] If the judge's decision is not arbitrary, it is because he or she can (or must) rely on the best arguments presented to him or her: "But, in order not to be arbitrary, [the judgment exercised in a particular situation] must draw its justification from the deliberation that it ends and the argumentative quality of that deliberation."[48] We should add that in the article "Interpretation and/or Argumentation," Ricoeur also asserts (this time following Habermas) that argumentation is directed towards a certain horizon that we allow ourselves to qualify as "objective," namely, that of "universal consensus," the "correctness" of the arguments presented, and so their quality, depending on their acceptability for a community.[49] Argumentation, and more specifically the probative strength and acceptability of the arguments, is also presented as a solution to the problem of the arbitrary character of the judge's decision-making power.

If we were to stop here, we might have the impression that Ricoeur's reflection on legal processes is split in two. The aim of truth does not exhaust the referential aim of the legal process: an aim of justice also flows through it. And a particular threat accompanies each of these two aims. On the one hand, it is the closing of the text that threatens the aim of truth and the appreciation of what really happened. On the other hand, it is the arbitrary power of the judge that threatens the aim of justice within the legal process, and, with it, the appropriateness of the rule he or she decides to apply. However, and this is what we are now proposing to examine, these two aims are interrelated and not disjointed in legal processes.

THE RULE OF LAW AND ITS EPISTEMOLOGICAL FUNCTION

We have already insisted on the idea that Ricoeur's developments of the assessment of past facts were first thought out according to the framework and the constraints of the historian's task. If Ricoeur announced an analogy between the phases of historiography and those at work in the judge's activity, he did not specify how this solution should work in the latter case.

The introduction of an additional aim—the aim of justice—which is absent from the historiographic process, occurs not without rendering such a transposition difficult. This difficulty results from the fact that the explanation/understanding phase and the documentary phase, which were originally supposed to constitute responses to the resistances opposed by narrative to the trial's aim of truth, must in fact be considered limited because of the aim of justice pursued by the trial.

It is in *Memory, History, Forgetting*, more specifically in the section entitled "The Historian and the Judge," that Ricoeur explicitly describes the tension between these two phases and the trial's aim of truth. "The legal stage is limited in principle," states Ricoeur, as it is a matter of judging "specific actions," that is, the "distinct and identifiable contribution of the protagonists," as well as individuals to whom these actions can be attributed.[50] The possibility of indicting someone would be directly dependent on one's ability to accurately isolate the prohibited conduct and to attribute it to an individual.

However, the explanation/understanding phase tends to breach this limitation. The "why" of human actions, as we have mentioned, is explained by laws and general regularities, but also by the currents or historical circumstances in which they are inscribed. Thus, an explanation introduces elements that are part of a context wider than the attribution of an action to an agent, to his or her desire and act. "Among the circumstances of the action," Ricoeur tells us, "will be included influences, pressures, constraints, and, in the background, the great social disorders"[51] which explains *why* an agent acted in this way. But the risk involved, he says, is "the exonerating effect of the excessive accommodation to circumstances."[52] Considering the action the result of larger historical processes is tantamount to no longer attributing it to the agent who committed it, but rather, to attributing it to circumstances or causes that go beyond the agent. This is why, recalls Ricoeur, the explanation and its appeal to external circumstances are often used as a defense.[53]

In a similar way, Ricoeur defends the idea that argumentation can also have an exculpatory effect. In *Memory, History, Forgetting*, it is the equal sharing of the rights to speak between the parties that tends to put on an equal footing the claims of the plaintiff and the defendant:

> By distributing the right to speak equally between the advocates on both sides, and by permitting the opposing narrations and arguments to be heard through this procedural rule, does not the court encourage the practice of a historically "balanced" judgment, tilting to the side of moral equivalence and, ultimately, to the side of exoneration?[54]

But the exculpatory effect of argumentation is not limited to the above. Elsewhere Ricoeur had already insisted that argumentation falls within the bounds of an ethics of discussion, which regulates the equal right to speak, but is also accompanied by the duty to recognize that the other party may have a better argument. To argue is to accept having to get behind the better argument, even when it refutes our own demand for justice.[55]

It therefore appears to us that explanation and argumentation, because they equate the complaint with circumstantial explanations and contrary arguments, lead to the suspension of a decision in indecision. And indecision must lead towards exoneration because of the presumption of innocence (in criminal cases) or the burden of proof most often lying with the plaintiff. To explain and to argue more, we could say, is also to exculpate more.

It could be tempting to use the documentary phase as a counterweight to these new resistances opposed to the aim of justice. To document more would be to judge better.

Yet, the documentary phase resists in its own way the aim of justice. Ricoeur himself suggested that the widening of the documentary evidence was a corollary to explanation by causes and reasons that are ever further from the accused.[56] The documentary phase would thus participate, at least indirectly, in the exculpatory effect of explanation. We also find this conflict between the aim of justice and the documentary phase in a recent debate, on which Ricoeur did not explicitly comment. Some consider that trials should adopt a "free regime of proof," so as to prevent judges and juries from inferring facts that are inaccurate, but that are essential to the narratives they construct of the facts in dispute.[57] Ricoeur, it seems to us, would most likely have endorsed this widening of the documentary evidence, which—one must remember—should, in his eyes, respond to the resistance opposed by the closing of our narratives to the trial's aim of truth. However, other writers have pointed out that one's assessment of the plausibility of narratives is influenced by the prejudices, myths, and stereotypes that one maintains.[58] Elements of evidence can therefore be prejudicial if they reinforce these generalizations in which we believe, leading us to wrongly choose a narrative sequence that serves them, and thus deceives us. Whether because the documentary phase takes us away from the case in dispute, or because it feeds our prejudices and stereotypes, documenting more is sometimes to exonerate or to wrongfully rule.

If we add the above-mentioned resistance that narrative itself opposes to the aim of justice—presenting events and characters not according to their properly legal content, but according to their contribution to the advancement of the story—then it is every methodological phase proposed by Ricoeur that appears problematic in relation to the idea of justice.

We will understand if the reader continues to find unsatisfactory the solution that Ricoeur explicitly proposed for these exonerating effects. His solution was, paradoxically, to appeal to the explanation/understanding phase and to the documentary phase, even though it is precisely these phases (as we have just noted) that bring their own package of resistances to the trial's aim of justice.[59]

However, Ricoeur has, it seems to us, at least sketched out another solution. If the aim of justice can win back its rights against the resistance opposed by all these methodological phases, it is mainly because of the particular "visibility" that rules of law give to the facts in dispute when they are applied to them. Ricoeur states:

> The trial begins by putting on stage the alleged facts with a view to representing them outside of their sheer having occurred and to making visible the infraction committed in relation to the rule of law. . . . Past acts are therefore represented solely in terms of the nature of the charges selected prior to the actual trial.[60]

There are at least two ways to interpret this passage. This particular visibility may simply mean that *already determined* facts obtain a supplementary qualification (i.e., legal/illegal; or just/unjust) following the application of a rule of law. For this reason, Ricoeur speaks of a simple "convergence," at the time of the verdict, between the interpretation of the facts and that of the appropriateness of the rule of law,[61] as if the rule of law were not already at work in the interpretation of the facts, but that interpretation happened to come across the rule of law at the end of its own journey by simply adding its own qualifications to the facts.

Elsewhere, however, Ricoeur mentions a "mutual condition[ing]" of the interpretation of facts and the interpretation of the norm.[62] He then asserts that "reading it [the personal story of an accused] in such a way is already oriented by the presumption that such interconnectedness places the case under some rule."[63] This means that there is a constant entanglement—and not a simple convergence—between the visibility of the facts and the rule of law.

Within this entanglement, the rule of law seems to act primarily as a norm of relevance for the facts in dispute. "The legal stage is limited in principle," said Ricoeur, because of "the prior selection of the protagonists and of the acts alleged."[64] But where does this preliminary selection come from, if not from the rule of law itself? Since it defines (in legislative texts or within precedents) the constituent elements of the offenses, the crimes, the rights, the obligations and so forth, the rule of law has the effect of delimiting precise facts and protagonists that can and should be staged during the litigation. A rule of law establishes that X does not have the right to do φ to Y, or that Y is entitled to α—and it is therefore on elements X, Y, φ and α that the legal process must concentrate. It must concentrate, for example, on the relationships between a landlord and a tenant, between an employer and an employee, between a murderer and a victim, as well as on certain facts: the presence or absence of good faith, premeditation, harassment, contract, consent, and so forth. Thus, evidence may be said to be "inadmissible" not only in relation to its probative value—as in the case, for example, of hearsay—but also because it is irrelevant with regard to the rules of law that are applied: it is not a matter of judging *that*.

What this means is that the legal corpus can act as a defense against the body of explanation, argumentation and documentation, the undue expansion of which is a threat, as we have seen, to a trial's aim of justice. When it comes to explaining, arguing and documenting, it is specifically about the constituent elements of the rule of law.

The legal corpus also imposes its constraints on the narratives of facts in dispute. Whereas from a narrative point of view the relevance of the facts and the characters is determined by their contribution to the advancement of a story, from a legal point of view it is determined by their connection to the constituent elements of the offenses, rights, and principles defined by the rule of law. Some will be included and others excluded, even if it does not make a "good" story or even if it does not contribute to the story's advancement. Most importantly, the rule of law colors the way in which these facts will have to be narrated. If, as Ricoeur suggests, there is a "multitude of ways" of telling a story,[65] the application of the rule of law has the effect of retaining only that which shows the specifically legal features of the dispute. It thus regulates the visibility of what is properly legal.

CONCLUSION

It goes without saying that this brief exposition will not have exhausted all of Ricoeur's reflections on the entanglement between narrative and law. Just think of how each of the protagonists will have to reintegrate this legal process into the narratives they make of their own lives.[66] Or consider the way in which certain legal processes are, as Ricoeur thought, stakeholders in the collective history, which is itself represented in narrative form.[67] Our purpose, however, was to link narrative to the epistemological challenges of legal processes, which, as we have noted, were of two kinds: those concerning the assessment of the truth of the facts in dispute, and those concerning the determination of the norm applicable to the dispute. Drawing on Ricoeur, we have observed that the methodological phases, which were presented as solutions to the narrative's resistance to the trial's aim of truth, nevertheless jeopardized its aim of justice. We have learned from the application of the rule of law to the facts in dispute that the rule of law could itself represent a counterweight to the resistances opposed to a trial's double aim of truth and of justice. This meant, however, that the legal norm is not limited to regulating which of our actions are legally correct. From an epistemological point of view, the legal norm also regulates what is to be seen in the trial, and so the scope and the content of the explanations, argumentations, documentations, and narratives at play.

Translated by Laura Kassar and Karl Racette

NOTES

1. Paul Ricoeur, *Time and Narrative*, trans. Kathleen McLaughlin Blamey and David Pellaeur, 3 volumes (Chicago: University of Chicago Press, 1984, 1985, 1988); Paul Ricoeur, *Oneself as Another*, trans. Kathleen Blamey (Chicago: University of Chicago Press, 1992).

2. Paul Ricoeur, *Memory, History, Forgetting*, trans. Kathleen Blamey and David Pellaeur (Chicago: University of Chicago Press, 2004), 236–37, 238, 277–78.
3. Ricoeur, *Memory, History, Forgetting*, 325.
4. Ricoeur, *Memory, History, Forgetting*, 275.
5. The difference between narrative and description can be enlightened by the difference between what Ricoeur calls the "picture" and the "sequence." Ricoeur, *Memory, History, Forgetting*, 262.
6. Ricoeur, *Memory, History, Forgetting*, 236.
7. Ricoeur, *Memory, History, Forgetting*, 325.
8. Ricoeur, *Memory, History, Forgetting*, 243.
9. Ricoeur, *Time and Narrative* (vol. 1), 43.
10. Ricoeur, *Memory, History, Forgetting*, 244.
11. Ricoeur, *Memory, History, Forgetting*, 245–46.
12. Ricoeur, *Memory, History, Forgetting*, 244–45.
13. Ricoeur, *Memory, History, Forgetting*, 325.
14. Ricoeur, *Memory, History, Forgetting*, 238.
15. Ricoeur, *Memory, History, Forgetting*, 237.
16. Ricoeur, *Memory, History, Forgetting*, 276.
17. Ricoeur, *Memory, History, Forgetting*, 237.
18. Ricoeur, *Memory, History, Forgetting*, 243.
19. Ricoeur, *Memory, History, Forgetting*, 244.
20. Ricoeur, *Memory, History, Forgetting*, 262–63, 276.
21. Nancy Pennington and Reid Hastie, "A Cognitive Theory of Juror Decision Making: The Story Model," *Cardozo Law Review* 13 (1991): 528.
22. Pennington and Hastie, "Cognitive Theory of Juror Decision Making," 528.
23. Ricoeur, *Time and Narrative* (vol. 1), 48.
24. Pennington and Hastie, "Cognitive Theory of Juror Decision Making," 528.
25. Pennington and Hastie, "Cognitive Theory of Juror Decision Making," 528.
26. Pennington and Hastie, "Cognitive Theory of Juror Decision Making," 527.
27. Ricoeur, *Memory, History, Forgetting*, 325.
28. Ricoeur, *Memory, History, Forgetting*, 325.
29. Ricoeur, *Memory, History, Forgetting*, 136.
30. Paul Ricoeur, *From Text to Action*, trans. Kathleen Blamey and John B. Thompson (Evanston, IL: Northwestern University Press, 1991), 142.
31. Ricoeur, *From Text to Action*, 109–10.
32. Ricoeur, *Memory, History, Forgetting*, 184–85.
33. Ricoeur, *Memory, History, Forgetting*, 184.
34. Paul Ricoeur, "Interpretation and/or Argumentation," in *The Just*, trans. David Pellaeur (Chicago: University of Chicago Press, 2000), 122.
35. Ricoeur, "Interpretation and/or Argumentation," 112.
36. Ricoeur, "Interpretation and/or Argumentation," 113.
37. Ricoeur, "Interpretation and/or Argumentation," 110.
38. Ricoeur, "Interpretation and/or Argumentation," 110, 125–26.
39. Ricoeur, *Memory, History, Forgetting*, 135.
40. Ricoeur, "Interpretation and/or Argumentation," 122, 126.

41. Ricoeur, "Interpretation and/or Argumentation," 113.
42. Ricoeur, "Interpretation and/or Argumentation," 113–14.
43. Ricoeur, "The Just Between the Legal and the Good," in this volume.
44. Ricoeur, "The Just Between the Legal and the Good," in this volume: 34.
45. Ricoeur, "The Just Between the Legal and the Good," in this volume: 35.
46. Ricoeur, "The Just Between the Legal and the Good," in this volume: 35.
47. Ricoeur, "The Just Between the Legal and the Good," in this volume: 35. In that sense, as we have already noted, both narrative and rhetoric are included in the critical and epistemological phase of interpretation/argumentation, even though on the scale of the truth assessment of facts in dispute, they respectively opposed resistances to the aim for truth of the trial.
48. Ricoeur, "The Just Between the Legal and the Good," in this volume: 35.
49. Ricoeur, "Interpretation and/or Argumentation," 117–18.
50. Ricoeur, *Memory, History, Forgetting*, 320–21.
51. Ricoeur, *Memory, History, Forgetting*, 321.
52. Ricoeur, *Memory, History, Forgetting*, 321.
53. Ricoeur, *Memory, History, Forgetting*, 324, 326.
54. Ricoeur, *Memory, History, Forgetting*, 325.
55. Ricoeur, "The Just Between the Legal and the Good" [195].
56. Ricoeur, *Memory, History, Forgetting*, 320–21.
57. Cf. Lisa Kern Griffin, "Narrative, Truth, and Trial," *Georgetown Law Journal* 101 (2013): 310; Robert P. Burns, "Fallacies on Fallacies: A Reply," *International Commentary on Evidence* 3, no. 1 (2005): 3.
58. Doron Menashe and Mutal E. Shamash, "The Narrative Fallacy," *International Commentary on Evidence* 3, no. 1 (2005): 29.
59. Ricoeur, *Memory, History, Forgetting*, 325–26.
60. Ricoeur, *Memory, History, Forgetting*, 318.
61. Ricoeur, *Memory, History, Forgetting*, 320.
62. Ricoeur, "Interpretation and/or Argumentation," 121.
63. Ricoeur, "Interpretation and/or Argumentation," 121.
64. Ricoeur, *Memory, History, Forgetting*, 321.
65. Ricoeur, "Interpretation and/or Argumentation," 121.
66. For other examples of applications of Ricoeur's narrative theory in judicial processes, see Christelle Landheer-Cieslak, "Paul Ricoeur et l'éthique du jugement judiciaire: Quelles relations entre justice et sollicitude?," *Revue interdisciplinaire d'études juridiques* 68, no. 1 (2012): 1–47; Marcin Pieniazek, "On Possible Applications of Paul Ricoeur's Thought in Legal Theory," *Archiwum filozofii prawa i folozofii spolecznei*, 1 (2015): 79–88.
67. Ricoeur, "The Historian and the Judge," *Memory, History, Forgetting*, 314–33.

BIBLIOGRAPHY

Burns, Robert P. "Fallacies on Fallacies: A Reply." *International Commentary on Evidence* 3, no. 1 (2005): 1–7.

Griffin, Lisa Kern. "Narrative, Truth, and Trial." *Georgetown Law Journal* 101 (2013): 281–335.
Landheer-Cieslak, Christelle. "Paul Ricoeur et l'Éthique du Jugement Judiciaire: Quelles Relations entre Justice et Sollicitude?" *Revue Interdisciplinaire d'Études Juridiques* 68, no. 1 (2012): 1–47.
Menashe, Doron Menashe, and Mutal E. Shamash. "The Narrative Fallacy." *International Commentary on Evidence* 3, no. 1 (2005): 1–45.
Pennington, Nancy, and Reid Hastie. "A Cognitive Theory of Juror Decision Making: The Story Model." *Cardozo Law Review* 13 (1991): 519–57.
Pieniazek, Marcin. "On Possible Applications of Paul Ricoeur's Thought in Legal Theory." *Archiwum filozofii prawa i folozofii spolecznei* 1 (2015): 79–88.
Ricoeur, Paul. *From Text to Action*. Translated by Kathleen Blamey, and John B. Thompson. Evanston, IL: Northwestern University Press, 1991.
Ricoeur, Paul. "Interpretation and/or Argumentation." In *The Just*. Translated by David Pellauer. Chicago: University of Chicago Press, 2000: 109–26.
Ricoeur, Paul. "The Just Between the Legal and the Good." Translated by Eileen Brennan, in *Reading Ricoeur through Law*, edited by Marc de Leeuw, George H. Taylor, and Eileen Brennan. Lanham, MD: Lexington Books, 2022, in this volume: 21–36.
Ricoeur, Paul. *Memory, History, Forgetting*. Translated by Kathleen Blamey, and David Pellauer. Chicago: University of Chicago Press, 2004.
Ricoeur, Paul. *Oneself as Another*. Translated by Kathleen Blamey. Chicago: University of Chicago Press, 1992.
Ricoeur, Paul. *Time and Narrative* (vol. 1). Translated by Kathleen McLaughlin, and David Pellauer. Chicago: University of Chicago Press, 1984.
Ricoeur, Paul. *Time and Narrative* (vol. 2). Translated by Kathleen McLaughlin, and David Pellauer. Chicago: University of Chicago Press, 1985.
Ricoeur, Paul. *Time and Narrative* (vol. 3). Translated by Kathleen Blamey, and David Pellauer. Chicago: University of Chicago Press, 1988.

Chapter Eleven

Laws and (Dis)empowerment
On Ricoeur's Phenomenology of Judging
Hans Lindahl

Ricoeur's contributions to the philosophy of law are rather fragmentary, spread out over a range of articles. One will find nothing like the large, systematic works he dedicates to, say, psychoanalysis, hermeneutics, religion, and some such. But one would be mistaken, or so I will argue, to treat his contribution to the philosophy of law in isolation from the main themes that occupied his attention. The significance of Ricoeur's work for the legal doctrine and philosophy of law can best be understood and assessed when read in the context of those themes. In the forthcoming pages I attempt one such reading of Ricoeur. Focusing on his interpretation of the act of judging, as outlined in an eponymously titled essay, I aim to show that it is informed by Ricoeur's phenomenological re-appropriation and collectivization of what Hans Blumenberg has identified as the principle of modern rationality, namely, the principle of self-assertion.[1] Building upon but finally going beyond and against Ricoeur, I will argue that the ultimate finality of the act of judging is restrained collective self-affirmation, which calls for asymmetrical, not reciprocal, recognition of the other in ourselves.

SELF-AFFIRMATION

Ricoeur's discussion of judgment is narrow and elegant. Narrow, because he focuses on evincing the *finality* of the act of judgment, rather than engaging in the broad discussion about the structure and dynamic of judgment, a discussion that includes thorny issues such as the copula between subject and predicate, and the relation between fact and norm. Instead, he appeals to the everyday meanings of the concept: to judge is "not just to opine, value, take as true, but in the final analysis, to take a stand."[2] Elegant, because Ricoeur moves from the short-term to the ultimate finality of judgment, showing how the former is contained in the latter. If to judge is to decide, and if to decide "is to separate, to draw a line between 'yours' and 'mine,'" then its short-term finality must be to end uncertainty in the face of conflict about the distribution of goods.[3] More fundamentally, the finality of judgments is to secure public peace, which he defines as realizing mutual recognition between the parties in conflict. On the one hand, whoever has won should be able to recognize herself in the other: "my adversary, the one who lost, remains like me a subject of right."[4] But, he adds, "such recognition will not be complete unless the same thing can also be said by the loser[:] ... he should be able to declare that the sentence that condemns him was not an act of violence but rather one of recognition."[5]

The common thread joining both finalities of the act of judgment is to settle conflict and the struggle for recognition to which it gives rise. The judge's task is to mediate between the parties in conflict, in principle enabling plaintiff and defendant to affirm each other as equal and free members of society, even though one party may lose and the other win. Therein lies the act's authoritativeness: the act of judging "manifest[s] the choice of discourse over violence."[6]

Assessing this interpretation of the two-tier finality of the act of judging requires digging more deeply into its structure and dynamic. I take my cue from Ricoeur's proposal to engage in a "kind of phenomenology"[7] of judging. Remarkably, the comment receives no further elaboration in his article. In what way might a phenomenology of the act of judging clarify why, for Ricoeur, its ultimate finality is to secure mutual recognition between the parties in conflict?

Edmund Husserl's *Experience and Judgment* yields the key to this question.[8] Husserl launches the book by announcing that he will sidestep a strictly logical inquiry into judgment with a view to uncovering its experiential foundations. His is a genealogical exploration that leads predicative judgments, as expressed in the logical form "x is y," back to the pre-predicative structures of experience. Here, then, is a first parallel: like Husserl before him, Ricoeur approaches judicial decisions from the perspective of the everyday meanings of the act of judging, meanings which attest to its rootedness in experience. We stumble here upon the central insight of phenomenological philosophy: the intentionality of experience, whereby something appears as something to someone. The act of judging has an intentional structure: to judge that "x is y" is to reveal something, x, as having the meaning y. Judgment is judgment *of* (something) and *as* (this or that). The intentional structure of judgment surfaces, albeit discreetly, in Ricoeur's remark that "[t]o judge is to opine. However, an opinion is expressed about something."[9]

There is a second parallel with Husserl, namely, his discussion of the modalizations of certainty. If, for Husserl, these modalizations encompass the spectrum going from doubt to possibility to certainty, so also for Ricoeur legal proceedings mark the progression from an initial situation of uncertainty towards legal certainty: the judgment decides, takes a stand, by definitively qualifying something as having this or that legal meaning: *la chose jugée*. Husserl's description of the passage from initial uncertainty to the certainty of a predicative judgment prefigures, word for word, Ricoeur's description of judging:

> as a rule an interest in confirmation [of what is experienced] will develop only where the simple certainty of belief has already been challenged for whatever motive, where it has perhaps given place to doubt, and where it is now a question of arriving at certainty from the doubt, of resolving it by a *decision,* and of taking a stand (*Stellung zu nehmen*) with regard to what has become doubtful.[10]

It pays to briefly follow Husserl's description of the trajectory leading from the situation of an initial, "simple certainty" to a decision that establishes what counts as certain in response to doubt about a percept. In normal situations, perception has a protentional or anticipative structure in which percepts appear to us in an "unobstructed process of intentions. The object . . . stands before us in a simple certainty of belief as existing and as being such and such."[11] But this perceptual process can be interrupted, either when the percept appears otherwise than as expected, e.g. not red but green, or when it becomes doubtful whether I see one thing or another, e.g. a human being or a mannequin. In Husserl's words, a "conflict" (*Widerstreit*) arises between two meanings—e.g. green/red, human being/mannequin—that is settled through a decision that takes a stand on the percept as having *this* (and not that) meaning. The experience of a perceptual obstruction (*Hemmung*) and the ensuing conflict of meanings to which it gives rise are the pre-predicative origin of the logical categories of negation and possibility.

Husserl's description of the interruption of the simple certainty of perception is of considerable interest for our inquiry. A first point concerns freedom, or rather its curtailment: when obstructed, the perceptual process "is no longer free."[12] Husserl makes clear that it is not only the perceptual process which is hindered; it is the *subject* who, having perceived freely under normal conditions, becomes unfree. The obstruction of perception, and the ensuing uncertainty about my capacity to adequately perceive something, are, for Husserl, the primordial experience of a loss of cognitive freedom. No less importantly, an obstruction bursts the twofold unity of the perceptual process. On the one hand, "[t]he ego is affected by [the obstruction]; it itself, as ego, and in its *own* way, is disunited with itself, is divided . . . ."[13] If the *subject* of the world becomes disunited, divided, with respect to itself, so also the *world* of the subject: "Every modalization of a certainty concerns the subject of the world; this concerns at the same time the entire system of certainty."[14] The experience of an obstruction is the experience of pluralization: "there emerges a consciousness of otherness."[15]

When confronted with the pluralization of experience, a predicative judgment strives to "reestablish" the unity of experience and therewith the unity of the subject and its world: "[i]f the unanimity of the perception is reestablished, if a single perception again unfolds in normal form, then the internal conflict of the ego with itself is resolved."[16] By reestablishing the unity of experience, a predicative judgment overcomes otherness, thereby recovering the subject's cognitive freedom. Significantly, Husserl characterizes the recovery of cognitive freedom in terms of self-preservation. "Striving for consistency of judgment and for certainty is thus a characteristic which is part of the general striving of the ego for self-preservation. The ego preserves itself when it can abide by its acts of position-taking, its 'validations,' its 'This is actually so,' 'That is valuable, good.'"[17] Earlier in the book, Husserl characterizes this striving as a "will to knowledge": overcoming the self-doubt to which the experience of an obstruction gives rise yields "a specific feeling of satisfaction in this enrichment [of perception] and, in relation to this horizon of expanding and heightening enrichment, a striving 'to come ever closer' to the object, to take possession of its 'self' ever more completely."[18] It is not exaggerated to say that Husserl's genealogy of predicative judgment is, most fundamentally, a celebration of the *will to cognitive power*, or more precisely, the will to self-affirmation of the knowing subject, in response to an initial experience of self-doubt and cognitive powerlessness: *I can* know ever more fully, overcoming otherness and plurality and reestablishing the "unbroken unity" of the perceptual world.[19]

COLLECTIVE SELF-AFFIRMATION

Ricoeur's reading of the dynamic—hence the finality—of the act of judging amounts, or so I will argue, to the practical collectivization of the will to self-affirmation of the knowing subject: to judge is to strive to affirm a collective as a unity in the face of an experience of collective self-doubt sparked by legal conflict. As I shall now show, Ricoeur defends the view that to reestablish the unity of a collective subject and of its legal order is to reestablish the freedom of the parties in conflict. An analysis of the famous *Mabo 2* case of the Australian Supreme Court will allow me in due course to critique the sufficiency of this reading of the act of judging.

But perhaps I am moving too quickly here. For Husserl's account of judgment is the account of a solitary ego, whereas Ricoeur focuses on intersubjectivity; Husserl deals with perception, whereas Ricoeur discusses judicial decisions; Husserl is interested in theoretical judging, whereas Ricoeur is interested in a modality of practical judging. Is it prudent, given these differences, to postulate an isomorphism between Husserl's theory of judgment and Ricoeur's interpretation of the finality of judgment?

Ricoeur's early essay, "Negativity and Primary Affirmation," yields a first confirmation of this isomorphism.[20] The essay is polemically oriented against Sartre, who "identif[ies] human reality with negativity."[21] Ricoeur resists the temptation to simply oppose positivity to negativity. Instead, he adopts a dialectical strategy, folding negation and negativity into the process of human self-affirmation. Whence the inaugural question of the essay: "does being have priority over the nothingness within the very core of man, that is, this being which manifests itself by a singular power of negation?"[22] As I read his intervention, Ricoeur takes up *à nouveaux frais* the famous proposition of Spinoza's *Ethics*, "A free man thinks of nothing less than of death, and his wisdom is a meditation on life, not on death."[23] Human self-affirmation, rather than negativity, is primary because "the specific experience of finitude at first presents itself as a correlative experience of limitation and of transgression of limitation."[24]

Significantly, Ricoeur illustrates the primacy of self-affirmation by recourse to an abridged phenomenology of perception. Human finitude manifests itself, as concerns perception, by way of an embodied *point of view*. Closely following Husserl, Ricoeur notes that perception is literally unilateral, hence inadequate, because the percept always and only presents itself from the angle correlative to my perspective on it. But, he asks, "[h]ow can I know my perspective as perspective in the very act of perceiving it if I did not somehow escape it?"[25] Even though I cannot see the other sides of a thing from any given point of view, I already anticipate them in an empty intention; I know them to be there, waiting to be perceived by me. Ricoeur explicitly characterizes this transcending as a *judging*: "Thus I judge of the thing itself by transgressing the face of the thing into the thing itself."[26] This anticipation of the whole percept is a reflexive transcending: I transcend the thing as given to me by "intend[ing] the thing in its meaning, beyond all point of view"; this transcending is reflexive because "I know that I am here; I am not merely the *Nullpunkt* but I also reflect on it."[27] The reflexive transcending deployed by perceptual judgments is a double negation: I know that the percept is *not* simply the silhouette that appears to me; by intending something as a unity, I "de-negate," as Ricoeur puts it, the unilaterality of the percept, hence its negativity. To affirm myself is to negate my point of view, transcending it in the direction of the percept.

Thus far, Ricoeur's analysis of the intentionality of perception and of pre-predicative judgment remains largely within the orbit of perception by the solitary ego. But Ricoeur pushes the analysis of de-negation a step further. For, he notes, I can only transcend the silhouette of a percept by anticipating other perspectives, perspectives which can be occupied by someone else. Perception is intersubjective through and through: "I transcend my point of view only by imagining this empty meaning of the signified thing, fulfilled by another presence, given to someone other than me." And in the same way that a percept is "not-this" silhouette, which I de-negate by anticipating it as a unity, so also "another is the not-I *par excellence*."[28]

Having shown how Ricoeur's analysis of the experience of perceptual negativity and its de-negation presuppose intersubjectivity, we can now elucidate the isomorphism that joins perceptual judging and judicial judging, and hence the theoretical and practical modalities of the act of judging. In the same way that Husserl begins with a freely flowing process of normal perception, so also Ricoeur's analysis of the act of judging presupposes an initial situation in which mutual expectations that individuals entertain with respect to one another are borne out by their behavior. They act *freely*; the limits laid down by the legal order in the form of obligations are limits to which individuals in principle assent in the course of their daily transactions. As such, these limits are the expression of practical freedom, albeit in the form of what, analogously to Husserl's "simple" perceptual certainty, I would like to call presumptive freedom—and the presumptive validity of legal order.

The emergence of conflict about what is to count as mine and thine interrupts the normal course of intersubjective relations, giving rise to a twofold experience of pluralization that is strictly parallel to Husserl's phenomenology of the obstruction of perception. On the one hand, the interruption of mutual expectations "divides," "disunites" the collective with respect to itself, as Husserl would put it: conflict bursts asunder the unity of a "We." On the other, conflict interrupts the unity of the legal order, because plaintiff and defendant can no longer agree on which rights and obligations ought to be allotted to whom. It sparks collective *self-doubt*, usually limited to the case at hand, but sometimes involving the broader community in those cases which—like *Roe v. Wade*[29] in the United States—expose deeply divisive issues: who are we and what do we stand for as a collective? Likewise, conflict announces itself as a moment of negativity and the obstruction of freedom for both parties: for the plaintiff, due to what she views as the misrecognition of her rights; for defendant, because plaintiff's demand for the recognition of a right encroaches on her capacity to carry on with her affairs.

Given this situation of initial uncertainty, the double finality of the act of judging comes into view: by deciding what is yours and what mine, a judge lifts uncertainty, taking a stand regarding what counts as certain for the case at hand. In so doing, the act of judging strives to overcome the negativity of conflict, such that plaintiff and defendant can recognize each other as free and equal members of the collective. If a struggle for the recognition of a right which has been threatened or violated marks an experience of *disempowerment*, the ultimate finality of the act of judging is to *empower* both individual and collective by "reestablishing" the "unbroken unity" (Husserl) of a "We" and of its legal order. By striving to reestablish the unity of a collective weakened by internal strife, the act of judging attests to a collective will to practical power, to the power of a collective to act as one: *We can* recognize each other as free and equal agents within the unity of a legal order: *e pluribus unum*. The ego's reflexive transcending as operative in a perceptual judgment, also holds sway in the act of judging as a practical self-transcending. In effect, the implicit reciprocity that Ricoeur ascribes to the intersubjectivity of perceptual processes is at work in the reciprocity of intersubjective recognition: "my ability to transport myself imaginatively into another perspective and my ability to judge my perspective finite are one and the same power of transcendence; another limits me only in the measure that I actively establish his existence."[30]

The interpretation of collective self-transcending as the emergence of reciprocal recognition between free and equal individuals is nothing other than the root condition of practical freedom as articulated in social contract theory: I am free to do everything that does not hinder the freedom of the other. By de-negating the negativity of conflict, that is, by overcoming the experience of plurality in a dialectical movement that incorporates different perspectives into the unity of a legal order, the act of judging "manifest[s] the choice of discourse over violence." I shall return to critique this reading of the social contract when discussing the representation and the emergence of collectivity.

Ricoeur's essay is placed in a section of *History and Truth* with the heading "The Power (*puissance*) of Affirmation." The heading could also have read, "The Affirmation of Power," or even "Power as Affirmation." In 1990, forty-five years after the publication of *History and Truth*, the celebration of human self-affirmation that plays out in the dialectic of self and other surfaces once again in *Oneself as Another*, where Ricoeur characterizes self-identity as "self-maintenance" (*maintien de soi*).[31] And in Ricoeur's last book, *The Course of Recognition,* he notes that self-recognition takes place when a person recognizes "that he or she is in truth a person 'capable' of different accomplishments."[32] The elemental notion of power as self-affirmation makes its final appearance in Ricoeur's meditations as capability. Like Husserl before him, Ricoeur's phenomenology of the act of judging is a late articulation of the concept of human power and empowerment that has its origins in the modern principle of self-preservation. Spinoza's *conatus* distils its mature metaphysical formulation: "Each thing, as far as it can by its own power, strives to persevere in its being."[33]

JUDGMENT AS (MIS)REPRESENTATION

What should we make of Ricoeur's phenomenology of the act of judgment? Should we endorse the view that its ultimate finality is to secure the mutual recognition of the parties in conflict? Is the finality of judging to be understood as the quest for practical certainty about legal order in the form of mutual recognition, and hence as the quest to overcome the contingency of legal orders which manifests itself in social conflict?

The key to this new set of questions turns on representation. Throughout his essay on judging, Ricoeur often refers to "society" as regards the broader context in which conflict takes place. But this is inaccurate: the judge adjudicates on behalf of a *collective*. To decide a conflict is to represent a collective as a unity in response to the pluralization arising from conflict. For, as Waldenfels points out, "[a] 'we' [cannot] say 'we' . . . . A political group only finds its voice by way of spokespersons who speak [and act, HL] in its name and represent it *as a whole*."[34] Thus, collective acts are acts by individuals or groups of individuals *ascribed* to a collective as its own acts—the *collective* judges, or so claims the judge.[35] Because there is no direct access to collective unity, all representations thereof are representational claims.

Does not the move to describe judging as a representational act stray from a phenomenology of judging and its focus on the intentional structures of experience? Not at all. Intentionality, albeit as collective intentionality, holds sway in representational acts and a fortiori in judging. When deciding a case, a judge claims to act on behalf of a collective (representation of) and takes a stand on what we hold in common, such that it is possible to separate what is yours from what is mine in the case at hand (representation as). In a sense, nothing changes regarding the structure of judgment, which, as noted earlier, is judgment of and judgment as.

But introducing representation into a phenomenology of the act of judging does more than simply support Ricoeur's account of judging as an act of collective self-affirmation; it also undercuts it. Let me first highlight three cardinal features of representation before assessing their implications for his analysis of the act of judging.[36]

1. Representation is common to *all* acts of law-making, not only to judging. This compensates for Ricoeur's methodological move to isolate the act

of judging from the wider process of legal ordering. What joins judging as the "endpoint" of legal ordering, and the enactment of, say, a constitution as the "initiating point" of legal ordering, is that both acts—and all other acts of law-making in between—claim to represent a collective as a unity.

2. The shift to representation clears the way for a genealogical inquiry into legal order from which Ricoeur prescinds by focusing exclusively on the act of judging. Assessing whether mutual recognition is the ultimate finality of judging can no longer be separated from an account of the *emergence* of legal order. As unity is always a represented unity, no group can emerge unless someone summons a manifold of individuals to view themselves as a collective. By definition this convocation cannot have been authorized in advance of the representational act; someone must seize the initiative to speak and act on behalf of a collective. But this unauthorized act only succeeds to the extent that those who it summons retroactively identify—recognize—themselves as the members of a collective.

3. There is no representation of collective unity without a more or less forceful inclusion and exclusion: "we" are represented as this (rather than that) collective. Here again, intentionality holds sway: if intending something as this (hence not as that) brings about a "significant difference" between the meant and its meaning,[37] so also representation effects a difference between the represented and its representations, such that some, many, or most emote "Not in our name!" when represented thus rather than so. Every collective is exposed to conflict because representation not only gives rise to *ourselves* as a group, but also to the *other* in ourselves. Representation is always also *mis*representation.

In some ways, these features of representational acts support Ricoeur's phenomenology of judging and its attendant thesis about collective self-affirmation. Human finitude, which Ricoeur elucidates in terms of the perspectival nature of perception, is rooted in the representational character of intentionality, perceptual or otherwise: something is represented as this, not as that. Ricoeur also refers to "closure" as an ingredient element of human finitude,[38] a closure that reappears, as concerns the first-person *plural* perspective, in the inclusion and exclusion wrought by the representation of collective unity. Collective finitude manifests itself in the *questionability* of every first-person plural perspective, which manifests itself in challenges by those who thereby becomes the other in ourselves. Remember Husserl's formulation: "there emerges a consciousness of otherness."[39]

Representational processes also offer a more precise account of how Ricoeur conceptualizes *responsiveness* to the experience of negativity. According to Ricoeur, the judge not only applies the general rule to the case at hand by way of a "determinative" judgment; she also seeks to articulate what, beginning from the case at hand, counts as the generality of the rule in a "reflective" judgment.[40] But, strictly speaking, this hybridization of two distinct forms of judgment does not work. By contrast, representation accounts for what Ricoeur wants to get at: when referring to a rule in the process of connecting fact to norm, the judgment represents the rule as meaning this (rather than that). Because representation precludes direct access to what is represented, including an irretrievable original meaning of the rule applied in judging, the re of representation means *anew*, where anew hovers somewhere between *again* and *new*. Although a court must claim that it is compelled to rule in a certain way because of precedent, it also always rewrites precedent at least minimally, if nothing else because the qualification of a rule as a precedent relevant to the case at hand bears the stamp of retroactivity, thereby opening up the possibility of rewriting the meaning of the precedent. As a result, in the course of representing rules when separating what is yours from what is mine, the act of judging can reconfigure what "we" hold in common, that is, what constitutes us as a unity.

To this extent, the act of judging is an act of collective self-affirmation: in the face of conflict, the collective can become aware of its limited perspective and transform itself through a judgment, including those who had been unjustifiably excluded from what is their own. The collective empowers those who had been treated unjustly by granting them rights, reaching out to them and bringing them into the fold of the law. Hear the late echoes of Husserl's thesis about the will to power: "a striving 'to come ever closer' to the [other in ourselves, HL]."[41]

JUDGMENT AS (MIS)RECOGNITION

We have reached the point at which Ricoeur's thesis about the ultimate finality of judgment stands strongest. We have also reached the point of inflection that leads toward the thesis's problematic nature.

To see why, consider the famous *Mabo 2* ruling of the Australian High Court, issued in response to a complaint brought against the State of Queensland by members of the Meriam people, who inhabit the Murray Islands in the Torres Strait.[42] The judgment reversed prior judgments by the Court, rejecting the view that, at the time of colonization, Australia was *terra nullius* and, consequently, that all rights were extinguished which the Meriam people—and a fortiori all Torres Strait Islanders and Aboriginal peoples—may have had in their lands. The Court explicitly characterized the conflict as a struggle for recognition by the Meriam people, portraying its decision as an act that redresses the misrecognition which they and Aboriginal peoples had suffered, first at the hands of colonial rule, and now under Australian common law. The decision is lengthy, its central finding terse: "[r]ecognition of the radical title of the Crown is quite consistent with recognition of native title to land . . ." (§ 52). As the Court explained, "[r]adical, ultimate or final title," as defined under English common law, means that "a sovereign enjoys supreme legal authority in and over a territory" (§ 50). Along these lines, the High Court held that "the Crown's acquisition of sovereignty over the several parts of Australia cannot be challenged in an Australian municipal court" (§ 83). But, it added, "the communal native title survives to be enjoyed by the members according to the rights and interests to which they are respectively entitled under the traditionally based laws and customs," provided that the community remains identifiable as such after colonization (§ 68).

The High Court's decision was issued in a period of political activism oriented to exposing the violence visited upon indigenous peoples by the Australian legal order. Most prominently perhaps, five months prior to *Mabo 2*, in January 1992, a group of activists proclaimed the sovereignty of Aboriginal peoples and invited the Australian government to engage in negotiations leading up to a treaty that would settle the land question between Aboriginal peoples and Australia.[43]

I will ignore the heated debate, public and scholarly, raised by *Mabo 2*. My sole interest is what light *Mabo 2* might cast on Ricoeur's thesis about the ultimate finality of judging. As the Court sees it, the recognition of native title to land entailed rejecting the *terra nullius* doctrine, as the doctrine breaches the Racial Discrimination Act of 1975 which proclaims the equality of all Australian citizens before the law. By positing that Aboriginals are entitled to the protection of their native title to land, the decision creates the conditions for Aboriginal and non-Aboriginal citizens to recognize each other as equal "subject[s] of rights"[44] (Ricoeur) under one legal order. That "[r]ecognition of the radical title of the Crown is quite consistent with recognition of native title to land . . ." means that the Court's recognition of the other (in ourselves) is an act of collective *self*-recognition. When confronted with our act of unjustifiable exclusion, we the Australian collective can include the other in ourselves as *one of us*. To this extent, the decision supports Ricoeur's account of collective self-affirmation and the ultimate finality of judging.

But does achieving their recognition as Australians on equal footing with all other Australians exhaust Aboriginal demands for recognition? What eludes Ricoeur's account of collective self-affirmation is the *mis*recognition of Aboriginals by such a decision. The point is not that the ruling falls short of fully recognizing them because, for instance, it upheld the right of the Australian government to extinguish native title to land by a subsequent act of the government (§ 2). Instead, the crux of the matter is that Aboriginals who demand sovereignty for their peoples are misrecognized because they are recognized as Australians. The Preamble to the Australian Constitution of 1900 reads as follows: "WHEREAS [we] the people of New South Wales, Victoria, South Australia, Queensland, and Tasmania, humbly relying on the blessing of Almighty God, have agreed to unite in one indissoluble Federal Commonwealth under the Crown of the United Kingdom of Great Britain and Ireland, and under the Constitution hereby established . . . ."[45] The Preamble seizes the initiative to convoke a manifold of individuals to view themselves as a collective, including them as members of the Federal Commonwealth. This constitutional enactment excludes Aboriginal peoples by including them as subject to Australian law; subsequently, Aboriginal non-citizens became excluded by being included as Australian citizens. All of this is elided when Ricoeur posits the "existence of written laws," the "presence of an institutional framework," and "the intervention of qualified, competent, independent persons," as preconditions that must be met if the act of judging is to live up to its ultimate finality.[46] For all these conditions are met in *Mabo 2*.

It will be argued that *Mabo 2* is an extreme case of a legal order tainted by colonization; one could supplement the preconditions posed by Ricoeur to exclude colonialism. Yes; but my point about the representational origins of legal orders is that no collective emerges absent a more or less forceful marginalization. *Mabo 2* is an extreme case of a more general problem. Every legal order has a normative blind spot called forth by the non-reciprocal emergence of legal reciprocity, which, like a birthmark, accompanies a collective throughout its career. The non-reciprocal origins of legal reciprocity return from ahead in the form of demands for recognition which refuse integration into the circle of reciprocity and mutual recognition available to that legal collective, yet which the latter cannot discard as unjustified other than by falling prey to a *petitio principii*. Just such a circular argument is at work in *Mabo 2*: "[r]ecognition of the radical title of the Crown is quite consistent with recognition of native title to land . . . ." What counts as a *justified* demand for recognition presupposes a first-person plural perspective—a point of view. Even though this perspective can be transformed, it does not allow for collective self-affirmation as the recognition of the other (in ourselves) "beyond all point of view"[47] (Ricoeur). Consequently, the boundaries that configure the unity of a collective and its legal order appear as *fault lines*, not merely as a limit to be de-negated by including who ought not to have been excluded, or by excluding who ought not to have been included.[48]

The Aboriginal demand for sovereignty challenges the authority of Australian courts to exercise authority over them, evoking the violent origins of the "radical title" whence, amongst others, the High Court draws its authority when ruling on *Mabo 2*. For, strictly speaking, the notion of a radical title vested in the Crown is an oxymoron. *Mabo 2* shows that, *pace* Simmel and all those who follow in his wake, the judge is never only, as he puts it, the non-partisan "third" party who either "produces the concord of two colliding parties" or "who balances, as it were, their contradictory claims against one another and eliminates what is incompatible in them."[49] Because the judge must claim to represent *us* as a whole, the judgment can aspire to impartiality *within* the cincture of collective unity, even when transforming its limits. Such would be the case if, say, Aboriginal peoples demand the recognition of rights as citizens of the Australian collective. By contrast, Australian courts cannot decide as non-partisan actors when responding to demands for *sovereignty* by Aboriginal peoples, as, in the face of such demands, the courts become both party to and judges of the conflict. The finitude of self-affirmation is about more than the collective's questionability and responsiveness in the face of conflict; it is about the finite questionability and finite responsiveness put on display by judging. Collective power and powerlessness go hand in hand: *we can* and *we cannot* include the other in ourselves as one of us.[50]

If we follow Ricoeur's account of the ultimate finality of legal order, the recognition of native title to land in principle allows Aboriginals to view *Mabo 2* "not [as] an act of violence but rather one of recognition."[51] For some—perhaps many—Aboriginals, such is more or less the case. But for those who demand Aboriginal sovereignty, and they are not few in number, *Mabo 2* is an act of violence *because* it is an act of recognition of the other as one of us. Theirs is a demand for the recognition of indigenous peoples as the other (in ourselves) *who is other than us*. Theirs is a challenge of "otherness" in the strong form of *strangeness*, that is, a challenge that cannot be accommodated in its own terms *within* the Australian legal order if the High Court is to reestablish—reaffirm—the "unbroken unity" of the Australian collective and of its legal order through an act of collective self-affirmation. The dialectic between collective self and other breaks down, such that, in a riff on *Oneself as Another*, there is no passage from "ourselves as another" to "ourselves as strange." A gap remains between the question about the Australian legal order raised by the Aboriginal peoples, and the question to which *Mabo 2* can respond when reaffirming Australian unity. Unless the ultimate finality of judging is *not* interpreted as "conquering ipseity,"[52] collective self-affirmation ends up conquering alterity, falling prey to legal imperialism as a project of expansive domination.

Although cases like *Mabo 2* starkly expose the danger of assimilation and domination ensconced in a phenomenology of judgment which too quickly assumes that its ultimate finality is to achieve mutual recognition within the (transformed) unity of a legal order, they do not force us to abandon the recognition of the other as the ultimate finality of judging. I propose that we reinterpret legal recognition of the other in terms of the double asymmetry which holds sway in the back-and-forth between a demand for recognition and the judicial response thereto. A theory of asymmetrical recognition acknowledges that responses to demands for recognition can be situationally fitting, while also showing, against theories of mutual recognition, that all such responses remain irreducibly contingent. Whereas de-negation ultimately privileges closure over openness, albeit in the teleological form of an all-inclusive closure, asymmetrical recognition points to an openness that is prior to, conditions, and survives all closure. Indeed, the linkage between question and response that plays out in struggles for recognition that are brought before a court is *irreducibly open* in a twofold sense: the question remains open because the response does not exhaust it; the response remains open because another response was possible.[53]

Collective self-affirmation cannot, on its own, adequately capture the ultimate finality of judging. Instead, judging should engage in what I would like to call *restrained* collective-self affirmation. Judging ought to recognize the other (in ourselves) as one of us and as other than us. More precisely, collective self-affirmation and the preservation of the other as *strange* constitute, I submit, the ultimate finality of judging, if judging is to promote public peace.

One of the ways in which collective self-restraint can be exercised is by suspending the application of the law to the case at hand, opening up a space for other ways of dealing with a demand for recognition recalcitrant to inclusion in the legal order it challenges. The Australian collective would exercise restrained collective self-affirmation in this strong sense were it to engage in negotiations with Aboriginal peoples to enact a coimperium over the land, both recognizing them as sovereign, hence recognizing them as other than "us," while also negotiating which domains of behavior are to be governed jointly, hence recognizing them as one of "us." As it stands today, Australian politics offers little hope of such a negotiation. On occasion, restrained collective self-affirmation can be more, rather than less, politically demanding than collective self-affirmation *tout court*.

NOTES

1. Hans Blumenberg, *The Legitimacy of the Modern Age*, trans. Robert M. Wallace (Cambridge, MA: The MIT Press, 1985).
2. Paul Ricoeur, "The Act of Judging," in *The Just*, trans. David Pellauer (Chicago: Chicago University Press, 2000), 128.
3. Ricoeur, "The Act of Judging," 131.
4. Ricoeur, "The Act of Judging," 130.
5. Ricoeur, "The Act of Judging," 131–32.

6. Ricoeur, "The Act of Judging," 130.
7. Ricoeur, "The Act of Judging," 127.
8. Edmund Husserl, *Experience and Judgment: Investigations in a Genealogy of Logic*, trans. James S. Churchill and Karl Ameriks (London: Routledge and Kegan Paul, 1973).
9. Ricoeur, "The Act of Judging," 127.
10. Husserl, *Experience and Judgment*, 272.
11. Husserl, *Experience and Judgment*, 87.
12. Husserl, *Experience and Judgment*, 291 (translation modified).
13. Husserl, *Experience and Judgment*, 290.
14. Husserl, *Experience and Judgment*, 291.
15. Husserl, *Experience and Judgment*, 88.
16. Husserl, *Experience and Judgment*, 291.
17. Husserl, *Experience and Judgment*, 291 (italics omitted).
18. Husserl, *Experience and Judgment*, 86.
19. Husserl, *Experience and Judgment*, 290. Husserl often refers to intentionality in terms of "*Ich kann,*" a formulation that Merleau-Ponty and Ricoeur take over as "*je peux.*"
20. Paul Ricoeur, "Negativity and Primary Affirmation," in *History and Truth*, trans. Charles A. Kelbley (Evanston, IL: Northwestern University Press, 2007), 305–28.
21. Ricoeur, "Negativity and Primary Affirmation," 305.
22. Ricoeur, "Negativity and Primary Affirmation," 305.
23. Baruch Spinoza, *The Ethics*, in *The Collected Works of Spinoza*, Vol. 1, 2nd printing, trans. Edwin Curley (Princeton, NJ: Princeton University Press, 1988), Book IV, Proposition 67. The Proof elucidates the Proposition in terms of self-preservation.
24. Ricoeur, "Negativity and Primary Affirmation," 306. The Hegelian overtones of this thesis are unmistakable: "the very fact that something is determined as a limitation implies that the limitation is already transcended." Georg Friedrich Wilhelm Hegel, *Science of Logic*, trans. John Niemeyer Findlay (London: Allen and Unwin, 1969), 134. The Hegelian dialectic underpinning Ricoeur's approach to judgment comes into full view in Paul Ricoeur, "Sanction, Rehabilitation, Pardon," in *The Just*, 133–145.
25. Ricoeur, "Negativity and Primary Affirmation," 308.
26. Ricoeur, "Negativity and Primary Affirmation," 309.
27. Ricoeur, "Negativity and Primary Affirmation," 309.
28. Ricoeur, "Negativity and Primary Affirmation," 313.
29. 410 U.S. 113 (1973).
30. Ricoeur, "Negativity and Primary Affirmation," 313.
31. Paul Ricoeur, *Oneself as Another*, trans. Kathleen Blamely (Chicago: Chicago University Press, 1992), 119.
32. Paul Ricoeur, *The Course of Recognition*, trans. David Pellauer (Cambridge, MA: Harvard University Press, 2005). In his later work, Ricoeur introduces the notion of *attestation*, namely, "assurance—the credence and the trust—of existing in the mode of selfhood." See Paul Ricoeur, *Oneself as Another*, trans. Kathleen Blamey

(Chicago: Chicago University Press, 2002), 302. This is, on the face of it, a more modest reading of the self's power than his early interpretation of self-affirmation. Yet the traces of this earlier conception of power are still clearly present in his last work, when Ricoeur discusses Axel Honneth's theory of recognition: "I accept the essence of this project. In my vocabulary, it is a question of seeking in the development of conflictual interactions the source for a parallel enlarging of the individual capacities discussed ... under the heading of the capable human being out to conquer his ipseity. The course of self-recognition ends in mutual recognition." Ricoeur, *The Course of Recognition*, 187. There is, I believe, an unmistakable connotation of self-affirmation in Ricoeur's reference to "conquering" ipseity, a reference that theories of recognition render extensive to collective ipseity. The chronological order of appearance of *Oneself as Another* (1990) and Ricoeur's essay in *The Just* (1991) confirms that self-affirmation, not self-attestation, holds sway in his depiction of the act of judging.

33. Spinoza, *Ethics*, Part III, Proposition 6.

34. Bernhard Waldenfels, *Verfremdung der Moderne: Phänomenologische Grenzgänge* (Essen: Wallstein Verlag, 2001), 140.

35. In Germany, for example, judicial rulings begin with the phrase "*Im Namen des Volkes*."

36. For a fuller account of representation see Hans Lindahl, "Inside and Outside Global Law: The Julius Stone Address 2018," *Sydney Law Review* 41 (2019): 1, 1–34.

37. Bernhard Waldenfels, *Bruchlinien der Erfahrung* (Frankfurt: Suhrkamp, 2002), 28–30.

38. Ricoeur, "Negativity and Primary Affirmation," 307.

39. Husserl, *Experience and Judgment*, 88.

40. Ricoeur "The Act of Judging," 129.

41. Husserl, *Experience and Judgment*, 86.

42. Mabo v Queensland (No 2) ("Mabo case") [1992] HCA 23; (1992) 175 CLR 1 (June 3, 1992), http://www6.austlii.edu.au/cgi-bin/viewdoc/au/cases/cth/HCA/1992/23.html.

43. For an analysis of Mabo 2 in tandem with the Aboriginal Tent Embassy, see Hans Lindahl, "Intentionality, Representation, Recognition: Phenomenology and the Politics of A-Legality:" in *Political Phenomenology, Experience, Ontology, Episteme*, eds. Thomas Bedorf and Steffen Herrmann, 256–76 (Abingdon: Routledge, 2020).

44. Ricoeur, "The Act of Judging," 131.

45. Commonwealth of Australia Constitution Act, chapter 12, Preamble.

46. Ricoeur "The Act of Judging," 127–28. Gadamer's interpretation of judging as "application" falls prey to exactly the same difficulty. See Hans-Georg Gadamer, *Truth and Method*, trans. Joel Weinsheimer and Donald G. Marshall (London: Continuum Books, 2005), 305–34.

47. Ricoeur, "Negativity and Primary Affirmation," 309.

48. See Hans Lindahl, *Fault Lines of Globalization: Legal Order and the Politics of A-Legality* (Oxford: Oxford University Press, 2013).

49. Georg Simmel, *The Sociology of Georg Simmel*, ed. and trans. Kurt. H. Wolff (New York, NY: The Free Press, 1950), 146–47.

50. Although well beyond the scope of this paper, this thesis is the point of departure for a critical examination of Blumenberg's claim that "[T]he rationality of the [modern] epoch is conceived as self-assertion, not as self-empowerment." See Blumenberg, *The Legitimacy of the Modern Age*, 97.

51. Ricoeur "The Act of Judging," 132.

52. Ricoeur, *The Course of Recognition*, 187.

53. See Hans Lindahl, *Authority and the Globalisation of Inclusion and Exclusion* (Cambridge: Cambridge University Press, 2018), 286–347, for an analysis and defense of asymmetrical recognition in a critical dialogue with Ricoeur.

BIBLIOGRAPHY

Blumenberg, Hans. *The Legitimacy of the Modern Age*. Translated by Robert M. Wallace. Cambridge, MA: The MIT Press, 1985.

Gadamer, Hans-Georg. *Truth and Method*, 2nd ed. Translated by Joel Weinsheimer and Donald G. Marshall. London: Continuum Books, 2005.

Hegel, Georg Friedrich Wilhelm. *Science of Logic*. Translated by John Niemeyer Findlay. London: Allen and Unwin, 1969.

Husserl, Edmund. *Experience and Judgment: Investigations in a Genealogy of Logic*. Translated by James S. Churchill and Karl Ameriks. London: Routledge and Kegan Paul, 1973.

Lindahl, Hans. *Authority and the Globalisation of Inclusion and Exclusion*. Cambridge: Cambridge University Press, 2018.

Lindahl, Hans. *Fault Lines of Globalization: Legal Order and the Politics of A-Legality*. Oxford: Oxford University Press, 2013.

Lindahl, Hans. "Inside and Outside Global Law: The Julius Stone Address 2018." *Sydney Law Review* 41 (2019): 1–34.

Lindahl, Hans. "Intentionality, Representation, Recognition: Phenomenology and the Politics of A-Legality." In *Political Phenomenology: Experience, Ontology, Episteme*, edited by Thomas Bedorf and Steffen Herrmann, 256–76. Abingdon: Routledge, 2020.

Mabo v Queensland (No 2) HCA 23; (1992) 175 CLR 1 (3 June 1992). http://www6.austlii.edu.au/cgi-bin/viewdoc/au/cases/cth/HCA/1992/23.html.

Ricoeur, Paul. "The Act of Judging." In *The Just*. Translated by David Pellauer, 127–32. Chicago: University of Chicago Press, 2000.

Ricoeur, Paul. *The Course of Recognition*. Translated by David Pellauer. Cambridge, MA: Harvard University Press, 2005.

Ricoeur, Paul. "Negativity and Primary Affirmation." In *History and Truth*. Translated by Charles A. Kelbley. Evanston, IL: Northwestern University Press, 2007.

Ricoeur, Paul. *Oneself as Another*. Translated by Kathleen Blamely. Chicago: University of Chicago Press, 1992.

Ricoeur, Paul. "Sanction, Rehabilitation, Pardon." In *The Just*. Translated by David Pellauer, 133–45. Chicago: University of Chicago Press, 2000.
Simmel, Georg. *The Sociology of Georg Simmel*. Translated and edited by Kurt H. Wolff. New York: The Free Press, 1950.
Spinoza, Baruch. "*The Ethics*." In *The Collected Works of Spinoza*. Translated by Edwin Curley. Princeton, NJ: Princeton University Press, 1988.
Waldenfels, Bernhard. *Bruchlinien der Erfahrung*. Frankfurt: Suhrkamp, 2002.
Waldenfels, Bernhard. *Verfremdung der Moderne: Phänomenologische Grenzgänge*. Essen: Wallstein Verlag, 2001.

Chapter Twelve

The "Crisis of Witnessing" and Trauma on the Stand

Attending to Survivors as an Obligation of Justice

Stephanie Arel

In *Memory, History, Forgetting*, Paul Ricoeur examines the relationship between the duty of memory and the idea of justice, constructing a sense of the just that implies a responsibility to the other, especially the suffering other. Ricoeur states, "[I]t is justice that turns memory into a project; and it is this same project of justice that gives the form of the future and of the imperative to the duty of memory."[1] The "exemplary value" of traumatic memories,[2] where trauma refers to the past, is to direct us toward future truth, justice, growth, and the good. If this is the case, then attention during a trial to the needs of the witness called to the stand to recall trauma becomes integral to justice and, therefore, an imperative of the law.

For Ricoeur, the root of justice is by design "turned toward others," so that its duties imply a moral and legal responsibility to the other.[3] In the field of law, then, an opportunity arises in the face of the tragic to be for the other: the vulnerable witness—a survivor of trauma—on the witness stand. The law can be for the other in this context in two senses. First, testimony allows the survivor the "possibility of speaking" and the "recovery and return of the voice," thereby producing growth in response to the traumatization itself.[4] Secondly, when the imperative in justice is to be "turned towards others," the legal process has an obligation. Listening to a survivor—a witness on the stand—demands consideration of Ricoeur's notion of "the good" as recognition of a lack or an absence on the ethical plane that practice seeks to fill but that is never completely attainable. This aim for the good, which must "never cease to be internal to human action," is to be sought in legal practice and, when considering legal testimony composed of a trauma narrative, anchors the legal in an ethical intent.[5]

Locating my chapter within the interrogation of the duties of memory and justice, where the aim for the good must "never cease to be internal to human action," I probe what trauma theorists call the "crisis of witnessing." The concept of the "crisis of witnessing" emerges from Shoshana Felman and Dori Laub's work negotiating the nature and function of memory alongside the act of witnessing. Their definition of the "crisis of witnessing" starts with the Holocaust, defined as a "uniquely devastating," "unprecedented," and "inconceivable" historical event that eliminated its own witnesses.[6] This event offers the lens through which we can view the crisis endured by those who witness other traumas. In seeking to escape this crisis, the witness must struggle with the fragmentation in memory that leads to the dual state of knowing and unknowing: a knowing deeply imprinted neurologically that lies incompatibly with a desire to forget, to pretend either that horror did not happen or that, if it did, the survivor escaped unscathed.[7] What does it mean, then, to ask of survivors struggling with traumatic memories and realities to face these traumas again on the witness stand? What protections do these individuals deserve from the legal system?

The first part of this chapter considers traumatic memory and the ways in which trauma affects the brain, showing how memory in trauma becomes imprinted and distinct but also often disassociated. The survivor attempts to forget, most often on a subconscious level. In the second section, I consider how traumas' effects manifest in their remembrance, articulated as the crisis of witnessing. On the basis of this crisis, I highlight the differences between types of testimony and how the effect on the witness of the retelling of traumatic memory challenges the legitimacy of current legal protections of testimony. In the last parts of the chapter, I consider justice from an ethical perspective, drawing on the traditional conception of justice as oriented for others, while underscoring how this system has an opportunity and an obligation to the witness recounting a trauma narrative on the stand. I question what is at stake for the witness who testifies to trauma, exploring what the legal system asks this person to endure. To probe these dilemmas, I draw on Ricoeur's ethical insistence that "aiming at a good life lived with and for others in just institutions" must take place after facing the reality of tragic conflict.[8]

TRAUMATIC MEMORY

In her hallmark book *Trauma and Recovery*, Judith Herman writes that "traumatic events are extraordinary, not because they occur rarely, but rather because they overwhelm the ordinary adaptation to human life."[9] The profuse reality of trauma allows it to create indelible memories which often are not integrated into a person's conscious life experiences.[10] This lack of integration—whether actuated by one-time or a chronic occurrence of trauma—is characteristic of someone who has endured trauma. Recognizing what happens to the body when it undergoes trauma initially, alongside how trauma makes an impact on memory and later recall, establishes the effects of recounting trauma as a witness in the legal system, especially in the instance when a witness testifies to personal victimization.

At its onset, a traumatic event represents imminent danger to the human person. Danger inspires fear, which stimulates the limbic system, specifically the amygdala, the area of the brain that perceives a threat whether through a sound, an image, or other sensory stimulus. The amygdala assesses the significance of the threat, working faster than the frontal lobe (the decision-making part of the brain), suppressing executive functions and inspiring the fight, flight, freeze mechanism.[11] This defensive, primitive measure overrides logical or critical thought processes not only during the traumatic event but also after the trauma. Once activated, the amygdala will continue to be sensitive to stimuli that trigger recall of the trauma. Triggers include images, sounds, or even thoughts associated with the particular experience. In such cases, the amygdala responds with alarm, even years after the trauma itself.[12] For instance, research has shown that those who were closer to the World Trade Center on September 11th, 2001 have heightened amygdala activation and an increased risk of mental health disorders decades after the event.[13]

When the most primordial part of the limbic system activates, taking over cognitive processes, it alters both how memory is encoded (whether it is frightening or not, for instance) and how it is stored. The amygdala plays a primary role in this process. Amygdala arousal and the release of stress hormones indicate an event is critical for survival, stimulating fear, action, and the necessity to remember. Such events are, therefore, saved and ready for easy recall.[14] This is the work of the right hemisphere of the brain, which stores traumatic memory, including the sensations it produces related to sound, touch, smell, and emotions. When past trauma emerges as memory, images of the trauma activate the brain's right hemisphere while deactivating the left.[15] As a result, survivors react automatically to present sensory stimuli identifiable with past trauma as if the past traumatic event were occurring in the present. Because of the way that information has been stored, survivors' bodies recall what "feels like intuitive truth—the way things are."[16] During traumatic recall, often occurring in the form of flashback, the part of the brain commonly called Broca's area, the brain's language comprehension area, goes offline. This emergence of traumatic memory poses a challenge to the ability to tell oneself that past events are *not* reoccurring in the present, because right brain activity and the amygdala suppress analytic thought, logic, language processing, and reasoning or executive functioning.[17]

The phenomenon of left-brain suppression and right brain hyperactivity facilitates a survivor's reaction to present stimulation as if past trauma had recurred. When a survivor "relives" past trauma as if it were occurring in the present, gaps in time result. Reliving is compounded by the disorganized way that the brain collects such memories. According to Van der Kolk, subjects remember "some details all too clearly (the smell of the rapist, the gash in the forehead of a dead child) but [they can] not recall the sequence of events or other vital details (the first person who arrived to help, whether an ambulance or a police car took them to the hospital)."[18] As a result, memories are fragmented, and recall is inconsistent and affective. By contrast, positive memories are more cohesive and do not emerge in the present as if they were occurring. For instance, weddings, births, and graduations maintain a narrative and cohesive structure with "a beginning, a middle, and an end," and when recalled evoke nostalgia because they remain in the past.[19]

After trauma, then, the brain neither stores memories nor recalls them in the same way that it does nontraumatic events. This leaves the survivor in a kind of double bind when pressed to recall such events—whether from a therapeutic standpoint or from a juridical one. This conundrum is made worse by what Herman calls the central dialectic of trauma: the will to deny and the will to proclaim.[20] She writes, "People who have survived atrocities often tell their stories in a highly emotional, contradictory, and fragmented manner which undermines their credibility and thereby serves the twin imperatives of truth-telling and secrecy. When the truth is finally recognized, survivors can begin their recovery."[21] Finding the truth, mourning what was lost, and reconstructing both the trauma narrative and relationships after trauma signify parts of the recovery process and introduce the survivor to the beginning of the crisis of bearing witness and to what we may call, following Ricoeur, the tragic dimension that lies there.

CRISIS OF WITNESSING

The "crisis of witnessing" indicates the complexity of reporting in language the experience of trauma. We label these accounts "testimony," a genre asserted by Holocaust survivor Elie Wiesel.[22] Understanding how trauma influences the storage and recall of memory, this testimony may not meet the requirements of legal testimony. Addressing testimony in the traditional legal sense, Felman articulates a conundrum when the legal conception of testimony intertwines with a trauma narrative that is a part of cultural self-understanding:

> The legal model of the trial dramatizes . . . a contained and culturally channeled, institutionalized, *crisis of truth*. The trial both derives from and proceeds by, a

crisis of evidence, which the verdict must resolve. What, however, are the stakes of the larger, more profound, less definable crisis of truth which, in proceeding from contemporary trauma, has brought the discourse off the testimony to the fore of the contemporary cultural narrative, way beyond the implications of its limited, restricted usage in the legal context?[23]

I offer three examples of trauma narratives that complicate the concept of testimony and its ethical implications in the legal context: the story of a Holocaust survivor, that of a survivor of 9/11, and the cross examination of a witness on the stand by Ted Bundy at his own trial.

In the first case, during a research visit to Poland, I witnessed a survivor of the Holocaust share her personal history. She did so with control and composure, displaying little to no emotion as she showed visitors pictures of the parents she hardly knew, both executed by the Gestapo. She was careful to differentiate the elements of her story that she had experienced first-hand from those that were recounted to her by neighbors, friends, and the nuns who saved her life. It was difficult to tell whether the emotional distance she projected between herself and the content of her story was a protective measure or simply a consequence of repeating the trauma narrative—she was frequently invited to tell her story at a local museum. In either case, the details of the story seemed elusive or debatable not only because she received the particulars secondhand but also because the story evoked little to no affect in her. The story itself appeared to evoke some affect in her audience, but she showed little to no emotion herself.

In the second case, retired firefighter Bill Spade tells a highly emotive account of his experience on September 11, 2001. He repeats this narrative for multiple audiences: students studying the horrific events of that morning, visitors of the 9/11 museum, staff working there, and even rescue service personnel in training. His story is compelling. He recalls the chaos after the attacks, the lack of radio transmissions, the collapse of the South Tower, and the intense fear of knowing that the North Tower would follow. He recalls crawling out from the debris of each collapse after believing he was going to die and having said mental goodbyes to his own family. He visibly mourns the reality that he alone survived, while his eleven colleagues from Rescue 5 in Staten Island died in the collapse of the North Tower. Spade displays high level of affect, often crying while sharing intimate details of his narrative.

The third example entails Ted Bundy questioning Officer Raymond Crew of the Florida State University's police department about what he reported seeing at the Chi Omega House when he responded to the attacks on four women there. Bundy does this of his own initiative, asking Crew to report "in as much detail" as he can recall about what he discovered. This request occurs prior to the call of witnesses to the stand whose role was to describe the crime scene. Bundy appears to relish the gore he solicits from his line of questioning. Footage of the inquiry shows people in the courthouse uncomfortable, shifting in their seats and looking incredulously at the allowance in the courtroom of an inquiry that demands of the witness to elaborate his gruesome discoveries. This retelling in the name of justice or fairness asked the witness to immerse himself in the trauma narrative. Different than the other two examples of trauma narratives told voluntarily and shared in the interest of not forgetting, this episode of evoking the details of trauma highlights the susceptibility of all witnesses to trauma and its impact when faced with the trauma narrative.

Simply recounting the trauma story can be retraumatizing to the witness; it can inspire dissociation, or it can lead to recovery. Discerning which effect storytelling has can be complex and often depends significantly on the experience and psychological state of the survivor. But we can examine the ways that each narrative interacts with the concept of a "crisis of witnessing." From a legal standpoint, the examples press the need to identify the danger of retraumatization when silence around trauma is broken by legal testimony, which, when compelled, distinguishes itself from voluntary testimony.

Unlike the death of an individual victim, the slaughter of large communities or races aims to silence those who survive. This attempt, though, leads these communities and races to promulgate "never forget" after mass atrocity. This phrase, initiated by responses to memory after the Holocaust, is now often assigned to remembering September 11, 2001 and other mass atrocities such as the Cambodian Genocide. Of the many interpretations of the saying, underlying one is the imperative to tell a trauma narrative with the goal that the persecutory action contained in that narrative is never repeated. In my examples, both the Holocaust survivor and Bill Spade spoke under this imperative of never forgetting. Raymond Crew had little choice but to answer the questions posed to him, even as we can extrapolate that he did so in an effort to bring justice to the victims of Ted Bundy's crimes. The differences in testimony—as oral autobiography or as compelled—underscore the complexity in telling trauma.

Further, after trauma, reality does not meet the expectation of living in a safe social reality and, if a person's body were violated, the body itself feels unsafe. In the best case, trauma leaves survivors perceiving the world as having changed; in the worst case, survivors endure a sense that the world is threatening. The perceptible change in the environment challenges integration of the trauma and adds to its unbelievability for the survivor. Annie Rogers expresses this conundrum as the "unsayable."[24] The unsayable emerges in the silences around trauma as well as in the words that survivors use to express horror or the unbelievable. Comprehending the unsayability of trauma is to be present in the crisis of witnessing, where silence operates to suppress survivors' experiences through death, trauma, and forgetting. Several times during her testimony, the Holocaust survivor shook her head in disbelief. This she did most poignantly when sharing a picture of her mother, lost to the ravages of the Holocaust. She portrayed in this moment the effect of trauma as provoking a sense of unbelievability. This state of unbelievability creates the internal dynamic of knowing and not knowing, a condition that is often supported by the mechanism of dissociation.

When death is evaded, especially in traumas of human design, survivors undergo various dimensions of what it means to be "silenced." Horror and helplessness alone have this silencing effect. But often, such as in the case of sexual violence, silencing through horror also has a secondary traumatic effect, when a survivor experiences a "concomitant" command projected by perpetrators that further violence or death will result if one does not remain silent.[25] This frightening realm of trauma supports mechanisms aimed at forgetting, explicitly or implicitly silencing survivors.

The crisis of witnessing, if it is defined as a suppression of memory which revolves around silence, implies that anyone who gives voice to the silence seeks justice. Justice entails *listening* to the voices who put words to the silence. In the realm of the law, this means being attentive to the vulnerability of the witness to trauma and its retelling.

RESPONDING TO TRAUMA IN THE REALM OF THE LAW

We cannot consider the duties or roles of memory and justice without encompassing the element of the tragic, which I put forth in the form of testimony communicated by someone who has endured a traumatic history but has survived to tell about it. My precept concurs with Ricoeur's conception of conviction delineated at the end of *The Just* when he asserts that the "the *apparent better* thing to do" in any circumstance includes confronting the tragic dimension of action from a place of wisdom.[26] In the case of trauma and the criminal justice system, this confrontation includes traversing and encountering the ambiguous and disconcerting terrain of traumatic memory.

To understand what is at stake for survivors of trauma in the act of retelling their stories, and specifically doing so on the witness stand, I turn to a framework offered by Ricoeur in both *The Just* and *Reflections on the Just*, which build from a structure developed in *Oneself as Another*. This framework will assist understanding how justice can respond to the event of trauma. Ricoeur writes in *The Just*:

> The first axis, which we can call the "horizontal" axis, is that of the *dialogical* constitution of the self.... The second, "vertical" axis is that of the hierarchical constitution of the *predicates* that qualify human actions in terms of morality.[27]

In the subsection that follows, I want to go beyond Ricoeur to show how, in the context of a trauma witness, these two axes may conflict. In the subsequent subsection, I return to build on Ricoeur to establish how, despite the potential for conflict, the two axes can ultimately be synthesized in the trial setting. Through the troubling example of the trial demands on a trauma witness, my goal is to deepen Ricoeur's consideration of the just as itself located at the juncture where the self who is the subject of legal rights cannot be distinguished from the moral question of the self who is worthy of these rights.[28]

The Conflict

In the courtroom, the horizontal axis of the dialogical constitution of the self and the vertical, hierarchical axis may intersect beneficially, but they also may conflict. The victim of trauma can be affected positively and negatively in the midst of this intersection. For the present subsection, I restrict the vertical axis to what Ricoeur describes as its deontological dimension: "What, in obligation, *obliges* is the claim for universal *validity* attached to the idea of the law."[29] In the next subsection, I incorporate Ricoeur's broader vision of the vertical axis as one of practical wisdom, where "the just then is no longer either the good or the legal, but the *equitable*."[30] I seek to argue that the equitable can be incorporated within the trial setting and so go beyond the procedural formality of the legal.

In the courtroom, when the act of testifying constitutes bearing witness, the witness becomes a medium for a category of proof offered verbally. In this context, testifying serves the legal purpose of asserting a fact. The legal frame exemplifies what Ricoeur considers the first trait of testimony, which "anchors all the other meanings" of testimony "in a quasi-empirical sphere ... because testimony is not perception itself but the report, that is, the story, the narration of the event. It consequently transfers things seen to the level of things said."[31] He continues:

> Testimony is a dual relation: there is the one who testifies and the one who hears the testimony. The witness has seen, but the one who receives his testimony has not seen but hears. It is only by hearing the testimony that he can believe or not believe in the reality of the facts that the witness reports. Testimony as story is thus found in an intermediary position between a statement made by a person and a belief assumed by another on the faith of the testimony of the first.[32]

This sense of testimony, Ricoeur tells us, takes place within the context of the trial which has its own "ritual" elements, including "swearing" or "promising."[33] All relies on "the quality of the witness, his good faith that a logic of testimony cannot do without."[34] The meaning of testimony is not exhausted by its quasi-empirical and quasi-juridical senses due to the displacement from "testimony-proof toward the witness." In question is who is a true witness or a faithful witness. Testimony then becomes an action that seeks to attest to the interior self, to conviction, and to good faith.[35]

Due to the trial emphasis on both the quasi-empirical nature of testimony in establishing facts and at the same time on the faithfulness of this witness, the vertical axis's search for truth as legal obligation may conflict with the horizontal axis's dialogical constitution of the self. Although the horizontal, dialogical constitution of the self can be enhanced in a legal setting—as Ricoeur rightly notes in his comments on South Africa's Truth and Reconciliation Commission[36]—from a traditional legal perspective the primary goal of justice revolves around ascertaining defendant guilt and providing society a sense of justice rather than providing justice for the witness. In the courtroom dealing with individual and/or societal trauma, the horizontal, dialogical constitution of the self of the witness may suffer at the vertical hands of the search for justice. I offer two more delineated and overlapping points here. First, the adversarial legal search for "truth" of the vertical axis may nullify the horizontal axis's dialogical constitution of the self. This problem is exacerbated in the context of trauma witness testimony, because the memory of trauma is not linear and narrative, as trial logic demands, which leads to vertical axis questioning of the truth of the testimony. Second, in probing the veracity of the testimony and its good faith, the trial may require the witness to re-enter a prior situation of trauma and so become retraumatized, which also undermines dialogical self-constitution. These insights into the negative consequences for self-constitution in the trial context go beyond Ricoeur's general view of courtroom dynamics.

As to the first point, in the courtroom the vertical axis's search for truth and law may trample the more horizontal dialogical constitution of the self. Instead of a dialogue between the parties to the trial, protection of oneself or entity may involve attempts to undermine the opposing party's self. The system is adversarial. Intense questioning and other tactics such as challenging the credibility of the witness become weapons that can be used lawfully, although not ethically, to dissuade witnesses from moving forward. Bundy's questioning of Crew provides an example of the kind of excessive badgering for details of traumatic scenes.

The credibility of the trauma witness is further susceptible to attack due to the way that the trauma memory is stored. *Black's Law Dictionary* defines memory as "the mental power to review and recognize the successive states of consciousness in their consecutive order."[37] But the courtroom's model of a coherent memory narrative is problematic in the context of a trauma witness. Acute recall of a traumatic memory can be marked by a singular image or contrarily as a mass of images that collide with one another so as not to make sense. Further, testimony of the trauma survivor intertwines with the way the survivor stores memory. Such testimony may not simply be composed of words that are heard, but also things felt, experienced, and therefore communicated through eye contact, body language, and other indicators. Memories may not come forward as narrative when they are linked to a traumatic event but instead emerge as hallucinations, as sensations such as abdominal pain, as voices warning of danger, or as nightmares.[38] These "fragments" of memory, although difficult to pinpoint in time, are exceedingly detailed, more detailed, as previously mentioned, than non-traumatic memory. Where the witness of trauma may falter in knowing precisely the timing of a particular event, he or she will often be able to retell sensory experiences—smell, sounds, colors—with great efficacy. Traumatic memories are thus easy to recall, but difficult to contextualize. The traumatic memory is fragmented and eludes cognition. When viewed in the way that memory functions after trauma and with the problematic nature of the "crisis of witnessing," discussed earlier, the legal model of memory as a linear construct represents a chronology that it is impossible to achieve when recalling trauma and can lead to misinterpretation of the witness's veracity and of the event being related. Narratives composed of non-linear, fragmented, affectively charged pieces potentially frustrate efforts in the courtroom to obtain the truth. These factors further complicate the effort to receive the trauma narrative in the courtroom drama.

A second and correlative problem of the vertical axis's search for truth is that the adversarial system may itself lead to retraumatization of a trauma witness. When survivors of trauma testify, remembering and retelling an account of victimization, they become witnesses who are asked to revisit and reexperience the original trauma, to endure amygdala activation and a stimulated sympathetic nervous system. Badgering of a witness may exacerbate these consequences. Survivors of rape put on the stand are particularly vulnerable to this kind of testimony, especially when questioned incessantly with the accused in the courtroom or if the examiner has characteristics in common with the accused that might elicit a flashback.[39] As another example, when Bundy asks Officer Crew for the details of the kill, he does not do so to support his argument, and yet he is permitted to continue as the Officer on the stand and the others in the courtroom grow visibly disturbed by the need to relive the gratuitous violence of Bundy's actions. While retelling of a trauma might or might not achieve the needs of courtroom examiners, such questioning can disrupt a witness's self-constitution. This risk of retraumatization rests at the heart of the conflict sustaining further suffering for the witness at the behest of the search for justice. The trauma of the crisis of witnessing is traditionally viewed as irrelevant to the effort to obtain a just result.

Synthesizing the Axes

Because the law seeks to ascertain the truth while the remediation process aims at making a legitimate grievant whole and a society just, the two axes ultimately should not be in conflict: the vertical demand for justice also must incorporate the horizontal dimension of the dialogical constitution of the self. If the role of the law includes individual redress, then it is not just the legal *result*—for example, conviction of an assailant—but also the legal *process*—the trial itself—that is integral to that goal. In this section, I respond to the prior section's demonstration of the existing conflict between the two axes in the context of trauma testimony by showing how these axes can be synthesized and reconciled in the same setting.

I begin by returning to Ricoeur and elaborate how he broadens the vertical axis beyond the procedural legal formalism exemplified in jurisprudential thinkers such as Rawls. As discussed in the prior subsection, a standard account is that the vertical axis is oriented to the deontological: to fairness as interpreting right or wrong on the basis of rules and procedures. Ricoeur, though, locates the deontological within the larger frame of teleology, focused on purpose and goal, and practical wisdom, considering how justice emerges in the face of difficult contexts such as the tragic.[40] While the trial process considers verifiable data and specific facts, Ricoeur asserts that it cannot exist independent of a wider pre-understanding of the just and unjust developing from Greek and Roman influence on the Judeo-Christian conceptions of the Golden Rule.[41] The Golden Rule as a principle of fairness is debated in the legal field because of its challenge to objectivity, and yet as an ethic of reciprocity it is foundational to many religious systems. As a prior understanding, the Golden Rule continually orients the judiciary process toward the teleological where "the good designates the *telos* of an entire life."[42] This "good" for Ricoeur relates intimately to the constitution of the self in relationship with the other of interpersonal relations and the other of justice mediated by the institution and their imbrication with the wish to live well with others. The vertical axis is broader than the narrow proceduralism discussed in the last subsection, and it converges with the "horizontal axis" of the dialogic constitution of the self.

Ricoeur describes the just as located between the legal and the good, in the sense where the legal is understood as proceduralism.[43] Eileen Brennan interprets Ricoeur to mean that the "idea of justice has two meanings—the good and the legal—and it orients a judicial practice in two corresponding directions—towards the good and towards the legal."[44] Building on Ricoeur, I want to show how in the courtroom setting of a trauma witness, the good can be incorporated into the vertical axis of the court's pursuit of the truth and interrelated with the good in the horizontal axis's orientation toward the dialogical constitution of the self. The legal judgment is one of practical wisdom, where "the just then is no longer either the good or the legal, but the *equitable*."[45] The just may be located between the legal and the good in the setting of trauma victim testimony to the extent that a trial provides legal protections not only for a criminal defendant but for the trauma witness. In turn, this protection of the trauma witness enhances the trial's search for truth. Protection of the trauma witness benefits both the horizontal, dialogical constitution of the witness's self and the vertical axis's pursuit of truth.

If a primary function of the law is to provide legal redress, this redress must be afforded the trauma witness as well as the criminal defendant. The trauma victim too must be "a subject of rights."[46] Ricoeur argues in *The Just* that justice includes a relationship which extends the notion of friendship—where the primary relationship is between you, as the other, and I—to embrace *any* other and I. Thinking about the other as the survivor on the witness stand becomes a decisive factor.[47] This orientation is enhanced by Ricoeur's avowal that "the moral priority belongs to the victims."[48] Orienting justice towards the good acknowledges the reality of tragedy and seeks protection of the most vulnerable.

To properly elicit the trauma witness's memory, the trial lawyers on both sides must engage with the witness in the dialogic construction of the witness's self. The criminal justice system has the inherent ability to contribute to the construction of identity, the forum to enable an understanding that the self is not reducible to its narrative, and the tools to show that accountability in the system not only lies with the storyteller but also with the person asking the questions or soliciting the story.[49] The legal system can participate in the ethical response to tragedy outlined by Ricoeur, in its request to hear legal testimony that is traumatic memory when it does so with the aim of supporting the hard work of memory and mourning. Ultimately, as Ricoeur asserts in *Memory, History, Forgetting*, mourning is the cost of remembering but leads to liberation in time.[50] In order to facilitate this liberation, one must return language "to speech that has been instructed by meaning."[51]

For the trial to take seriously trauma witness testimony, it must begin in Ricoeur's assertion that "[t]he truthful ambition of memory has its own merits, which deserve to be recognized before any consideration is given to the pathological deficiencies and nonpathological weaknesses of memory."[52]

It is this "truthful ambition" that must be an initial presupposition of what underlies survivor accounts of their personal, tragic histories. For the vertical axis's search for justice to converge with the horizontal axis's dialogical constitution of the self, those involved in litigation then have the further responsibility to understand and perceive the psychological phenomena of survivor testimony that might inform their practices and procedures. Understanding the nature of traumatic memory, which removes the survivor from the present affectively and cognitively because the past action of attack is believed to be occurring in the present moment, affords the system an opportunity to utilize such memory intelligently for the good of all. The criminal justice system must acknowledge survivors as witnesses who may find themselves suspended between truth and the non-cohesive processes of the brain in constructing the narrative of tragic action. When we listen to the testimony of a survivor, we hear not only fact, but bodies and pain, which may transpose historical fact into a noncommensurable personal truth. At the center of remembering and then recounting of the trauma narrative lies the enigma of the way that the brain stores trauma, which is not necessarily as narrative words for easy recall. The non-linear nature of the traumatic memory does not make the memory false but rather in need of responsible questioning and gathering of data to make the fragments fit together with larger narratives. This effort demands systematic verification of facts and efforts to collect plausible opposing viewpoints, while making explicit this protocol for the witness. The suggested procedural protections for the trauma victim on the witness stand extend current witness rights—for instance, protections against being badgered or being subject to lengthy cross-examination[53]—and these procedural protections would merge with the legal goal of truth and the ethical imperative to understand the risk of re-subjecting a witness to the effects of trauma.

Telling the story of the story of trauma is necessary in the construction of truth and of self-identity, of putting back the pieces of the self after trauma and making sense of the experience. The retelling allows the trauma witness indeed to become "a subject of rights"[54] and to recover a sense of agency, an ability to do something, in the ability to remember, to tell the truth. The Holocaust survivor constructed a narrative from fragments of her own memory, stories told to her, and realities that she knew existed during the Holocaust to illustrate and explain her experience. The story and the act of telling her story ratified her sense of being a capable human person in the world. Furthermore, her testimony combatted the crisis of witnessing for her. In the case of 9/11 survivors, those who share their narratives do so with the desire to help themselves integrate the reality of their trauma stories with their current lives and to help others understand the day of 9/11, its costs, and the importance of remembering the day's victims.

For Ricoeur, as Eileen Brennan points out, the arguments that take place in the courtroom form part of *practice*. Justice is an exercise in "social practice,"[55] not just a matter of theory, procedural form, or doctrine. The interrogation of the survivor on the witness stand forms a critical part of the dialogue: but for the witness there would be no conversation. Ricoeur makes the very interesting claim that exchanging arguments before a court is an ethically motivated "communication activity" and "a remarkable example of the dialogical employment of language."[56] When the survivor is at the center of the discourse about justice, then the procedural form of justice challenged by Ricoeur fails to make sense. The trial cannot succeed without a presupposition and concern for the good; in this case the good emerges in what is essential for the constitution of the traumatized self, through dialogic encounters. Both the self of the trauma victim and the trauma victim's testimony are constructed not simply by the narrative recounted, but also supported by the verbal exchanges that Ricoeur notes are characteristic of the courtroom environment. The vertical and horizontal axes converge.

The meaning of justice and the act of testifying have implications for the "crisis of witnessing," which must be considered with the duty of memory to highlight the ethical obligation of participants in the criminal justice system to heed the difficulty, both affectively and neurologically challenging, in recounting traumatic memory. Acknowledging this difficulty lies alongside the demands of legal testimony. Drawing attention to traumatic memory as it emerges in the courtroom expands the point of view of justice oriented in terms of fairness towards the good, connoting the influence of the Golden Rule. It is also here where we must orient justice and decide what the facts presented as personal truth do, enact, or effect for the person, as survivor and witness, and for the case at stake. In the example of the Holocaust survivor, her testimony does not fail to highlight an unspeakable reality nor to meet its goal of teaching listeners of the threat and reality of crimes enacted upon human bodies. Memory's duty is in this education and subsequent mourning part and parcel of justice. It is, as Ricoeur asserts, a duty of justice to legitimate the duty of memory.[57]

CONCLUSION

Throughout Ricoeur's oeuvre, he constructs a sense of just institutions which have at their base an obligation to the other, especially the suffering other. Ricoeur reprehends systems that dissociate consolation and reconciliation of this suffering. When this kind of system flourishes, he writes, "victims are marginalized. The success of the system is its failure. Suffering, as what is expressed by the voices of lamentation, is what the system excludes."[58] Ricoeur's critique in this passage takes place at the social or cultural level, but when traumatic memory is considered, the concept of dissociation becomes even more alarming. Dissociation of traumatic memory leads to more trauma. Furthermore, as I have discussed, the physical reaction to trauma affects the ability of survivors to give objective, factual testimony. Survivor testimony differs in this respect from traditional legal testimony and its expectations, but I have argued that it is still essential, and its vertical and horizontal requirements demand attention from the criminal justice system. Even a simple awareness by those in the legal profession of the effects of retelling a trauma narrative on the witness stand begins to have an ameliorative impact on the conflict between the horizontal and vertical planes.

Understanding the nature of traumatic memory should lead to improvement in the trial use of it. The atmosphere of the trial, which Ricoeur considers a forum for dialogue in recognition of the other, offers a space or a foundation from which we can envision respect and consideration for people who have traumatic memories. This respect manifests in maintaining a propulsion toward the support of the "*dialogical* constitution of the self" on the horizontal plane and on the vertical plane "placing the stamp of prudence on goodness" where prudence is the "art of a fair decision in situations of uncertainty and conflict, hence in the tragic setting of action."[59] The crisis of witnessing imposes a steep toll on the witness, a toll that requires recognition and balance by the legal system. In the event of the retelling of trauma on the witness stand, the law has the opportunity to enable an understanding that the self is not reducible to its narrative and to show that an obligation in the system to ensure that the truth is told is not only in the hands of the testifier but also in the hands of the examiner.

NOTES

1. Paul Ricoeur, *Memory, History, Forgetting*, trans. Kathleen Blamey and David Pellauer (Chicago: University of Chicago Press, 2004), 88.
2. Ricoeur, *Memory, History, Forgetting*, 88.
3. Ricoeur, *Memory, History, Forgetting*, 89.
4. Shoshana Felman and Dori Laub, *Testimony: Crises of Witnessing in Literature, Psychoanalysis, and History* (New York: Routledge, 1992), xix.
5. See Olivier Abel, "The Political Ethics of Paul Ricoeur: Happiness and Justice" (paper presented at Union Theological Seminary, New York, October 1992), accessed December 12, 2018, http://olivierabel.fr/supplement/the-political-ethics-of-paul-ricoeur-happiness-and-justice.php.
6. Felman and Laub, *Testimony*, xvii.

7. See Felman and Laub, *Testimony*, passim, but particularly 46.

8. Paul Ricoeur, *Oneself as Another*, trans. David Pellauer (Chicago: University of Chicago Press, 1992), 172.

9. Judith Lewis Herman, *Trauma and Recovery* (New York: Basic Books, 1997), 33.

10. Cathy Caruth, ed., *Trauma: Explorations in Memory* (Baltimore: Johns Hopkins University Press, 1995), 256.

11. Bessel A. Van der Kolk, *The Body Keeps the Score: Brain, Mind, and Body in the Healing of Trauma* (New York: Viking, 2014), 61.

12. Van der Kolk, *The Body Keeps the Score*, 42.

13. See Barbara Ganzel et al., "The Aftermath of 9/11: Effect of Intensity and Recency of Trauma on Outcome," *Emotion* 7, no. 2 (2007): 227–38.

14. Elizabeth A. Phelps, "Human Emotion and Memory: Interactions of the Amygdala and Hippocampal Complex," *Current Opinion in Neurobiology*, 14 (2004): 198–99.

15. Van der Kolk, *The Body Keeps the Score*, 44.

16. Van der Kolk, *The Body Keeps the Score*, 45.

17. Van der Kolk, *The Body Keeps the Score*, 45.

18. Van der Kolk, *The Body Keeps the Score*, 195. Incidentally, and worth reporting, when asked questions regarding the sensory details of positive memories, subjects came up short. Negative replies were total to questions such as: do you recall how your husband's body felt on your wedding night? By contrast, powerful emotional responses and recall were elicited when asked questions about how a rapist's body smelled.

19. Van der Kolk, *The Body Keeps the Score*, 195.

20. Herman, *Trauma and Recovery*, 1.

21. Herman, *Trauma and Recovery*, 1.

22. Shoshana Felman, "Education and Crisis, or the Vicissitudes of Teaching," in *Testimony: Crises of Witnessing in Literature, Psychoanalysis, and History*, eds. Shoshana Felman and Dori Laub (New York: Routledge, 1992), 6.

23. Felman, "Education and Crisis," 6.

24. See Annie Rogers, *The Unsayable: The Hidden Language of Trauma* (New York: Random House, 2006).

25. Eric D. Lister, "Forced Silence: A Neglected Dimension of Trauma," *American Journal of Psychiatry* 139, no. 7 (1982): 872.

26. Ricoeur, *The Just*, trans. David Pellauer (Chicago: University of Chicago Press, 2000), 155.

27. Ricoeur, *The Just*, xii.

28. Ricoeur, *The Just*, 1.

29. Ricoeur, *The Just*, xvii.

30. Ricoeur, *The Just*, xxiv.

31. Paul Ricoeur, "The Hermeneutics of Testimony," in *Essays on Biblical Interpretation*, ed. Lewis S. Mudge (Philadelphia: Fortress Press, 1980), 123.

32. Ricoeur, "The Hermeneutics of Testimony," 123.

33. Ricoeur, "The Hermeneutics of Testimony," 124.

34. Ricoeur, "The Hermeneutics of Testimony," 128.
35. Ricoeur, "The Hermeneutics of Testimony," 128–29.
36. Ricoeur, *Memory, History, Forgetting,* 483–85.
37. Henry Campbell Black, *Black's Law Dictionary*, ed. Bryan A. Garner (Minneapolis: Thompson Reuter, 11th Ed., 2019), 771.
38. Van der Kolk, *The Body Keeps the Score*, 25.
39. In literature about rape and incest, triggers of past trauma elicit flashbacks and can be instigated by the encounter with particular individuals or situations, see The Havens, "A Self-Help Guide for Survivors of Rape and Sexual Assault," March 2019, accessed October 4, 2019, https://www.kch.nhs.uk/Doc/pl%20-%20819.2%20-%20a%20self-help%20guide%20for%20survivors%20of%20rape%20and%20sexual%20assault.pdf; Judith Herman, *Trauma and Recovery*, 37, 232. Such intrusive memories are retraumatizing, especially when the emotional valence of a situation is high and/or when power is wielded—as in the case of a trial. See Rose Mary Lynn Ubell, "Myths and Misogyny: The Legal Response to Sexual Assault" (Master of Studies in Law Research Papers Repository, University of Western Ontario, 2018) especially chapter 4, 52–72, https://ir.lib.uwo.ca/mslp/4.
40. Ricoeur, *The Just*, xiv–xxi.
41. Ricoeur, *The Just*, 56.
42. Ricoeur, *The Just*, xv.
43. Paul Ricoeur, "The Just Between the Legal and the Good," this volume: 21–36.
44. Eileen Brennan, "Doing Justice to Justice: Ricoeur's Discovery of the Juridical Plane," *Philosophy Today* 58, no. 4 (2014): 594.
45. Ricoeur, *The Just*, xxiv.
46. Ricoeur, *The Just*, 2.
47. Ricoeur, *The Just*, xiii.
48. Ricoeur, *Memory, History, Forgetting*, 89.
49. Basia D. Ellis and Henderikus J. Stam, "Addressing the Other in Dialogue: Ricoeur and the Ethical Dimensions of the Dialogical Self," *Theory and Psychology* 20, no. 3 (June 2010): 428.
50. Ricoeur, *Memory, History, Forgetting*, 71–74.
51. Ricoeur, *Memory, History, Forgetting*, 496.
52. Ricoeur, *Memory, History, Forgetting*, 21.
53. See National Crime Victim Law Institute, "Practical Tips and Legal Strategies for Easing Victims' Concerns about Testifying," *NCVLI News*, Winter, 2007–2008.
54. Ricoeur, *The Just*, 2.
55. Brennan, "Doing Justice to Justice," 595.
56. Brennan, "Doing Justice to Justice," 594.
57. Ricoeur, *Memory, History, Forgetting*, 89.
58. Paul Ricoeur, "Evil, A Challenge to Philosophy and Theology," trans. David Pellauer, *Journal of the American Academy of Religion* 53, no. 4 (1985): 643. In this passage, Ricoeur is critiquing Hegel's philosophy of history, not the legal trial, but I would contend that the message is more generalizable.
59. Paul Ricoeur, *Reflections on the Just*, trans. David Pellauer (Chicago: University of Chicago Press, 2007): 60, 63.

BIBLIOGRAPHY

Abel, Olivier. "The Political Ethics of Paul Ricoeur: Happiness and Justice." Paper presented at Union Theological Seminary, New York, October 1992. Accessed December 12, 2018. http://olivierabel.fr/supplement/the-political-ethics-of-paul-ricoeur-happiness-and-justice.php.

Black, Henry Campbell. *Black's Law Dictionary*. Edited by Bryan A. Garner. Minneapolis: Thompson Reuter, 11th Ed., 2019.

Brennan, Eileen. "Doing Justice to Justice: Ricoeur's Discovery of the Juridical Plane." *Philosophy Today* 58, no. 4 (2014): 591–606.

Caruth, Cathy, ed. *Trauma: Explorations in Memory*. Baltimore: Johns Hopkins University Press, 1995.

Ellis, Basia D., and Henderikus J. Stam. "Addressing the Other in Dialogue: Ricoeur and the Ethical Dimensions of the Dialogical Self." *Theory and Psychology* 20, no. 3 (June 2010): 420–35.

Felman, Shoshana. "Education and Crisis, or the Vicissitudes of Teaching." In *Testimony: Crises of Witnessing in Literature, Psychoanalysis, and History*, edited by Shoshana Felman and Dori Laub, 1–56. New York: Routledge, 1992.

Felman, Shoshana, and Dori Laub. *Testimony: Crises of Witnessing in Literature, Psychoanalysis, and History*. New York: Routledge, 1992.

Ganzel, Barbara et al. "The Aftermath of 9/11: Effect of Intensity and Recency of Trauma on Outcome." *Emotion* 7, no. 2 (2007): 227–38.

The Havens. "A Self-Help Guide for Survivors of Rape and Sexual Assault." March 2019. Accessed October 4, 2019, https://www.kch.nhs.uk/Doc/pl%20-%20819.2%20-%20a%20self-help%20guide%20for%20survivors%20of%20rape%20and%20sexual%20assault.pdf.

Herman, Judith Lewis. *Trauma and Recovery*. New York: Basic Books, 1997.

Lister, Eric D. "Forced Silence: A Neglected Dimension of Trauma." *American Journal of Psychiatry* 139, no. 7 (1982): 872–76.

National Crime Victim Law Institute. "Practical Tips and Legal Strategies for Easing Victims' Concern about Testifying." *NCVLI News*, Winter, 2007–2008.

Phelps, Elizabeth A. "Human Emotion and Memory: Interactions of the Amygdala and Hippocampal Complex." *Current Opinion in Neurobiology*, no. 14 (2004): 198–202.

Ricoeur, Paul. "Evil, A Challenge to Philosophy and Theology." Translated by David Pellauer. *Journal of the American Academy of Religion* 53, no. 4 (1985): 635–48.

Ricoeur, Paul. "The Hermeneutics of Testimony." In *Essays on Biblical Interpretation*, edited by Lewis S. Mudge, 119–54. Philadelphia: Fortress Press, 1980.

Ricoeur, Paul. *The Just*. Translated by David Pellauer. Chicago: University of Chicago Press, 2000.

Ricoeur, Paul "The Just between the Legal and the Good," in this volume, 21–36.

Ricoeur, Paul. *Memory, History, Forgetting*. Translated by Kathleen Blamey and David Pellauer. Chicago: University of Chicago Press, 2004.

Ricoeur, Paul. *Oneself as Another*. Translated by Kathleen Blamey. Chicago: University of Chicago Press, 1992.

Ricoeur, Paul. *Reflections on the Just*. Translated by David Pellauer. Chicago: University of Chicago Press, 2007.

Rogers, Annie. *The Unsayable: The Hidden Language of Trauma*. New York: Random House, 2006.

Ubell, Rose Mary Lynn. "Myths and Misogyny: The Legal Response to Sexual Assault." 2018. Master of Studies in Law Research Papers Repository, University of Western Ontario, 4. https://ir.lib.uwo.ca/mslp/4.

Van der Kolk, Bessel A. *The Body Keeps the Score: Brain, Mind, and Body in the Healing of Trauma*. New York: Viking, 2014.

Chapter Thirteen

The Interaction Between Love and Justice in the Legal System

Walter Salles

INTRODUCTION

My thesis is that elements of love—at least in a certain sense—can be incorporated within the law, and the law can help to preserve the possibility of love within society.[1] The departure points for my reflection are from Paul Ricoeur's well-known essays on love and justice. My claim is that Ricoeur went too quickly to theological aspects of love to oppose the logic of superabundance to the logic of equivalence, and consequently he does not consider sufficiently the possibility of love orienting judicial practice. Unlike Ricoeur, I insist on an anthropological rather than theological perspective in order to show why love matters for justice. The orientation of love allows us to imagine new ways to live with one another. My goal is to show that love can be more integrated into law in its day-to-day operations, even if it is realized only occasionally. I intend to defend that the tension between both logics, superabundance and equivalence, does not entail a necessary opposition, for love and justice can interact with each other.

I develop my argument in three parts. Part I examines Paul Ricoeur's own arguments on the dialectic between love and justice. Part II incorporates some secondary commentary on why love matters for justice. I refer particularly to arguments from Martha Nussbaum, Elizabeth Mertz, and Susan Daicoff, who defend the need to take into account noneconomic factors in legal practice. In part III, I build upon parts I and II to show that we can amend Ricoeur's treatment of the dialectic between love and justice to show that love can motivate the exercise of justice in legal practice. My conclusion will suggest that the way in which Ricoeur exposes dimensions of the judicial system authorizes us to venture beyond his thesis and endorse the interaction between love and justice.

HOW RICOEUR SEES THE INTERRELATION BETWEEN LOVE AND JUSTICE

In this first Part, I will focus my reflection on Paul Ricoeur's arguments on the dialectic of love and justice in three main essays:[2] "The Logic of Jesus, the Logic of God," "Love and Justice," and "Thou Shalt Not Kill: A Loving Obedience."[3] Ricoeur explores this dialectic in a concentrated fashion in these essays, which have a religious background, more specifically what Ricoeur calls the logic of Jesus and God. His main claim is that this dialectic expresses an opposition between two logics: one of superabundance, which is identified with love, and the other of equivalence, which is associated with the exercise of justice in the legal system. This logic of superabundance reverses the human logic of equivalence, which finds in the famous law "an eye for an eye" (*lex talionis*) its most ancient expression of the victory over endless vengeance.[4] This law was a principle developed in early Babylonian law. This principle was present in both biblical and early Roman law. It means an equivalence between the punishment received by criminals and those injuries that they had inflicted upon their victims.

For Ricoeur, thinking about the dialectic between love and justice is an attempt to locate love in contemporary society. Ricoeur's arguments are concerned with the fact that he sees love from within the context of biblical faith, and consequently love is placed on a transcendent level. He locates love in the religious context of the Judeo-Christian tradition, particularly having as background the commandment of love for God and for the neighbor (Deuteronomy 6:5; Luke 10:27). In order to explore this aspect, Ricoeur suggests the reading of Matthew 5:39b-42 from within the economy of the gift.[5] This logic will take the love of enemies as an extreme attitude (Matthew 5:44).

What does love mean in these essays? If we consider them together, we can state summarily that Ricoeur presents the dialectic between love and justice as one way of finding a way between two extremes: simply an exaltation of love on the one hand and on the other a demonstration of love as simply sentimental platitudes.[6] The exaltation is presented by biblical tradition: everything we do without love has no value, love endures all things, love never fails, love is greater than faith and hope.[7] The sentimentality is so intimate that it is not expressed in social practices but a feeling that is easily exhausted in simple words.

Love is expressed in attitudes such as gratuity, compassion, and mercy, and it is moved by a logic that bursts the logic of equivalence that commands our every day of exchange, commerce, and penal law.[8] Love is governed by the economy of gift, a gift that for Ricoeur always manifests itself as an excess in relation to justice.[9] This notion of excess allows Ricoeur to state that love is commanded by a logic that is not in accordance with the logic of our ordinary ethics. The economy of the gift develops a logic of superabundance that raises love to a condition of the hyperethical. Being hyperethical does not mean that love is nonmoral. It means above all that love is not subordinate to the logic of equivalence—I give in order that you will give. Consequently, love can also correct the utilitarian tendency expressed by reciprocity: give to receive in return. The "in order that" no longer has a place in the economy of gift, because the lover expects nothing in return.[10]

The influence of love on justice may occur when we have to take a side in conflicts between a respect for law or a solicitude for the individuals involved, or in the case where the choice is about the lesser evil. In these situations, "love comes to plead in the name of compassion and generosity in favor of justice."[11] The influence of love also occurs when it contributes to the effective universalization of the moral.[12] Love presses justice to enlarge the circle of mutual recognition. "The vis-à-vis of justice is faceless others . . . [T]he vis-à-vis is no longer you, but each and all."[13] Another effect of the pressure that love makes on justice concerns itself with the recognition of persons as always unique. In this sense, love is the guarantor of singularity, otherness, and mutuality.

By contrast, Ricoeur insists that justice is governed by the logic of equivalence.[14] This second logic is the human logic, our tendency to establish an exact proportion between crime and punishment, the penalty being equal to the mistake, for example. The circumstance of justice as social practice arises when "a higher court is asked to decide between the claims of parties with opposed interests or rights."[15] Justice encompasses at the same time the judicial apparatus (court, lawyers, judges, laws, etc.) and the ideal of justice. Ricoeur sees justice, above all, from within its distributive dimension. Therefore, he gives to the idea of distribution an amplitude that surpasses the realm of economic aspects and includes roles, tasks, rights, and duties. Thus, we have the most general formula of justice: "to render each his or her due."[16] Another important aspect of justice is equality of rights and the proportional equality of responsibilities that indicates both the strength and the limits of justice.[17]

Ricoeur also insists on the idea that the logic of equivalence that governs justice is opposed to the gratuity that characterizes love. This is because justice bases its security on the submission to the rule of equivalence, and gratuity is freed from this rule. Although Ricoeur defends the existence of a disproportion between love and justice, for him this disproportion can open a space for practical mediations capable of supporting a more basic moral project of justice.[18]

Some years after writing these essays, Ricoeur spent several pages in *The Course of Recognition*, in particular in chapter 3, on mutual recognition,[19] to talk about the economy of the gift with an explicit reference to the dialectic between love and justice. Ricoeur states again that the economy of gift is characterized by the attitude of giving without expecting anything in return, that is, the expression of gratuity.[20] Giving without expecting anything in return is the only desire of love.[21] In an exchange of gifts between two people, Ricoeur asks whether an obligation to give in return in the second act would not annul the gratuitous nature of the original gift, in that in the first act someone gives without expecting anything in return. For Ricoeur, this exchange of gifts is characterized by a creative tension between gratuity and obligation that is governed by love, by a loving obedience.[22] This tension characterized by gratuity and obligation will help us to understand why love matters for justice.

LOVE AS MOTIVATION FOR THE EXERCISE OF JUSTICE

Why do emotions matter for justice? The attempt to answer this question has inspired a significant debate, as Martha Nussbaum shows in her book, *Anger and Forgiveness*.[23] I would like to take into account just one aspect of this book that is presented in the introduction, when she talks about the Greek tragedy *Oresteia*, which was composed by the playwright Aeschylus. This tragedy narrates the mythico-religious establishment of the human tribunal in Athens by the goddess Athena. In this tragedy, the Erinyes play a key role as ones charged with punishing mortals.

According to Nussbaum, two important transformations take place at the end of Aeschylus's play. First, Athena introduces legal institutions to replace and terminate the endless cycle of blood vengeance and announces that blood guilt will now be settled by law, rather than by the Erinyes. Athena establishes a court of twelve judges (citizens of Athens) and offers Orestes a human judgment based on a sense of justice. Hence, a legal system replaces the act of vengeance. Second, often neglected, the Erinyes are not dismissed. Instead, Athena persuades them to join the city, giving them a place of honor in recognition of their importance for the legal institutions and the welfare of the city. But the condition of this honor is that they abandon their focus on vengeance and adopt a new range of sentiments, in particular benevolent sentiments toward the entire city. Perhaps the most fundamental transformation of all is the requirement that justice be regulated using the law by human beings, by the citizens, and justice becomes a human prerogative no longer associated with vengeance.

Ricoeur points to this change of perspective when he suggests that forgiveness must accompany justice in its effort to eradicate, on the symbolic plane, both the sacred and the savage elements of vengeance, by which blood calls for blood, as an attitude of justice. In fact, on the deepest symbolic plane, it is a matter of distinguishing *Dikē* (non-vengeful justice) and *Themis* (the ultimate and shadowy refuge of sacred vengeance). This is what *Oresteia* teaches us when, at the end of the play, the Erinyes (the avenging furies) also become the Eumenides (the benevolent spirits). The Erinyes and the Eumenides are one and the same.[24] The Eumenides protect the city of Athens from passions (emotions) that inspire fratricidal struggles derived from the desire of vengeance that lead human beings to destruction. It is in Athens that justice is connected to law enforcement instead of vengeance.

Aeschylus offers us suggestive images, not a theory or answers for our contemporary problems of justice or more specifically for the interaction between love and justice. One of these perspectives is precisely the migration from vengeance, fruit of pure emotion, to justice as the practice of argumentation and discernment. Personal emotions, although legitimate, cannot be taken as the sole criterion for the fulfillment of justice, because the offended normally desires an exacerbated punishment of the wrongdoer. In this sense, judicial practice can be understood as a set of alternatives which a society assumes in order to guarantee life together based on just institutions in opposition to the practice of doing justice with one's own hands.

Another important perspective offered by Aeschylus points to the need to take emotions into account, especially the desire for justice. Elizabeth Mertz contends in her book, *The Language of Law School*,[25] that students of law are encouraged to put aside emotional and ethical conflicts in the name of an alleged neutral or technical language of law. Yet, she continues, it is very important to consider that legal texts and laws do not exist entirely apart from human stories, conflicts, and pain, that is, moral dilemmas and social injustices. The technical aspect of the legal profession sometimes provokes disinterest over noneconomic and affective dimensions.[26] This position can lead to a narrowing of legal practice which does not allow inquiry into the building of law and the relevance of emotions for justice.

The balance between language, emotions and a technical approach of law is an unstable situation, as demonstrated by the well-known contest between the literal interpretation of legal texts and the need to assess the sense of justice in line with the challenges of the contemporary world. From this long and broad debate, which involves such renowned jurists as Antonin Scalia,[27] I would like to retain only two points. First, legal practice must be interested in the human as a whole. Second, there is a need to instill in law professionals, as a purpose of legal practice, the desire for a just society.

This conviction is in line with Susan Daicoff's criticism when she affirms that lawyers are more focused on the economic bottom line and are less swayed by noneconomic, psychological factors.[28] Lawyers tend to evaluate whether to settle a lawsuit on the basis of a traditional economic model of litigation. From this perspective, to bring about justice means to be focused on maximizing expected economic return, regardless of the emotional aspects of a case. My thesis does not intend to devalue the economic aspect of the legal process. Rather, it aims to draw attention to other litigant needs that involve noneconomic aspects, such as the restoration of human dignity. In many cases, while punishment is indispensable, total reparation is not feasible and monetary restoration is not enough, nor does the punishment of the wrongdoer undo the evil committed. More is necessary to move toward justice as a form of deterrence.

Love may be a motivation for the pursuit of justice. I offer two examples from the United States: The National Memorial for Peace and Justice (Alabama), dedicated to remembering the tragic experience of slavery, and the United States Holocaust Memorial Museum (Washington, D.C.). The intent of both museums is, above all, to promote human dignity and to prevent dehumanizing actions, and thus to do justice to the memory of those who suffered such a dehumanization process. The two museums rise the question "how was this possible?" and do not seek to search for the guilty. They also do not attempt an answer to the question of the origin of evil, but rather seek to motivate us to fight against evil, which is understood as an experience of injustice. This motivation, as is well known, also inspired Ricoeur's philosophical project, which is based in part on the principle that no matter how radical evil is, it will never be as original as love.[29] The persons who are capable of bringing about evil during their lives are also capable of loving and being just.

Thus, the interaction between love and justice requires an anthropological optimism, even though also realist, according to which the guilty is capable of something different from their wrongdoings or faults. They are worth more than their acts. This optimism addresses the desire for justice and for the possibility of love as motivating the practice of justice. The next step is precisely to show how this is possible within legal practice as an outgrowth of Ricoeur's work.

A READING FROM WITHIN THE LEGAL SYSTEM

In the previous part of this chapter, I demonstrated the importance of emotions for justice, more specifically why love matters for justice. I also explained how a juridical reading helps us think about the importance of emotions for the legal system. In this third part, I will go beyond Ricoeur to argue for a possible interaction between love and justice inside the legal system.

Ricoeur did not want to completely separate love from justice. However, the way Ricoeur understands the dialectic between love and justice sometimes makes it difficult to know what might be the role of love in the legal system, because he sees love as an external interference: "It is as though the economy of the gift sought to infiltrate the economy of equivalence."[30] This statement suggests that love comes from a higher level, like an exception that infiltrates our daily life. Sometimes it seems that this highest level of love is accessible only for special people such as Martin Luther King Jr., or Mother Teresa of Calcutta. In general, as we have seen, Ricoeur approaches love and justice by means of contrast. For example, he says that "the logic of superabundance bursts the logic of equivalence"[31]; there is a "disproportionality between love and justice"[32]; and "it is in contrast to justice that Agape presents its credentials."[33]

My difficulty with Ricoeur is that in the relationship between love and justice, he describes love as an obligation,[34] as if being just was not a natural unfolding of love. As the background for my own reflections, I on the other hand claim that love leads us to be just or that justice is an expression of love, and both refer to the other person. I will develop my reflection on the interrelation between love and justice oriented to love of the other. I explore four basic ideas of love related to justice: gratuity; recognition of human dignity; restorative justice; and just institutions.

My first consideration addresses Ricoeur's argumentation on the notion of gratuity that he assumes belongs to the sphere of the gift. He claims that to give without wanting anything in return is the main characteristic of love. I agree with Ricoeur when, in both "A Loving Obedience" and "Love and Justice," he warns us about the danger of the first act of giving, giving unconditionally, destroying the gratuity of the second act, giving in return, if the second actor is forced to return love.[35] According to Ricoeur, only love itself can engender love. "The commandment to love is love itself."[36] In this sense, both acts, the initial gift and the gift in return, should be motivated by the same logic of gratuity, by the same logic of gift. But unlike Ricoeur, I consider that in love there is also the expectation of reciprocation. We often experience the feeling of ingratitude if the act of love is not given back. Nevertheless, in my opinion, the gratuity of love consists in not conditioning my act on the act of recognition by the other. By contrast, in a contract, moved by the logic of equivalence and reciprocity, when one party breaks the contract, the other is no longer obliged to comply with the contractual terms. In the economy of the gift, however, even if the second action—the giving in return—does not occur, the first actor is obliged by love to continue loving and giving from a loving obedience. The gratuity is not in the expectation, but in the non-conditioning of the act of the first giver to the return.

Further, we can experience love both in the interpersonal encounter and inside of institutions. But it is important to take into account the different expectations in each act of love. If on the one hand I hope to be reciprocated in my love by my children and my wife, on the other hand I, as professor, do not expect to be loved by my students. Instead, I hope that my love for my students helps them to become good professionals and just citizens. Considering the gratuity of love in this sense has helped, for example, Bryan Stevenson[37] and Max Kenner[38] to see the role of love in the legal system. They expect their loving efforts to facilitate a return—helping incarcerated persons to be treated by them and the legal system with great dignity—but this return does not always happen. The possible lack of a return does not prevent them from continuing, moved by a feeling of giving, loving, and being just.

My second consideration concerns the way an act of recognition can turn into justice from within institutional practices of justice. According to Ricoeur, a legal recognition occurs, for example, when during a legal process my adversaries present their arguments and I am willing to listen to them. In this context, both victim and defendant have the opportunity to admit that the sentence declared by a judge is not an act of violence or vengeance, but rather one of recognition, one of justice.[39] But if we take into account the importance of emotions for justice, we can talk about restorative forms of redress as well. In this sense, recognition is, above all, a recognition of noneconomic needs, more specifically a recognition of human dignity, and recognition of the possibility of the human being to be good and just.

The notion of recognition as a form of reeducation is one of the aspects that I consider fundamental in thinking about the direct effects of love in the sphere of justice. I would like to focus on the educational role of punishment from what Ricoeur himself develops in his reflection on condemnation in the legal system.[40] One of the fundamentals of this role is to believe in the capacity of a person to be more than the perpetrator of a wrong. With a focus on the future, the act of recognition believes that the guilty person is capable of something better than his or her offenses and faults.[41] Reeducation has to do with the notion of care for the other. In judicial practice, this means to restore the capacity of the convicted to be a citizen, in a double sense: regaining rights and duties after the purgation of the penalty and the possibility of living in community under the perspective of the virtue of justice.

For example, the Brazilian criminal code in its article 59 states that the judge must impose the penalty taking into account what is "necessary and sufficient for the disapproval and prevention of crime."[42] This provision is interpreted by many jurists as a way not only to punish but also to reeducate the convicted. In the United States, Max Kenner states that prisoners learning the liberal arts encourages them critical thinking and self-discipline.[43] It is necessary to find ways to help people to leave prison ready to work and to contribute to their families and society. The educational role of a system of punishment shows how it is possible in the legal system to live according to another logic, far from the logic of equivalence or the mere application of punishment. The notion of punishment as reeducation is oriented to the improvement of the guilty along with expiation and promotes the reeducation of the culpable instead of working as mere vengeance.

My third consideration concerns the definition of justice in relation to the logic of equivalence. In my view, Ricoeur pushes too hard on the notion of justice as redistributive justice from the perspective of an arithmetic logic and its deontological orientation. It is necessary to seek an equilibrium between this perspective and justice as restoration of human dignity to better understand how love matters for justice. Ricoeur himself allows us to think in this direction when he asks about the possibility of living according to the logic of the superabundance in our day to day lives.[44] One of the signs of this possibility that he offers concerns the reeducation of the guilty in the sphere of criminal law. The just punishment opposes vengeance to rehabilitation of the culpable. In this case, the logic of superabundance aims not to reduce punishment to a logic that seeks the simple arithmetic equivalence between crime and punishment.

According to some experts, while there is a broad consensus on the meaning of distributive justice (goods, status, honors, occupation) and on retributive justice (to give to each one what is due to each), the same consensus does not obtain on the meaning of restorative justice.[45] The importance of taking into account restorative justice is based on the idea that this conception of justice seeks to transform the experience of evil into the possibility of good.[46] The challenge is to find the social significance of restorative justice when it has little or no effect on the amount of economic restitution. For example, when someone unjustly loses a certain amount of money, justice means to obtain this amount back. In this conception of justice frequently there is no place for noneconomic factors. At the same time, economic factors are insufficient to pull people out of a situation of anger, rancor, resentment, or a desire for revenge. The restoration of personal dignity requires another action, and that lies beyond economic retribution. Restoring dignity to the offended is not reduced to an economic issue. Attempting such restoration, if possible, would go far beyond receiving a sum of money stipulated by the judicial authorities or the incarceration of the guilty. While those forms of redress are necessary, they are also insufficient.

My fourth and last consideration points to the concept of just institutions. I agree with Ricoeur that love cannot be institutionalized inasmuch as it is not reducible to the logic of equivalence.[47] But human relationships are mediated by institutions in which love can manifest itself. Private life, for example, needs the jurisdictional organs and administrative apparatus of the legal system. For example, civil registrations of birth, marriage, and death are often the recognition of human dignity inside institutions, and such an attitude is often a recognition of love. Through birth registration, the law recognizes parenthood, it gives a name and citizenship to a child, it offers the beginning of a history of life. Through marriage registration two persons promise to respect the rights and obligations of a life together. Death registration offers respect to the memory of a person. Death is not a simple extinction but at the end of a history that deserves to be remembered and narrated.

The experience of love through institutions can happen also in attitudes that go beyond what is strictly legal, such as the attitude of a doctor who, moved by compassion for the suffering of a person, acts beyond a professional role. According to Bryan Stevenson, "An absence of compassion can corrupt the decency of a community, a state, a nation. Fear and anger can make us vindictive and abusive, unjust and unfair, until we all suffer from the absence of mercy, and we condemn ourselves as much as we victimize others."[48] An attitude of compassion has led Stevenson to succeed in removing a few persons from imposition of the death penalty. His life is a testimony that our commitment to the rule of law and justice cannot be measured only by the logic of equivalence. A just legal system should seek a just solution for an unjust situation.[49]

Both the personal levels of the expression of love—to be just and moved by compassion and gratuity—and its institutional expressions are fundamental for building a just society. In this sense, justice refers to both the victim and the wrongdoer. In relation to the victim, justice prevents the endless violence of vengeance, which consists in the victim pretending to do justice with his/her own hands and constituting a simulacrum of justice.[50] This attitude, the punishment imposed by the victim him/herself, moved by a sentiment of vengeance and anger, adds violence to violence and dehumanizes both the victim and the aggressor. In this sense, justice intends to discipline vengeful desire. In regard to the wrongdoer, justice makes punishment an educational act that aims at both the reeducation of the aggressor and the dissuasion of other practices of transgression of the law as experiences of evil.[51]

While I agree with Ricoeur that love and justice arise in different practices motivated by distinct logics, the logic of gift and the logic of equivalence, this contrast does not entail the impossibility of interaction between love and justice in the legal system if we consider love as gratuity, and recognition and justice as restorative justice. Love concerns human life and common action in the world, and so it can be lived in the common life with and for others in just institutions. It is precisely this possibility of interaction that allows us to state, with Ricoeur, that the first thing that love entails is for us to be just. Yet going beyond Ricoeur, if love requires us to be just, this justice is not reduced to the logic of equivalence and can interact with the logic of gift, with love. Love should be understood as gratuity, recognition, and the restoration of human dignity in just institutions.

CONCLUSION

One of Ricoeur's great contributions to the debate on justice is his effort to create a dialogue with secular contemporary society on the basis of an optimistic anthropology. According to this perspective, the human being is capable of something beyond the evil committed or the injustice done to the other. One of the ways chosen by Ricoeur to develop this aspect points to the dialectic between love and justice, in which there is always an excess of love in relation to justice or, as Ricoeur himself likes to say, a disproportion between the logic of superabundance and the logic of equivalence. In my opinion, though, his insistence on this excess or disproportion makes it difficult to understand why love matters to justice. Therefore, in the interaction between love and justice, I chose to focus on love anthropologically as a human capacity to recognize human dignity in oneself and in the other person, and on being just as what love requires us, above all, to do. This way allows us to say that love can enlighten the practice of justice without intending to replace justice by love. It also excludes the simple exaltation of love and its reduction to mere sentimentalism.

My essential point is that the interaction between love and justice can be thought of as occurring within the law. Throughout this chapter, I have tried to show that some elements of love act as internal aspects of justice. A bridge can be built between love and justice, since both experiences or practices reside within the same world of action. Moreover, both love and justice are fundamentally open to the other: I love another person, and I am just to another person. It is the regard for otherness that commands these two actions. Therefore, the search for a just society can be nourished by love insofar as it means to look more primarily to the other rather than to one's own interest. For Ricoeur, this anthropological concept has as background the religious origin of love, but love as Agape should not limit the possibility of realizing a broader love in human actions or prevent us from perceiving love as something inherent in our institutions. Love can be incorporated into the legal system and can motivate the search for justice.

Let me offer one last consideration as I conclude. If on the one hand Ricoeur often refers to the Bible to talk about love as Agape, on the other hand he does not offer a similar biblical reference when he talks about justice. However, as Ricoeur well knows, the idea of justice appears throughout the Bible. For the biblical tradition, justice shall come down from Heaven, and at the same time it is part of daily life and the organization of society. Justice is not an external intrusion into our daily lives. Why, then, does Ricoeur not refer to this biblical tradition to speak about justice when he approaches the dialectic between love and justice? This question requires separate research, which would encompass both the desire for justice and the practice of justice. Such research might in turn provide the basis for investigation into how it might be possible to extend a hermeneutics of Biblical texts and symbols to lay legal institutions, such as a court of law.

NOTES

1. The impetus of my thesis is George Taylor's reflection in the unpublished text, "Ricoeur and Limits of Law?"

2. For my retrieval of Ricoeur's usage of the expression "love and justice" and of both words individually, I have drawn upon the Digital Ricoeur Website (www.digitalricoeur.org). For more details on this platform, see George H. Taylor and Fernando Nascimento, "Digital Ricoeur," *Études Ricoeuriennes / Ricoeur Studies* 7 (2016): 124–45.

3. Paul Ricoeur, "The Logic of Jesus, the Logic of God," in *Figuring the Sacred: Religion, Narrative and Imagination*, trans. David Pellauer, ed. Mark I. Wallace (Minneapolis: Fortress Press 1995), 279–83; Paul Ricoeur, "Love and Justice," in *Figuring the Sacred: Religion, Narrative and Imagination*, trans. David Pellauer, ed. Mark I. Wallace (Minneapolis: Fortress Press, 1995), 315–29; Paul Ricoeur, "Thou Shalt Not Kill: A Loving Obedience," in *Thinking Biblically*, trans. David Pellauer (Chicago: The University of Chicago Press, 1998), 111–38.

4. Ricoeur, "The Logic of Jesus, the Logic of God," 280.

5. Ricoeur, "The Logic of Jesus, the Logic of God," 280.

6. Ricoeur, "Love and Justice," 315.

7. 1 Corinthians 13.

8. Ricoeur, "The Logic of Jesus, the Logic of God," 281.

9. Ricoeur, "Love and Justice," 316, 325, 329; Ricoeur, "Thou Shalt Not Kill," 124.

10. Ricoeur, "Love and Justice," 328. As I return to in the text, Ricoeur revisits this theme in his last book, *The Course of Recognition*, in particular in chapter 3, where he addresses the topic of mutual recognition to deepen the notion of a gift economy. See Paul Ricoeur, *The Course of Recognition*, trans. David Pellauer (Cambridge, MA: Harvard University Press, 2005), 150–246.

11. Ricoeur, "Thou Shalt Not Kill," 127.

12. Ricoeur, "Thou Shalt Not Kill," 128.

13. Ricoeur, "Thou Shalt Not Kill," 131–32.

14. Ricoeur, "The Logic of Jesus, the Logic of God," 283, 328; Ricoeur, *The Course of Recognition*, 251.
15. Ricoeur, "Love and Justice," 321.
16. Ricoeur, "Love and Justice," 322.
17. Ricoeur, "Love and Justice," 323.
18. Ricoeur, "Thou Shalt Not Kill," 125.
19. Ricoeur, *The Course of Recognition*, 150–247.
20. Ricoeur, "The Logic of Jesus, the Logic of God," 281–82.
21. Ricoeur, *The Course of Recognition*, 224.
22. Ricoeur, *The Course of Recognition*, 245.
23. Martha Nussbaum, *Anger and Forgiveness: Resentment, Generosity, Justice* (Oxford: Oxford University Press, 2016); see also Martha Nussbaum, *Political Emotions: Why Love Matters for Justice* (Cambridge: Harvard University Press, 2015).
24. Paul Ricoeur, *The Just*, trans. David Pellauer (Chicago: The University of Chicago Press, 2000), 145.
25. Elizabeth Mertz, *The Language of Law School: Learning to "Think Like a Lawyer"* (Oxford: Oxford University Press, 2007).
26. Mertz, *The Language of Law School*, 217.
27. Antonin Scalia, *A Matter of Interpretation: Federal Courts and the Law* (Princeton: Princeton University Press, 1997); Antonin Scalia and Bryan A. Garner, *Reading Law: The Interpretation of Legal Texts* (Saint Paul: Thomson/West, 2012); John F. Manning, "Justice Scalia and the Idea of Judicial Restraint," *Michigan Law Review* 115 (2017): 747–82.
28. On this aspect, see Susan S. Daicoff, *Lawyer, Know Thyself: A Psychological Analysis of Personality Strengths and Weaknesses* (Washington: American Psychological Association, 2004); and Susan Daicoff, "Law as Healing Profession: The Comprehensive Law Movement," *Pepperdine Dispute Resolution Law Journal* 6 (2006): 1–61.
29. Paul Ricoeur, *The Symbolism of Evil*, trans. Emerson Buchanan (New York: Harper and Row, 1967), 156, 233, 252; Paul Ricoeur, *Fallible Man*, trans. Charles A. Kelbley (New York: Fordham University Press, 1986), 145.
30. Ricoeur, "Thou Shalt Not Kill," 127.
31. Ricoeur, "The Logic of Jesus, the Logic of God," 282.
32. Ricoeur, "Love and Justice," 316.
33. Ricoeur, *The Course of Recognition*, 220. As is well-known, Ricoeur uses the term *agape* in consonance with its religious origin, that is, as the Biblical Christian tradition understand love.
34. Ricoeur, "Thou Shalt Not Kill," 127.
35. Ricoeur, *The Course of Recognition*, 232–33, 243.
36. Ricoeur, "Love and Justice," 319.
37. He is an American lawyer who dedicates his professional life to the legal assistance to poor people and incarcerated. See Bryan Stevenson, *Just Mercy: A Story of Justice and Redemption* (New York: Spiegel and Grau, 2014).
38. He is founder and executive director of the Bard Prison Initiative (BPI) which has with a mission of offering liberal arts education to inmates nationwide.

39. Ricoeur, *The Just*, 131–32.
40. Ricoeur, *The Just*, 137–40.
41. Paul Ricoeur, *Memory, History, Forgetting*, trans. Kathleen Blamey and David Pellauer (Chicago: The University Chicago Press, 2004), 493. This also is the motivation of the work of Bryan Stevenson. He relates, for example, in the introduction of his book *Just Mercy*, that if love is the motivation, justice is the instrument. Stevenson, *Just Mercy*, 3–18.
42. www.jusbrasil.com.br. Article 59 of Penal Code—Decree Law 2848/40.
43. www.cuspconference.com/presenters/max-kenner.
44. Ricoeur, "The Logic of Jesus, the Logic of God," 283.
45. Antoine Garapon, "La Justice Comme Reconnaissance," *Revue le Genre Humain* 43 (2004): 181; Antoine Garapon, "Justice et reconnaissance," *Esprit* (Mars-Avril 2006): 231–32.
46. Garapon, "La Justice Comme Reconnaissance," 181–82, 187–88.
47. Paul Ricoeur, "The Socius and the Neighbor," in *History and Truth*, trans. Charles Kelbley (Evanton: Northwestern University Press, 1965), 101.
48. Stevenson, *Just Mercy*, 18.
49. David Pellauer, "Looking for the Just," *Études Ricoeuriennes / Ricoeur Studies* 3, no. 1 (2012): 136.
50. Ricoeur, *The Just*, 127–32.
51. Ricoeur, *The Just*, 140–42.

BIBLIOGRAPHY

Daicoff, Susan. "Law as Healing Profession: The Comprehensive Law Movement." *Pepperdine Dispute Resolution Law Journal* 6 (2006): 1–61.

Daicoff, Susan S. *Lawyer, Know Thyself: A Psychological Analysis of Personality Strengths and Weaknesses*. Washington: American Psychological Association, 2004.

Garapon, Antoine. "Justice et Reconnaissance." *Espirit* 323 (Mars-Avril 2006): 231–48.

Garapon, Antoine. "La Justice Comme Reconnaissance." *Revue le Genre Humain* 43 (2004): 181–204.

Manning, John F. "Justice Scalia and the Idea of Judicial Restraint." *Michigan Law Review* 115 (2017): 747–82.

Mertz, Elizabeth. *The Language of Law School: Learning to "Think Like a Lawyer."* Oxford: Oxford University Press, 2007.

Nussbaum, Martha. *Anger and Forgiveness: Resentment, Generosity, Justice*. Oxford: Oxford University Press, 2016.

Nussbaum, Martha. *Political Emotions: Why Love Matters for Justice*. Cambridge: Harvard University Press, 2015.

Pellauer, David. "Looking for the Just." *Études Ricoeuriennes / Ricoeur Studies* 3, no. 1 (2012): 132–43.

Ricoeur, Paul. *Fallible Man*. Translated by Charles A. Kelbley. New York: Fordham University Press, 1986.

Ricoeur, Paul. *The Just*. Translated by David Pellauer. Chicago: The University of Chicago Press, 2000.

Ricoeur, Paul. "The Logic of Jesus, the Logic of God." In *Figuring the Sacred: Religion, Narrative and Imagination*, edited by Mark I. Wallace, translated by David Pellauer, 279–83. Minneapolis: Fortress Press, 1995.

Ricoeur, Paul. "Love and Justice." In *Figuring the Sacred: Religion, Narrative and Imagination*, edited by Mark I. Wallace, Translated by David Pellauer, 315–29. Minneapolis: Fortress Press, 1995.

Ricoeur, Paul. *Memory, History, Forgetting*. Translated by Kathleen Blamey and David Pellauer. Chicago: The University Chicago Press, 2004.

Ricoeur, Paul. "The Socius and the Neighbor." In *History and Truth*. Translated by Charles Kelbley, 98–109. Evanston: Northwestern University Press, 1965.

Ricoeur, Paul. *The Symbolism of Evil*. Translated by Emerson Buchanan. New York: Harper and Row, 1967.

Ricoeur, Paul. "Thou Shalt Not Kill: A Loving Obedience." In *Thinking Biblically*. Translated by David Pellauer, 111–38. Chicago: The University of Chicago Press, 1998.

Scalia, Antonin. *A Matter of Interpretation: Federal Courts and the Law*. Princeton: Princeton University Press, 1997.

Scalia, Antonin, and Bryan A. Garner. *Reading Law: The Interpretation of Legal Texts*. Saint Paul: Thomson/West, 2012.

Stevenson, Bryan. *Just Mercy: A Story of Justice and Redemption*. New York: Spiegel and Grau, 2014.

Taylor, George H. *Ricoeur and the Limits of Law?* (Unpublished).

Taylor, George H., and Fernando Nascimento. "Digital Ricoeur." *Études Ricoeuriennes / Ricoeur Studies* 7 (2016): 124–45.

Chapter Fourteen

Forgiveness at the Border of the Law

Olivier Abel

Forgiveness is a late and somewhat marginal theme in Ricoeur's work, even a theme "at the limit." Its first, slightly sketched occurrence can be found in "Reflections on a New Ethos for Europe," first published in 1992.[1] One can rightly note that it is a subject that he approached carefully, after long detours. To illustrate this reticence, when in 1989 I asked him to write a text for the edited collection on forgiveness that I was preparing,[2] he replied that it was not a theme he had worked on sufficiently.

However, numerous texts point towards this question at each stage of his oeuvre and in various guises: the theme of "redemption," for instance, not as a moral and individual redemption but as something that informs political institutions, economic mediations, and the social imaginary as a whole; or the idea of compromise; and there is even the theme of festive forgiveness, of a forgiveness that does not involve work.[3]

My purpose in this study will be to try to unravel and present three quite different semantic configurations, three questioning knots or constellations, in which forgiveness takes different meanings, but which all have a link with justice. The last one, which takes shape in the 1990s culminating with *Memory, History, Forgetting* (2000), is the most evident and explicit, and centers on forgiveness and the sharing of memories and forgetting. Difficult forgiveness is practiced in political debates about just memory. Another constellation, which takes shape around "Love and Justice" and *Oneself as Another* (1990), is concerned precisely with justice. The third constellation, deconstructing the idea of punishment, revolves around the archaic conversion of vengeance into forgiveness, of the Erinyes into Eumenides in Aeschylus's *Oresteia*, a scene that is often cited in Ricoeur's writings since the 1950s.

FORGIVENESS AND JUST MEMORY

In *Memory, History, Forgetting*, Ricoeur starts with the now famous observation: "I continue to be troubled by the unsettling spectacle offered by an excess of memory here, and an excess of forgetting elsewhere, to say nothing of the influence of commemorations and the abuses of memory—and of forgetting. The idea of a policy of the just allotment of memory is in this respect one of my avowed civic themes."[4] Such will be the first configuration into which forgiveness has to find its path, between an abuse of memory and an abuse of forgetting.

It is, however, in an apparent shift of perspective that Ricoeur places the most important reflection of his entire oeuvre on forgiveness in the Epilogue of this book:

> Forgiveness raises a question that in its principle is distinct from the one that, beginning with the preface of this book, has motivated our entire undertaking, namely, the question of the representation of the past. . . . It is twofold: on the one hand, it is the enigma of a fault held to paralyze the power to act of the "capable being" that we are; and it is, in reply, the enigma of the possible lifting of this existential incapacity, designated by the term 'forgiveness.'"[5]

In this Epilogue of about sixty pages on "Difficult Forgiveness," most of the themes of Ricoeur's reflection on forgiveness come together. He starts with an in-depth analysis of fault, i.e., the terrible clinging of the subject to the wrong he or she has committed, as if existence itself were sin and unhappiness. This is viewed from the height of an unconditional forgiveness, as a given, a "there is," an "it happens," and in a type of language—like the language of love, of joy, of wisdom, or of madness[6]—that borders on the hymnic. Ricoeur proposes then a journey through different forms of responsibility—criminal guilt, political guilt, and moral guilt—which we may map with the help of the categories of guilt identified by Jaspers, discussed by Ricoeur in an important article of 1949.[7] Only metaphysical guilt is missing in this discussion, but it was fully covered in the first section, on fault and forgiveness.

This "Odyssey" of the spirit of forgiveness is presented as the "passage through institutions"[8] which support and carry those different forms of responsibility (the juridical question of criminal imprescriptibility, the political question of civic responsibility, the question of absence of a "third party" for moral guilt). It is remarkable that in this journey forgiveness has to undergo the trial of justice and not short-circuit it.[9] Ricoeur talks about the "conditionality of the request for forgiveness" faced with the unconditionality of forgiveness.[10] The problem is thus to link the asymmetrical verticality between fault and forgiveness, on the one hand, and the horizontality of a restored reciprocity on the other. Forgiveness comes back as what surpasses exchange, enveloping it as it were by its unpredictable excess (one is here in the logic of the gift). Yet at the same time forgiveness lies at the basis of exchange, mutuality, which brings out its most originary signification.

It is precisely the dialectic of forgiveness and promise, picked up from Arendt, which unbinds us (forgiveness) from the irreversible past, to bind us (promise) in the face of the unpredictable future. But it is not any longer only a question of unbinding a subject from his or her debts, from the consequences of his or her acts: it is a question of "unbinding the agent from his act."[11] If fault was a powerlessness to act, or a desensitizing, an "incapacitation,"[12] forgiveness does not present itself here as a capacity like any other,[13] but as a restitution or a restoration of capacities.

One needed this long and difficult path that I called above a shift of perspective in order to return in the end to the question of just memory, to happy memory, and to forgetting. In memory, it is the moment of happy recognition; in history, it is the moment of mourning which ends in recollection at the gravesite; in forgetting, it is the moment of idleness, without worry. One will note that if forgiveness sets the tone of the Epilogue, it is rather as a figure of tragic wisdom or as an "eschatology of the representation of the past. Forgiveness—if it has a sense, and if it exists—constitutes the horizon common to memory, history and forgetting. Always in retreat, this horizon slips away from any grasp. It makes forgiving difficult: not easy but not impossible. It places a seal of incompleteness on the entire enterprise."[14] The grammatical mode is neither the indicative of description nor the imperative of prescription but the optative of the wish (494).[15]

In this final overlapping of themes, I want to highlight those that concern precisely this question of memory and forgetting. The theme of forgiveness linked to the idea of a just memory had already appeared in a text published in 1992, "Reflections on a New Ethos for Europe." In that text, Ricoeur tries to "formulate the problem of the future of Europe in terms of imagination," the problem being "a matter of combining 'identity' and 'alterity' at numerous levels . . . according to an increasing order of spiritual density."[16] At the first level, we find the model of translation which points to an ethos of mutual hospitality, to live in another's home, receiving the other in one's home, taking into account the other's own "customs, fundamental beliefs and deepest convictions,"[17] without thinking that we have understood them all. At a second level, one finds the model of exchange of memories, where our "identity is mingled with that of others in such a way as to engender second order stories which are themselves intersections between numerous stories," according to the idea that we are "'entangled in stories.'"[18] It is certainly not "a matter of actually reliving the events that happened to others; the inalienable character of life experiences renders this chimerical 'intropathy' impossible. More modestly, but also more energetically, it is a matter of exchanging memories at the narrative level where they are presented for comprehension" and making "space for several stories [concerning] the same past"[19] in an effort of plural interpretation and of narrative hospitality, but also of "discerning past promises which have not been kept."[20] One could say that the healing supposes the installation of a plural narration, where I also allow the other tell me his or her story, as if just memory were never alone: one can no more remember alone than one can pardon oneself alone.

It is precisely at a third and final level that we find the model of forgiveness, which builds on this mutual revision of the past and this mutual freeing not only from broken promises but also from mutual wounds, and which asks us to imagine the suffering of others. This imagining is what corrects the abuses and perversions of a narrative identity that can crush others. Ricoeur clarifies: "Forgiveness, in its full sense, certainly far exceeds political categories. It belongs to an order—the order of charity—which goes even beyond the order of morality. Forgiveness falls within the scope of an economy of the gift [which] belongs to what we would be able to term the 'poetics' of the moral life."[21] The poetical power of forgiveness consists in breaking temporal irreversibility "by lifting the burden of guilt which paralyses the relations between individuals who are acting out and suffering their own history."[22] On this path one must avoid two pitfalls:

> The first would be that of confusing forgiveness and forgetting. On the contrary, we can forgive only where there is no forgetting, where the humble have been released from a promise (speech has been restored to those humiliated). "Shattering the debt and forgetting" is the subtitle of the book mentioned earlier. Nothing would be more loathsome than what Jankélévich called the forgetful forgiveness.... The second pitfall would be to take forgiveness under its worst aspect. The first relation that we have to forgiving is not the exercise of an easily granted forgiveness—that which once again is reduced to forgetfulness—but the difficult practice of responding to a request for forgiveness.[23]

This necessitates a difficult pathway, and this is why sometimes for

> the victims of imprescriptible crimes—crimes that they consider to be unforgivable—there is no other advice than to wait for better times. These times will see the first cathartic effect of the drawing-up of wrongs suffered by the injured, who will see the offender attain full understanding of the crimes that he or she has committed. There is a time for the unforgivable and a time for forgiveness.[24]

Forgiveness, Ricoeur concludes, is the only way to cancel debt and forgetfulness and thus to lift the barriers to the exercise of justice and recognition.

Ricoeur says something similar again in his 1994 text, "Sanction, Rehabilitation, Pardon." Talking about the finality of forgiveness, he writes: "Its 'project' is not to wipe away memory. It is not forgetting. On the contrary, its project, which is to overlook [*briser*] the debt, is incompatible with that of overlooking what is forgotten. Pardon is a kind of healing of memory, the end of mourning. Delivered from the weight of debt, memory is freed for great projects. Pardon gives memory a future."[25]

Another fulcrum for this first semantic constellation on forgiveness is a 1998 article on "La crise de la conscience historique et l'Europe"[26] ("The Crisis of the Historical Conscience and Europe"). Ricoeur speaks of the crisis of memory and distinguishes between repetitive memory, "which encloses peoples into resentment and hate," and a remembering that is "active, selective, interrogative, reflective."[27] He also distinguishes two kinds of forgetfulness, an evasive one and "a voluntary forgetfulness, related to forgiveness, which belongs to the therapeutic of vengeance. . . . It is not a paradox to say that this forgetfulness is a consequence of the critical memory which we set against memory-repetition."[28]

Forgiveness must not, however, be captured exclusively by the conundrum of memory and forgetfulness, even if the latter seems dominant in Ricoeur's last works. In "The Difficulty to Forgive,"[29] he had already written that what he had underestimated, in an enterprise aiming to locate forgiveness as an extension of a dialectic of forgetting and memory, was "the roots of the problem in a multiplicity of regions of the known."[30] He then tried to classify these difficulties in an increasing order of perplexity: those of memory and those of forgetting, of course, but also those of guilt, because "[t]he wounds that forgiving could want to cure are not those of a failing memory, but rather a bad conscience, a guilty conscience [and not just] a wound at the core of self-esteem, but an injury inflicted to our bonds with the others."[31] And then there are the difficulties of living in common, the lesions of the social bond, ending with the deepest issues of historical violence, the relationship to enemies, and so on. We come up against the impossibility of forgiveness. "Nevertheless,"[32] *there is* forgiveness, or at least "scattered signs"[33] of forgiveness, that can be found in each of these stages. The praise of forgiveness then picks up those difficulties on the other side, in the reverse order. Forgiveness is sometimes only a rare gesture in the relationship between friend and foe; at the level of being in common, forgiveness "helps justice to be always more fair, that means more universal, more equal, more attentive to the singularity of each case,"[34] with a belief in the lenient exception. Can we then separate the I, or rather the self, from the fault? It would be forgiveness, the capacity to unbind oneself from the past to bind oneself again toward the future through a promise. After having praised a "good oblivion,"[35] of a "divine insouciance,"[36] Ricoeur observes finally that "[w]ithin memory lies the most secret resistance to forgiveness,"[37] and that is what makes forgiveness a work of remembering and of mourning, of recognizing that the past is past. "The Difficulty to Forgive" ends with a reference to *The Gay Science* by Nietzsche, to play that does not labor any more, where wisdom "cannot occur without a certain amount of folly."[38] One sees how this text is still contemporaneous with *Memory, History, Forgetting* and its Epilogue.

LOVE AND JUSTICE: FORGIVENESS AS VIEWFINDER OF JUSTICE

The second configuration which seems to appear in the links between forgiveness and justice is both earlier (it culminates in texts of 1990s but starts much earlier) and more deeply rooted in Ricoeur's thought. We have just seen that forgiveness is turned not only towards just memory but also towards what "presses on justice from within, demands that it be always more just, i.e. more universal, more equal, and more attentive to the singularity of each case," with a sense of the lenient exception. Note well: "exception" here is not the sign of a vertical sovereignty, some power of mercy that would be in the hands only of one magistrate, but a formula of wisdom—a wisdom not without a touch of madness, yet still an ordinary wisdom shared with all whose experience has taught them the prudent art of *adjustment*. Ricoeur continues in that way in *Oneself as Another:* "Practical wisdom consists in inventing conduct that will satisfy the exception required by solicitude, by betraying the rule to the smallest extent possible."[39] Solicitude is the capacity for ordinary exception. But this ordinary exception is the limit on which the law never stops forming, deforming, and reforming itself.

That is why, at the heart of this second layer or configuration, it will be a matter of showing in what way, if forgiveness cannot be institutionalized, forgiveness in Ricoeur is nonetheless the chief seeker for justice and the law, to recall from within their intention, and to show from without their limits. In "Love and Justice" this magnificent sentence occurs: "[T]he tenacious incorporation, step by step, of a supplementary degree of compassion and generosity in all of our codes—including our penal codes and our codes of social justice—constitutes a perfectly reasonable task, however difficult and interminable that may be."[40] One could add the suggestion that, just as the rapprochement between love and justice deforms their semantic field, forgiveness for Ricoeur oscillates between a radical figure of love of neighbor and an ordinary figure of practical wisdom that seeks minute readjustments if not compromises rather than total solutions. It is that ambiguity which interests me in Ricoeur, as if forgiveness brings together distant spheres and draws from that rapprochement innovative meanings. This oscillation can be seen in the selection of texts of the 1990s, "Love and Justice" and in particular *Oneself as Another*. Ricoeur's thought moves between the more hymn-like pole that borders sometimes on madness and the more sapiential pole of practical wisdom, a wisdom that draws its prudence from the journey through tragedy.

The idea is not new in Ricoeur's work that love seeks a justice that is both more universal and more singular than the justice that is always established within a given political body, is historically and geographically limited, and that always follows general rules. In fact, in law's verticality when it protects the widow and the orphan, and in its horizontality when it seeks the common rule, equal and reciprocal, it is never sufficiently singularized, adjusted to each individual, and never sufficiently universalized, proposing a sufficiently total redistribution, never ample enough nor radical enough. "[I]n comparison to love of neighbor, the social bond is never as profound or as comprehensive."[41] These are the two directions in which love and forgiveness work on the limits of the law, through a constant pressure, imposing a slight "slant." In *The Course of Recognition* once more, love consists in letting go of offenses, in not retaliating, and Ricoeur seeks out the Dostoevskyian figure of the Idiot to describe the works of love.[42]

To be sure, in order to situate this theme precisely, one has to measure also Ricoeur's tremendous distrust with regard to love, or rather—when love claims to reduce everything to itself and to understanding everything—with regard to any premature synthesis between the religious ethic of compassionate agape and the ethic of the magistrate. We find this already at the end of "State and Violence," a text of the 1950s published in *History and Truth*: "[U]ntil the last day, love and coercion will walk along side by side as the two pedagogies, sometimes converging, sometimes diverging, of mankind. The end of this duality would be the total 'reconciliation' of man with man. But this would also be the end of the State, because this would be the end of history."[43] Yet we know since "Freedom in the Light of Hope" that "true evil, the evil of evil, is not the violation of an interdict, the subversion of the law, disobedience, but fraudulency in the work of totalization."[44] This is why love cannot short-circuit justice nor the constitutive conflictual nature of the political world, but at the same time forbids justice to take itself for the last judgment.

In "Reflections on a New Ethos for Europe," Ricoeur also writes:

> We have said that these considerations do not have their primary employment in the political sphere whose principle is justice and reciprocity, and not charity and the gift. Could we not suggest, nevertheless, that the order of justice and

reciprocity can be touched by that of charity and the gift—touched, that is to say, affected, and, if I may say, moved to pity? Have we not some examples of this in the sphere of penal justice, with the royal pardon, prescription and sentence reductions? And are there not further examples found in the social sphere in certain affective expressions of solidarity? . . . But to the same degree that charity exceeds justice we must guard against substituting it for justice.[45]

In *Memory, History, Forgetting*, Ricoeur writes again: "love . . . proves to be foreign to the world and, for this reason, not only apolitical but antipolitical."[46] In all of these texts, the dialectic between love and justice is tense, and even if the two logics correct one another up to a certain point, one is never very far from tragedy, as if the actual political order of justice were abutted and limited by another *metapolitical* (or theological?) realm, which allows complaint, but also devoted love or even self-sacrifice.

In *Oneself as Another*, forgiveness, explicitly thematized but borrowing the words Hegel used for Sophocles's *Antigone*, appears in the interlude on the tragedy of action,[47] where it becomes really a theme of practical wisdom, when the protagonists, after having avoided the worst, attempt to escape from tragedy. Reading Hegel, Ricoeur observes that forgiveness supposes "an actual renunciation by each party of his partiality,"[48] that "narrowness of the angle of commitment,"[49] a topic that Ricoeur had previously picked up in Karl Mannheim and discussed in the *Lectures on Ideology and Utopia*.[50] Ricoeur writes: "[T]he genuine reconciliation occurs only at the very end of this itinerary, at the outcome of the conflict between judging consciousness and acting man; this reconciliation rests on an actual renunciation by each party of his partiality and has the value of a pardon in which each is truly recognized by the other." He continues: "Now it is precisely this reconciliation through renouncement, this pardon through recognition, that tragedy—at least the tragedy of *Antigone*—is incapable of producing. If the ethical powers served by the protagonists are to continue to subsist together, the *disappearance* of their particular existence is the full price to be paid."[51] This disappearance is thus not accomplished in synthesis—the measure for which Hegel is commonly accused[52]—but rather in the confrontation between the acting consciousness and the judging consciousness. Ricoeur comments: "[T]he 'pardon' resulting from the mutual recognition of the two antagonists who admit the limits of their viewpoints and renounce their partiality denotes the authentic phenomenon of conscience. It is along the path to this recognition that the critique of the moral vision of the world is found."[53]

We could add here that if forgiveness supposes being aware of the narrowness of one's point of view (and that is already an enlargement, as Kant observed[54]), it also presupposes that one internalizes the plurality of voices to make room in one's story for the possibility of the story of the other. How does identity intersect with alterity? Narrative identity in its variations meets two limits. With time one becomes other than oneself: we are dealing with the unpredictable as well as the irreversible; and one is dealing with oneself as another. The subject must then both maintain itself as "ipse" despite alteration, in the very alteration (that is the promise), and make space for the other, including the other self, oneself as another (that is forgiveness). The one who forgives, like the one who is forgiven, accepts oneself as another. One's identity supposes this "disidentification": we touch on the death of oneself, on the birth of another; but at the same time on the impossibility of this death and this birth *by* oneself. One must recognize oneself and be recognized as another in order to recognize oneself as a self. As Hannah Arendt remarked, it is difficult to see oneself in another way: that is one of the reasons why it is practically impossible to forgive oneself.[55]

Later in *Oneself as Another*, at the end of the last study on ipseity and alterity, Ricoeur returns to this reading of Hegel:

> In this way, the phenomenon of split consciousness crosses through the entire *Phenomenology of Spirit*, from the moment of the desire of the other, passing through the dialectic of master and slave, all the way to the double figure of the beautiful soul and the hero of action. It is important, however, that the ultimate reconciliation leaves us puzzled with respect to the identity of that other in "openly confessing itself by the vision of itself in the other." . . . Hegel, the philosopher of mind, leaves us here in a state of indecision, halfway between an anthropological reading and a theological reading. The ultimate equivocalness with respect to the status of the Other in the phenomenon of conscience is perhaps what needs to be preserved in the final analysis.[56]

THE CONVERSION OF THE TRAGIC

But the practical wisdom coming from the tragic has already started us on the road of a third configuration, deeper still, and perhaps also earlier in Ricoeur. This is the one that brings forgiveness to the archaic and pre-juridical scene of vengeance. We shall start with the most recent texts and work back to the older ones. In "Le juste, la justice et son échec" ("The Just, Justice, and its Failure") (2004), Ricoeur talks about the incapacity to give a convincing justification of the right to punish. In the dialectic of crime and punishment, law "exhibits its limits, its spiritual poverty, and even its failure."[57] To understand what scandalizes Ricoeur—and one senses that this indignation goes back to his adolescence, his outrage over the Sacco and Vanzetti affair in 1927, his vibrant and radical non-violence—one examines his deconstruction of punishment in "Interpretation of the Myth of Punishment," which summarizes the problem: "What is most rational in punishment, namely, that it fits the crime, is at the same time most irrational, namely, that it erases it."[58] There is something sacred, magical, in this idea that one wrong can wipe out another, and Ricoeur never ceased to protest against this sacrality of retribution.

But at the same time, and this is the penal paradox:

> if there is an intellectual scandal, it is that penal law represents one of the more remarkable conquests of rationality at the level of social transactions engaged with violence. The Greek tragedy of Oresteia demonstrates it: the irruption of the *Diké*, the emblematic figure of the penal reason entrusted to a human tribunal. Even the sacred fury of the Erinyes has to convert into benevolence under the tutelage of the Eumenides. This conquest of rationality at the penal level is so important that one can take it as example of all the other advances of the law.[59]

Justice stops the cycle of vengeance, by introducing the just distance and the third party, which forbids one to take personal revenge. If in most cultures vengeance is homogeneous with the ceremonial counter-gift, can we, like Seneca,[60] banish all violence and even all anger, and how can we place ourselves under "the utopian horizon of non-violent justice"?[61]

Let us go back a notch. The topic is the same in "Justice and Vengeance" (1997), where Ricoeur notes the irresistible resurgence of the spirit of vengeance at the expense of the meaning of justice.[62] He desires a just distance in "the mediation of an institution capable of incarnating the third person"[63] and in the "ceremony carried out in language" that the trial is.[64] But the primacy conferred on discourse is not without a remainder, and "[a] residual degree of violence remains."[65] The penal imposition of a legal violence which responds to a primitive violence does not prevent that "[a] fair penalty remains a punishment, a kind of suffering. In this sense, the punishment as a type of penalty reopens the way to the spirit of vengeance."[66]

In "Sanction, Rehabilitation, Pardon" (1994), Ricoeur questions the difference between justice, which interposes the third party of the judiciary institution, and vengeance, which "short-circuits the two forms of suffering, that undergone by the victim and that inflicted by the avenger."[67] At the end of a long detour, Ricoeur concludes by insisting that "pardon does not belong to the juridical order,"[68] but, as we saw in Part One above, "gives memory a future,"[69] and, as we saw in Part Two, has "a kind of secondary effect on the juridical order."[70] (He then mentions "all the manifestations of compassion, of good will, at the very heart of the administration of justice."[71]) Finally, he asks, and this is our theme in Part Three: "Does it not come down to pardon to accompany justice in its effort to eradicate on the symbolic plane the sacred element of vengeance . . . ?" Ricoeur continues:

On the deepest symbolic plane, what is at stake is the separation between *Dike*, the justice of humans, and *Themis*, the ultimate and shadowy refuge of the equation of Vengeance (with a capital V) and Justice (with a capital J). Does it not belong to pardon to exercise over this malicious sacred the catharsis that makes a benevolent sacred emerge from it? Greek tragedy, that of the Orestia in the first place, teaches us that the Erinyes (the avenging furies) and the Eumenides (the benevolent spirits) are one and the same.[72]

They are "the same!" The wonder is that with forgiveness, as with vengeance, we are dealing, in a radically inseparable manner, with the tragic and murky depths that are also the depths of goodness and benevolence that need to be awakened, restored. The knot that Ricoeur does not fully untie is that if justice and vengeance—but also justice and forgiveness—are of different orders, forgiveness is far nearer to vengeance than people think. Arendt remarked that one can only forgive that which can be punished, but at the base of this observation, which seems to grant the right to forgive, wrongly, only to the one who exerts the power to punish, there lies a more profound insight: that the right to forgive (if it can be called a right) belongs to the one who could want to take revenge. Nobody can forgive as a third party: forgiveness thus short-circuits the institutional mediations and appropriate distances, and this is why Ricoeur talks also of the "sometimes monstrous failure of all efforts to institutionalize forgiveness."[73]

In "Evil, a Challenge to Philosophy and Theology" (1985), Ricoeur speaks of wisdom not from the point of view of Greek tragedy but thinking of Job. The lament rises in a complaint against the deity, contesting not the stories but the alleged explanations of evil that which would reduce it to retribution.[74] That is what Job contests, but the finale of the Book of Job, facing the greatness of creation, presents itself as a pure lamentation, from which all that it might contain of accusation has been purged. Ricoeur comes back to this at the end of his essay. After having attempted through the labor of imputation and action to alleviate "the suffering inflicted by people on other people,"[75] one finally discovers the remainder of non-imputable suffering: To say: "'I don't know why things happened as they did; chance and accident are part of the world.' This would be the zero degree, so to speak, in the catharsis of the complaint."[76] Ricoeur continues: "To love God for nought is to escape completely the cycle of retribution to which the lamentation still remains captive, so long as the victim bemoans the injustice of his or her fate. [But] I do not want to separate these individual experiences of wisdom from the ethical and political struggle against evil."[77] And he links those experiences with actions of non-violent resistance, which traverse the political realm as a call, but which cannot be given institutional form.

In a less known but important text, "Le droit de punir"[78] ("The Right to Punish") (1958), Ricoeur shows the pre-Christian origin of this ancient magical law of retribution, which weighs down on all our old codes, and states that "this struggle against the theology of vengeance is absolutely contemporaneous with law."[79] Punishment draws its energy from the archaic appeal for vengeance, but law adds to it measure, limits, and forms.

> The old ferocious religion which wanted to repay Iphigenia's death by that of her father, Agamemnon, then the death of Agamemnon by that of Clytemnestra, the unfaithful wife, then that of Clytemnestra the mother by that of Orestia, the son, until the vengeful Erinyes miraculously become Eumenides, when Athena founded the human tribunal, the Aeropagus. This is how Oresteia, Aeschylus' play ends: the sacred tribunals will finally forgo the bloodletting conflicts and a lay, human, civil tribunal will grant Orestia the right to live. I think one finds here an admirable symbol: one needs a lay tribunal to affirm that gods are good.[80]

Here again, as in this entire series of texts, it is a question of dismantling the penal logic of retribution, or rather of de-divinizing it. It is because there is a divinity that is terrible that one needs to measure the transformation taking place in the divine to produce a benevolent divinity. The transformation in the gods is analogous to what takes place in humans, if not mutual. Ricoeur ended this 1958 lecture by saying: "justice is instituted by God when justice renounces being divine and accepts being human, and only human."[81]

Finally, we can go back to two texts written in 1953, "Sur le tragique"[82] ("On the Tragic"), and "Culpabilité tragique, culpabilité biblique"[83] ("Tragic Guilt, Biblical Guilt"). Ricoeur discovered the "theological" dimension of Greek tragedy, the oscillation between a cruel divinity (Prometheus protests his innocence just as Job does!) and a merciful one. This is the movement that in Aeschylus goes from *Prometheus Bound* to *Prometheus Unbound*, which shows that "the divine is also at work; he tears himself away from his center of darkness and chaos, and reaches, through violence and pain, towards his center of light and order."[84] The gods can blind Xerxes, the enemy, who then becomes their victim. But on the other side Prometheus's anger is also full of *hubris*,[85] and humans are trapped too in this work of distress and wisdom. At the beginning of the *Oresteia*, the chorus cries out:

> Zeus, whosoe'er he be,—if by this name it well pleaseth him to be invoked, by this name I call to him.... who leadeth mortals the way of understanding, Zeus, who hath stablished as a fixed ordinance that "wisdom cometh by suffering." But even as trouble, bringing memory of pain, droppeth o'er the mind in sleep, do to men in their despite cometh wisdom.[86]

The *Oresteia* is woven around the question of how one may deliver the city from the powers of vengeance without neglecting the rites that appease them, how the archaic divine may be integrated into the democratic city. The terrible Erinyes, goddesses of vengeance, compared to bloodthirsty she-hounds, are on the track of Orestes, murderer of his own mother. Faced with Athena's merciful judgment which thwarts their vengeance they cry out: "Ah, cruel indeed the wrongs of the woeful daughters of Night, bereft of honour and distressed."[87] But Athena answers: "Let me prevail with you not to bear it with sore lament. For ye have not been vanquished."[88] Gradually the chorus calms down: "Methinks thou wilt win me by thy spells; my anger departs from me."[89] They will slowly be assuaged to the point of becoming the caring Eumenides, and the tragedy ends with a new "alliance" through which Athena makes space for the goddesses: "In loving zeal towards these my burghers I act thus, installing here among them divinities powerful and hard to please. For to their office it hath fallen to hold dominion over all things mortal."[90] In return, the chorus of the Eumenides ask: "May no hurtful wind blow to the destruction of the trees . . . and may no scorching heat, blasting the budding plants, pass the borders of its proper clime; may no deadly blight draw near to kill the fruit."[91] "Grant that lovely maidens may live each to find her mate give, O ye Fates divine, our sisters by one mother, ye divinities whose award is just, who have a common part in every home."[92] For Nicole Loraux, the (metapolitical) presence on the edge of the city of those figures of the widow and the orphan, Antigone or Electra, recalls to us the other stage, that of the fundamentals of the human condition.[93]

But what complicates things once more, and we shall end our reflection with this, is precisely that with Sophocles's *Antigone*, we no longer have only the opposition between the divinities of vengeance and the peaceful divinity of the city. If Antigone represents the chthonic powers of the earth and the dead,[94] with Creon the city is also deadly and refuses the burial owed the dead. "[T]he city is not the place for reconciliation any more: it is the closed city that rejects Antigone into defiance."[95] In Sophocles's *Oedipus Rex*, only duration succeeds in "wearing out wrath," and this phrase is the closest expression of tragic forgiveness, a meditation which "leads from pain to acquiescence and wisdom."[96] This is very close to the attrition of Achilles's anger, finally turned around and converted, at the end of the *Iliad*, into compassion for Hector's father.

We know that Ricoeur never ceased to re-read until his final days Simone Weill's superb commentary on that passage: "Perhaps they [the peoples of Europe] will yet rediscover the epic genius, when they learn there is no refuge from fate, learn not to admire force, not hate the enemies, nor to scorn the unfortunate. How soon this will happen is another question."[97]

Translated by Anne Bernard Kearney, who thanks Joseph S. O'Leary for his assistance with the translation.

NOTES

1. Paul Ricoeur, "Reflections on a New Ethos for Europe," in *Paul Ricoeur: The Hermeneutics of Action*, trans. Eileen Brennan, ed. Richard Kearney (London: Sage Publications, 1996) [1992], 3–13. [Ed.: References throughout are provided to English translations, where available, with years of publication of the original given in brackets. Dates in the text refer to original dates of publication.]

2. Olivier Abel, ed., *Le Pardon, Briser la Dette et l'Oubli*, Paris, Autrement, 1991.

3. Paul Ricoeur, *The Course of Recognition*, trans. David Pellauer (Cambridge, MA: Harvard University Press, 2005), 232ff.; *Memory, History, Forgetting*, trans. Kathleen Blamey and David Pellauer (University of Chicago Press, 2004), 505–06.

4. Ricoeur, *Memory, History, Forgetting*, xv.

5. Ricoeur, *Memory, History, Forgetting*, 457.

6. Ricoeur, *Memory, History, Forgetting*, 467.

7. Paul Ricoeur, "La culpabilité allemande," *Christianisme Social* 57, no. 3–4 (1949): 150–57.

8. Ricoeur, *Memory, History, Forgetting*, 470.

9. Ricoeur, *Memory, History, Forgetting*, 472–73.

10. Ricoeur, *Memory, History, Forgetting*, 482.

11. Ricoeur, *Memory, History, Forgetting*, 489.

12. Ricoeur, *Memory, History, Forgetting*, 457.

13. After reading *Oneself as Another* and *The Course of Recognition*, one may ask: if we find in those texts the power of saying, of telling stories, of taking responsibility, of remembering, and of promising, why does Ricoeur not consider a power of forgiving? Ricoeur offers us here a first interpretation of the lack of power. Another possible interpretation is that forgiveness always depends on how it is received. The pragmatics (in Austin's sense) of forgiveness is essentially perlocutionary, and thus it is a powerless speech-act par excellence.

14. Ricoeur, *Memory, History, Forgetting*, 457.

15. It is the register of Kant's third *Critique*, one could say, that of resistible communicativeness, which knows itself to be referred to this receiver without being able to constrain him or her. (See the remark on the pragmatics of forgiveness in note 13.)

16. Ricoeur, "Reflections on a New Ethos for Europe," 3–4.

17. Ricoeur, "Reflections on a New Ethos for Europe," 5.

18. Ricoeur, "Reflections on a New Ethos for Europe," 6, quoting and translating the title of Wilhelm Schapp, *In Geschichten Verstrickt* (Frankfurt: Klostermann, 2012) [1953].

19. Ricoeur, "Reflections on a New Ethos for Europe," 7.

20. Ricoeur, "Reflections on a New Ethos for Europe," 8.

21. Ricoeur, "Reflections on a New Ethos for Europe," 10.

22. Ricoeur, "Reflections on a New Ethos for Europe," 10.

23. Ricoeur, "Reflections on a New Ethos for Europe," 11, citing Abel, ed., *Le Pardon: Briser la Dette et l'Oubli*.

24. Ricoeur, "Reflections on a New Ethos for Europe," 11.

25. Paul Ricoeur, "Sanction, Rehabilitation, Pardon," in *The Just*, trans. David Pellauer (University of Chicago Press, 2000), 144.

26. Paul Ricoeur, "La crise de la conscience historique et l'Europe," Ética e o Futuro da Democracia, Lisboa, Edições Colibri / S.P.F. (1998), 26–35.
27. Ricoeur, "La crise de la conscience historique et l'Europe," 30.
28. Ricoeur, "La crise de la conscience historique et l'Europe," 31.
29. Paul Ricoeur, "The Difficulty to Forgive," in *Memory, Narrativity, Self and the Challenge to Think God*, eds. Maureen Junker-Kenny and Peter Kenny, London (Transaction Publishers, 2004) [1999], 6–16. [Ed.: This essay is an abbreviated translation of Paul Ricoeur, "Les difficultés du pardon," *Bulletin de Littérature Ecclésiastique* 10, no. 3 (2000): 199–214, the publication of a 1999 lecture. Where the translation includes language cited in the present text, references are provided to the English text. Otherwise, references are to the original French text.]
30. Ricoeur, "Les difficultés du pardon," 199.
31. Ricoeur, "The Difficulty to Forgive," 8.
32. Ricoeur, "The Difficulty to Forgive," 10. In a great number of Ricoeur's texts, of which a systematic survey could be made, the term "nevertheless" (used in a similar way by Frank Kermode), signals a turn, almost a change of perspective, but always in the optative mode, not the indicative or prescriptive.
33. Ricoeur, "Les difficultés du pardon," 205.
34. Ricoeur, "The Difficulty to Forgive," 12.
35. Ricoeur, "The Difficulty to Forgive," 14–15.
36. Ricoeur, "Les difficultés du pardon," 210.
37. Ricoeur, "The Difficulty to Forgive," 15.
38. Ricoeur, "The Difficulty to Forgive," 16.
39. Paul Ricoeur, *Oneself as Another*, trans. Kathleen Blamey (Chicago: University of Chicago Press, 1992) [1990], 269.
40. Paul Ricoeur, "Love and Justice," in *Figuring the Sacred*, trans. David Pellauer, ed. Mark I. Wallace (Minneapolis: Fortress Press, 1995) [1990], 329.
41. Paul Ricoeur, *History and Truth*, trans. Charles A. Kelbley (Evanston, IL: Northwestern University Press, 1965) [1964], 108. On the theme concerning what Ricoeur calls the ecclesial utopia, see Paul Ricoeur, *Plaidoyer pour l'utopie ecclésiale* (Geneva: Labor et Fides, 2016) [1967], particularly 51–55.
42. Ricoeur, *Course of Recognition*, 224–25.
43. Ricoeur, "State and Violence," in *History and Truth*, 246.
44. Ricoeur, "Freedom in the Light of Hope," in *The Conflict of Interpretations*, ed. Don Ihde (Evanston, IL: Northwestern University Press, 1974), 423. This is also the reason why, in upholding the idea of ordinary *dissensus* at every level of democracy, Ricoeur talks of "the impossibility of an absolute third party." Ricoeur, *Memory, History, Forgetting*, 314.
45. Ricoeur, "Reflections on a New Ethos for Europe," 10–11.
46. Ricoeur, *Memory, History, Forgetting*, 488.
47. The theme was already evoked in the Fourth Study on the Aporias of Ascription, concerning Aristotle. For Aristotle "the criteria of the voluntary—and all the more so, those of choice—are from the start criteria of moral and juridical imputation. Compulsion and ignorance have an explicit value of excuse, of discharge from responsibility. If the voluntary deserves praise and blame, the involuntary calls for pardon and pity." Ricoeur, *Oneself as Another*, 99.

48. Ricoeur, *Oneself as Another*, 248.

49. Ricoeur, *Oneself as Another*, 243.

50. Paul Ricoeur, *Lectures on Ideology and Utopia*, ed. George H. Taylor (New York: Columbia University Press, 1986), 166.

51. Ricoeur, *Oneself as Another*, 247–48.

52. Ricoeur, *Oneself as Another*, 247.

53. Ricoeur, *Oneself as Another*, 343.

54. Immanuel Kant, *Critique of the Power of Judgment*, trans. Paul Guyer and Eric Matthews, ed. Paul Guyer (Cambridge: Cambridge University Press, 2000), § 40.

55. Ricoeur picks up these themes in *Memory, History, Forgetting*, 486 and 493.

56. Ricoeur, *Oneself as Another*, 353.

57. Paul Ricoeur, "Le juste, la justice et son échec," in *Ricoeur* (Paris, Editions de l'Herne, 2004), 293.

58. Paul Ricoeur, "Interpretation of the Myth of Punishment," in *The Conflict of Interpretations: Essays in Hermeneutics* (Evanston, IL: Northwestern University Press, 1967), 358.

59. Ricoeur, "Le juste, la justice et son échec," 293.

60. Ricoeur, "Le juste, la justice et son échec," 297.

61. Ricoeur, "Le juste, la justice et son échec," 301.

62. Paul Ricoeur, "Justice and Vengeance," in *Reflections on the Just*, trans. David Pellauer (Chicago: University of Chicago Press, 2007 [1997]), 223.

63. Ricoeur, "Justice and Vengeance," 224.

64. Ricoeur, "Justice and Vengeance," 226.

65. Ricoeur, "Justice and Vengeance," 228.

66. Ricoeur, "Justice and Vengeance," 229.

67. Ricoeur, "Sanction, Rehabilitation, Pardon," 134.

68. Ricoeur, Sanction, Rehabilitation, Pardon," 144.

69. Ricoeur, Sanction, Rehabilitation, Pardon," 144.

70. Ricoeur, Sanction, Rehabilitation, Pardon," 145.

71. Ricoeur, Sanction, Rehabilitation, Pardon," 145.

72. Ricoeur, Sanction, Rehabilitation, Pardon," 145.

73. Ricoeur, *Memory, History, Forgetting*, 488.

74. Paul Ricoeur, "Evil, a Challenge to Philosophy and Theology," *Journal of the American Academy of Religion* 53, no. 3 (1985) [1984]: 638.

75. Ricoeur, "Evil, a Challenge to Philosophy and Theology," 645.

76. Ricoeur, "Evil, a Challenge to Philosophy and Theology," 646.

77. Ricoeur, "Evil, a Challenge to Philosophy and Theology," 647–48.

78. Paul Ricoeur, "Le droit de punir," *Cahiers de Villemétrie* 6 (March–April 1958): 2–21.

79. Ricoeur, "Le droit de punir," 12.

80. Ricoeur, "Le droit de punir," 16.

81. Ricoeur, "Le droit de punir," 21.

82. Paul Ricoeur, "Sur le tragique," *Lectures 3: Aux Frontières de la Philosophie* (Paris, Seuil, 1994 [1953]): 187–209.

83. Paul Ricoeur, "Culpabilité tragique, culpabilité biblique," *Revue d'Histoire et de Philosophie Religieuses* 33, no. 4 (1953): 285–307.

84. Ricoeur, "Sur le tragique," 189–90.
85. Ricoeur gives this account: "this abduction was a blessing; but this blessing is an abduction." Ricoeur, "Culpabilité tragique, culpabilité biblique," 296. Hence the tragic duo that Prometheus, with his titanic refusal, forms with Io, for whom suffering is, in a manner of speaking, purely passive.
86. Ricoeur, "Culpabilité tragique, culpabilité biblique," 288, citing Aeschylus, *Agamemnon*, trans. Herbert Weir Smyth (Cambridge, MA: Harvard University Press, 1963), ll. 160–62, 176–81.
87. Aeschylus, *Eumenides*, trans. Herbert Weir Smyth (Cambridge, MA: Harvard University Press, 1926), ll. 791–92.
88. Aeschylus, *Eumenides*, ll. 794–95.
89. Aeschylus, *Eumenides*, ll. 900.
90. Aeschylus, *Eumenides*, ll. 927–31.
91. Aeschylus, *Eumenides*, ll. 938–42.
92. Aeschylus, *Eumenides*, ll. 960–64. The biblical texts offer a comparable scene in Exodus 32: Yahweh threatens to destroy his people, but Moses succeeds in calming him, in wooing him, in unbinding him from his threats and his wrath. In short, Moses manages to convert the terrible divine into a compassionate divine.
93. Nicole Loraux, *La voix endeuillée* (Paris: Gallimard, 1999).
94. Ricoeur comments: "The phrase 'let the dead bury the dead' ruined the tragic Antigone." Ricoeur, "Sur le Tragique," 192.
95. Ricoeur, "Culpabilité tragique, culpabilité biblique," 302.
96. Ricoeur, "Culpabilité tragique, culpabilité biblique," 302.
97. Simone Weil, "The *Iliad*, or the Poem of Force," in *On Violence: A Reader*, ed. Bruce B. Lawrence and Aisha Karim (Durham, NC: Duke University Press, 2007), 390, [378–90].

BIBLIOGRAPHY

Abel, Olivier, ed. *Le pardon, briser la dette et l'oubli*. Paris, Autrement, 1991.
Aeschylus. *Agamemnon*. Translated by Herbert Weir Smyth. Cambridge, MA: Harvard University Press, 1963.
Aeschylus. *Eumenides*. Translated by Herbert Weir Smyth. Cambridge, MA: Harvard University Press, 1926.
Kant, Immanuel. *Critique of the Power of Judgment*. Translated by Paul Guyer and Eric Matthews, edited by Paul Guyer. Cambridge: Cambridge University Press, 2000.
Loraux, Nicole. *La voix endeuillée*, Paris, Gallimard, 1999.
Ricoeur, Paul. *The Course of Recognition*. Translated by David Pellauer. Cambridge, MA: Harvard University Press, 2005.
Ricoeur, Paul. "La crise de la conscience historique et l'Europe." Ética e o Futuro da Democracia, Lisboa, Edições Colibri/S.P.F. (1998): 26–35.
Ricoeur, Paul. "La culpabilité allemande." *Christianisme Social* 57, no. 3–4 (1949): 150–57.

Ricoeur, Paul. "Culpabilité tragique, culpabilité biblique," *Revue d'Histoire et de Philosophie Religieuses* 33, no. 4 (1953): 285–307.

Ricoeur, Paul. "The Difficulty to Forgive." In *Memory, Narrativity, Self and the Challenge to Think God*, edited by Maureen Junker-Kenny and Peter Kenny, 6–16. London: Transaction Publishers, 2004 [1999].

Ricoeur, Paul. "Les difficultés du pardon." *Bulletin de Littérature Ecclésiastique* 10, no. 3 (2000): 199–214.

Ricoeur, Paul. "Le droit de punir." *Cahiers de Villemétrie* 6 (March–April 1958): 2–21. Republished in *Foi et vie* 104, no. 1 (2005): 75–96.

Ricoeur, Paul. "Evil, a Challenge to Philosophy and Theology." *Journal of the American Academy of Religion* 53, no. 3 (1985): 635–48.

Ricoeur, Paul. "Freedom in the Light of Hope." In *The Conflict of Interpretations*, edited by Don Ihde, translated by Robert Sweeney, 402–24. Evanston, IL: Northwestern University Press, 1974.

Ricoeur, Paul. *History and Truth*. Translated by Charles A. Kelbley. Evanston, IL: Northwestern University Press, 1965.

Ricoeur, Paul. "Interpretation of the Myth of Punishment." In *The Conflict of Interpretations: Essays in Hermeneutics*, translated by Robert Sweeney, 354–77. Evanston, IL: Northwestern University Press, 1974.

Ricoeur, Paul. "Le juste, la justice et son échec." In *Ricoeur*, 287–306. Paris: Editions de l'Herne, 2004.

Ricoeur, Paul. "Justice and Vengeance." In *Reflections on the Just*. Translated by David Pellauer, 223–31. Chicago: University of Chicago Press, 2007.

Ricoeur, Paul. *Lectures on Ideology and Utopia*. Edited by George H. Taylor. New York: Columbia University Press, 1986.

Ricoeur, Paul. "Love and Justice." In *Figuring the Sacred*, Translated by David Pellauer, edited by Mark I. Wallace. Minneapolis, Fortress Press, 1995.

Ricoeur, Paul. *Memory, History, Forgetting*. Translated by Kathleen Blamey and David Pellauer. University of Chicago Press, 2004.

Ricoeur, Paul. *Oneself as Another*. Translated by Kathleen Blamey. Chicago: University of Chicago Press, 1992.

Ricoeur, Paul. *Plaidoyer pour l'Utopie Ecclésiale*. Geneva: Labor et Fides, 2016.

Ricoeur, Paul. "Reflections on a New Ethos for Europe." In *Paul Ricoeur: The Hermeneutics of Action*. Edited by Richard Kearney, Translated by Eileen Brennan, 3–13. London: Sage Publications, 1996.

Ricoeur, Paul. "Sanction, Rehabilitation, Pardon." In *The Just*. Translated by David Pellauer, 133–45. University of Chicago Press, 2000.

Ricoeur, Paul. "State and Violence." In *History and Truth*. Translated by Charles A. Kelbley, 234–46. Evanston, IL: Northwestern University Press, 1965.

Ricoeur, Paul. "Sur le tragique." In *Lectures 3: Aux Frontières de la Philosophie*, 187–209. Paris: Seuil, 1994.

Schapp, Wilhelm. *In Geschichten Verstrickt*. Frankfurt: Klostermann, 2012 [1953].

Weill, Simone. "The *Iliad*, or the Poem of Force." In *On Violence: A Reader*, edited by Bruce B. Lawrence and Aisha Karim, 378–90. Durham, NC: Duke University Press, 2007.

Chapter Fifteen

Law and Evil in Paul Ricoeur's Thought

Bertrand Mazabraud

Ricoeur's thought confronted the "challenge" of evil from the start, for considerations that were biographical as much as philosophical. The phenomenology of the will struggled to grasp how one passes from a fallibility of the will to an empiric of the fault,[1] which is why Ricoeur grafted hermeneutics onto the phenomenological wild stock in the "symbolism of evil."[2]

In this hermeneutics of the confession of fault (i.e., defilement, sin, and guilt) and in the myths of evil, two areas of meaning receive more attention. The first is the figure of "tragic evil," the second the figure of the "servile will," with the latter constituting the "intentional *telos* of the whole symbolism of evil."[3] Each of these two figures allows for criticism of the other without completing, reducing, or subsuming it.

Ricoeur guards against a figure of tragic evil that would give way to gnosis and be recovered in logic—a mistake for which he criticizes Hegel.[4] Rather, he retains tragic myths, a figure of evil that cannot be brought back to the ethical without remainder—that is, an evil that cannot be managed by people, who are subject to its enigma. This figure of tragic evil refers to a suffering not related to the deprivation of freedom, and as such is opposed to the moral vision defended by Kant.[5]

Later, however, Ricoeur will rethink and reclaim the Hegelian reading of tragic evil, conceived of as the fate of a consciousness separated into, on the one hand, the acting consciousness, limited in its particularity, and, on the other hand, the judging consciousness, limited by the abstraction of the universality of the rule. And Ricoeur also retains the resolution of this evil as a confession of the one-sidedness of points of view, the recognition of their limitations and their partiality.[6]

However, the second figure of evil—which corresponds to that of "radical evil"—is itself forgotten by tragic evil, and this forgetting is even more prejudicial. Indeed, the tragic was not the root of evil—or rather it did not explain how one passes from "this possibility" to "the reality of evil," which is "the whole riddle of fault."[7] In contrast, radical evil is situated primarily in the dissymmetry at the heart of human interactions, between the agent and the patient, each interaction offering an occasion for evil.[8] To interpret this figure of evil, Ricoeur follows the teachings of Kant (*Religion within the Bounds of Bare Reason*)[9] and Nabert (*Essai sur le mal*).[10]

Ricoeur retains the Kantian analysis that evil is linked neither to passions (desire) nor to reason, the two being innocent.[11] The site of evil will be the will, because without this, "the use or abuse of the human being's power of choice in regard to the moral law could not be imputed to him, and the good or evil in him could not be called moral."[12] Consequently, as Ricoeur argues while commenting on Kant, the foundation of evil cannot be located in a natural tendency, but only in a rule that the will gives to itself, that is, in a maxim.[13]

In other words, the foundation of evil resides in the *perversion of maxims of the will*, where evil is radical and at the root of freedom: "I see in Kant the complete philosophical manifestation that the supreme evil is not the gross infraction of a duty but the malice that makes pass for virtue what is virtue's betrayal. The evil of evil is the fraudulent justification of the maxim by apparent conformity with law—it is the semblance of morality."[14] Evil is therefore related to the moral law, but according to a subversion of the relation to the law. And yet here too this figure of evil does not explain the passage from the fallibility of the will to the empiric of fault, even if it allows for a link with human freedom.

On the one hand, then, there is the figure of tragic evil, not reducible without remainder to the ethical and resting on a plurality of points of view and on values that cannot be chosen without prejudice to others. On the other hand, there is the figure of radical evil, which connects evil with the possibility of freedom, consists in the perversion of maxims of action, and passes off as law that which is only self-love. And there is also the idea that if the focus is on one figure, the other figure is obscured, but does not disappear.

In addressing the problem of evil, which he describes as a "challenge" to philosophy and theology,[15] Ricoeur constantly insists on the disparity between the evil that is committed and the evil that is suffered, casting suspicion on their overly hasty synthesis: the correlation between violence and penal retribution. As Ricoeur says, "Violence, in this sense, constantly re-creates the unity of moral evil and suffering."[16] The same goes for the logic of penal retribution: "All suffering is deserved because it is the punishment for some individual or collective sin, known or unknown."[17] We should note that penal law responds to violence by posing the unity between the evil that is suffered and the evil that is committed. This problem of an equivalence between evil suffered and evil committed is the problem of the search for a law, and it refers mainly to the figure of radical evil, while tragic evil lets equivalences go, or rather learns that this search may be in vain.

Ricoeur's legal thought often does not clearly distinguish between moral law and juridical law.[18] He retains three distinctive traits of legality: the structuring role of prohibition, the claim to universal validity, and the ordering of human plurality. Following Kant, he distinguishes juridical law from moral law in terms of the goal of conformity versus respect, and in terms of external versus internal constraint.[19]

Whatever the meaning of the law, evil in its relationship with it finds two entry points. Ricoeur either thinks that the law is necessary to oppose the evil of violence, the power of one person over another, or he thinks of the law as inflicting evil in the administration of punishment. In the first case, the law constitutes the deontological moment that is essential for preventing the ethics of self-affirmation from turning into bad faith and abuses that could ensue in our relations with others (the subject of part I). In the second case, the law, which should prevent or contain evil, is in charge of inflicting evil, which for Ricoeur constitutes an aporia (part II).

In both cases, the relation of law to evil is focused on the figure of radical evil. Thus, it exposes itself, on the one hand, to succumbing to this kind of evil and, on the other hand, it can only obscure tragic evil, which recalls the limits of law and requires corrective action in the concrete application of law.

LAW AGAINST EVIL

In *Oneself as Another*, but also in *The Just* and *Reflections on the Just*, Ricoeur supports the primacy of the ethical aim over that of morality.[20] The deontological moment, that of the law—in the double sense of moral and juridical law—only corresponds to the second moment of the ethical route between, on the one hand, the aim of the good life and, on the other hand, practical wisdom in concrete situations.[21] Ricoeur's ethics of a "good life, with and for others, in just institutions"[22] begins with Aristotelian considerations, which already contain almost all requirements. The "just," understood following Aristotle as "the lawful and the equal,"[23] allows for the articulation of the virtuous disposition at the personal and institutional levels.[24] So, why does Ricoeur think it is necessary to pass through the deontological moment—why is it "necessary to subject the ethical aim to the test of the norm?"[25] For one reason ever renewed: evil, in the figure of radical evil. If Aristotelian ethics dealt with the figure of tragic evil, it was not of any help to a failing freedom. The concern of the law will be to place evil outside of the law (see the next section). With radical evil corresponding to a perversion of maxims, nothing prevents juridical law, instead of limiting violence, from extending it in other ways under the seal of legitimacy (see the subsequent section).

Evil Outside of the Law: Law Against Evil

The law is required to oppose the harm that one person does to another. It passes through the sieve of moral law, the aim of a good life, the realization of which, through perversion, can be detrimental to others. The law will be, first of all, the prohibition of violence (see the subsequent section). In establishing a prohibition, however, the law does not only limit evil: it also opens up a space for interaction and interlocution, structures this space, and participates in the condition in which people live (see the subsequent section).

The Law as a Catalogue of Prohibitions

The test of legality is necessary because the desire for a good life can go astray. There would need to be a regenerated freedom—that is the hope[26]—to be able to trust in the single desire for a good life. Ricoeur explains these errant ways both in terms of the *penchant for evil* at the root of freedom and in terms of the *opportunity* for this penchant to be satisfied in the power that one exercises over another.

Radical evil, as has already been mentioned, consists in a subversion of the relation to the moral law, a perversion that smuggles in a subjective maxim of action as the universal rule.[27] If respect is an affect of reason itself, the mark of reason among feelings, which makes it possible to have an inclination towards duty, evil is also an inclination, a tendency in real opposition to that of respect.[28] There would therefore be a "bad maxim" that would be the subjective foundation of all bad maxims.[29] Thus, as Ricoeur argues, "does it not follow from evil and from the inscrutable constitution of (free) will that there is, consequently, a *necessity* for ethics to assume the features of morality? Because there is evil, the aim of the 'good life' has to be submitted to the test of moral obligation, which might be described in the following terms: 'Act solely in accordance with the maxim by which you can wish at the same time that what *ought not to be*, namely evil, will indeed *not exist*.'"[30]

In the light of evil, which is commonplace in human relations, the first formulation of the Kantian categorical imperative ("act only on that maxim whereby you can at the same time will that it become a universal law")[31] is reformulated in negative terms by Ricoeur: because it is evil, it *ought* first to be prevented. The universalization test is therefore purely negative; it aims at separating, among the maxims of subjective actions, those that are perverted, like the expression of self-love, from those that are valid.[32] In other words,

Ricoeur finds symmetry in Kantian reasoning. If the *Factum der Vernunft* presents the fact of the moral structure of reason, with the positive formulations of the categorical imperative, inversely, due to the "fact of evil," the moral law is required in its negative formulations and, we might add, directly juridical because supposing an external constraint.

But this failure of desire would not require legality so insistently if it were not situated in the fundamental dissymmetry that constitutes human relations.[33] More precisely, Ricoeur sees in the power of one over another the opportunity for the penchant for evil to be realized: "The occasion of violence, not to mention the turn toward violence, resides in the *power* exerted *over* one will by another will . . . The power-over, grafted onto the initial dissymmetry between what one does and what is done to another—in other words, what the other suffers—can be held to be the occasion par excellence of the evil of violence."[34] Ricoeur can then review all opportunities for the evil of violence. All have in common the diminution or destruction of the power-to-do of others.[35] These evils are innumerable in their form—they affect the body, language, mine and yours, intimacy, and vulnerability. Ricoeur thinks of their common point, like Spinoza, as a diminution of the power of others. This diminution of being would perhaps find its paroxysm in torture, which aims, through the diminution of the power to act, at self-respect itself.[36]

Ricoeur adds, "In each case, morality replies to violence. And if the commandment cannot do otherwise than to take the form of a prohibition, this is precisely because of evil: to all the figures of evil responds the *no* of morality. Here, doubtless, resides the ultimate reason for which the negative form of prohibition is inexpungible."[37] This "no" of morality, this catalogue of prohibitions, finds its origin in a more originary "yes." If the deontological moment (moral and juridical legality) is second, it is because it stands on the original ground of the ethical, on a disposition toward the good that cannot distort the penchant for evil. Ethics had emphasized solicitude for others as the basis of justice, and it is this solicitude for others that is at work in the negative formulation of prohibitions: it aims at protecting others and at reestablishing reciprocity between patient and agent.[38]

The law that is required for opposing evil imposes a limit on the power of one over another. In so doing, it not only keeps the penchant for evil contained, but it establishes a space for interaction based on reciprocity.

The Law as Guarantor of a Regulated Space for Speech

If Ricoeur detects in the law the negative side of solicitude for others in the face of violence, he also insists on the structuring dimension of the law. This structuring dimension is twofold. First, it opens up a distance between one and the other, which prevents movements of fusion/rejection, in order to adapt itself to mutual recognition. But, from a more juridical point of view, it is also the condition in which everyone acts within institutions, with the penal dimension of law giving way to its civil dimension.

In establishing prohibitions, the law also opens up a space of exchange between them. This is how Ricoeur, following Lévi-Strauss, points out that the prohibition against incest establishes the distinction between the social bond of alliance and the simply biological bond of reproduction. The same would apply to the prohibition of murder, which, by removing the victim's right of revenge, establishes a distance between the crime and the punishment. Or again, the same would apply to the prohibition against testifying falsely, which, in protecting language, establishes a bond of mutual trust between the members of a community.[39] This distance between persons is also an opportunity for *distanciation*, this serving in the given historical situation as the possibility of a second reflexivity.[40] In other words, if the law opposes the evil of violence, it also imposes a space for interlocution between agent and patient, where the word of one counts as much as the word of the other. Justice is understood precisely as this substitution of speech for violence, and that is the purpose of the law.[41]

States, if they have first limited violence through law, also establish and guarantee a civil space, which does not necessarily depend on coercion. Ricoeur does not ignore this positive dimension of law, understood as the rule of law: "the State, as the organization of the community, gives a legal form to what seems to us to constitute the neutral third party in ethical intention, namely, the rule."[42] And he continues to follow this logic: "The essential contribution of the State is in effect to catalogue all the roles, all the masks of the social character, and to establish rights and duties; this is principally how the State is the rule of law and how it imposes real conditions of equality before the law."[43]

The catalogue in question is no longer only that of prohibitions—this is the moral foundation of juridical rules—but also a catalogue of roles and prerogatives—which is the societal foundation of juridical rules. However, if the law moves away from taking charge of evil, the latter is on the lookout, because with the second catalogue of rules, it is the public space that is at stake, but subject to political decisions. However, political decisions—like all decisions—can fail and be the occasion for evil, even the greatest evil.

The Law of Evil

The law was required for keeping evil contained, for preventing the desire for a good life from being realized to the detriment of others. However, if the moral law cannot be affected by evil, whether under the formulation of the universalization test or under the second formulation of the respect for persons as ends in themselves, this is not the case for juridical laws. These, as we have seen, can be founded in part on the moral law, but they are put into effect only in the historical framework of States. Therefore, in this gap between the moral foundation and the historic decision, nothing prevents a political regime with bad laws from being established. But even independently of the enactment of bad laws, the formalism of the law tends to obscure tragic evil, which was not silenced.

Evil Laws: From Radical Evil to the Banality of Evil

The State, as an organization of a historical community capable of *decision-making*,[44] is susceptible to failure. Laws are enacted by people; they are expressions of the will and are, therefore, occasions for evil.[45] Between the moral foundation of juridical law, on the one hand, and its historic enforcement by the State, on the other hand, political decision can fail. When it fails, the *power over* others is generalized to all the members of the community, ensuring an unprecedented extension of evil, with the guarantee of external constraint.

This figure of evil can take the specifically political form of totalitarian evil. Democracy, according to Ricoeur, is based on conflict regulated by discussion and ever greater participation of citizens in the exercise of power.[46] Now, the temptation in totalitarianism is to aim to immediately resolve the tensions inherent in democracy. Faced with the void of foundation, with negotiated conflict, and with provisional laws under discussion, totalitarian regimes offer the dream of an immediate resolution of divisions. Ricoeur, commenting on the figure of "radical evil," insisted on the connection to a wish for a synthesis of reason: "evil shows its true face—the evil of evil is the lie of premature syntheses, of violent totalizations."[47] This ever-increasing demand for synthesis spurs on theoretical reason, and is necessary for all scientific activity, but it has disastrous effects on the practical level, as it forces the plurality to become a unity. "[A]s soon as the exigency for a single truth enters into history as a goal of civilization, it is immediately affected with a mark of violence. For one always wishes to tie the knot too early. The *realized* unity of the true is precisely the initial lie. Now this culpability which is linked to the unity of the truth—this lie of *the* truth—appears when the goal of unifying coincides with the sociological phenomenon of *authority*."[48]

As a result, evil laws keep evil and violence within the whole political community. The law is perverted to the point of commanding murder, as under the Nazi regime, or ordering false testimonies, as under the Bolshevik regime.

The formalism of law, however, has a double effect with respect to the generalization of evil. First, as Arendt remarks, totalitarian regimes would abolish the gap between the law and the case, by governing all cases directly and by doing away with juridical discourse itself.[49] With the suppression of this gap, the exigency of thought, according to the modalities of reflective judgment, is also suppressed. This absence of thought allows for the passage from radical evil to the banality of evil. In other words, and on the contrary, for a regime of terror to be able to operate, laws must not limit it, if only because of the problem of "ignorant law," which invites us to rethink the law.[50]

Then the law, by accepting maxims of egregious actions (torture, slavery, murder, etc.), is not neutral in its discursive texture. It legitimizes and makes acceptable the treatment of certain categories of persons in society; it stabilizes violence, the limit, but makes it ordinary and again ensures the banality of evil.

In this gap between the moral foundation of juridical laws and their historic enforcement by human authorities, the law can fail, especially since the political regime is itself based on perverted principles. However, this support for the figure of radical evil even in the content of laws pushes the figure of tragic evil into the background.

Tragic Evil Obscured by the Formalism of Law

The law opposing evil presents it as its opposite, the objective. It tends to rationalize it by naming it. However, this attempt to theorize evil by inserting it into a coherent system is doomed to failure.[51] Here Ricoeur takes up Nabert's characterization of evil as *unjustifiable*. This should not be understood as a falsification of justification, or even as the refusal to ask the question of justification, but as the fact that all normative approaches divide and qualify experiences of evil, and insert them into the binary of norm-transgression. As a result, if such an approach makes evil intelligible, it also conceals it in equal measure, permitting it to continue on in the margins—evil as such being unjustifiable, not susceptible of rationalization.[52]

This is the tragic limit of any attempt by the law to completely oppose evil, since evil escapes categorization. This limit is especially tragic since the law is itself deluded as to its own capacities. But another tragic limit is added to this management of evil, in that the law must sometimes arbitrate between "bad and worse."[53]

If the enactment of a juridical law is the occasion for evil, in most cases this occasion is realized. According to Ricoeur, the ends of political communities are incompatible with one another, in such a way that the political domain is, ultimately, that of the undecidable.[54] Deciding will always be choosing to support one end rather than others. This tragedy of action—which is extended to the level of the enactment of laws, but also to their application—lies in the combination of the heterogeneity of goods and the impossibility of supporting them all at the same time. "The historical realization of one value cannot be obtained without wronging another; the tragedy in all human action is that one cannot support all values at once . . . One must choose, so prefer, so exclude."[55] One person may claim that the good of highest priority is health, while another may claim that it is education, another security, and so on. On the one hand, these laws are not necessarily founded on the moral imperative—this domain of political action is indifferent.[56] On the other hand, these laws can—even when founded on the moral imperative—oppose one another. However, the relegation of goods not considered priorities by the law entails allowing evil to continue under their guises.

The law was required for confronting the evil that one person does to another, for containing it, but the law's pretensions are not within its means. This contradiction at the heart of the law is paradigmatically manifested in what Ricoeur calls the aporia of punishment: an evil founded on law.

LAW RESPONSIBLE FOR EVIL

The penal sanction appeared to Ricoeur, from his early works, as an aporia that, in his later works, was considered a failure: "Its justification, as a legally inflicted suffering, constitutes the blind spot of any judicial system which, from there, becomes a penal system. By blind spot I also mean an intellectual scandal, insofar as, in my opinion, all attempts at the rational justification of punishment and the pain of punishment seem to have failed."[57] However, if the penal law fails to justify punishment, while constituting the rational foundation, it is, as we have seen, because of the impossibility for the law to pin down evil, whether it is under the figure of radical evil or tragic evil (see the section below). This failure is not a renunciation, but a call to think and to act, taking up the aporia of evil.[58] The law alone succumbs to evil and needs a corrective, informed by the logic of superabundance (see the subsequent section below).

The Law as Justification of Evil: Punishment

Ricoeur has been consistently thinking and rethinking punishment, this evil inflicted in response to an evil suffered. Initially, the penal sanction was considered a conquest of rationality in comparison with the magico-religious vision of revenge. In contrast to the figure of Job, this conquest of justice—the logic of *individual* compensation for a fault—lets go of "innocent suffering," the scandal of evil: a no-fault suffering, evil imputed without reason, unjustifiable. If Ricoeur concedes that the only rational foundation for punishment is (1) violation of the law, he nevertheless thinks that (2) punishment signifies the failure of justice: the punishment would never have enough reasons to justify itself because ultimately it would be only further suffering.

The Law as the Rational Foundation of Punishment

The analysis of punishment explains four constitutive moments:[59] (1) it is a suffering, (2) directed by a desire that thereby affects another desire, (3) the rationality of which rests on a *presumed* equivalence between the evil suffered and the evil committed, i.e. what the punishment is *held to be for* (*for* the value, the price of the crime), and (4) the guilty is *presumed* to be *identical* in the evil of the fault committed and in the evil suffered from the punishment; it is in that individual that the punishment would cancel out the fault. And Ricoeur uncovers the enigma of the rationality of the punishment, in that it supposes an equivalence of values between the evil committed and the evil suffered, although these seem to be incommensurable.[60]

However, that which affirms this equivalence, that which mediates it, is the law. And Ricoeur logically found in Kantian thought and especially in Hegelian thought the rational foundation of punishment in the law.

The fact remains, however, that this road towards the rational foundation of punishment leaves us at a disadvantage on the path to its execution. In spite of expectations to the contrary, why can we not be content with a reminder of the law? And it is with respect to the pragmatics of punishment, the *how to* punish, that Ricoeur's proposal takes on all of its acuity. If "an act in return" is needed, why is it not a simple word, but rather an imposition of suffering? The aporia denounced by Ricoeur seems to be more about the spiritual indigence of the reason for punishment. If there is an aporia, that of the equivalence between the evil suffered and the evil committed, it is also in the impossibility of deriving from the right to punish—rationally founded, *a priori*— the modalities of punishment, which are then historically contingent.

In Ricoeurian terms, if the scandal persists in the rational foundation of punishment, it is because there exists on the path of its application an incommensurability between the evil suffered and the evil committed, which is intensified by the incommensurability between the offending desire and the punished desire. The punishment to reaffirm the law will fix the *ipse*-identity to the *idem*-identity of the guilty person. Punishment does not allow the guilty person to show that she is better than her action. It stops at the threshold of forgiveness, which alone makes it possible to envision untying the guilty person from her fault to develop it in a higher sense.[61]

Thus, the punishment must be spiritualized; it must be opened up to its *ends*, which would put an *end* to the suffering inflicted. Ricoeur then suggests, for want of an impossible elimination of punishment, the reduction of its harshness. In this regard, the link of mutuality, of common recognition, could serve as a spur for articulating all the ends of the punishment.[62] This is, in other words, the lesson that Ricoeur takes from Hegel concerning tragic evil, in disarming the one-sidedness of the points of view of the "judging consciousness" and the "acting consciousness." The law alone will succumb to its curse: where there is law, there is fault. To contain evil, without succumbing in its turn, the law has to be revitalized with the sense of justice—a sense that is more original and can guide it in its applications.

The Law in Need of Justice

There is a certain hesitation in Ricoeur's thought on justice, depending on whether it is theorized in the philosophical register or the theological register. In the first case, justice is thought of as articulating the good and the legal, that is, solicitude for others and the law (understood as reciprocity due to each). In the second case, the paradox is externalized between justice confused with legality (the reciprocity of the rule) and love (*agapē*), which is a logic of superabundance. Whether it is under one or the other, the law remains defective if it does not listen to justice to think through its enactment or its application. At first, (1) it attests itself as equity, in order (2) to signal towards the logic of superabundance of *agapē*.

The Defects of the Law as Occasion for Equity

The law, because of evil, can only apply precisely as equity.[63] For Ricoeur, equity would contract two qualities: it would designate *phronesis* in the domain of justice; and it would mean solicitude for others at the risk of being excluded from the rule.

Ricoeur discovers, classically, in Book V of the *Nicomachean Ethics* the resources for thinking of equity as a corrective of the law. To follow Aristotle: "the equitable is just, but not the legally just but a correction of legal justice. The reason is that all law is universal but about some things it is not possible to make a universal statement which will be correct."[64] Therefore, equity is a corrective provision that presupposes the law, where it has failed either because of its generality or because of a conflict between the laws to be applied.

Now, to follow Ricoeur, it would be necessary to go further: equity would be solicitude working in the generality of the rule. Ricoeur brings equity close to *phronesis*, both of them apprehending the situation in its singularity.[65] With equity, the priority in the tension between the share due to each and the solicitude for others leans toward the latter.[66] A correlation between the rule and the exception appears, a correlation that could well be principled and dynamic. No rule without solicitude; no solicitude without the rule.

In this regard, it should be noted that radical evil also consisted of an "exception": the tendency of each to exclude themselves from the reciprocity of the rule. Now, with equity, the exceptional movement is the inverse: it does not abolish the law but corrects it for others—and this is because the scrupulous and dogmatic application of laws can lead to evil. Therefore, it is the defects inherent in the laws (their generality or conflicts in their application) that constitute the opportunity to avoid evil, guided by equity.

This attempt at thinking between the law and the exception for the other takes up the correlation between the logic of equivalence and the logic of superabundance, each of which cannot proceed without the other.

The Law Listening to Charity

Detached from *agapē*, the law would mark only a relative cessation of conflicts, secured by the fear of constraint. *Agapē* would show itself to be of another order and of another language than that of the norm: it would be the power of metaphorization.[67] This is how the "commandment" of love could be understood. It would be a metaphorical use of the law, situating the latter in a supra-ethical order and leaving it more closely connected to supplication, to the objurgation of tenderness: "Love me!"[68] *Agapē* advances the one-sidedness of a gift that is excluded from all reciprocity. *Agapē* evaluates the other as being worth *more*, placing her higher.[69]

Agapē does not stop at a utopia critical of ordinary justice; it also refers to a resource for the interpretation of laws, towards ever more solicitude, which pleads the singularity of the other against the reciprocity due to all others. The leitmotif is thus the same but with a change of accent.[70] On the one hand, solicitude becomes a hermeneutical resource for inventing the solution to the case, by always drawing the rules to take into account the singularity of the other—in other words, equity. On the other hand, justice is the extension of solicitude to all third parties through institutions, to the point where Ricoeur comes to hope that *agapē* might inspire ever more codes of laws.[71]

But *agapē*, the logic of superabundance, even going as far as loving one's enemy, needs the law in order to be audible. Ricoeur maintains that the logic of equivalence allows for the emergence of the logic of superabundance, it being the foundation on which its power of metaphorization acts.[72] Without the resources of the rule of equivalence, the commandment to love one's enemies would risk turning against itself. Would it not make cowardice and generosity, baseness and self-denial, ambiguous, justifying the exploitation of the most vulnerable? In other words, the law would be the guardian of *agapē*, which in its excess would be inaudible and without response.

Therefore, *agapē*, if it must be kept in order, can offer its hermeneutical resources to the law in its application, and these resources translate concretely into actual decisions.[73] It is therefore together that the logic of equivalence and the logic of superabundance can find their way.[74]

CONCLUSION

The law was necessary to stand up to the evil of violence—the evil that one commits against another—because of the tendency of each person's desire to achieve a good life, so valuable, to the detriment of others. However, the negative formulation of the moral law, which is the foundation of juridical prohibitions as well, proves a fragile dam in the face of evil. On the one hand, all attempts to categorize evil in the binary of norm-transgression allow evil to continue. On the other hand, in the gap between the moral law and juridical law, which is produced by people in history, juridical law can be badly done, but also bad. Moreover, the law apprehends evil only under its figure of radical evil and cannot take on the management of tragic evil.

All of these tensions between law and evil crystallize around the question of punishment. Since it is well founded rationally, there must be punishment. And yet, it is powerless by itself to reconcile the guilty person and the victim, let alone society. It fixes the guilty person in an *idem*-identity without the prospect of learning anything from her fault. And the punishment is only an addition to the evil that has been inflicted.

Therefore, the law needs thought, a thought that is oriented by justice, to apply itself, correct itself, and avoid evil. This thought is that of a tension between equality before the law and the exception for the other. Solicitude for others without the law would be absurd; the law without solicitude would be unlivable. This tension between the generality of the rule and the exception of the case, between the consideration of all persons and such-and-such person, also allows for the articulation of a "fine dialectic" between the judging consciousness following the laws and the consciousness acting according to its conviction, in order to maintain an open space for reconciliation and mutual recognition.

Translated by Norah Woodcock

NOTES

1. Paul Ricoeur, *Fallible Man*, trans. Charles Kelbley (New York: Fordham University Press, 1986 [1960]), 141–46.
2. Paul Ricoeur, *The Symbolism of Evil*, trans. Emerson Buchanan (Boston: Beacon Press, 1967 [1960]), 3ff.
3. Ricoeur, *The Symbolism of Evil*, 151–52.
4. Paul Ricoeur, *The Conflict of Interpretations: Essays in Hermeneutics*, ed. Don Ihde (Evanston: Northwestern University Press, 1974 [1969]), 287–314; Paul Ricoeur, "Hegel et le mal," *Dossier* 90.02, ff. 12488–12524, Fonds Ricoeur.

5. Ricoeur, *The Conflict of Interpretations*, 307–08.
6. Paul Ricoeur, *Oneself as Another*, trans. Kathleen Blamey (Chicago: University of Chicago Press, 1992 [1990]), 342–45.
7. Ricoeur, *Fallible Man*, 142.
8. Ricoeur, *Oneself as Another*, 219–20.
9. Immanuel Kant, *Religion within the Bounds of Bare Reason*, trans. Werner S. Pluhar (Indianapolis: Hackett, 2009).
10. Jean Nabert, *Essai sur le mal*, (Paris, Cerf, 1997 [1955]).
11. Paul Ricoeur, *Figuring the Sacred: Religion, Narrative, and Imagination*, trans. David Pellauer, ed. Mark I. Wallace (Minneapolis: Fortress Press, 1995), 77.
12. Kant, *Religion within the Bounds of Bare Reason*, 21 (AK VI, 21).
13. Kant, *Religion within the Bounds of Bare Reason*, 20 (AK VI, 20).
14. Ricoeur, *The Conflict of Interpretations*, 303.
15. Ricoeur, *Figuring the Sacred*, 249.
16. Ricoeur, *Figuring the Sacred*, 259.
17. Ricoeur, *Figuring the Sacred*, 252.
18. Paul Ricoeur, *The Just*, trans. David Pellauer, (Chicago: University of Chicago Press, 2000 [1995]), 148.
19. Ricoeur, *The Just*, 150–51.
20. Ricoeur, *The Just*, 148.
21. Ricoeur, *Oneself as Another*, 169 ff. and 240 ff.; Paul Ricoeur, *Reflections on the Just*, trans. David Pellauer (Chicago: University of Chicago Press, 2007), 59–60.
22. Ricoeur, *Oneself as Another*, 239; Ricoeur, *Reflections on the Just*, 59–60.
23. Aristotle, *Nicomachean Ethics*, V 1130 6, trans. W. D. Ross, in *The Complete Works of Aristotle*, ed. Jonathan Barnes (Princeton: Princeton University Press, 1984).
24. Ricoeur, *Oneself as Another*, 199–202.
25. Ricoeur, *Oneself as Another*, 203.
26. Ricoeur, *The Conflict of Interpretations*, 402 ff.
27. Ricoeur, *Oneself as Another*, 216.
28. Kant, *Religion within the Bounds of Bare Reason*, 33 (AK VI, 30).
29. Ricoeur, *Oneself as Another*, 217.
30. Ricoeur, *Oneself as Another*, 218.
31. Immanuel Kant, *Groundwork for the Metaphysics of Morals*, trans. Thomas Kingsmill Abbott, ed. Lara Denis (Peterborough: Broadview, 2005), 81 (AK IV, 421).
32. Ricoeur, *Oneself as Another*, 215.
33. Ricoeur, *Oneself as Another*, 219; Paul Ricoeur, *Lectures 1. Autour du politique* (Paris: Seuil, 1991), 263.
34. Ricoeur, *Oneself as Another*, 220.
35. Ricoeur, *Oneself as Another*, 220.
36. Ricoeur, *Oneself as Another*, 220.
37. Ricoeur, *Oneself as Another*, 221; Ricoeur, *Lectures 1*, 264.
38. Ricoeur, *Oneself as Another*, 224–25.
39. Ricoeur, *The Just*, 144.

40. Paul Ricoeur, *From Text to Action: Essays in Hermeneutics II*, trans. Kathleen Blamey and John B. Thompson (Evanston: Northwestern University Press, 1991), 259–61.

41. Paul Ricoeur, "Le Juste, la justice et son échec," in *Cahier de l'Herne: Paul Ricoeur* (Paris: Éditions de l'Herne, 2004), 293.

42. Ricoeur, *From Text to Action*, 326.

43. Ricoeur, *Lectures 1*, 104.

44. Ricoeur, *From Text to Action*, 322.

45. Paul Ricoeur, *History and Truth*, trans. Charles A. Kelbley (Evanston: Northwestern University Press, 1965), 254 ff.

46. Ricoeur, *From Text to Action*, 326.

47. Ricoeur, *The Conflict of Interpretations*, 439.

48. Ricoeur, *History and Truth*, 176.

49. Hannah Arendt, *The Origins of Totalitarianism* (San Diego: Harcourt Brace and Company, 1958), 462.

50. Arendt, *The Origins of Totalitarianism*, 462.

51. Ricoeur, *Figuring the Sacred*, 249.

52. Nabert, *Essai sur le mal*, 22–61.

53. Ricoeur, *The Just*, 155.

54. Ricoeur, *Lectures 1*, 168; cf. also Ricoeur, *The Just*.

55. Ricoeur, *Lectures 1*, 169.

56. Ricoeur, *Lectures* 1, 183.

57. Ricoeur, "Le Juste, la justice et son échec," 294.

58. Paul Ricoeur, "Evil, a Challenge to Philosophy and Theology," *Journal of the American Academy of Religion* 53, no. 3 (1985): 258.

59. Ricoeur, *The Conflict of Interpretations*, 354–55.

60. Ricoeur, *The Conflict of Interpretations*, 355.

61. Paul Ricoeur, *Memory, History, Forgetting*, trans. Kathleen Blamey and David Pellauer (Chicago: University of Chicago Press, 2004), 489–93.

62. Ricoeur, "Le Juste, la justice et son échec," 304.

63. Paul Ricoeur, "From Metaphysics to Morals," *Philosophy Today* 40, no. 4 (1996): 458.

64. Aristotle, *Nicomachean Ethics*, V, 10, 1137b10-14; cf. also 1138a1-3.

65. Ricoeur, *Oneself as Another*, 261.

66. Ricoeur, *Oneself as Another*, 268–9.

67. Paul Ricoeur, "Love and Justice," in *Figuring the Sacred*, 317.

68. Ricoeur, "Love and Justice," 319.

69. Ricoeur, "Love and Justice," 317; Paul Ricoeur, *The Course of Recognition*, trans. David Pellauer (Cambridge: Harvard University Press, 2005), 239.

70. Ricoeur, "Love and Justice," 323–24.

71. Ricoeur, "Love and Justice," 329.

72. Ricoeur, "Love and Justice," 324.

73. Paul Ricoeur, *Figuring the Sacred*, 279.

74. Ricoeur, "Love and Justice," 329.

BIBLIOGRAPHY

Arendt, Hannah. *The Origins of Totalitarianism*. San Diego, Harcourt Brace and Company, 1958.
Aristotle. "Nicomachean Ethics." In *The Complete Works of Aristotle*, edited by Jonathan Barnes, translated by W. D. Ross. Princeton: Princeton University Press, 1984.
Hegel, G. W. F. *Elements of the Philosophy of Right*. Translated by H. B. Nisbet, edited by Allen W. Wood. Cambridge: Cambridge University Press, 1991.
Kant, Immanuel. *Groundwork for the Metaphysics of Morals*. Translated by Thomas Kingsmill Abbott, edited by Lara Denis. Peterborough: Broadview, 2005.
Kant, Immanuel. *Religion within the Bounds of Bare Reason*. Translated by Werner S. Pluhar. Indianapolis: Hackett, 2009.
Nabert, Jean. *Essai sur le mal*. Paris: Cerf, 1997.
Ricoeur, Paul. *The Conflict of Interpretations: Essays in Hermeneutics*. Edited by Don Ihde. Evanston: Northwestern University Press, 1974.
Ricoeur, Paul. *The Course of Recognition*. Translated by David Pellauer. Cambridge: Harvard University Press, 2005.
Ricoeur, Paul. "Evil, a Challenge to Philosophy and Theology." *Journal of the American Academy of Religion* 53, no. 3 (1985): 635–48.
Ricoeur, Paul. *Fallible Man*. Translated by Charles Kelbley. New York: Fordham University Press, 1986.
Ricoeur, Paul. *Figuring the Sacred: Religion, Narrative, and Imagination*. Translated by David Pellauer, edited by Mark I. Wallace. Minneapolis: Fortress Press, 1995.
Ricoeur, Paul. "From Metaphysics to Morals." *Philosophy Today* 40, no. 4 (1996): 443–58.
Ricoeur, Paul. *From Text to Action: Essays in Hermeneutics II*. Translated by Kathleen Blamey and John B. Thompson. Evanston: Northwestern University Press, 1991.
Ricoeur, Paul. "Hegel et le mal," *Dossier* 90.02, ff. 12488–12524, Fonds Ricoeur.
Ricoeur, Paul. *History and Truth*. Translated by Charles A. Kelbley. Evanston: Northwestern University Press, 1965.
Ricoeur, Paul. *The Just*. Translated by David Pellauer. Chicago: University of Chicago Press, 2000.
Ricoeur, Paul. "Le Juste, la justice et son échec," *Paul Ricoeur*. Paris: Éditions de l'Herne, 2004, 287–306.
Ricoeur, Paul. *Lectures 1. Autour du politique*. Paris: Seuil, 1991.
Ricoeur, Paul. *Lectures 3. Aux frontières de la philosophie*. Paris, Seuil, 1994.
Ricoeur, Paul. *Memory, History, Forgetting*. Translated by Kathleen Blamey and David Pellauer. Chicago: University of Chicago Press, 2004.
Ricoeur, Paul. *Oneself as Another*. Translated by Kathleen Blamey. Chicago: University of Chicago Press, 1992.
Ricoeur, Paul. *Reflections on the Just*. Translated by David Pellauer. Chicago: University of Chicago Press, 2007.
Ricoeur, Paul. *The Symbolism of Evil*. Translated by Emerson Buchanan. Boston: Beacon Press, 1967.
Soual, Philippe. *Le sens de l'État: Commentaire des Principes de la philosophie du droit de Hegel*. Louvain: Peeters, 2006.

Index

abortion, right to, 8, 116, 121n47
accountability, 4, 79–81, 126, 127–30, 131, 220
action:
   capacity of, 162–63
   philosophy of, 75–76
Aeschylus, *Oresteia*, 232–33, 245, 254, 255, 256–57
"Aesthetic Judgment and Political Judgment according to Hannah Arendt" (Ricoeur), 66–67
Alexy, Robert, 4, 147
alterity, 130, 136n40, 165, 203, 247, 252, 253
amygdala, effects of trauma on, 211–12
Anger and Forgiveness (Nussbaum), 232
Antigone (Sophocles), 252, 257, 261n94
Arendt, Hannah, 4, 28, 41, 43, 60, 66, 71, 132, 247, 253, 255, 269
argumentation, 62–64, 113–14, 146–47, 180, 181–82, 183, 188n47
Aristotle, 2, 4, 21, 23, 24, 25, 29, 34, 35, 35n2, 38, 140, 150, 165, 259n47, 265;
   Nicomachean Ethics, 3, 23, 141, 273
Arthos, John, 154n66
artificial intelligence, 76, 83

"The Ascription of Responsibility and Rights" (Hart), 7
Atienza, Manual, 4
attestation, 75, 84, 129, 205n32
Augustine, 43
Austin, John, 1, 125
authority, 60–61, 65, 73n28, 132;
   experience of, 137n54
   juridical, 60–61
   superiority of, 132–34
autonomy, 9, 76, 83–84, 126, 127–30, 131–32, 134
"Autonomy and Vulnerability" (Ricoeur), 128

Basic Norm, 137n54
Bell, Derrick, 119n4
Bentham, Jeremy, 125
between-ness of law, 9, 139–40;
   Gadamer's, 139–42, 144, 145–46
   Habermas,' 142–44, 145
   Ricoeur's, 144–50
Black's Law Dictionary, 217
"black swan" events, 108, 119n6
Blumenberg, Hans, 191, 207n50
Bohman, James, 166
Boltanski, Luc, 4;
   De la justification, 5, 37–52
Bossuet, Jacques-Bénigne, 44

Bourdieu, Pierre, 93, 94, 95
Brandeis, Louis, 72n25
Brennan, Eileen, 35, 103, 219–20, 222
Breyer, Stephen, 72–73n25
Bundy, Ted, 213–14, 217, 218
"butterfly effect," 108, 118

Camus, Albert, 100
Cane, Peter, 79–80
capacities, 77–78, 79–80, 162–65
certainty, 193–94
charity, 248, 251–52, 274
Chicago School, 2
Christianity, 107, 119n4
cities, 42–45, 48–50, 97–98
City of God (Augustine), 43
coherence criterion, 178
collective unity, 194–99
commitments, 130
community, historical, 67–68, 70
compromise, 12, 48–50, 54, 245, 251
The Concept of Law (Hart), 1
consent, 127
constitutionalism, 2–3, 55
contingency, 115;
 narrative and, 109–12
contractualism, 26–27, 54
conversion, of goods, 46–48
convictions, 31–32
The Course of Recognition (Ricoeur), 77, 197, 231, 251
courts, 95–96;
 birth of, in Greece, 96–97, 99
Crew, Raymond, 213–14, 217, 218
"The Crisis of the Historical Conscience and Europe" (Ricoeur), 249
"crisis of witnessing," 11, 210, 212–15, 218–19, 222–23
critical distanciation, 154n66
critical theory, 139, 142–44, 145, 147
Critique of Judgment (Kant), 113
culpability, 130–32

Daicoff, Susan, 229, 233
deductive reasoning, 145

De la justification (Boltanski and Thévenot), 5, 37
democracy, 8–9, 25, 53–55, 70, 99, 102, 142–43, 157–60, 163–64, 166, 169, 269
de-negation, 195–96, 197, 204
Derrida, Jacques, 7, 95, 102;
 "Force of Law: The 'Mystical Foundation of Authority,'" 94
Deweer, Dries, 161
Dewey, John, 159
Dierckxsens, Geoffrey, 79
differentiation, 41–42
"The Difficulty to Forgive" (Ricoeur), 249
discord, 41, 42, 98
discourse, 34–35, 148–50
dissent, 5
distanciation, 154n66, 268
distribution:
 principles of, 28–29
 society as a system of, 24–25, 29, 31
Doctrine of Right, 66–67
domination, 5, 38–39, 41, 46
Dosse, François, 19
Durkheim, Émile, 2, 24
Dworkin, Ronald, 2, 4, 5, 7, 14n27, 62–63, 72n17, 115, 121n40, 147, 180–81

École nationale de la magistrature, 19
economy of scale, 41–42
egalitarianism, 25, 29, 38, 46
embodiment, 76, 83, 195
episteme, 139, 140–42
equality, 5, 24, 38n3, 69;
 complex, 38–39, 46, 48
 justice as, 38
 numerical, 25, 35n2, 38
 procedural, 55
 proportional, 25, 26, 29
equitability, 146, 150, 220
equity, 273–74
equivalence, logic of, 101–2, 230–32, 239, 274

Essai sur le mal (Nabert), 264
esteem, 161
ethics, 35, 54–55;
ethical life, 9
  law and, 135
  responsibility and, 164
Ethics (Spinoza), 195
evil:
  expressions of, 127–28
  god, myth of, 100–101
  law against, 265–71
  law of, 268–71
  law responsible for, 271–74
  origin of, 99
  radical, 13, 263–64, 266, 269–70
  reality of, 69
  suffered vs. committed, 264–65
  symbolism of, 12–13, 91, 263
  tragic, 13, 263–64, 265, 270–71
  of violence, 266–67, 275
  and will, 264.
  See also punishment
"Evil, a Challenge to Philosophy and Theology" (Ricoeur), 255
evolution, 109–10, 115
Experience and Judgment (Husserl), 192–94
explanation, 139, 145–46, 151n3, 179, 180, 183–84

facts:
  coherence criterion, 178
  in dispute, assessment of truth of, 174–76
  interpretation of, 184–85
  and norms, inseparability of, 142–44
fairness, 5, 27, 219, 222
Felman, Shoshana, 210, 212
15th Amendment, 68
1st Amendment, 118
"Force of Law: The 'Mystical Foundation of Authority'" (Derrida), 94
forgetting, 246–49
forgiveness, 12;
  and justice, 250–53
  and memory, 246–50
  as a powerless speech-act, 258n13.
  See also pardon
formalism, 5, 9, 28;
  imperfect vs. perfect, 23, 25–26
  of law, 269–71
  minimal, 46
  as an understanding of rights, 160–61, 164
Foucault, Michel, 7, 94, 102
Francis of Assisi, 66
Francken, Theo, 167–68
Frankfurt School, 147
freedom, 68–69, 128;
  of speech, 157, 158–60, 163, 166
Freedom and Nature (Ricoeur), 127
"Freedom in the Light of Hope" (Ricoeur), 251
French Revolution, 2
friendship, 24, 38n3
From Text to Action (Ricoeur), 179, 181
Fuller, Lon, 2

Gadamer, Hans-Georg, 9, 113, 139–42, 144, 145, 146, 147, 150, 154n66
Garapon, Antoine, 4, 19, 33, 134
Garland, Merrick, 118
Gasché, Rodolphe, 152n21
The Gay Science (Nietzsche), 250
Geertz, Clifford, 43
Gerry, Elbridge, 121n50
gerrymandering, 8, 107, 115, 116–19, 121n50
Golden Rule, 219, 222
Goldwater, Barry, 108
the good:
  idea of, 26
  the just and, 23–25, 219–20
good life, 3, 11, 23, 210, 265–66;
  justice vs., 53, 54, 72n17
goods:
  commercial, 44
  common, 44–45
  conversion of, 46–48

distribution of, 24–25, 29, 31–33, 47
  social, 39–40, 42–43, 46
Gould, Steven Jay, 109–10, 115
gratuity, 231–32, 235–36, 240n10
Greece, birth of court in, 96–97, 99
guilt, 246, 249

Habermas, Jürgen, 4, 9, 139, 140, 142–44, 145, 146, 147, 152n23, 154n66, 181
"hard cases," 7, 62, 66, 180
Hart, H.L.A., 1, 2, 4, 80–81;
  "The Ascription of Responsibility and Rights," 7
Hastie, Reid, 177–78
Haydon, Graham, 80
Hayek, Friedrich, 2
Hegel, Georg, 4, 9, 68–69, 126, 134, 252, 263, 272;
  Philosophy of Right, 2, 125
Heidegger, Martin, 140, 142, 152n21
Hénaff, Marcel, 104n27
Herman, Judith, *Trauma and Recovery*, 210, 212
hermeneutics:
  of authority, 133
  of discourse, 148–50
  juridical, 61–64
  of law, Gadamer's, 139–42, 144, 145–46, 154n66
  legal, 113
  Ricoeur's theory of, 111
  of self, 79, 83, 125
  of symbolic order, 133
higher authority, 32–33
historical inquiry, 139, 151n3
historiography, 173–75, 177, 178
history, course of, 107–9, 115
History and Truth (Ricoeur), 95, 197, 251
Hobbes, Thomas, 2, 4, 44
Höffe, Ottfried, 4
Holmes, Oliver, 2
Honneth, Axel, 205–6n32

humanity:
  common, 49–50
  respect for, 161
  task of, 8, 107, 112
human rights, 2, 98, 162
humiliation, 77–78
Husserl, Edmund, 10, 195, 196, 199, 200;
  Experience and Judgment, 192–94

identity, narrative, 129–30, 163, 252
imagination, 7, 8, 64–66, 110, 111, 114–15, 120n18, 134, 137n70, 146, 247
impartiality, 3, 65, 133–34, 135, 137n70
imputability, 78–79, 84–85, 131
individualism, 24, 27
inequality, 29–30
injustice, sense of, 3, 21
innovation, 8, 33, 83, 111, 114
Institut des hautes études sur la justice (IHEJ), 19
intentionality, 198–99
interpretation, 62–64, 72n25, 113–15, 141, 146–48, 180–81, 184–85, 188n47
"Interpretation and/or Argumentation" (Ricoeur), 181–82
"Interpretation of the Myth of Punishment" (Ricoeur), 253–54
Isocrates, 38

Jacob, Robert, 98
Jaspers, Karl, 100
Job, 255
Johnson, Lyndon, 108
judges and judging, 10, 99, 145;
  phenomenology of, 192–94
judgment:
  act of, 152n21, 191–92, 197–98
  determinative, 114
  legitimacy of, 73n28
  as (mis)recognition, 200–204
  as (mis)representation, 198–200
  perceptual, 195–96

predicative, 193–94
reflective, 62, 63, 65–67, 68–70, 72n24, 113–15, 119, 145, 180. *See also* impartiality
judicatory imaginary, 114
judicial system, 32–35, 99
jurisprudence, 1–2
the just:
   and the good, 23–25, 219–20
   and the legal, 25–30, 219–20
   vs. unjust, 3–4, 22, 219
The Just (Ricoeur), 2, 7, 19, 75, 77–78, 80, 91, 113, 125, 160, 180, 215–16, 220, 265
just distance, 3, 33–34, 59, 61, 70–71, 127, 134, 254
justice:
   aim of, 173–74, 182–86
   arguments of, 21, 34–35
   channels of, 21, 32
   distributive, 25, 28–29, 42, 237
   emotions and, 232–34
   as equality, 38n3
   forgiveness and, 250–53
   generativity of, 7, 91, 95, 102–3
   vs. the good life, 53, 54, 72n17
   idea of, 21
   law in need of, 273–74
   and logic of equivalence, 101–2, 230–32, 239
   and love, 11–12, 101–2, 229–40, 250–53, 274
   moral vs. legal, 4–5
   occasions of, 21, 30–31
   and politics, 55
   principles of, 28–30
   procedural, 5, 26–28, 33–34
   reason and, 67–71
   restorative, 237
   retributive, 237
   ritual part of, 98
   sense of, 3, 21
   and the state, 54–55
   substantive, 5
   "swollen" sense of ordinary, 98–99
   symbols of, 7–8
   trial as first form of, 96
"Justice and Vengeance" (Ricoeur), 254
justification, 37, 41–42, 48–49
just institutions, 9, 67–68, 135, 161, 170n7, 222–23, 237–38
"The Just, Justice, and its Failure" (Ricoeur), 253
"The Just Between the Legal and the Good" (Ricoeur), 4–5, 19, 181

Kant, Immanuel, 2, 4, 5, 9, 27, 28, 64, 127–28, 131–32, 134, 136n24, 263; *Critique of Judgment*, 113; *The Metaphysics of Morals*, 26; *Religion within the Bounds of Bare Reason*, 264
Kavanaugh, Brett M., 60, 118
Kelsen, Hans, 4, 82, 86n18, 137n54; *Pure Theory of Law*, 78
Kennedy, Anthony, 118
Kenner, Max, 236, 241n38
King, Martin Luther, Jr., 8, 107, 111, 119n2, 235
knowledge, situated, 9

The Language of Law School (Mertz), 233
Last Judgment, 95–96, 98–99, 101
Laub, Dori, 210
law:
   Austin on, 1
   as a catalogue of prohibitions, 266–67
   as a "chain novel," 7
   and ethics, 135
   against evil, 265–71
   of evil, 268–71
   formalism of, 269–71
   as guarantor of regulated space for speech, 267–68
   Hart on, 1
   interpretation of, 62–63, 72n25

Kant's theory of, 26
moral vs. juridical, 12–13, 264–69, 275
narrative and, 112–16
natural, 2, 107
in need of justice, 273–74
between-ness of, 9, 139–56
normativity of, 1
and politics, 135
responsible for evil, 271–74
rule of, 167–68, 179–86, 268
settled, 64–65, 72n25. *see also* precedents
soft-, 82–83
subject of, 126, 128, 134–35
and symbols of justice, 7–8
victories in, 116
"lawfare," 138n75
lawyers, 233–34
Lectures on Ideology and Utopia (Ricoeur), 252
the legal, the just and, 25–30, 219–20
legalism, 26
legal realism, 2, 143
legal reasoning, 4, 6, 9, 10, 125
Leibniz, Gottfried, 2
Levinas, Emmanuel, 7, 36n3, 94, 95, 102
Lévi-Strauss, Claude, 39, 93, 268
liminality, 6, 126, 128
logic, 110, 115–16, 146, 150, 160, 181, 211, 217, 229–31
"The Logic of Jesus, the Logic of God" (Ricoeur), 230
love:
  as Agape, 239, 273, 274
  anthropological optimism of, 12
  gratuity as an act of, 235–36
  institutional expressions of, 237–38
  and justice, 11–12, 101–2, 229–40, 250–53, 274
  and logic of superabundance, 101–2, 230–32, 239, 273, 274
"Love and Justice" (Ricoeur), 230, 235, 245, 250–51

"A Loving Obedience" (Ricoeur), 235
Lyotard, Jean-François, 111–12

Mabo 2 case, 10–11, 194, 200–204
Machiavelli, Niccolò, 2
Mannheim, Karl, 252
Marx, Karl, 60
Mauss, Marcel, 93
maximin principle, 30, 31
mediators, 28, 29, 30;
  political, 33
memory:
  defined, 218
  forgiveness and, 246–50
  "never forget" saying, 214
  sensory details of, 212, 224n18
  traumatic, 210–12, 218, 220–21, 223
Memory, History, Forgetting (Ricoeur), 151n3, 178, 182–83, 209, 220, 245, 246, 250, 252
Mertz, Elizabeth, 229;
  The Language of Law School, 233
metaphor, 110, 112, 114–15
The Metaphysics of Morals (Kant), 26
metaphysics of otherness, 9–10, 160, 165–69
migration, 8, 167
minorities as others, 157–60, 165, 167–68
morality, 3;
  law and, 145
  phenomenology of moral experience, 132
  political vs. ethical, 53
  respect for humanity, 161
  responsibility and, 164.
  See also ethics
moral reasoning, 136n24, 145
Mother Teresa, 235
myths:
  "aliveness" of, 92
  demythization, 94
  drama of creation, 99–100
  evil god, 100–101
  latent existence of, 92–93

soul exiled in the body, 101
trial origins, 95–96

Nabert, Jean, 270;
   Essai sur le mal, 264
Nagel, Thomas, 133, 137n70
narrative(s):
   and assessment of truth of facts in dispute, 174–76, 186
   and contingency, 109–12
   vs. description, 187n5
   of facts, 63
   founding, 133
   hospitality, 247–48
   identity, 129–30, 163, 252
   and law, 112–16
   postmodern, 111
   resistances of, against the aim of truth, 176–79, 186
   Ricoeur's theory of, 8, 111–12
   testimony as, 10
   tradition as a form of, 111
   trauma, 11, 212–15, 221
nationality, 47
National Memorial for Peace and Justice, 234
natural law, 2, 107
"Negativity and Primary Affirmation" (Ricoeur), 195
Nicomachean Ethics (Aristotle), 3, 23, 141, 273
Nietzsche, Friedrich, *The Gay Science*, 250
19th Amendment, 68
norms, 9, 71, 93, 113, 139, 140, 142–44, 151, 164, 168, 179
Nozick, Robert, 48
Nussbaum, Martha, 229;
   Anger and Forgiveness, 232

Obama, Barack, 108, 118
obedience, 60–61, 128
objectivity, 181–82
obligation, 131–32, 136n41, 235.
   See also responsibility

Oedipus Rex (Sophocles), 257
Oneself as Another (Ricoeur), 3, 76, 84, 102, 125, 130, 170n7, 197, 215, 245, 250–51, 252, 265
"On the Tragic" (Ricoeur), 256
order, 99–100, 132–34
Oresteia (Aeschylus), 232–33, 245, 254, 255, 256–57
otherness:
   of conscience, 168–69
   consciousness of, 194
   exclusion of, 159
   of the flesh, 166
   metaphysics of, 9–10, 160, 165–69
   of other people, 167, 203–4
   rights and, 9–11
   suffering other, 11, 209, 222–23

pardon, 232–33, 248, 249, 252, 254–55, 259n47.
   See also forgiveness
Pennington, Nancy, 177–78, 179
perception, 195–96
Perelman, Chaïm, 148
Pericles, 24, 38
personalism, 9, 161, 164, 169
personhood, 77.
   See also self
persuasion, 148–49, 152n21, 177
phenomenology:
   of action, 165
   of alterity, 165
   of judging, 192–94, 197–98
   of moral experience, 132, 133
   of otherness, 165–69
   of perception, 195–96
   superiority of authority, 132–33
philosophical anthropology, 6, 8–9, 95, 126
Philosophy of Right (Hegel), 2, 125
Philosophy of the Will (Ricoeur), 91, 127
Plato, 2, 21, 23, 165
pluralism, 3, 5, 6, 37–38, 46, 48–49, 53–55

"The Plurality of Instances of Justice" (Ricoeur), 5–6
poetics, 9, 113, 139, 146, 148–49, 248
poiesis, 140
political paradox, 41, 46–51;
   and juridical authority, 60–61
   Ricoeur's, 2–3, 6
   of the state, 7
political power, 40–41, 45, 47–48
politics:
   justice and, 55
   law and, 135
   victories in, 116.
   See also democracy
polytheism, 104n38
populism, 108
positivism, 1–2, 5, 26, 28, 62, 181
Posner, Richard, 2
power:
   in-common, 127
   constitutive, 132–34
   judiciary, 61
   lack of, 129
   political, 40–41, 45, 47–48
   sovereign, 5, 6, 45.
   See also state
practical reasoning, 145
practical verification, 166
pragmatism, 157–60, 166, 169
praxis, 33, 140, 152n21
precautionary principle, 82
precedents, 59, 61–62, 64–67, 70–71, 115.
   See also stare decisis
proceduralism, 33–34
promises, 130, 162, 248
prophetic monotheism, 104n38
The Providence of Jurisprudence Determined (Austin), 1
punishment, 253–57, 264–65, 271–73;
   as reeducation, 236–37.
   See also vengeance
Pure Theory of Law (Kelsen), 78

racism, 107, 119n4
Rasmussen, David, 143
Rawls, John, 4, 24, 25, 27–30, 31, 37, 46, 48, 53, 54, 132, 219;
   Theory of Justice, 5
Raz, Joseph, 2
Reagan, Ronald, 108
reason and reasoning:
   and justice, 67–71
   traditions of, 145
recognition, 76–78, 81, 134, 200–204, 205–6n32, 231–32, 236–37, 240n10
reconciliation, 102, 252
reeducation, 236–37
reflection, 152n21
"Reflections on a New Ethos for Europe" (Ricoeur), 245, 247–48, 251–52
Reflections on the Just (Ricoeur), 91, 160, 215, 265
refugees, 167–69
regulation, 82–83
Religion within the Bounds of Bare Reason (Kant), 264
representation, 198–200
respect, 9, 28, 40, 55, 75, 161, 164, 168, 223, 266, 269
responsibility:
   as a capacity, 77–78, 163–64
   imputation and, 78–79, 84–85, 131
   prospective, 79–83, 84–85
   retrospective, 79–83
   rights and, 7, 75–76
   role-, 80, 81
   virtue-, 80–81.
   See also obligation
rhetoric, 148–49, 150, 177, 188n47
"Rhetoric-Poetics-Hermeneutics" (Ricoeur), 148–50
Ricoeur, Paul:
   "Aesthetic Judgment and Political Judgment according to Hannah Arendt," 66–67
   "Autonomy and Vulnerability," 128

The Course of Recognition, 77, 197, 231, 251
"The Crisis of the Historical Conscience and Europe," 249
"The Difficulty to Forgive," 249
"Evil, a Challenge to Philosophy and Theology," 255
Freedom and Nature, 127
"Freedom in the Light of Hope," 251
From Text to Action, 179, 181
History and Truth, 95, 197, 251
"Interpretation and/or Argumentation," 181–82
"Interpretation of the Myth of Punishment," 253–54
The Just, 2, 7, 19, 75, 77–78, 80, 91, 113, 125, 160, 180, 215–16, 220, 265
"The Just, Justice, and its Failure," 253
"The Just Between the Legal and the Good," 4–5, 19, 181
"Justice and Vengeance," 254
Lectures on Ideology and Utopia, 252
"The Logic of Jesus, the Logic of God," 230
"Love and Justice," 230, 235, 245, 250–51
"A Loving Obedience," 235
Memory, History, Forgetting, 151n3, 178, 182–83, 209, 220, 245, 246, 250, 252
"Negativity and Primary Affirmation," 195
Oneself as Another, 3, 76, 84, 102, 125, 130, 170n7, 197, 215, 245, 250–51, 252, 265
Philosophy of the Will, 91, 127
"The Plurality of Instances of Justice," 5–6
"Reflections on a New Ethos for Europe," 245, 247–48, 251–52
Reflections on the Just, 91, 160, 215, 265
"Rhetoric-Poetics-Hermeneutics," 148–50
"The Right to Punish," 256
The Rule of Metaphor, 110
"Sanction, Rehabilitation, Pardon," 249, 254
"State and Violence," 251
The Symbolism of Evil, 7, 91–92, 95, 101, 127
"Thou Shalt Not Kill," 230
Time and Narrative, 110, 129
"On the Tragic," 256
"Tragic Guilt, Biblical Guilt," 256
"Uncanniness Many Times Over," 165
"Who is the Subject of Rights?" 160–61
"The Right to Punish" (Ricoeur), 256
rights:
  Aboriginal, 10–11, 200–204
  ascription of, 157–65, 169
  to be free, 136n24
  distribution of, 68
  formalist approach to, 160–61, 164
  as forms of recognition, 157
  otherness and, 9–11
  personalist approach to, 160–61, 164
  and responsibility, 7
  subject of, 75–76, 81–82, 83–84, 126, 160–61, 221
Roe v. Wade, 116, 118, 196
Rogers, Annie, 214
Rousseau, Jean-Jacques, 27, 101;
  Social Contract, 44, 50
The Rule of Metaphor (Ricoeur), 110

Saint-Simon, Henri de, 44
"Sanction, Rehabilitation, Pardon" (Ricoeur), 249, 254
Sartre, Jean-Paul, 195
Scalia, Antonin, 118, 233

Scheler, Max, 32
scriptural representation, 175
self:
   dialogical constitution of, 216–22
   hermeneutics of, 79, 83, 125
   moral, 126
   responsibility as a capacity of, 77–78, 79–80
   sense of, 130–31
   as a subject of law, 126, 128, 134–35
   as a subject of rights, 75–78, 81–82, 84
self-affirmation, 191–94, 205–6n32;
   collective, 194–98, 204
Seneca, 254
singularity, 77, 129, 130–32, 136n40, 274
situated knowledge, 9
Smith, Adam, 43
Social Contract (Rousseau), 44, 50
society:
   "civil," 33
   as a system of distribution, 24–25, 29, 31
soft-law, 82–83
Solon, 24, 29, 38
sophia, 140
Sophocles:
   Antigone, 252, 257, 261n94
   Oedipus Rex, 257
sovereign power, 5, 6, 45.
   See also Mabo 2 case
Spade, Bill, 213, 214
speech, 166;
   capacity of, 162
   freedom of, 157, 158–60, 163
   law as guarantor of regulated space for, 267–68
Spheres of Justice (Walzer), 5, 37–52
Spinoza, Baruch, 129, 198;
   Ethics, 195
Spirit, Hegel's philosophy of, 68–69
stare decisis, 59, 71, 72–73n25.
   See also precedents

state:
   authority, legitimacy of, 132–33
   and evil, 269–70
   as higher authority, 32–33
   juridical power of, 37
   just, 54–55
   political paradox of, 7
   privilege of legitimate violence by, 59–61, 67–71
"State and Violence" (Ricoeur), 251
Stevenson, Bryan, 236, 238, 241n37, 242n41
storytelling, 10, 214.
   See also narrative(s)
suffering, 3, 11, 13, 69, 209, 222–23, 238, 248, 255, 264, 271–72
superabundance, logic of, 101–2, 230–32, 239, 273, 274
surplus value, 60
symbolic order, 132–34
The Symbolism of Evil (Ricoeur), 7, 91–92, 95, 101, 127
symbols and symbolism:
   aporia of, 93–94
   of evil, 12–13, 91, 263
   latent existence of, 92–93
   Ricoeur's philosophy of, 7–8
synthesis of the heterogeneous, 175

techne, 140–42, 151
testimony, 216–17;
   as narrative, 10, 176
   trauma and, 11, 212–15, 222
Theory of Justice (Rawls), 5
Thévenot, Laurent, 4;
   De la justification, 5, 37–52
"Thou Shalt Not Kill" (Ricoeur), 230
Tillich, Paul, 100, 101
Time and Narrative (Ricoeur), 110, 129
Tocqueville, Alexis de, 25
Torah, 127
tradition, 111, 114
tragic, conversion of, 253–57

"Tragic Guilt, Biblical Guilt" (Ricoeur), 256
trauma:
    "crisis of witnessing," 210, 212–15, 218–19
    and memory, 210–12, 218, 220–21, 223
    and narrative, 11
    unsayability of, 214–15
Trauma and Recovery (Herman), 210, 212
trials, 34–35, 95–98;
    documentary phase of, 183–84
    spectacle of, 100–101
Trump, Donald, 108, 159
trustworthiness, 130
truth:
    aim of, 173–74, 182–86
    assessment of in facts in dispute, 174–76, 186
    resistances of narrative against aim of, 176–79, 186
    search for, 216–22
Tushnet, Mark, 115–16

"Uncanniness Many Times Over" (Ricoeur), 165
uncertainty, 10, 23, 30, 82, 192–94, 197, 223
understanding, 139, 141, 145–46, 151n3, 180, 183
United States Holocaust Memorial Museum, 234
unity, 8, 10, 111, 175, 194–99

values, 31–32, 33
Van der Kolk, Bessel A., 212

veil of ignorance, 28, 29, 30
vengeance, 70, 91, 97, 134, 147, 230, 232–33, 253–57
victories, legal and political, 116
violence:
    evil of, 266–67, 275
    inevitability of, 95
    internal vs. external, 133
    legitimate, by the state, 59–61, 67–71
virtue:
    justice as, 23–24, 34
    -responsibility, 80–81
voluntary, vs. involuntary, 259n47
voluntary self-regulatory instruments, 82–83
vulnerability, 126, 128–29, 134

Waldenfels, Bernhard, 198
Walzer, Michael, 4, 31;
    Spheres of Justice, 5, 37–52
"we, the people," 3, 5, 6, 10–11
Weber, Max, 2, 4, 24, 31, 43
Weill, Simone, 257
Whitford v. Gill, 117–19
"Who is the Subject of Rights?" (Ricoeur), 160–61
Wiesel, Elie, 212
will, 127, 132, 194, 263–64, 267
witnesses:
    retraumatization of, 218–19, 225n39
    right of, 220–21
    testimony of, 176
witnessing, crisis of, 11, 210, 212–15, 218–19, 222–23
worlds, 45–46, 48–49

About the Contributors

Olivier Abel studied with Michel Henry, Vladimir Jankélévitch, Emmanuel Levinas, but principally with Paul Ricoeur (Masters, Doctorate, and HDR). He is professor of ethics at the Institut Protestant de Théologie of Montpellier, having taught in Chad and Istanbul, then in Paris (1984 to 2014) where he now plays host to the Fonds Ricoeur. Research associate at the Arts and Language Research Center of the École des Hautes Études en Sciences Sociales, he is a member of the editorial board of the journal *Esprit*, and a former member of the National Ethics Advisory Committee. His published works include, *Paul Ricoeur, la promesse et la règle* (Michalon, 1996); *L'éthique interrogative* (Presses Universitaires de France, 2000); *La conversation* (Gallimard, 2006); *Pierre Bayle* (Michalon, 2017); and *Le vertige de l'Europe* (Labor et Fides, 2019).

Stephanie Arel is currently an instructor at Fordham University. She previously held an Andrew W. Mellon Fellowship at the National September 11 Memorial and Museum and New York University. She was also a fellow of the UBIAS phase II on Human Dignity held jointly at the Hebrew University in Jerusalem and the ZiF in Bielefeld, Germany. She is the author of *Affect Theory, Shame, and Christian Formation* (2016) as well as co-editor of *Post-Traumatic Public Theology* (2016) and *Ideology and Utopia in the 21st Century: The Surplus of Meaning in Ricoeur's Conception of the Dialectical Relationship of Ideology and Utopia* (2018). She has written extensively on Paul Ricoeur and is past president (2018–2020) of the Society for Ricoeur studies.

Eileen Brennan studied Philosophy in Dublin and Paris and is a lecturer in philosophy and education at Dublin City University. She has written widely

291

in the field of hermeneutics with particular concentration on the work of Paul Ricoeur. A former editor of *Études Ricoeuriennes/Ricoeur Studies*, she has translated a number of books and papers by contemporary French thinkers.

Marie-Hélène Desmeules is an assistant professor of philosophy at the Université de Sherbrooke, Québec. Her research lies at the intersection of phenomenology, ethics, and law. She is particularly interested in how legal norms affect our lived experience. As a postdoctoral researcher at the New School for Social Research, a position funded by the Social Sciences and Humanities Research Council (Canada) and the Fonds de recherche du Québec–Société et culture, she mobilized phenomenology's resources to examine the ethical issues raised by the norm of consent. She recently translated with Julien Farges (CNRS): Edmund Husserl, *Normativité et déconstruction. Digression dans les "Leçons sur l'éthique" de 1920* (Paris: Vrin, 2020).

Geoffrey Dierckxsens is currently head of the Interdisciplinary Research Lab for Bioethics (IRLaB) at the Department of Contemporary Continental Philosophy at the Institute of Philosophy of the Czech Academy of Sciences (CAS) in Prague. He recently was a visiting scholar in the international exchange program, SAIA, at the Institute of Philosophy of the Slovak Academy of Sciences in Bratislava and received the Lumina Quaeruntur Award for prospective researchers. He obtained his PhD in 2015 at the University of Antwerp (Belgium), worked as an associated researcher at the École des Hautes Études en Sciences Sociales (EHESS) in Paris and as a postdoc at the IP CAS Prague. Geoffrey Dierckxsens specializes in French phenomenology and hermeneutics, in particular as applied to bioethics and cognitive theory. His publications include Paul *Ricoeur's Moral Anthropology: Singularity, Responsibility and Justice* (Lexington Books, 2017), "Responsibility and the Physical Body: Paul Ricoeur on Analytical Philosophy of Language, Cognitive Science, and the Task of Phenomenological Hermeneutics" (*Philosophy Today*, 2017), and "Prostheses as Narrative Technologies: Bioethical Considerations for Prosthetic Applications in Health Care" in *Interpreting Technology: Ricoeur on Questions Concerning Ethics and Technology*, Rowman and Littlefield, 2021.

Antoine Garapon served as a judge in the French juvenile justice system for many years. He is a member of the editorial board of the journal *Esprit* (which is how he met Paul Ricoeur); and he founded the Institut des Hautes Études sur la Justice [IHEJ] in Paris in 1991. Paul Ricoeur delivered the IHEJ's inaugural lecture, "The Just Between the Legal and the Good," as well as numerous others that were then brought together in two volumes: *The Just* (University of Chicago Press, 2000) and *Reflections on the Just* (University of Chicago Press, 2007). He is the author of several books including, *Le gardien des promesses,* with a preface by Paul Ricoeur (Odile Jacob, 1996); *Juger en Amérique et en France*, co-authored with Ioannis Papadopoulos and with a foreword by Justice Stephen Breyer (Odile Jacob, 2003); and *Justice digitale. Révolution graphique et rupture anthropologique*, co-authored with Jean Lassègue (PUF, 2018). He also manages the collection *Bien commun* for the publishing company Michalon and has a weekly programme "Esprit de justice" on France Culture.

Guido Gorgoni is assistant professor in legal theory at the University of Padua, Italy. He teaches the course "Digital Citizenship and Law." He has worked on the evolution of the legal idea of responsibility, in particular, the idea of prospective responsibility, explored along with Paul Ricoeur's thought. His research activity deals also with the evolution of legal systems and regulation, on the Precautionary Principle and the idea of Responsible Research and Innovation. More recently his research has turned also towards Digital Citizenship and Digital Constitutionalism.

Marc de Leeuw teaches legal philosophy at the Faculty of Law and Justice at the University of New South Wales (Sydney). His research concerns issues in philosophical anthropology, phenomenology of law, biolegality, environmental law, and AI. He has been a visiting fellow at Yale University (New Haven), University of California-Berkeley, and the Institute for Advanced Study (Princeton). His books include *Personhood in the Age of Biolegality* (Palgrave MacMillan, 2019); *Biolegality: A Critical Intervention* (Palgrave MacMillan, 2022); and *Paul Ricoeur's Renewal of Philosophical Anthropology* (Rowman and Littlefield, 2021).

Hans Lindahl holds the chair of the philosophy of law at Tilburg University, the Netherlands, and a chair of global law at the Law Department of Queen Mary University of London. His research is primarily oriented toward issues germane to globalization processes, such as the concept of legal order in a global setting; a politics of boundary-setting alternative to both cosmopolitanism and communitarianism; transformations of legal authority and political representation; immigration and global justice; collective identity and difference. In dealing with these topics Lindahl draws on (post-)phenomenology and theories of collective action of analytical provenance, while also seeking to do justice to the nitty-gritty of positive law.

Bertrand Mazabraud is a French magistrate. He has a PhD in private law (University of Paris II—Assas) and a PhD in philosophy (University of Poitiers). Formerly a judge in the French juvenile justice system, he currently holds the position of global coordinator for humanities at the École Nationale de la Magistrature. He also teaches moral and political philosophy and business ethics at the Institut Catholique de Paris. His doctoral dissertation in philosophy—later published under the title, *De la juridicité. Le droit à l'école de Ricoeur* (Presses Universitaires de Rennes, 2017)—took a phenomenological hermeneutical approach to exploring the concept of law and paid particular attention to Paul Ricoeur's writings. Other published works, also taking a philosophical approach to law, focus mainly on judicial rationality, judgments, and sanctions. He has written on transitional justice and terrorism, and his most recent works consider the concepts of danger, emergency, and authority in democracies.

Francis J. Mootz III is Professor of Law at University of the Pacific, McGeorge School of Law, where he previously served as Dean. He has also taught at the William S. Boyd School of Law at University of Nevada, Las Vegas, Penn State Dickinson School of Law, William and Mary School of Law, and Western New England University. He has written extensively on legal argumentation, drawing from Hans-Georg Gadamer's philosophical hermeneutics, Paul Ricoeur's critical hermeneutics, and Chaim Perelman's new rhetoric. He developed his core themes in *Rhetorical Knowledge in Legal Practice and Critical Legal Theory* (2006) and *Law, Hermeneutics and Rhetoric* (2010).

Walter Salles was a post-doctoral student at the School of Law at the University of Pittsburgh (USA) and the Faculty of Theology at the Pontifical Catholic University of Rio de Janeiro (Brazil). He holds a PhD in Sciences of Religion, a Master in Theology, and graduated in philosophy and theology. His research focuses on the thought of Paul Ricoeur with an emphasis on Ethics, Hermeneutics, and Religion. He is a Member of the Society for Ricoeur Studies (SRS) and the Iberoamerican Association of Ricoeurian Studies (ASIER). He is also a freelance translator for Loyola Publisher.

Roger W. H. Savage is a professor at the University of California, Los Angeles, specializing in aesthetics, hermeneutics, and politics. His books include *Paul Ricoeur's Philosophical Anthropology as Hermeneutics of Liberation: Freedom, Justice, and the Power of Imagination*; *Music, Time, and Its Other: Aesthetic Reflections on Finitude, Temporality, and Alterity*; and *Hermeneutics and Music Criticism*. He also edited *Paul Ricoeur and the Lived Body* and *Paul Ricoeur in the Age of Hermeneutical Reason: Poetics, Praxis, and*

Critique. He was a Fulbright scholar and a Moore Institute visiting fellow at the National University of Ireland, Galway, and he is a founding member and a past president of the Society for Ricoeur Studies.

George H. Taylor is an emeritus professor of law in the United States at the University of Pittsburgh. He specializes in legal hermeneutics and hermeneutics more generally. He studied as a graduate student under Paul Ricoeur, and he is the editor of Ricoeur's *Lectures on Ideology and Utopia* and co-editor of Ricoeur's *Lectures on Imagination*. With Francis J. Mootz, he also co-edited *Gadamer and Ricoeur: Critical Horizons for Contemporary Hermeneutics*. He has written on Ricoeur extensively.

www.ingramcontent.com/pod-product-compliance
Lightning Source LLC
Chambersburg PA
CBHW020110010526
44115CB00008B/778